Overleaf — Recipes for this favorite Southern dish vary in ingredients and methods of cooking. See recipe for Sour Dough Chicken Pie on Page 131.

The

SOUTHERN COUNTRY COOKBOOK

By
The Editors of
The Progressive Farmer Magazine
Under the Direction of
Lena Sturges, Foods Editor

Contents

Introduction

The heart of the South has been the people of her farms and ranches. And from their country kitchens have come foods unexcelled by the world's most sophisticated cuisines.

These foods reflect the people who have created them — stable and imaginative, honest and ambitious, dependable and delightful.

A warm climate and rich soil have given abundantly to an equally warm people who have brought from the soil the best of nature's foodstuffs, and combined them with the ingredients of the lands and cultures of their forefathers, and blended them into a rich way of life unique in the history of man.

Within the South the result may be called Creole or Southwestern or Tidewater, but to the world across that famous line it is all Southern.

For over three-quarters of a century, *The Progressive Farmer* has felt it a worthy endeavor to serve such a people. Our readership is what we are all about, and our readers have been more than generous with us — sharing their recipes that we might share them with others.

Through this book we hope to repay them.

We have compiled the best from not only their kitchens, but from those of the women who preceded them as well. We hope you will, in turn, treasure our *SOUTHERN COUNTRY COOKBOOK*, and then pass it on to your daughters someday in the well-worn state all good cookbooks eventually reach.

It has been an undertaking of no small significance. Writers, editors, artists, and cooks have written and edited, illustrated and designed, tested and tasted to the limits of their professional skills.

We have a lot of faith in the results, and from test kitchens and typewriters we'd like to say a special word of thanks to the people who really made this collection possible — those who have made, and will continue to make, the Southern country kitchen a very special place.

Favorite Oldtime Southern Foods

When the "soul food" fad swept the country, Southerners smiled and said, "Why, that's just staple food."

Black-eyed peas and pot likker, collard greens and pigs' feet were born of hard times when any edible green and every part of an animal from head to feet and the "chitlins" in the middle were about all that was available.

Ingenuity transformed them into dishes as desirable as they were expedient.

In fact, many of these traditional Southern foods make up what has been described as the first genuinely American cuisine utilizing native foods.

In times past, pork, corn, and wild greens predominated, and filled not only the dinner plate but dietary needs as well. Even if they were served every day, the variety of greens available — kale, collard, turnip, mustard, and dandelion — provided at least some change of pace.

Sweet potatoes have long had a place on the Southern menu. Many a Southerner less notable than the fictional Miss O'Hara literally lived on them. From biscuits to cake and pie, sweet potatoes appeared as often as greens and in innumerable forms.

Molasses was the sweetening in breads and vegetables; and wild berries, fruit, and nuts became dessert.

Necessity was the mother of a cuisine still very much a part of today's prosperous South.

A Soul Food dinner can be a gourmet's delight. Shown clockwise from upper right: Sweet Potato Pie, recipe on Page 327; Fresh Turnip Greens, Page 189; Fried Ham and Red-Eye Gravy, Page 128; Black-Eyed Peas with Ham Hock, Page 177; Country Cornbread, Page 195.

Sassafras Tea

Wash the sassafras roots, cut into
2- to 3-inch pieces; place in a deep pan,
cover with cold water, and boil for
about 12 to 15 minutes. Strain and serve
hot. Add lemon and sugar, if desired.
The tea is a delicate pink and is delicious as a cold beverage.

*Note: Sassafras tea may be substituted for 1 cup
of liquid in plain cakes. Use a strong brew as a
flavoring for desserts and candies.*

Crackling Bread

2 **cups self-rising cornmeal**
2 **cups crisp cracklings, cut into size of
   large lima bean**
   Boiling water
   Shortening to grease skillet
   All-purpose flour

Put cornmeal into large mixing bowl,
add cracklings, and mix thoroughly.
Add enough boiling water to make a
medium stiff dough. Heat a well greased
iron skillet, sprinkle liberally with flour,
and pour in dough. Bake in a preheated
450° oven for 25 minutes or until brown.
Serve hot.

Georgia Sunlight Bread

Early on hot sunny days in June or July,
7 a.m. is the best time to start, take
1 teacup full of morning's milk. Scald it
with 1 teacup of boiling water. Let cool.

Put ½ teaspoon salt, ½ teacup meal,
½ cup flour, and 1 teaspoon sugar in
bowl. Do not beat the mixture, but stir it
leaving lumps to dissolve. Cover and put
in a warm place near your stove. Maybe
set bowl in warm water. By 8 or 9
o'clock maybe, put in hot place in sun.
Go to the yeast. Stir it at least three
times before 10 o'clock. Keep it moved
in hotter place. After 9 o'clock will do
to stop stirring, just so you get it out
early. If you see bubbles, don't stir any
more. Cover and leave it until near as
you can go to 2 p.m. It should rise all
over in small puffs.

Now go hurriedly to tray of sifted flour.
Sprinkle more salt, more sugar, to
taste; some lard, not too heavy. Knead
very well. Place dough in greased pan.
Go back to sun and let rise again. Bake.
You will lose if it comes a cloud, or
rains much.

Breadcrumb Pancakes

   1 **tablespoon butter or margarine**
1½ **cups buttermilk**
   1 **cup dry breadcrumbs**
   2 **eggs**
   ½ **cup all-purpose flour**
   1 **teaspoon soda**
   ½ **teaspoon salt**
   ½ **cup blueberries or strawberries**

Melt butter or margarine, add to milk,
and pour over crumbs. Add well beaten
eggs and dry ingredients sifted together.
Mix well. Add blueberries. Drop by
tablespoonfuls onto hot, greased griddle. Small cakes are easier to manage.

Hash Biscuits

Make hash, preferably of beef, with
additions of finely cut Irish potatoes and
onions. Add plenty of meat stock to the

hash. Split cold biscuits into halves, drop them into the hash just long enough before serving for them to get as warm as the hash, or split the biscuits in half and toast with butter before adding to the hash.

Cush

2 tablespoons meat drippings
2 tablespoons butter
3 cups broken-up cornbread
2 cups broken-up biscuits
   Salt and pepper to taste
1 teaspoon ground sage
1 chopped onion
2 eggs
   Milk

Heat meat drippings and butter in a heavy skillet. Add cornbread and biscuits, salt and pepper, sage, onion, and eggs. Stir and brown lightly. Then add milk to make a soft, mushy batter and cook until fairly dry. Cush may be baked at 350° for about 15 to 20 minutes.

'Lasses Hole in Biscuit

An oldtime, after school favorite was made from thick buttermilk biscuits left-over from breakfast. A hole was punched in center of biscuit and filled with syrup. This was a very satisfying snack.

Dried Beef (Comanche Indian Method)

When you kill a beef, leave some for drying. Cut meat in long, thin strips, and hang it up on a pole to dry. Then pound the meat almost into a powder. Children like to chew on these strips.

Calf's Head Dressed As Terrapin

This recipe was published in *The Progressive Farmer*, December 25, 1894. It was also published in *Carolina Cooking* in 1845.

Have the head split open and thoroughly cleaned. Put into a stew pan with just water enough to cover it, and 6 or 8 small onions. Let it cook until quite tender. Take up the head and cut it into pieces as you would terrapin. Put ¼ pound of butter in a frying pan and strip into it 1 teaspoonful flour. Stir until it browns, then add three onions chopped fine, cayenne, black pepper, salt, marjoram, and a little of the water in which the head was boiled. Into this gravy put the pieces of meat. Hard cook 6 or 8 eggs, chop them fine, and mix all through the gravy. Garnish with forcemeat balls, made of veal or cold turkey, and a little of the brains mixed. Season as usual. Roll into balls, fry in boiling fat and drain. Make the rest of the brains into brain cakes, seasoning with salt and pepper.

Barbecued Goat

Dress goat carefully. If hair gets in contact with meat, it imparts an unpleasant flavor. Add salt, pepper, chili powder, cumin seed, and cover goat with a layer of lard. Wrap and tie meat in maguey leaves. Cover with clean white sack and wrap in a tow sack. Put in pit where fire has been burning several hours. Lay covered meat in a layer of ashes over hot coals, cover with dirt, and leave meat in ashes all night.

Hog's Head Cheese

Prepare meat as for souse. Remove all bones, and run meat through food chopper. For 5 pounds meat, use the following:

2 *cups broth in which meat was boiled*
5 *teaspoons salt*
3 *teaspoons black pepper*
3 *teaspoons red pepper*
3 *teaspoons ground allspice*
2 *teaspoons ground cloves*

Mix thoroughly. Put into pans and press with weight overnight. Head cheese may be sliced, covered with vinegar, and stored in glass jars.

Fried Salt Pork

"Fat back," "poor man's chicken," or whatever, the meat should be selected with care. A streak of lean is most preferred, although many discriminating cooks use the pure fat.

Allow 3 or 4 slices for each serving. Use only thick slices. Cover with boiling water, bring to a boil, discard the salt water. Drain, and dip slices in cornmeal. Fry in hot shortening until slices are golden brown. Drain on a paper towel. Serve with milk gravy, sliced tomatoes, or fried green tomatoes.

Often served for breakfast, the fried pork may also be served for patio or outside suppers.

To make milk gravy, pour off drippings, leaving about 2 tablespoons in frying pan. Add 2 tablespoons flour, and stir until brown. Add 2 cups milk slowly; stir and cook slowly until gravy is done. Serve with hot spoon cornbread, hot biscuits, cornbread, grits, or hominy.

Chitterlings

First, split the intestines. Then clean thoroughly in several changes of warm water. Soak overnight in salt water made by adding 1 teaspoon salt to 1 quart water. Cut into 2-inch lengths. Boil until tender. Dip in a light batter made of 1 egg, flour, and milk; or roll in meal, and fry.

Ham and Egg Pie

Begin with a layer of ham, using bits of ham from a ham bone. Lay on a layer of dumpling strips, and follow with a layer of sliced, hard-cooked eggs. Repeat until the baking dish is two-thirds full. Season with salt and pepper. Cover with milk and bake at 350° for about 30 minutes.

Colorful drinks poured over crackling ice are always refreshing. See beverage recipes beginning on Page 32.

8 Oldtime Foods

Liver Pudding

1 **pound liver**
½ **hog's head**
1 **large onion**
    Salt, red and black pepper
    Sage to taste

Dress and cook liver and hog's head until very tender. Remove hog's head meat from bones, and grind with liver and onion. Add seasonings. Press into mold and chill. May be served with grits or hominy or used in sandwiches.

Pig's Feet

Dress pig's feet and tie each separately in cheesecloth. Cover with boiling water. Season with 1 teaspoon salt for each quart of water. Simmer for about 4 hours, or until feet are tender. Serve feet cold with salt, pepper, and French salad dressing. Or split in half, dip in batter, and fry. Boiled pigs' feet may be pickled and served.

Pigtail with Turnip Greens

Clean pigtail thoroughly, salt to taste, and brown in shortening. Add about 1 cup water, cover and simmer slowly until tender, about 1½ to 2 hours. Serve with turnip greens.

Souse

Reserve the head, feet, and ears of one hog. Remove eyes and brains. Slit head in half. Wash and scrape thoroughly, and remove excess fat. Singe pig's feet, wash, and scrape. Singe, wash, and clean ears thoroughly with hot water. Cover meat with hot water, and boil until meat drops from bones. Remove bones. Drain meat, and season with 1 teaspoon each of salt, black pepper, and sage for each quart. Place meat in a mold or bowl. When cool, souse will be firm and jellied. Serve cold with vinegar. Or dip in beaten eggs and breadcrumbs and brown in hot shortening.

Scrapple

1 **pound pork**
4 **cups water**
2 **teaspoons salt**
⅔ **cup cornmeal**
1 **large onion**
    Pepper
2 **to 3 teaspoons ground sage**

Cook meat, covered, in boiling salted water at simmering until meat falls from bones. Remove meat from broth. Cut or grind into small pieces. Strain broth into top of a double boiler. Add cornmeal, and cook over direct heat for 5 minutes, stirring constantly to prevent lumping. Add meat, chopped onion, and season to taste. Cook over boiling water for 1 hour. Pack into mold or small loafpans. Serve cold, or slice and pan fry with or without batter.

This South Carolina Scrapple recipe is typical, although some lean beef is often added to the pork. Often the broth from boiled meat from head cheese or souse is thickened and cooked with cornmeal, seasonings, and onion.

Colcannon

Combine equal parts of cabbage cooked with pork, cooked Irish potatoes, and 1 cup cream.

Brined Corn

Use firm-grained roasting ears, not in the hard stage but not too milky. Use when starch grain is well formed, but not hard. Cut two rows from cob, but do not scrape. Use six parts corn to one part salt. Place in a bag or sack inside a stone jar. Weight well, use jar cover with a stone. Cover with a cloth. Set in a cool place. Will keep even in the hottest weather.

To serve: Add milk, sugar, butter or margarine, and pepper, and simmer; or bake at 350° for about 1 hour.

Lye Hominy

Use 8 cups sweet, flat corn. (Most early varieties of sweet corn have the flat kernels.) Dissolve 2 ounces of concentrated lye in 1 gallon of boiling water in an iron kettle. Drop corn into this solution and boil rapidly for 25 to 30 minutes. Drain and put into a pot of cold water. If possible, allow water to run over it for 3 to 4 hours to remove all traces of lye. If this isn't possible, wash through about six changes of fresh water. After this, place in a barrel churn and turn the churn for 5 to 10 minutes to remove hulls and black eyes. After removing the hulls, place the corn in an enamel kettle, cover with clear boiling water, and cook until tender. Wash again and remove any hulls or eyes that failed to come off in the churn. The hominy may now be seasoned for serving.

To Cook Dried Corn

For a family of eight, wash 2 cups of corn through one water, and put to soak overnight in clean, cold water (if impossible to soak so long, place over a kettle of hot water for 2 to 3 hours); when softened, cook for 5 to 10 minutes in water in which it was soaked, adding as soon as boiling, 2 tablespoons butter, 1 of flour, and a little salt and pepper. Another good way to finish is the following: Take the yolk of one egg, 1 tablespoon milk, pinch of salt, thicken with flour quite stiff so as to take out with a teaspoon, and drop in little dumplings no larger than an acorn; cover tightly and cook for 5 to 10 minutes; have enough water in kettle before adding dumplings, as cover should not be removed during cooking

Fried Pumpkin or Squash Blooms

Gather the blossoms while they are still in the large bud just ready to open. Wash carefully and press together flat. Dip in eggs, then in cornmeal or cracker crumbs. Add salt and pepper to taste. Fry in hot shortening until brown. Serve as a vegetable fritter.

Green Corn Pie

Grate several ears of green corn on a potato grater, enough to make about 3 cups of mush (the corn may be a little older and less tender than for roasting). Add the yolks of 2 eggs, a large spoonful of butter, pepper and salt, and the juice of 6 to 8 tomatoes scalded and pressed through a colander. Mix all well. Have ready young chickens stewed, as for chicken pie, or slices of cold veal and ham, or shrimp, or whatever you choose. Line a baking dish with half the batter, put the meat in the center, cover with rest of batter, and bake for about half an hour.

To make corn fritters: Keep back several spoonfuls of the above batter, add 1 egg, a little more salt, and the grains of 4 or 5 ears of parboiled young corn, cut from the cob. Mix together and fry as fritters.

Oklahoma Dried Corn (Comanche Indian Method)

To prepare dried corn, start off with a great quantity of green corn. First, build a large fire and let it burn down to a nice bed of coals. Remove silks, but leave most of the shucks on the ears. Put the corn directly on the coals. Keep turning the corn with a garden rake to keep corn from scorching. When corn is roasted and cooled, remove shucks, and cut corn from the cob with a very sharp knife. Spread kernels on a clean sheet and let dry in the sun for about 3 days.

Caution: Bring the corn in at night. Store in fruit jars, and seal lids. Corn may be stored in the freezer.

Poke Greens (or Sallet)

Poke greens for 4 to 6 servings
 4 *thick slices bacon*
¾ *to 1 teaspoon salt*
12 *tender young onions, chopped*
 2 *hard-cooked eggs, chopped*

Select tender, young poke greens. Clean thoroughly and rinse three times. Parboil twice and discard water. This is a most important step. Cover with water in large kettle and cook until greens are tender but not mushy. Fry bacon until crisp; remove from drippings, and set aside. Add poke greens, salt, and chopped onions to drippings. Cook over low heat for 20 minutes. To serve, sprinkle crumbled bacon and chopped hard-cooked eggs over greens.

Poke Stalk Pickle

To pickle poke stalk, use only tender stalks not over 6 inches high. Cut into 3-inch lengths. Trim off leaves. Cook in clear water for about 5 minutes. Discard water. Cover again with salted water and boil for about 5 minutes. Discard water. Pack stalks vertically in jars.

Cover with this solution:
To each pint of vinegar add ½ teaspoon mustard seed and 2 tablespoons sugar. Heat to boiling, pour over pickles, and seal.

Beef, ham, fish, or lamb can be made into delectable stews. For beef stew with an oriental flavor, see Teriyaki Stew recipe on Page 44.

Corn in Cane Juice

Shuck (or husk) fall roasting ears, silk, wash and dry the ears of corn. Carefully drop into boiling sorghum juice at syrup-making time. Leave for 15 minutes. Dip out and eat with salt and butter.

Canned Boiled Peanuts

Select well filled out "boiling peanuts" and wash them. Bring to a boil. Put peanuts into quart jars to within ½ inch of top of jar. Fill jars with boiling water and add 2 tablespoons salt to each jar. Cook at 10 pounds pressure for 30 minutes. Cool and store.

Boiled Peanuts

Select and wash young, green peanuts in the shell. Add 1 tablespoon salt to each quart of water, and boil peanuts for 2½ to 3 hours.

Leather Britches or "Shucky Beans"

Select young, tender green beans that contain small bean seed as large as can be obtained without the pods being tough. String and break off each end of the pods.

Thread a large needle with No. 40 sewing thread. Tie both ends of thread together forming a large knot. Take a pod and pierce needle through center bean seed. Continue to put needle through all the pods in the center. When string is full finish off by going through center seed in last pod. Prepare as many strings as you have beans. Hang strings over a wire or rope stretched across porch or upstairs or in the garage. Do not let them get damp with rain or fog. As soon as they are dry enough to crimp or rattle, place them in plastic bags and tie securely so no insects can get in them. Be sure they are perfectly dry or they will mold and be unfit for use.

To cook: The day before the beans are to be served, take about two strings of beans, wash carefully, cover with cold water and soak overnight. Next morning put beans in cooker, an iron pot improves the flavor. Boil hard for 30 minutes. Drain well, wash under running water, return to cooker, add two teaspoons of salt, ¼ to ½ pound of fatback or salt pork or a ham bone, and about ¼ cup of dried, yellow-eyed beans. Cover with hot water, bring to a boil, reduce heat to simmer, and cook until done, about 3 hours. Add more water as necessary. Cook until most water is absorbed and beans are just dry. Serve hot with cornbread.

Tomato Gravy

Split freshly baked, hot, crisp biscuits and place in a serving dish. Spoon hot, slightly salted canned tomatoes over the biscuits. Over this pour hot cream gravy.

Make cream gravy by pouring fresh milk into hot fat. Fat from fried salt pork has a better flavor, but bacon fat may be used. Proportion: About four times as much milk as fat, or 1 tablespoon fat to 4 tablespoons milk. Tomato juice may be substituted for canned tomatoes.

Southern Baked Peaches

8 *medium-ripe peaches*
½ *cup sugar*
1 *cup hot water*

Place peaches in casserole or pan; add sugar and water. Cover and bake at 300° for 30 minutes. Remove cover and bake for 10 minutes to brown. Serve with cream.

Vinegar Cobbler

Mix sugar, water, and vinegar to taste. Bring to a boil. Roll biscuit dumplings very thin and cut into strips. Drop into boiling liquid, cover pan and cook for about 15 minutes.

Watermelon Ice

Take the heart of a large, sweet, ripe melon, put into a chopping tray and chop rather fine, then add to it 1 cup powdered sugar, and turn into container of ice cream freezer. Pack freezer with ice and salt. Turn crank for 5 minutes or until the melon is icy cold and in the condition of soft snow. Serve in glasses.

Roasted Eggs

Roll each egg in four layers of wet paper (brown, or newspaper) and put down in the hot ashes; cover well. Let stay until the outer layer is well scorched; let cool until it may be handled; then remove the paper.

Eggless, Milkless, Butterless Cake

2 *cups raisins*
1 *cup sugar*
1 *cup water*
½ *cup shortening*
2 *cups all-purpose flour*
1 *teaspoon baking powder*
¼ *teaspoon salt*
1 *teaspoon ground cinnamon*
1 *teaspoon ground nutmeg*
½ *teaspoon ground cloves*
1 *teaspoon soda*
1 *tablespoon boiling water*

Mix raisins, sugar, and water and boil for 3 minutes; add shortening. When cold, add flour, baking powder, salt, cinnamon, nutmeg, and cloves (sifted together), and soda, dissolved in boiling water. Bake in a greased loafpan at 350° for 30 minutes.

Dried Whole Persimmons

Select fully ripened persimmons; rinse, drain, and place them about ¼ inch apart on a wire or cheesecloth frame, and dry in the sun. A fruit evaporator may be used, if preferred. When properly dried, the persimmons resemble dates in texture. Pack the dried fruit in glass jars which have been sterilized and then dried in a warm oven. Seal tightly and store in a cool, dry place.

Corncob Jelly

12 medium red corncobs
2 quarts water
1 (1¼-ounce) package powdered pectin
3 cups sugar

Wash the corncobs and cut into 4-inch lengths. Put into container, add 2 quarts water, and bring to a boil. Reduce heat and boil slowly for 35 to 40 minutes.

Strain the juice. Measure 3 cups of juice into large container. Add the powdered pectin and bring to a boil. Add sugar and again bring to the boiling point. Boil for 5 minutes. Skim, and pour into hot, sterilized glasses or jars, and seal.

Transparent Pudding

Lay in a deep dish any kind of dried sweetmeats. Rub ½ pound butter and ½ pound sugar together; beat 8 eggs well, and add them; then pour this mixture upon the sweetmeats, and bake in a 300° oven for 30 minutes. Turn it out of the dish, so that the preserves are at the top of the pudding. When quite cold, ice it; and it may be garnished to suit the fancy of the cook.

Pear Waffle Syrup

4 cups sweetened juice from canned pears
Juice of 1 lemon
1½ (2½-ounce) packages powdered pectin

Add lemon juice to pear juice and bring to a boil. Add fruit pectin and let come to a full rolling boil. Pour into jars immediately.

Hannah's Eggless Fruitcake

1 cup dried apples
1 cup firmly packed brown sugar
1 cup white sugar
3 cups all-purpose flour
1½ teaspoons soda
2 teaspoons baking powder
½ teaspoon salt
¾ cup butter
½ cup chopped roasted peanuts
2 cups raisins
1 cup black walnuts
1 cup chopped gumdrops
1 cup buttermilk
½ teaspoon ground cinnamon
2 teaspoons vanilla extract
1 cup boiling water

Steam dried apples for 10 minutes, chop and set aside. Put next six ingredients into large mixing bowl, mix together and add butter, roasted peanuts, raisins, black walnuts, steamed apples, chopped gumdrops, and buttermilk. Beat well for 3 minutes, add cinnamon and vanilla. Then add boiling water. Bake at 300° for about 2 hours. Stays moist longer than most fruitcakes.

Appetizers & Snacks

Foods have changed with the life-styles they must serve. We make frequent reference to the slower pace of former days, but the hours saved by modern manufacturing, marketing, and appliances allow the homemaker many extra hours for entertaining.

Whereas for great-grandmother entertaining meant a seated dinner on Sunday, today it may be as informal and as easy as carrying a tray of hors d'oeuvres from kitchen to family room.

As entertaining has relaxed, so have the foods associated with it, Even a formal dinner today is not complete without a preliminary appetizer course.

Appetizers offer a hostess her greatest chance for creativity — as simple as a bowl of popcorn, or as elaborate as seafood canapés with hot sauce. Strive for variations in texture, taste and color, and by all means utilize the additional interest offered by garnishes.

Within the family routine, snacks are in demand for TV fans, and sandwich meals are more often requested than just accepted.

Fondue has become increasingly popular as a snack-type food and can serve as the main dish itself. Beef and cheese are the most popular fondue choices; and while no young homemaker would consider her kitchen complete without this rather nonproverbial pot, fondue is still considered a novel way to entertain.

Fondue or finger sandwiches, the only inherent trouble in serving appetizers is getting guests to leave the snacks for the dinner table.

Sandwich Suggestions

Fresh or day-old bread is usually better for sandwiches. For very thin slices, freeze the bread, and slice before it thaws.

When making sandwiches a day ahead, spread softened butter or margarine on slices before adding mayonnaise or salad dressing and filling. This will help keep the bread from becoming soggy. Spread filling to edge of bread. Crusts should be cut off (if desired) after filling has been spread so that sandwiches will retain their shape.

To keep openface or unwrapped sandwiches moist, cover with moisture-vaporproof material and place in refrigerator. Dainty sandwiches may be stacked several layers deep, if desired, but cover each layer with waxed paper. Never use a dampened towel to cover sandwiches.

Use Softened Cream Cheese with:

Chopped cooked dried prunes, apricots
Chopped crisp bacon, pickle relish
Dried beef, minced onion, chili sauce
Chopped dates or figs, peanuts
Chopped green pepper, olives, celery
Finely chopped peanuts, minced onion, mayonnaise
Grated cucumbers

Use Chopped Chicken with:

Apple, celery, mayonnaise
Nuts, green olives, mayonnaise

Use Peanut Butter with:

Chopped crisp bacon, raw apple
Grated raw carrot, chopped raisins, chopped celery
Chopped dates, chopped figs, lemon juice, sliced or mashed bananas
Deviled ham, chopped dill pickles, mayonnaise
Any kind of fruit preserves

Mix Hard-Cooked Eggs with:

Grated raw carrot, sliced ripe olives, mayonnaise
Chopped chicken, celery, onions, mayonnaise
Deviled ham, chopped pickles, mustard, mayonnaise
Tuna or salmon, celery, pickle relish, mayonnaise

Combine Cheese with:

Grated American cheese, dried beef, chili sauce
Bleu cheese, sliced turkey or ham
Swiss cheese slices, deviled ham, pickles
Cottage cheese, celery, green pepper
Sharp cheese spread, sliced salami, mustard

Cheese Dip

2 cups shredded Cheddar cheese
2 tablespoons bleu cheese
¼ cup salad dressing or mayonnaise
2 tablespoons prepared mustard
2 tablespoons horseradish
3 to 4 tablespoons milk

Blend cheeses together. Add salad dressing or mayonnaise, mustard, and horseradish and beat until well blended. Add enough milk to make dip the right consistency. Yield: about 1½ cups.

Chili-Cheese Dip

1 (2-pound) loaf processed
  American cheese
2 medium onions, chopped
2 tablespoons butter or margarine
2 (15½-ounce) cans chili without beans
  Chili powder to taste
  Dash Tabasco sauce

Melt cheese in top of double boiler.
Brown chopped onions in butter or
margarine; add to cheese with other
ingredients. Blend well. Serve
hot. Yield: 4 pints.

Cottage Cheese Dip

1 (12-ounce) package cream-style
  cottage cheese with chives
3 to 6 drops Tabasco sauce
  Chopped parsley or chives

Place cheese and Tabasco sauce in
blender, and blend until fluffy (or beat
with rotary or electric beater). Garnish
with parsley or chives. Yield: 1½ cups.

Cottage Cheese Dip With Relishes

1 (12-ounce) carton cottage cheese
½ cup skim milk
2 tablespoons freshly squeezed
  lime juice
½ teaspoon salt
1 clove garlic, crushed
1 teaspoon onion juice
  Dash curry powder
  Fresh vegetables

Rub cottage cheese through fine sieve.
Blend in milk. Add the next five
ingredients and mix well. Chill. Cut
carrot strips, squash slices, cauliflowerets,
and radishes, and chill. Arrange
vegetables on plate with dip. Yield:
12 to 15 servings.

Calico Cheese Dip

1 cup cottage cheese
2 hard-cooked eggs, finely chopped
¼ cup commercial sour cream
2 teaspoons prepared mustard
1 teaspoon onion salt
½ teaspoon curry powder
½ teaspoon garlic salt
3 tablespoons minced green pepper
1 tablespoon finely chopped pimiento

Beat cheese until almost smooth. Add
eggs, sour cream, mustard, onion salt,
curry, and garlic salt and blend until
smooth. Stir in green pepper and
pimiento. Mix well and chill. Yield:
1¾ cups.

Avocado Dip No. 1

¾ cup sieved avocado
1 clove garlic
1½ teaspoons freshly squeezed
  lemon juice
3 tablespoons minced parsley
¾ teaspoon celery seed
¼ teaspoon salt
  Few drops Tabasco sauce
1 teaspoon grated onion
½ teaspoon prepared mustard

Cut avocado into halves and remove seed
and skin. Force fruit through a sieve.
Rub bowl with cut garlic and discard
garlic. Add avocado and other
ingredients, blend well. Chill. Yield:
1 cup.

Avocado Dip No. 2

1 cup mashed avocado pulp
1 (8-ounce) package cream cheese
3 tablespoons freshly squeezed
   lemon juice
1 teaspoon finely chopped onion
1 teaspoon salt
   Dash Worcestershire sauce

Gradually add the avocado to the softened cream cheese, blending until smooth. Add the lemon juice, onion, salt, and Worcestershire sauce. Mix until well blended. Yield: 2½ cups.

Green Dragon Dip

1 ripe avocado
1 (3-ounce) package cream cheese
3 tablespoons mayonnaise or
   salad dressing
   Few drops freshly squeezed lemon
   juice or vinegar
¼ teaspoon seasoned salt
⅛ teaspoon pepper
   Grated onion (optional)

Peel, pit, and mash avocado. Mix with remaining ingredients and blend well. Add grated onion, if desired. Chill before serving. Yield: 1 cup.

Holiday Dip

1 (0.58 ounce) package onion soup mix
1 pint commercial sour cream
4 ounces bleu cheese, crumbled
¾ cup chopped pecans
   Potato chips

Combine onion soup mix and sour cream, then blend thoroughly. Fold in remaining ingredients. Serve with potato chips. Yield: 1½ cups.

Denver Dip

1 (8-ounce) package cream cheese
2 chicken bouillon cubes
⅓ cup hot water
2 teaspoons instant minced onion
2 teaspoons freshly squeezed
   lemon juice
1 tablespoon chopped pimiento
1/16 teaspoon dried dill seed (optional)

Beat cream cheese until soft. Crush bouillon cubes in water. Add instant minced onion and let stand for a few minutes. Add bouillon-onion mixture gradually to cream cheese, mixing until well blended. Stir in lemon juice, pimiento, and dill. Chill. Yield: 1⅓ cups.

Deviled Ham Dip

2 (2¼-ounce) cans deviled ham
1 cup commercial sour cream
2 teaspoons capers, chopped (optional)
1½ tablespoons chopped pimiento
⅛ teaspoon black pepper
   Few drops Tabasco sauce

Combine all ingredients. Chill before serving. Yield: 2 cups.

Smoky Cheese Dip

1 (8-ounce) package cream cheese
2 tablespoons freshly squeezed
   lemon juice
1 teaspoon liquid smoke
2 tablespoons cream
¼ teaspoon garlic salt

Combine all ingredients well with mixing spoon or electric blender. Chill before serving. Yield: 1 cup.

Sour Cream Dip

    1   cup commercial sour cream
    ¼   cup salad dressing or mayonnaise
    1   tablespoon vinegar
    ½   teaspoon salt
    ¼   teaspoon curry powder

Combine all ingredients and chill.
Yield: 1¼ cups.

Peanut Butter

Shell the peanuts; roast just enough
so that the hulls may be slipped off
easily; remove all the hulls by gently
rolling, fanning, and screening. Grind
peanuts very fine in any sort of mill,
passing through several times if
necessary. Pack into cans, bottles or jars,
and seal if not for immediate use. Some
manufacturers add a little salt and a
small amount of olive oil; others do not,
according to taste. For small quantities
of butter, a good meat grinder will
answer the purpose. If the nuts are
ground fine enough, no additional oil
will be necessary for easy spreading.

Party Dip

    2   tablespoons butter or margarine
    3   tablespoons all-purpose flour
    ½   teaspoon salt
    1   cup milk
    ½   cup shredded Cheddar cheese
    ½   cup mayonnaise or salad dressing
    ¼   cup catsup
    ¼   teaspoon Worcestershire sauce

Melt butter or margarine in top of
double boiler, electric skillet, or chafing
dish. Blend in flour and salt. Slowly add
milk, stirring constantly to insure a
smooth sauce. Blend in cheese,
mayonnaise or salad dressing, catsup,
and Worcestershire sauce and cook
until cheese melts and sauce thickens.
Yield: 2 cups.

Peanut Butter Dip

    ½   cup smooth peanut butter
    1   cup commercial sour cream
    ⅛   teaspoon salt
    1   teaspoon horseradish
    2   tablespoons prepared mustard

Combine all ingredients and mix well.
Yield: 1 cup.

Double-Ring Sandwiches

    2   hard-cooked eggs, chopped
    ⅓   cup chopped, cooked bacon
    3   tablespoons mayonnaise or
        salad dressing
    3   slices whole wheat bread
    3   slices white bread
    1   tablespoon soft butter or margarine
   12   slices stuffed green olives

Combine eggs, bacon, and mayonnaise
or salad dressing. Cut each slice of
the whole wheat and white bread into
two 2-inch rounds with a cookie cutter,
then cut the center from half of the
rounds to form circles. Spread butter or
margarine on rounds, then spread
with 1 tablespoon egg-bacon filling.
Place a circle of bread over filling, and
place a slice of stuffed olive in the
center of each circle. Yield: 12 party
sandwiches.

Egg Salad

2 tablespoons prepared mustard
⅛ teaspoon paprika
2 tablespoons mayonnaise or
   salad dressing
4 hard-cooked eggs, diced
2 tablespoons chopped celery
2 tablespoons chopped olives
1 tablespoon chopped sweet pickle
1 tablespoon chopped pimiento

Add mustard and paprika to mayonnaise or salad dressing. Combine all other ingredients and fold in mayonnaise or salad dressing. Yield: 1½ cups or filling for 6 sandwiches.

Grilled Cheese Sandwiches

Thin-sliced sandwich bread
Sliced cheese
1 teaspoon butter or margarine for
   each sandwich

Assemble all materials. Melt butter or margarine in small saucepan, brush generously on both sides of bread. Put one or two slices cheese between two slices buttered bread. Melt a small amount of butter or margarine in heavy skillet. Put sandwich into skillet and cook slowly over low heat until brown. Turn, and brown other side of sandwich. Yield: 1 sandwich.

Franks and Cheese

4 weiners
2 slices Cheddar cheese
4 slices bacon
4 hot dog buns
   Mustard or chili sauce

Slit each weiner to make a pocket. Cut cheese into four even slices. Put slice of cheese in each weiner; wrap weiner with bacon slice. Fasten both ends of bacon to weiner with toothpicks. Bake at 350° for 20 minutes. Serve on hot dog buns with mustard or chili sauce. Yield: 4 servings.

Pimiento Cheese Sandwich Filling

1 (5⅓-ounce) can evaporated milk
½ pound processed American
   cheese, diced
1 (3-ounce) can pimientos
¼ teaspoon salt
   Pickles (optional)
   Chopped olives (optional)
   Grated onion (optional)

Put milk into top of double boiler. Add diced cheese, and keep hot until melted. Drain pimientos and mash. Add to cheese and milk with the salt. Pickles, chopped olives, or grated onion may be added, if desired. Yield: 1¾ cups or filling for 10 sandwiches.

Chicken Salad Tea Sandwiches

⅔ cup chopped, cooked chicken
¼ cup chopped celery
⅛ teaspoon salt
3 tablespoons mayonnaise or
   salad dressing
2 tablespoons chopped green olives
4 slices thin-sliced sandwich bread
4 teaspoons soft butter or margarine

Combine chicken, celery, salt, mayonnaise or salad dressing, and olives. Spread each slice of bread with 1 teaspoon butter or margarine, then with 3 tablespoons chicken salad mixture. Trim crusts and cut each slice crosswise into four finger sandwiches. Yield: 16 open-face finger sandwiches.

Minced Chicken

Thin-sliced sandwich bread
1½ cups minced, cooked chicken
1 hard-cooked egg, sieved
½ teaspoon grated onion
⅓ cup mayonnaise or salad dressing
Salt and pepper

Buy unsliced bread and have it sliced very thin lengthwise at the bakery. Combine minced chicken, sieved hard-cooked egg, seasonings, and mayonnaise or salad dressing. Spread sliced bread with soft butter or margarine; add filling, and cover with buttered bread. Trim crusts; cut into small squares, triangles, strips, etc. Yield: about 75 small sandwiches.

Egg-Avocado Pinwheel Sandwiches

3 hard-cooked eggs, chopped
1 tablespoon freshly squeezed lemon juice
3 tablepoons mayonnaise or salad dressing
3 tablespoons minced avocado
¼ teaspoon salt
⅛ teaspoon dry mustard
2 lengthwise slices from unsliced sandwich loaf
2 tablespoons soft butter or margarine

Combine chopped eggs, lemon juice, mayonnaise or salad dressing, avocado, salt, and dry mustard. Spread 1 tablespoon butter on each slice. Spread buttered bread with ½ cup egg-avocado mixture. Trim crusts and cut each slice crosswise into equal halves. Roll each half slice of bread up like a jellyroll. Wrap each roll in waxed paper, twisting ends of paper. Place on a flat surface so that roll rests on last turn of bread; chill. To serve, unwrap and cut each roll into six slices. Yield: 24 pinwheel sandwiches.

Sloppy Joes

1 pound ground beef
½ cup chopped celery
½ cup chopped onion
¼ cup chopped green pepper
1 clove garlic, minced (optional)
2 cups canned tomatoes
2 teaspoons salt
¼ teaspoon chili powder
1 teaspoon Worcestershire sauce
Hamburger buns

Brown meat in heavy skillet; add celery, onion, green pepper, and garlic; cook for 5 minutes. Add the tomatoes and seasonings. Cover and simmer for 30 minutes. Serve over split toasted hamburger buns. Yield: 4 to 6 servings.

Meat Salad

2 cups ground ham or beef
2 tablespoons chopped pickle
¼ cup chopped celery
¼ cup mayonnaise or salad dressing

Combine all ingredients and mix well. Yield: 2 cups or filling for 8 sandwiches.

Canapes with Lemon-Herb Glaze

Canape Combinations

Pumpernickel bread with cream cheese and sliced smoked salmon
Buttered salty rye with sliced egg and caviar
Salty rye with horseradish, chili sauce, tiny shrimp

Place on a rack and top each canape with 2 to 3 tablespoons Lemon-Herb Glaze.

Lemon-Herb Glaze

1⅔ cups water
⅛ teaspoon peppercorns
½ bay leaf
½ teaspoon dried dill
1 (3-ounce) package lemon-flavored gelatin
½ teaspoon salt
   Dash cayenne pepper
3 tablespoons vinegar

Bring water to simmer; add peppercorns, bay leaf, and dried dill. Cover, and simmer for about 10 minutes. Strain. Dissolve gelatin, salt, and cayenne in the hot liquid. Add vinegar. Chill until slightly thickened. Spoon mixture over canapes.

Deviled Ham and Carrot Filling

2 (4½-ounce) cans deviled ham
½ cup grated carrots
¼ teaspoon pepper
¼ cup pickle relish
¼ cup salad dressing or mayonnaise
½ teaspoon salt

Combine all ingredients and mix well. Yield: Filling for 4 sandwiches.

Ribbon Sandwiches

Spread a slice of white bread with deviled ham and carrot filling. Cover with whole wheat slice. Spread with egg and celery filling. Cover with a white slice. Firmly press together. Wrap in moisture-vaporproof paper and store in refrigerator until ready to serve. To serve, trim crusts and cut into ¾-inch slices.

Shrimp Tea Sandwiches

½ cup pimiento cream cheese
½ teaspoon chili sauce
⅓ cup finely chopped, cooked shrimp
½ teaspoon freshly squeezed lemon juice
5 slices bread
5 teaspoons soft butter or margarine
10 strips pimiento

Combine pimiento cream cheese, chili sauce, shrimp, and lemon juice. Trim crusts and cut each slice of bread into two 2-inch diamonds with a cookie cutter. Spread each diamond with ½ teaspoon butter or margarine, then with 1 tablespoon shrimp mixture. Yield: 20 openface sandwiches.

Surprise Hamburgers

1 pound ground beef
6 slices onion
6 tablespoons chili sauce
  Salt and pepper
6 hamburger buns

Shape ground beef into 12 patties. Place a slice of onion and a tablespoon chili sauce on six of the patties. Put another patty on top, and pinch the two edges firmly together. Sprinkle with salt and pepper. Broil hamburgers in broiler or in skillet. Toast both halves of buns; place hamburger in hot toasted buns. Serve while hot. Yield: 6 servings.

Chili-Cheese Rounds

1 (8-ounce) package cream cheese
½ pound Cheddar cheese, shredded
2 cloves garlic, minced or mashed
1 cup finely chopped pecans
2 tablespoons chili powder
  Crackers

Cream together the cheeses and garlic until blended; mix in pecans. Shape into two rolls, about 1½ inches in diameter. Roll in chili powder. Wrap each roll in waxed paper or aluminum foil and chill. To serve, slice into thin rounds and serve with crackers. Yield: about 150 rounds.

Dipsy Doodle

1 cup cottage cheese
¼ cup shredded sharp cheese
3 tablespoons chili sauce
½ teaspoon garlic salt
  Crackers, potato or corn chips

Mix cheeses, chili sauce, and garlic salt together until well blended. Chill. Spread on crackers, or use as a dip for crackers, potato chips, or corn chips. Yield: 1⅓ cups.

Mystery Snacks

½ cup cornmeal
1 cup all-purpose flour
1 teaspoon salt
⅓ cup shortening
½ cup shredded sharp cheese
¼ cup milk

Combine cornmeal, flour, and salt. Cut in shortening and cheese until mixture resembles coarse crumbs. Add milk, stirring lightly only until dry ingredients are dampened.

Knead gently for a few seconds on lightly floured board. Roll out to ⅛-inch thickness. Cut into strips, triangles, diamonds, or other fancy shapes. Place on baking sheet and bake at 375° for 12 to 15 minutes or until delicately browned. Serve warm or cold. Yield: 3 dozen.

Cheese Ball

2½ pounds cream cheese
2½ pounds American cheese, shredded
¼ pound bleu cheese
2 tablespoons Worcestershire sauce
½ cup mayonnaise
10 drops Tabasco sauce
  Onion salt and garlic salt to taste
  Chopped walnuts

Thoroughly mix all ingredients except walnuts. Shape into balls and roll in chopped walnuts. Chill until firm and ready to serve. Yield: 3 cheese balls.

Tuna Salad Sandwiches

1 (7-ounce) can tuna fish
4 hard-cooked eggs, minced
1 cup finely chopped celery
½ finely chopped green pepper
1 tablespoon chopped onion
  Mayonnaise or salad dressing to
  moisten, about ½ cup
16 to 20 slices bread

Drain oil from fish and break tuna into small pieces with a fork. Chop eggs, celery, green pepper, and onion. Mix with tuna in mixing bowl. Add mayonnaise or salad dressing. Keep in refrigerator until ready to spread. Yield: 8 to 10 sandwiches.

Canape Spread

1 (8-ounce) package cream cheese
¼ cup mayonnaise
1 teaspoon prepared mustard
1 teaspoon Worcestershire sauce
  Few drops Tabasco sauce
1 teaspoon prepared horseradish
1 hard-cooked egg, minced
2 tablespoons minced stuffed olives
1 (4½-ounce) can deviled ham
  Crackers

Soften cream cheese. Add mayonnaise, mustard, Worcestershire, and Tabasco and whip until fluffy. Blend in other ingredients and chill. Serve on crisp crackers. Yield: About 2 cups.

Cheese Straws

1 pound American cheese
¼ pound butter or margarine
2 cups self-rising flour
⅛ teaspoon red pepper

Grind cheese, mix with butter or margarine, and stir well. Add flour and red pepper and mix well. Make into a roll and put in cookie press. Bake on greased cookie sheets at 400° for 8 to 10 minutes. Yield: 3 dozen.

Cheese Snacks

¼ pound butter or margarine
¼ pound sharp cheese, shredded
1 tablespoon Worcestershire sauce
1½ cups all-purpose flour
¼ teaspoon cayenne pepper
¼ teaspoon paprika
1 teaspoon salt
  Pecan halves
1 egg white, beaten

Blend butter or margarine with shredded cheese until smooth. Add the Worcestershire sauce. Combine dry ingredients and add to butter mixture. Mix thoroughly and shape into small balls. Place on ungreased cookie sheet and press with fork. Brush pecan halves with egg white; place on top of Cheese Snacks. Bake at 325° for 25 minutes. Yield: 50.

Onion-Cheese Munchies

1 (8-ounce) package cream cheese
1 tablespoon grated onion
1 tablespoon prepared mustard
1 egg
  Plain salted crackers

Let cream cheese soften to room temperature. Add onion, mustard, and egg. Whip thoroughly. Spread cheese mixture over crackers, being careful to completely cover each cracker. Place crackers on a cookie sheet. Toast under broiler for a few minutes or until cheese turns light brown. Serve warm. Yield: 1 cup.

Sweet Cracker Treat

1 egg white
3 tablespoons sugar
¼ teaspoon almond extract
  Dash salt
12 crackers
  Strawberry halves

Beat egg white until stiff but not dry. Gradually add sugar. Stir in almond extract and salt. Spoon onto 12 crackers; bake on ungreased baking sheet at 300° for 15 minutes. Garnish with strawberry halves. Yield: 6 servings.

Spread de Luxe

2 (3-ounce) packages cream cheese
4 teaspoons anchovy paste
1 hard-cooked egg, sieved
1½ teaspoons grated onion
¼ teaspoon salt
⅛ teaspoon paprika
2 teaspoons parsley flakes
¼ teaspoon Tabasco sauce
2 tablespoons light cream

Blend all ingredients, adding a little more cream if necessary to make a mixture of spreading consistency. Yield: 1½ cups.

Apple-Wiches

Wash an apple for each person; slice each apple into six slices. Dip apple

slices in orange juice or lemonade and drain on paper towel. Place a slice of aged cheese between two apple slices to make a sandwich; serve with hot tea or coffee as a snack.

Variation

Spread one side of each apple slice with peanut butter and fit two slices together.

Nibblers

1 (6-ounce) package pretzel sticks
2 (8-ounce) cans salted peanuts
4 cups crisp rice cereal
4 cups crisp oat cereal
1½ cups butter or margarine
¼ cup Worcestershire sauce
1 tablespoon garlic salt
1 tablespoon onion salt
1 tablespoon celery salt

Break pretzel sticks into small pieces and mix with peanuts and cereals in a large roasting pan. Heat butter or margarine until melted and stir in Worcestershire sauce, garlic, onion, and celery salts. Pour over cereal mixture and mix thoroughly. Cover and bake at 225° for 1 hour. Remove cover and bake for another hour, stirring occasionally. Yield: 4 quarts.

Prune Bums

12 large dried prunes
4 tablespoons peanut butter

Place prunes in bowl. Cover with hot water and soak for 30 minutes. Slit one side and lift out seed. Stuff each prune with peanut butter. Press to close. Yield: 1 dozen.

Fruit Sweets

1 (8-ounce) package pitted dates
1 (3½-ounce) can flaked coconut
½ cup chopped nuts
½ pound dried figs
1 tablespoon orange juice
1 teaspoon grated orange rind

Put dates, coconut, nuts, and figs through food chopper. Knead in the orange juice and rind. Press into greased loafpan, or shape into balls. Shaped small balls may be rolled in toasted, chopped coconut, or finely ground nuts. Yield: 6 to 8 servings.

Orange Snackies

1 cup softened butter
1 (1-pound) box sifted powdered sugar
   Grated rind of 1 orange
½ cup orange juice or frozen orange juice
   concentrate, undiluted
1½ loaves sandwich bread

Blend butter, sugar, and grated orange rind. Gradually add orange juice and whip thoroughly. Trim edges off breads slices and cut each slice into halves or quarters. Spread bread with orange mixture and toast under the broiler until lightly browned. Serve warm or cold. Yield: 4 dozen.

Popcorn Balls

5 quarts popped popcorn
2 cups sugar
½ cup white corn syrup
⅓ teaspoon salt
1½ cups water
1 tablespoon vanilla extract

Discard any grains of the corn that are not tender, and put the perfect kernels in a large pan. Combine sugar, corn syrup, salt, and water in a saucepan, stir until well mixed, and then bring to boil. Boil without stirring to 260° or until candy threads from the spoon. Add vanilla. Remove from heat and pour slowly over corn, stirring and turning it with a spoon so every kernel will be coated with syrup. Make the sugared corn into balls and wrap in waxed paper. Yield: about 20 balls.

Rainbow Popcorn Balls

1 cup light corn syrup
½ cup sugar
1 (3-ounce) package fruit-
   flavored gelatin
½ pound salted peanuts, coarsely ground
9 cups popped corn

Combine syrup and sugar and bring to a boil; remove from heat. Add gelatin, and stir until dissolved. Add peanuts and pour over popcorn, mixing well. Shape into balls. Yield: about 4 dozen (1½-inch) balls.

Molasses Popcorn Balls

1½ quarts popcorn (popped)
¼ teaspoon salt
½ cup light molasses
½ cup dark corn syrup
1½ teaspoons vinegar
1½ tablespoons butter or margarine

Put the popcorn into a very large bowl, and sprinkle with salt. Combine molasses, corn syrup, and vinegar in a saucepan; cook, stirring occasionally, until a drop of mixture forms a soft ball in cold water (240°). Continue cooking, stirring constantly, to 270° or until a little mixture in cold water is slightly brittle. Remove from heat, add butter or margarine, and stir only enough to mix. Pour over popcorn, tossing to coat each kernel. Shape into balls. Yield: 10 (2½-inch) popcorn balls.

Party Mix

⅔ cup butter or margarine
1 tablespoon Worcestershire sauce
¼ teaspoon salt
⅛ teaspoon garlic salt or powder
2 cups bite-sized shredded wheat
2 cups bite-sized shredded rice
2 cups salted peanuts
Pretzel sticks

Melt butter or margarine in shallow pan over low heat. Stir in Worcestershire sauce, salt, and garlic salt. Add other ingredients; mix gently until all pieces are covered with butter or margarine. Bake at 300° about 30 minutes, stirring gently every 10 minutes. Spread out to cool. Yield: 8 cups.

Popcorn

Corn may be popped in a metal popper, a skillet, or an electric popper. After popping, sprinkle with salt, and add melted butter or margarine and stir to coat kernels. A cup of corn makes from 15 to 20 cups when popped.

Metal popper: Do not try to pop too much at a time because if the popper becomes too full, corn will not have room to pop. Shake popper constantly, and cook over low heat.

Skillet: Melt 2 tablespoons shortening or heat 2 tablespoons salad oil in the skillet. Add ½ cup corn, cover, and shake the skillet over the heat until corn is popped.

Electric: Follow the directions of the manufacturer, but be sure that you do not add too much corn.

Beef Fondue

1½ pounds beef tenderloin, ¾ inch thick
Fresh parsley
Buttery-flavor cooking oil

Arrange beef cubes on platter and border with parsley. Heat oil on range to 400°; pour into fondue pot to depth of 2 inches. Place pot on table and keep hot over canned heat. Spear meat with fondue fork or skewer and hold in hot oil until browned as desired. Dip in desired sauce. Yield: 4 to 6 servings.

Variations

1. Chicken Fondue: Cut 3 whole chicken breasts (boned and skinned) into ½-inch cubes. Cook chicken in hot oil until lightly browned, ½ to 1 minute.

2. Shrimp Fondue: Cook 2 pounds medium shrimp (shelled and deveined) in hot oil until lightly browned, about ½ to 1 minute.

Teriyaki Steak for Fondue

- 1 pound sirloin steak
- ⅔ cup soy sauce
- ¼ cup white wine
- 2 tablespoons sugar
- ½ tablespoon ground ginger
- 1 clove garlic, minced

Cut steak into ¾-inch cubes. Combine other ingredients and put in a dish with a cover. Add steak cubes and marinate for at least 30 to 40 minutes. Spear meat with fondue fork and cook in hot oil until as done as desired. Yield: 4 to 6 servings.

Pizza Spread

- ½ pound ground beef
- ¾ teaspoon salt
- ⅛ teaspoon pepper
- ¼ teaspoon ground oregano
  Dash garlic salt
- ¼ cup chopped ripe olives
- 1½ teaspoons chopped onion
- ¼ cup grated Parmesan cheese
- 1 (3-ounce) can tomato paste
  Sliced bread
  Sliced American cheese

Put ground beef into cold skillet and cook over low heat until meat is well done, stirring constantly. Add other ingredients except bread and sliced cheese and cook for 5 minutes longer over low heat. Cool and store in refrigerator until ready to use.

To make pizzas, spread mixture on bread, covering entire area, and top with a slice of American cheese. Bake at 375° for 10 to 15 minutes, or until cheese is melted. Yield: 8 servings.

Peppered Nuts

Sauté 1 pound pecan halves in a little butter or margarine. Add 2 teaspoons Worcestershire sauce, a few dashes of Tabasco, salt, and white pepper. Roast at 300° for 20 minutes, or until brown. Yield: 1 pound nuts.

Salted Pumpkin Seeds

Remove stringy fiber that clings to pumpkin seeds. Spread seeds on a baking sheet and roast at 300° for 15 to 20 minutes. Do not brown. Melt a little butter or margarine in a skillet; add seeds and brown lightly, shaking the pan constantly. Drain on absorbent paper towels and salt lightly.

Biscuit Pizza Snacks

- ½ to ¾ pound sausage
- 1 tablespoon crushed oregano
- 1 clove garlic, minced
- 1 (10-count) package refrigerated biscuits
- 1 (3-ounce) can tomato paste
- 1 cup shredded sharp Cheddar cheese
- ¼ cup grated Parmesan cheese
  Sliced stuffed olives

Brown sausage; drain. Add oregano and garlic. On a greased baking sheet flatten refrigerated biscuits to 4-inch circles with the bottom of a floured custard cup, leaving a rim around edges. Fill with sausage and tomato paste. Sprinkle with shredded cheese. Bake at 425° for about 10 to 12 minutes. Top with a slice of stuffed olive. Yield: 10 pizzas.

Pickled Eggs

15 to 18 hard-cooked eggs
3 cups white vinegar
1 cup water
1 teaspoon salt
  Pickling spices, if desired

Carefully shell eggs. Bring vinegar, water, salt, and spices (if desired) to boiling point. Place eggs in hot sterilized jars and cover with boiling liquid. Seal immediately.

To pickle eggs with beet vinegar, drain liquid from jars of pickled beets and use this instead of vinegar and water in recipe. Yield: about 2 quarts.

Egg-Peanut Spread

6 hard-cooked eggs, finely chopped
½ cup finely chopped roasted peanuts
2 tablespoons finely chopped pimiento
2 tablespoons finely chopped olives
1 tablespoon finely chopped chives
¾ teaspoon salt
¼ cup mayonnaise
¼ cup milk
¼ teaspoon Worcestershire sauce

Combine all finely chopped ingredients and salt. Stir mayonnaise, milk, and Worcestershire sauce together. Blend with eggs and other ingredients. Stir well. Serve with crackers and potato chips. Yield: 2 cups.

Surprise Spread

1 (6-ounce) jar peanut butter
3 tablespoons chili sauce
4 teaspoons Worcestershire sauce
½ cup chopped stuffed olives
¼ teaspoon Tabasco sauce

Blend all ingredients thoroughly and chill. Yield: 1½ cups.

Bordelaise Sauce

2 medium carrots, chopped
2 medium onions, chopped
2 sprigs parsley, chopped
¼ cup butter
2 tablespoons all-purpose flour
1 cup dry white wine
1½ cups consomme
½ teaspoon salt
½ teaspoon pepper
¼ teaspoon thyme
1 bay leaf
1 cup dry red wine
1 teaspoon freshly squeezed lemon juice

Sauté carrots, half of the chopped onion, and parsley in butter in medium saucepan until golden brown. Add flour and cook until slightly brown, stirring constantly. Add white wine, consomme, and seasonings. Bring to a boil; cover and simmer for 15 minutes.

Meanwhile, put remaining onion and red wine into an 8-inch skillet. Bring to a boil and cook for about 10 minutes until 2 tablespoons of liquid remain. Drain liquid from carrot mixture into red wine. Add lemon juice and cook 10 to 15 minutes until reduced to about 1 cup. Serve warm. Yield: 1 cup.

Hot Mustard Sauce

½ cup dry mustard
½ cup hot water
1 tablespoon oil
1 teaspoon salt

Combine ingredients and allow to stand at room temperature for 15 minutes to develop flavor. Yield: about 1 cup.

Curry Sauce

1 cup commercial sour cream
½ cup mayonnaise
1 tablespoon chopped fresh parsley
2 teaspoons curry powder
1 teaspoon freshly squeezed
   lemon juice
½ teaspoon Worcestershire sauce
½ clove garlic, crushed
¼ teaspoon salt

Blend all ingredients until smooth; chill. Serve as dip for cooked beef, chicken or shrimp. Yield: 1½ cups.

Red Devil Sauce

1 (15-ounce) can or 2 (8-ounce) cans
   tomato sauce with tomato bits
4 teaspoons sugar
2 tablespoons thinly sliced green onions
   (tops included)
2 tablespoons red wine vinegar
1 clove garlic, crushed
   Few drops red pepper sauce, if desired

Combine all ingredients; chill. Serve as dip for cooked beef, chicken, or shrimp. Yield: about 2 cups.

Barbecue Sauce

2 (8-ounce) cans tomato sauce
2 tablespoons brown sugar
¼ cup vinegar
2 tablespoons Worcestershire sauce
1 teaspoon salt
1 teaspoon dry mustard
1 teaspoon chili powder
1 tablespoon paprika
⅛ teaspoon cayenne pepper
2 tablespoons chopped green onion tops

Combine all ingredients except green onion tops. Simmer for 15 minutes, stirring occasionally. Serve hot with onion sprinkled on top. Yield: 2½ cups.

Chili Sauce

½ cup chili sauce
1 teaspoon horseradish
½ teaspoon steak sauce

Combine all ingredients. Cover and refrigerate at least 1 hour. Yield: ½ cup.

Beverages

Berries, fruits, and even roots from native Southern plants have been the basis of many Southern beverages. Sassafras tea has been served in the South since the time the white man first reached these shores. Although it might not have palatable characteristics, it has through the years proven to be a most popular beverage.

Before the days of the home freezers, berries were made into concentrated mixtures called "acids" or "shrub." These concentrates were diluted at the time of serving to make a basis for fruit punch or were served on their own merits.

Only the most recent cookbooks have dropped the term "sweet" from the designation of milk in a recipe, for early settlers were familiar with sweet milk, clabber, and buttermilk, and each served its purpose well. Some were interchangeable in recipes. Seldom do we now see a recipe calling for sour milk; buttermilk is about the only form of sour milk that is used in a day when dairy farmers have their milk delivered to their doors the same as city friends and relatives. Thus, our recipes call for "milk" or "buttermilk."

The South boasts two of the largest citrus-producing areas in the country, Florida and Texas. A country kitchen would as soon be without bread as without lemons in the summertime. The South probably uses more lemonade than any other section of the country and citrus juices are the base for many punches served at parties or to drop-in guests.

For festive occasions, real eggnog is a must, especially for gatherings at Christmas or New Year's. Eggnog became a Southern favorite because early settlers had an abundance of fresh cream and eggs on the farm. However, today's rural families may buy the eggs and cream, as well as the "nog" which is served. And served it is — and in no other place with more genuine hospitality.

Coffee

There are many types of coffeemakers. Use the one that suits your family best. Whatever method you prefer for making coffee, these rules will help you.

1. Start with a sparkling clean coffeemaker; rinse it just before using.
2. Start with fresh, cold water.
3. Measure coffee and water accurately. For each serving, allow 2 level tablespoons coffee to ¾ measuring cup of water for each serving.
4. Be sure your coffee is the proper grind for your coffeemaker.
5. Your coffeemaker will give best results at full capacity. For small amounts, use a small coffeemaker, if possible.
6. Time coffeemaking carefully, according to the type coffeemaker you are using. This is taken care of if you use an automatic coffeemaker.
7. Serve coffee immediately after brewing.

Drip Coffee

Place the required amount of pulverized or drip-grind coffee in the strainer and place in position. Pour boiling water over it. The water will drip through the coffee very slowly.

Boiled Coffee

Measure the coffee into the pot and add the white of an egg or just the eggshell. Add a little cold water, and mix well. Pour on boiling water in the correct amount and place on the heat to boil. As soon as the coffee boils up, reduce the heat and allow the coffee to settle. Add a little cold water to allow grounds to settle. Remove eggshell and serve hot.

Percolated Coffee

Place cold water in the percolator. Put ground coffee in the strainer. As the coffee heats, the water bubbles up through the hole in the strainer and trickles down through the coffee. Coffee is usually percolated 5 to 10 minutes according to the strength desired.

Coffee Made in Vacuum-Type Coffeemaker

Measure drip-grind coffee in upper part of coffeemaker. Measure water into lower bowl. Place upper bowl snugly on lower bowl. When water in lower bowl is heated, most of it rises to upper bowl. When all but a small amount has risen or when water in upper bowl starts to bubble, turn off heat. Let coffeemaker stand until brew returns to lower bowl.

Instant Coffee

When only a few cups of coffee are needed, make coffee right in the cup. When several cups are to be served, make all at once in a large pot. Make the coffee according to the label directions.

Iced Coffee

Make coffee double strength, and pour hot coffee over ice cubes; or make coffee full strength, let cool, and pour over ice cubes. Use sugar and cream as desired.

Blackberry Shrub

4 cups blackberry juice
  Sugar syrup
1 cup grape juice
  Juice of 2 lemons

Strain juice from canned blackberries, pressing through as much pulp as possible, and measure. If you use fresh berries, prepare juice by cooking berries with just enough water to keep them from burning, and strain. Sweeten to taste with sugar syrup; add grape juice, lemon juice, and chill. Fill glasses one-third full and add water or crushed ice. Yield: 1½ quarts.

Note: Fresh raspberries or loganberries, as well as canned berries, may be used.

Christmas Party Punch

1 (12-ounce) can frozen orange juice
  concentrate
1 (6-ounce) can frozen lemonade
  concentrate
1 (18-ounce) can pineapple juice
6 cups water
6 pints cranberry juice cocktail

Add water to frozen concentrates as directed on cans. Mix all ingredients well. Serve in punchbowl over ice. Yield: 50 servings.

Quick Fruit Punch

1 (46-ounce) can sweetened orange juice
1 (46-ounce) can sweetened
  pineapple juice
4 cups ginger ale

Chill thoroughly. Mix well. Add ginger ale last. Yield: 30 servings.

Fruit Juice Punch

3 cups sugar
3 quarts water
1 cup strong tea
  Juice of 12 lemons
  Juice of 12 oranges
4 cups grape juice
1 (8-ounce) can crushed pineapple
8 cups ginger ale

Boil sugar and water 8 minutes. Chill; add tea, juices, and pineapple. Set in refrigerator to mellow. Just before serving, add the ginger ale. Yield: 50 servings.

Ginger Ale-Sherbet Punch

6 quarts ginger ale
7 pints sherbet (mint or orange)
2 or 3 pints vanilla ice cream (optional)

Combine 1 quart ginger ale and 1 pint sherbet, beating well before adding any more. Continue adding in these proportions as needed.

For extra "body" to the punch, add 2 or 3 pints of vanilla ice cream every so often. Yield: 50 (½-cup) servings.

Golden Punch

2 cups freshly squeezed lemon juice
6 cups orange juice
8 cups apple juice
4 cups sugar syrup, or sweeten to taste
1 quart orange sherbet (optional)

Combine all ingredients and chill. Add 1 quart orange sherbet just before serving, if desired. Yield: about 30 servings.

Hot Fruit Punch

> 4 teaspoons tea leaves
> 2 cups boiling water
> 2 cups sugar
> 2 cups orange juice
> 1 cup freshly squeezed lemon juice
> 1 cup pineapple juice
> 2½ quarts boiling water
>   Orange and lemon slices

Steep tea in boiling water for 5 minutes. Strain. Add sugar to hot tea and let cool. Prepare fruit juices and keep in a glass quart jar, covered tightly, until ready to use. Then add boiling water; mix all ingredients in punchbowl and garnish with orange and lemon slices. Serve while hot. Yield: 32 small servings.

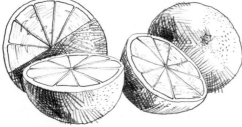

Fruit Punch

> 1 cup water
> 2 cups sugar
> 1 cup strong, hot tea
> 2 cups fruit syrup
> 1 cup freshly squeezed lemon juice
> 2 cups pineapple juice
>   Ice water
> 1 cup maraschino cherries
> 4 cups ginger ale

Boil water and sugar for 5 minutes; add tea, fruit syrup, and juices. Let stand for 30 minutes; add ice water to make 1½ gallons of liquid. Add cherries and ginger ale. Serve in punchbowl with large piece of ice. Yield: 50 servings.

Citrus Punch

> 1½ cups sugar
> 3 cups water
> 1 tablespoon instant tea
> 1½ cups lime juice
> 2 (46-ounce) cans blended grapefruit and orange juice
>   Ice cubes
> 4 cups ginger ale

Combine sugar and water in saucepan; place over low heat and stir until sugar is dissolved. Add to instant tea. Add juices; chill. Pour into punchbowl; add ice cubes; stir until ice is partially melted. Just before serving, add ginger ale. Garnish with lime slices and maraschino cherries. Yield: 44 (½-cup) servings.

Mint Punch

> 1 cup powdered sugar
> 4 lemons
> 24 sprigs of mint, chopped fine
> 1 cup sugar
> 12 stalks mint
> 8 cups ginger ale
> 4 cups water
> 4 cups shaved ice

Mix powdered sugar, lemon juice, and mint sprigs and set aside for 2 hours. Combine granulated sugar, mint stalks, water, and cut up rind of the 4 lemons. Boil together about 5 minutes; allow to cool. Stir the two mixtures together and strain. To 1 quart of this stock add, just before serving, 2 quarts of ginger ale, 1 quart shaved ice. Stock may be made several days ahead of use and stored in refrigerator. Yield: 1 gallon punch.

Strawberry Punch

1 (10-ounce) package frozen strawberries
1 (6-ounce) can frozen orange juice concentrate
1 (6-ounce) can frozen lemonade concentrate
3 cups cold water
1 (12-ounce) bottle ginger ale
  Ice cubes
1 cup fresh strawberries
3 orange slices

Thaw strawberries. Combine orange juice, lemonade, and water; chill. Add thawed strawberries and ginger ale when ready to serve. Pour over ice cubes in punchbowl. Garnish with whole fresh strawberries and orange slices. Yield: 2 quarts.

Pineapple-Lime Punch

3 quarts unsweetened pineapple juice
  Juice of 8 lemons
  Juice of 8 oranges
  Juice of 3 limes
2 cups sugar
4 quarts ginger ale
2 quarts plain soda water
  Green food coloring (optional)

Combine fruit juices and sugar. Chill thoroughly. Just before serving, add ginger ale and soda water. Tint a delicate green, if you wish. Yield: 35 cups.

Mulled Cider

8 cups apple cider
½ cup brown sugar, firmly packed
12 whole cloves
2 (2-inch) cinnamon sticks

Combine all ingredients in a saucepan. Bring to a boil; simmer for 5 minutes. Strain and serve hot in mugs or cups. Yield: 12 servings.

Hot Cider

1 gallon sweet cider
  Juice of 4 oranges
  Juice of 5 lemons
2 cups sugar
½ teaspoon ground nutmeg
3 teaspoons ground allspice
1 teaspoon ground cinnamon
4 sticks cinnamon

Mix cider, orange juice, lemon juice, and sugar in saucepan. Tie nutmeg, allspice, and ground cinnamon in a cheesecloth bag. Add to liquid, and let boil. Remove spice bag and then float cinnamon sticks on top. Serve hot. Yield: 30 servings.

Spiced Lemonade

¾ cup sugar
¾ cup water
12 whole cloves
1 (3-inch) stick cinnamon
6 lemons
4 cups water
  Decorated ice cubes

Boil sugar and ¾ cup water about 5 minutes. Combine 1 cup of the syrup with spices and cook 5 minutes. Strain. Add juice of lemons and quart of water. Chill. Pour over ice cubes when ready to serve. Lemon-decorated ice cubes or cubes with whole cloves frozen in them will add appeal to this summertime favorite. Yield: 6 servings.

Ginger Orange Ice

1½ cups cold water
1½ cups sugar
 ¼ teaspoon ground ginger
 ⅛ teaspoon ground cinnamon
  1 cup orange juice
 ¼ cup freshly squeezed lemon juice
 ¼ cup finely cut crystallized ginger
 ½ cup top milk
  1 egg white

Combine water, sugar, ground ginger, and cinnamon in a small saucepan. Stir over low heat until sugar is dissolved. Bring to a boil for 5 minutes. Let cool. Add fruit juices and crystallized ginger. Pour into freezing tray of refrigerator and freeze to mushlike consistency. Remove to a bowl. Add top milk and egg white beaten stiff. Beat well. Return to refrigerator tray and freeze, stirring every 30 minutes until mixture is set. Serve in chilled sherbet glasses. Yield: 6 to 8 servings.

Orange Frosted

  1 (6-ounce) can frozen concentrated orange juice
 ¼ cup sugar syrup
    Shaved ice
    About ⅓ cup water

Put 3 tablespoons undiluted concentrate and 1 tablespoon sugar syrup into each 12-ounce glass; mix well. Fill two-thirds full with ice. Fill with water; stir vigorously. Garnish with mint. Yield: 4 servings.

Sugar Syrup

1 cup sugar
1 cup water

Combine sugar and water in saucepan over low heat; stir until sugar is dissolved. Yield: about 1¼ cups.

Grape Juice-Lime Cooler

 ¼ cup chilled grape juice
  1 tablespoon sugar or corn syrup
  2 tablespoons chilled milk
    Carbonated water

In each glass, blend grape juice and sugar or corn syrup. Slowly stir in chilled milk. Add carbonated water to fill glasses within 1½ inches of top. Top with a scoop of frozen lime sherbet, and serve at once. Yield: 1 (8-ounce) glass.

Limeade Julep

1 (6-ounce) can frozen limeade concentrate
   Shaved ice

Put 3 tablespoons undiluted limeade concentrate into each 12-ounce glass. Fill to top with shaved ice; let stand 15 minutes. To serve immediately, fill almost to top with shaved ice, and add ¼ cup cold water. Stir. Yield: 4 servings.

Tomato Juice Cocktail

  1 quart canned tomato juice
  1 teaspoon sugar
    Juice of 1 lemon
 ½ cup kraut juice
 ¼ teaspoon grated horseradish or ½ teaspoon chili sauce
    Salt and pepper to taste

Mix ingredients together. Chill and serve. Yield: 8 (4-ounce) servings.

Cucumber-Tomato Cocktail

    1 medium cucumber
    2¼ cups tomato juice
    2 tablespoons chopped scallions and tops
    1 teaspoon Worcestershire sauce
       Juice of 1 lemon
    2 teaspoons grated horseradish
    ⅛ teaspoon Tabasco sauce
    ½ teaspoon salt
    ⅛ teaspoon black pepper
       Parsley or watercress
       Lemon wedges

Peel cucumber and grate into tomato juice; add remaining ingredients. Cover, place in refrigerator for 2 hours. Strain, and serve garnished with parsley or lemon. Yield: 6 to 8 servings.

Hot Chocolate (or Cocoa)

    4 tablespoons cocoa
    4 tablespoons sugar
    ⅛ teaspoon salt
    4 cups milk

Blend cocoa, sugar, and salt, and make syrup by using a part of the milk. Add syrup to remaining milk and heat to just below the boiling point. Serve hot, with a dash of cinnamon, or a marsh-mallow in each cup. Yield: 4 servings.

Chocolate Milk Shake

    1 cup cold milk
    2 tablespoons chocolate syrup
       (commercial or homemade)

To the cold milk, add 2 tablespoons chocolate syrup. Shake or beat well. Yield: 1 serving.

Chocolate Syrup

    4 squares unsweetened chocolate
    1 cup boiling water
    1 cup sugar

Melt 4 squares chocolate over hot water. Add 1 cup boiling water, and cook directly over low heat until thick and smooth, stirring constantly. Add 1 cup sugar and continue cooking for 3 or 4 minutes. Cool and store. Yield: 1¼ cups.

Banana Milk Shake

    6 bananas
    6 cups milk
    1 teaspoon vanilla extract
       Ground nutmeg

Mash ripe bananas with a fork in a big bowl. When soft, beat them with a rotary beater. Add cold milk and vanilla and beat until drink is very frothy. Dust with nutmeg. Yield: 6 servings.

Coffee Milk Shake

    1 cup strong fresh coffee
       Pinch salt
       Ice cubes
    2 large scoops vanilla ice cream
    1½ tablespoons sugar
       Whipped cream
       Shaved chocolate

Pour hot coffee over ice cubes to cool. Then put coffee, salt, ice cream, and sugar into mixing bowl. Beat just long enough to blend. Serve in a tall glass. Garnish with whipped cream and shaved chocolate. Yield: 1 serving.

Fruit Milk Shake

1 or 2 bananas
½ cup orange juice
¼ cup freshly squeezed lemon juice
1 cup canned pineapple juice
4 cups milk (use whole milk or 2 cups evaporated milk and 2 cups water)

Mash bananas, and add fruit juices. Chill thoroughly and pour into cold milk. Beat with egg beater. Serve cold. Yield: 4 servings.

Peppermint Milk Shake

¼ pound peppermint stick candy
⅛ teaspoon salt
4 cups chilled milk
   Whipped cream
   Crushed peppermint candy

Crush candy thoroughly. Add salt and 1 cup of milk; cover. Chill for 2 or 3 hours. Stir occasionally until candy dissolves. Before serving, add remaining milk. Shake, and top with whipped cream and crushed candy. Yield: 4 servings.

Cherry Coolie

1 (3-ounce) package cherry-flavored gelatin
1 cup boiling water
½ cup cold water
   Ginger Ale
   Vanilla ice cream

Dissolve gelatin in boiling water. Add cold water. Stir well, and use this mixture as a syrup. Put 4 tablespoons syrup in a glass and fill glass two-thirds full with ginger ale. Add vanilla ice cream and stir to blend. Yield: 6 glasses.

Eggnog

4 eggs
4 tablespoons honey
   Pinch salt
3 cups whole milk

Beat eggs until thick and lemon colored. Add honey, salt, and milk and mix well. Serve cold. Yield: 4 servings.

Orangenog

1½ cups chilled orange juice
1 tablespoon freshly squeezed lemon juice
3 tablespoons sugar
2 cups chilled milk

Mix first three ingredients and stir slowly into milk. For egg-orangenog: Add fruit juice mixture gradually to 2 well beaten eggs, then stir into diluted milk and mix as directed for orangenog. Yield: 4 servings.

Mocha Foam Drink

2 squares unsweetened chocolate or ⅓ cup cocoa
2½ cups milk, divided
1 teaspoon instant coffee
1 cup hot water
   Dash salt
⅓ cup sugar
8 marshmallows

Place chocolate or cocoa and ½ cup of the milk in saucepan. Heat slowly, stirring constantly, until a smooth paste is formed. Add remaining 2 cups milk, and blend. Dissolve coffee in hot water, and add chocolate mixture. Add salt and sugar. Heat, and stir until mixture is scalded. Add marshmallows, and beat until marshmallows are melted and mixture is foamy. Yield: 6 servings.

Spiced Hot Chocolate Milk

  4 *cups chocolate milk*
  ¼ *teaspoon crushed cardamom*
  ¼ *teaspoon ground mace*
  ½ *teaspoon ground nutmeg*
  2 *cinnamon sticks*

Combine all ingredients; heat to serving temperature over low heat, stirring occasionally. Remove cinnamon sticks. Pour into mugs and garnish as desired. Yield: 4 to 6 servings.

Witches' Brew

  4 *cups milk*
  3 *sticks whole cinnamon*
  ¼ *cup sugar*
  ½ *cup quick chocolate drink mix*
  4 *cups hot coffee*

Bring milk, cinnamon sticks, and sugar to simmering point in large saucepan. Reduce heat and cook 10 minutes until cinnamon flavor is released. Add chocolate mix to the hot milk; combine with hot coffee. Yield: 8 servings.

Peach Crush

  2 *cups very ripe peaches*
  6 *cups milk*

Mash ripe peaches and add to chilled milk. Beat with rotary egg beater or blender until mixture is smooth. Pour over crushed ice. Bananas or other fruits may be used. Yield: 6 servings.

Peanut Butter Milk

1 ½ *cups nonfat dry milk solids*
  2 *tablespoons sugar*
  6 *cups cold water*
  ⅓ *cup peanut butter*

Combine milk solids and sugar; add cold water, and shake or beat until smooth. Add a small amount of mixture to peanut butter and mix until smooth. Continue adding milk until all the mixture is used. Chill thoroughly. Yield: 6 servings.

Spiced Milk

1 ½ *cups nonfat dry milk solids*
  ½ *teaspoon ground cinnamon*
  ½ *teaspoon ground nutmeg*
  1 *tablespoon sugar*
  ¼ *teaspoon salt*
  6 *cups milk*

Add dry ingredients to milk and beat, stir, or shake until smooth. Serve cold. Yield: 6 servings.

Hot Spiced Milk

1 cup milk
1 tablespoon molasses
  Dash of ground cinnamon
  Ground allspice or nutmeg

Combine milk, molasses, and spices. Heat thoroughly. Pour into cup and dust with additional spices. Omit additional spices and use a stick of cinnamon for stirring, if desired. Yield: 1 serving.

Instant Spiced Tea Mix

½ cup instant tea
2 cups orange-flavored instant breakfast drink
1 (3-ounce) package sweetened lemonade mix
1 teaspoon ground cloves (optional)
1 teaspoon ground cinnamon (optional)
2 cups sugar

Combine ingredients in large bowl and mix well. Spoon into jars and seal. To serve, add 2 teaspoons to a cup of boiling water. Yield: about 40 cups.

Hot Spiced Tea

1 cup sugar
1 cup water
2 sticks cinnamon
½ cup orange juice
½ cup pineapple juice
¼ cup freshly squeezed lemon juice
6 cups water
6 tea bags or 6 tablespoons tea

Combine sugar, water, and cinnamon, and boil for 5 minutes. Add fruit juices and tea made by steeping tea bags in hot water 5 minutes. Grated rind may be added, if desired. For a mild cinnamon flavor, remove sticks from syrup before adding juices and tea. Serve piping hot. Yield: 10 to 12 servings.

Iced Tea-Ade

8 cups boiling water
12 teaspoons tea leaves
24 mint leaves, crushed
1 teaspoon grated lemon rind
1 cup sugar
2 cups water
½ teaspoon salt
⅜ cup freshly squeezed lemon juice

Pour boiling water over tea leaves and add crushed mint leaves. Steep 3 to 5 minutes and strain the tea and chill. Prepare lemon ice by combining lemon rind, sugar, water, salt, and lemon juice. Place over heat and stir until the sugar is dissolved. Then boil for 5 minutes. Place in refrigerator tray and freeze. When ready to serve, fill each iced tea glass one-fourth full with the lemon ice or lemon sherbet. Add the tea. Serve with sugar and garnish with mint. Yield: 8 servings.

Hot Tea

1 cup boiling water
1 teaspoon tea
½ teaspoon sugar
  Lemon or cream

Pour briskly boiling water over tea, cover, and steep 3 to 5 minutes. Strain, and add sugar and sliced lemon or a small amount of cream. Yield: 1 serving.

Soups, Stews, & Chowders

Wise cooks have always known that the most efficient way to stretch meat and vegetables is to pull out the soup pot and fill it with anything that happens to be available and edible, and ladle out an imaginative far-reaching result.

In the South of earlier years, the ingredients ranged from squirrels to black-eyed peas; the pot was a heavy, black iron kettle, and what was ladled out became tradition.

The most notable of Southern soups and stews were concocted with crowds in mind, reflecting the life-style of a gregarious people who gathered at the slightest excuse — from a political rally to a church meeting.

Brunswick stew, containing whatever the hunters happened to have killed that day, is still a favorite choice wherever men gather in the South. Although the ingredients today are usually more easily obtained than squirrels and hog's heads, the hearty conversation and spicy taste remain.

Undoubtedly the most famous Southern stew is the Kentucky burgoo of political rally fame. This thick soup of vegetables, supported by beef or chicken, originated in Europe and came to America with Flemish and Belgian sailors. It is an undisputed fact, however, that its citizenship now belongs to Kentucky, and it is a matter of speculation as to how many elections have been won on the strength of the burgoo rather than on what the candidate had to say.

While the early settlers of Kentucky were throwing in whatever they had to produce a burgoo, the never-to-be-outdone Creoles were utilizing their teeming supplies of seafood in bouillabaisse and gumbo.

If it seems a little unbelievable that an assortment of diverse foods from field, stream, and forest can go into a big pot and come out a perfect blend of flavors, watch someone stand over a steaming kettle of burgoo or Brunswick stew and you'll know that what goes in with the meat and vegetables is a magic spice called ingenuity.

Beef Stew No. 1

    2   tablespoons shortening
    1   pound boneless beef, cut into
        1½-inch cubes
    1   onion, chopped
    1   medium turnip, diced
    1   cup canned tomatoes
    ¼   cup catsup
    1½ teaspoons salt
    ¼   teaspoon pepper
    3   cups broth, or 3 beef bouillon cubes
        dissolved in 3 cups hot water
    2   cups cubed, peeled potatoes
    2   cups sliced, peeled carrots
    6   small whole onions, peeled

Heat shortening in heavy kettle. Brown
meat cubes on all sides in shortening.
Add chopped onion, turnip, tomatoes,
catsup, seasonings, and broth. Cover,
bring to a boil; reduce heat, and simmer
until meat is tender, about 1½ hours.
Add vegetables and more water just to
cover, if necessary. Cover and simmer until vegetables are tender. Add
more salt and pepper to taste. Yield:
6 servings.

Beef Stew No. 2

    2   to 2½ pounds very lean beef
    2   tablespoons vegetable oil
    2   large onions, diced
        Water
    5   large potatoes, cut into eighths
    4   or 5 large carrots, cut into 2-inch slices
        Salt and pepper to taste
        Garlic salt (optional)
        Diced celery (optional)
    1   (1-pound) can tomatoes

Cut beef into cubes; brown with diced
onions in vegetable oil in a heavy Dutch

oven. Add about 2 cups boiling water,
and simmer until meat is tender. Add
other ingredients, and cook until vegetables are tender. Yield: 6 servings.

Beef Stew with Dumplings

    1½ pounds lean beef (boned chuck,
        round, flank, or rump)
    1½ teaspoons salt
    ⅛   teaspoon pepper
    3   tablespoons all-purpose flour
    3   tablespoons shortening
    4   cups water
    ½   teaspoon Tabasco sauce
    12 small white onions, peeled
    6   medium carrots, scraped and
        quartered
    1½ cups all-purpose flour
    2   teaspoons baking powder
    ¾   teaspoon salt
    ¾   cup milk

Cut beef into 1½-inch pieces. Blend together ½ teaspoon of the salt, pepper,
and flour. Roll pieces of meat in blended
mixture. Put shortening in a heavy kettle; add beef, and brown on all sides.
Add water, ½ teaspoon of the salt, and
Tabasco sauce. Cover; simmer for 2 to
2½ hours until meat is almost tender.
Add remaining ½ teaspoon salt, onions,
and carrots; cover, and cook until vegetables are tender. For dumplings, sift
together flour, baking powder, and salt.
Add milk; stir only until blended. Drop
by spoonfuls on top of piece of meat or
vegetable in stew. Cook uncovered for
10 minutes; cover tightly, and cook over
low heat for 10 minutes longer. Yield:
6 servings.

Grits–Beef Stew

2½ pounds beef for stew
1 cup all-purpose flour
2 tablespoons salt
½ teaspoon pepper
6 tablespoons shortening
2 cloves garlic, minced
4 cups boiling water
3 cups cooked tomatoes
1 teaspoon Worcestershire sauce
18 small white onions, peeled and quartered
7 carrots, peeled and cut into 2-inch strips
2 cups cooked green peas
1 cup uncooked grits

Cut meat into 1½-inch cubes. Combine flour, salt, and pepper; coat meat well with this mixture. Melt shortening in Dutch oven; add meat and brown. Add garlic, boiling water, tomatoes, and Worcestershire sauce. Cover and simmer for about 2 hours or until meat is tender. Add onions and carrots, and cook an additional 20 minutes. Add more salt, if needed. Add peas and uncooked grits; cook for 15 minutes. Yield: 8 servings.

Quick Chili

1 tablespoon shortening
½ cup chopped onion
1 pound ground beef
1 green pepper, chopped
1 (10½-ounce) can condensed tomato soup
1 teaspoon salt
4 teaspoons (or more) chili powder
⅛ teaspoon black pepper
1⁄16 teaspoon ground red pepper
1 (1-pound) can red kidney beans

Melt shortening in heavy skillet. Add onion and cook until brown, then add ground beef and brown. Stir frequently so there will be no lumps of meat. Add green pepper, tomato soup, salt, chili powder, black and red pepper, and kidney beans. Heat mixture thoroughly and serve piping hot. Yield: 6 servings.

Oven-Cooked Beef Stew

1 pound beef stew meat
   Salt, pepper, all-purpose flour
3 tablespoons shortening
2 medium onions, chopped
1¾ cups water
1 (10½-ounce) can condensed tomato soup
1 small bay leaf
2 whole cloves
1 stalk celery, sliced
4 carrots, sliced
1 cup canned peas
3 medium potatoes, cut into eighths
   Salt and pepper

Cut meat into 1-inch cubes; sprinkle with salt and pepper, and dredge with flour. Melt shortening in skillet and brown meat thoroughly. Transfer meat to a 2-quart casserole. Lightly brown chopped onions in the hot shortening; add to meat. Heat water with tomato soup and pour over meat. Add seasonings and sliced celery. Cover and bake at 325° for 1½ hours, or until meat is nearly tender. Add sliced carrots, peas, and potatoes cut in eighths; sprinkle with salt and pepper, and mix in with beef and gravy. Cover and continue baking for 45 minutes. Yield: 4 to 6 servings.

Teriyaki Stew

2 pounds lean stew beef, cut in 2-inch cubes
¼ cup cooking oil
  Boiling water
2 bay leaves
  Salt and pepper to taste
1 teaspoon bottled brown bouquet sauce or soy sauce
1 whole stalk celery
1 carrot
1 onion
1 bunch celery, cut in 2-inch-long strips
1 bunch small carrots, cut in 2-inch lengths
4 medium potatoes, cut in quarters
12 whole small onions
4 tablespoons Worcestershire sauce
1 tablespoon cooking sherry (optional)
1 pound fresh mushrooms, cut in halves
1 (10-ounce) package frozen peas or 1 pound fresh peas
3 tablespoons instant blending flour for thickening

Brown beef in cooking oil in skillet. Put in deep pot and cover with boiling water; add seasonings, whole stalk celery, carrot, and onion. Cook slowly until meat is tender (at least 1 hour).

Remove bay leaves, celery, and carrot. Add cut celery, carrots, potatoes, and small onions. Cook about 20 minutes or until onions are tender. Additional water may be added with the vegetables if necessary. Add Worcestershire sauce, sherry, mushrooms, and frozen peas; cook several minutes. Mix flour with enough water to make a thin and fairly clear gravy; add to mixture and stir until thickened. Serve hot over rice. Yield: 6 to 8 servings.

Southern Hash

4 or 5 raw potatoes
2 medium onions
4 tablespoons shortening
½ cup tomatoes
1 cup meat stock or gravy
2 cups cooked, chopped meat
  Salt
  Pepper

Put potatoes and onions through a food chopper. Melt shortening, add potatoes, onions, and tomatoes, cover pan, and cook until potatoes are done. Stir occasionally to prevent sticking. Add chopped meat and season with salt and pepper. Heat thoroughly and serve hot. Yield: 6 servings.

Brunswick Stew No. 1

1 (4- to 5-pound) hen
2 pounds boneless stew meat
1 pound onions
3 pounds potatoes
2 (16-ounce) cans tomatoes
2 (17-ounce) cans cream-style corn
1 (17-ounce) can green peas
1 (17-ounce) can lima beans
1½ bottles catsup
1 (14-ounce) bottle Worcestershire sauce
½ cup vinegar
¾ cup freshly squeezed lemon juice
4 teaspoons Tabasco sauce
2 teaspoons salt
  Black pepper

Put hen and stew meat in a saucepan with water to cover. Cook until well done or meat leaves the bone. Grind and set meat aside. Put onions and potatoes through food grinder and add to the broth. Cook until well done. Add meat and other ingredients. Cook over low heat until well done and thick (about 2 to 3 hours). Serve hot; or cool, pour into containers, and freeze. Yield: 5 to 6 quarts.

Brunswick Stew No. 2

3 squirrels, or 2 rabbits
5 quarts boiling water
1 pound salt pork, cut into strips
1 large onion, minced
4 cups chopped tomatoes
2 cups green lima beans
2 cups corn
8 to 12 diced potatoes
1 tablespoon salt
1 teaspoon black pepper
⅛ teaspoon cayenne pepper
4 teaspoons sugar
½ cup butter or margarine
4 tablespoons all-purpose flour

Cut squirrels or rabbits into serving-size pieces. Drop pieces into boiling water in a large kettle; add salt pork and minced onion. Cover and simmer for 2

hours, removing film at beginning of cooking. Add vegetables and seasonings and bring to a boil; cover and simmer 1 hour longer, stirring occasionally to prevent burning. Make a paste of butter or margarine and flour; shape into small balls and drop into stew. Boil for 10 minutes, stirring to make a smooth stew. Add more seasoning, if necessary. Yield: 12 servings.

Chicken and Oyster Gumbo

12 cups water
 1 (3- to 5-pound) chicken
⅓ cup shortening
½ cup all-purpose flour
 1 large onion, chopped
    Salt, black and red pepper
½ cup chopped green onion tops
⅓ cup chopped parsley
 3 dozen oysters
 1 tablespoon filé
    Cooked rice

Pour water into large pot. Cut chicken into serving-size pieces, and brown in hot shortening. When brown, put in pot with water; add flour to the shortening, and brown very slowly. Add onion. Let cook until slightly brown and clear; add to chicken and seasonings. Cook very slowly until chicken is tender, stirring often. Add green onion tops and parsley. Cook for 10 minutes; add oysters; let cook until oysters curl. Remove from heat, add filé, and stir; serve at once. To serve, place a serving of cooked rice in soup plate, add a piece of chicken, fill plate with gumbo. Yield: 10 to 12 servings.

Chicken Stew No. 1

1 (3- to 4-pound) stewing chicken
  Salt and pepper
½ cup shortening
3 tablespoons all-purpose flour
2 cups chopped onions
½ cup chopped celery
½ cup chopped green peppers
2 cups water
1 (4-ounce) can mushrooms
¼ cup chopped onion tops or shallots
2 tablespoons chopped parsley
  Cooked rice

Disjoint chicken; salt and pepper the pieces. Brown quickly in the shortening, and remove chicken after browning. Add flour to shortening and brown. Add onions, celery, and peppers; cook slowly until tender. Return chicken to pan. Add water and mushrooms. Cover, and simmer for about 2½ to 3 hours. Add onion tops or shallots about 10 minutes before done. Add parsley 5 minutes before removing from heat. Serve with cooked rice. Yield: 8 servings.

Chicken Stew No. 2

1 (5- to 6-pound) chicken, cut up
6 cups hot water
1 medium onion, sliced
1 tablespoon salt
½ teaspoon pepper
2 teaspoons ground allspice
3 cups sliced celery
1 cup uncooked regular rice
  Finely minced giblets

Heat water in a heavy kettle. Add seasonings, onion, and chicken. Cover, simmer for about 2 to 2½ hours or until just tender. Add celery, rice, and giblets.

Cover and cook for 20 minutes or until rice is tender. Thicken if desired. Yield: 6 servings.

Louisiana Bouillabaisse

2½ pounds firm-fleshed fish (black bass, gaspergou), or whole pan fish (perch or bream, etc.)
  Salt and pepper
1 cup chopped onions
½ cup chopped onion tops
2 tablespoons finely cut garlic
1 cup chopped celery
¼ cup chopped parsley
1¼ cups cooked tomatoes
2 tablespoons freshly squeezed lemon juice
2 tablespoons Worcestershire sauce
2 tablespoons all-purpose flour
1½ pounds cleaned shrimp
1 pound crabmeat

Bone fish and cut into serving-size pieces. Season with salt and pepper. Prepare the onions, garlic, celery, and parsley, and mix together thoroughly. Pour off some of the juice from the tomatoes and add lemon juice and Worcestershire sauce. Mix well. Add flour gradually to tomato juice mixture and make into a thin paste.

Brush olive oil or salad oil on bottom and sides of pot. A black iron pot with heavy lid is ideal for this, but an electric skillet can be used.

Place a layer of seasoned fish in the pot. Spoon the flour-tomato mixture over all the fish. Put a layer of vegetable seasoning next. Mash a few tomatoes and sprinkle over vegetables. Put a second layer of fish, the vegetable mixture, and tomatoes until all the fish and vegetable mixture is used up. Size of the pot will determine the layers. It is possible there will be only one layer.

Place lid on pot and cook over medium heat until juice starts to boil, then reduce immediately to low heat.

Cook, covered, for 45 minutes to 1 hour, or until fish flakes easily with fork. With an electric skillet, start fish at 350°. As soon as it starts to boil, reduce to 225°; cook for 45 minutes to 1 hour, or until done. Ten minutes before stew is done, add shrimp and crabmeat. Yield: 8 to 10 servings.

Fresh Vegetable and Chicken Stew

1 (4- to 5-pound) chicken
2 to 3 tablespoons shortening
2 cups hot water
1 tablespoon salt
¾ teaspoon black pepper
12 small white onions
1 cup sliced carrots
1 cup fresh peas, lima beans, or snap beans
1 cup diced potatoes
⅓ cup all-purpose flour
½ cup water

Cut chicken into serving-size pieces and brown on all sides in hot shortening. Place in Dutch oven or saucepan with water, salt, and pepper. Cover and cook for 1 hour, or until chicken is tender. Add vegetables about 30 minutes before cooking time is up. Combine flour with the ½ cup water and stir into stew. Cook until medium thickness. Yield: 6 servings.

Court Bouillon de Poisson

½ cup shortening
⅓ cup all-purpose flour
1 teaspoon chopped onion tops
1 large onion, finely chopped
1 clove garlic, minced
1 medium green pepper, finely chopped
1 stalk celery, finely chopped
Celery seed
Bay leaves
Cayenne pepper, black pepper, and salt
1 cup canned tomatoes
6 cups water
Enough fish to serve 6 persons (gaspergou, red snapper, perch, or trout)
Hot cooked rice

Melt shortening in heavy skillet or Dutch oven. Add flour and cook to a deep brown, stirring constantly. Add onion tops, onion, and garlic, and cook slowly until onions are shriveled, but not scorched. Add pepper, celery, celery seed, a few bay leaves, cayenne and black pepper, and salt. Cook a few minutes longer; add tomatoes and cook slowly, stirring constantly until the vegetables separate from the shortening. Add 6 cups water and let cook over low heat until all ingredients are soft and blend with the liquid (about 1 hour). Add fish (cut into serving-size pieces) about 30 minutes before serving; cook slowly, allowing fish to become tender but not broken. Serve with hot cooked rice. Yield: 6 servings.

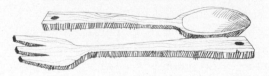

Georgia Stewed Catfish

½ cup butter or margarine
  Salt
12 small to medium catfish
1¾ cups hot water, divided
¼ cup all-purpose flour
2 cups milk
  Salt and pepper

Melt butter or margarine in a roasting pan over medium heat. Salt the catfish and arrange them so they lie flat in the pan. Add ¾ cup hot water, place pan in oven, and bake at 425° until fish are done and lightly browned. Remove from oven and continue cooking on top burner of range. Add 1 cup water and bring to the boiling point. Make a paste of flour and milk; add to water in fish pan to make gravy. Add salt and pepper. Yield: 6 servings.

Pine Bark Fish Stew

6 slices bacon
6 medium onions, chopped
2½ cups canned tomatoes
3 pounds fish
  Salt
  Black and red pepper
1 (6-ounce) can tomato paste
4 cups water
3 tablespoons butter or margarine
1 teaspoon Worcestershire sauce
1 cup catsup

Fry bacon until crisp. Remove from pan. Fry onions slowly in bacon drippings until brown. Add sieved tomatoes to tomato paste and let boil until tomatoes are thoroughly cooked (about 5 minutes). Add onions, bacon drippings, water, and butter or margarine. Boil for

10 minutes. Drop in fish which has been cut into eight pieces; season well with salt, black and red pepper, Worcestershire sauce, and catsup. Boil slowly until the fish is tender, then break bacon into small pieces and drop into stew. Yield: 6 to 8 servings.

Caesar Stew

2 pounds boneless shoulder of lamb
1½ cups boiling water
3 tablespoons onion flakes
1 bay leaf
3 pounds spinach, chopped
3 cups diced tomatoes
1½ teaspoons salt
1 teaspoon rosemary leaves
½ teaspoon ground black pepper
2 tablespoons all-purpose flour
2 tablespoons cold water

Trim excess fat from lamb and cut into 1-inch cubes. Brown meat on all sides in fat trimmed from lamb. Add boiling water, onion flakes, and bay leaf. Cover and cook for 1 hour or until meat is tender. Add chopped spinach to lamb with tomatoes, salt, rosemary, and pepper. Cook for about 10 minutes or until spinach is done. Blend flour with cold water and add to stew. Cook for 1 minute or only until slightly thickened. Serve as a one-dish meal. Yield: 6 servings.

Irish Stew

2 pounds boned shoulder of lamb, cut
   into 2-inch pieces
4 cups water
2 sprigs parsley
1 bay leaf
2 celery tops
2 teaspoons salt
2 cups cubed rutabagas
3 medium potatoes, peeled and halved
6 small onions, peeled
2 tablespoons all-purpose flour
3 tablespoons water

Put lamb into saucepan with water,
parsley, bay leaf, celery tops, and salt.
Cover; simmer for 1½ hours, or until
lamb is tender. Add cubed rutabagas,
halved potatoes, and onions; cover,
and cook until vegetables are tender.
Then set aside and make a smooth paste
of flour and water. Gradually add to
stew, stirring constantly until thickened.
Yield: 6 servings.

Lamb and Lentil Stew

2 pounds boned shoulder of lamb
2 tablespoons shortening
4 cups water
1½ cups dried lentils
1 teaspoon salt
1 bay leaf
1 tablespoon chopped parsley
1 onion, finely chopped
6 small carrots, scraped and cut
   into 2-inch lengths
1 clove garlic, minced
6 small onions, peeled
⅛ teaspoon powdered thyme
½ teaspoon salt
⅛ teaspoon pepper

Cut lamb into 2-inch pieces, add to
shortening in heavy kettle; brown
well. Add water, lentils, salt, bay leaf,
parsley, chopped onion, carrots, and
garlic. Cover, and simmer over low heat
for 2 hours or until meat and lentils are
tender. Add whole onions, thyme, salt,
and pepper. Cover and continue to cook
the stew until vegetables are tender.
Yield: 6 servings.

New Year's Eve Oyster Stew

5 tablespoons butter
3 dozen oysters, shucked and
   with liquid
2 tablespoons Worcestershire sauce
1 teaspoon salt
¼ teaspoon seasoned pepper
6 cups whole milk or half milk and
   half cream
½ bunch parsley, minced
   Paprika to taste
   Butter

Heat the butter in a deep, heavy kettle.
When it bubbles, add oysters, Worcestershire sauce, salt, and seasoned
pepper. Cook gently until the edges
of the oysters begin to curl (about a
minute). Heat the milk until hot but not
boiling; combine with the oysters and
simmer briefly but do not boil. Let stand
to blend the flavors. When ready to
serve, heat until hot but not boiling.
Pour into a warm tureen and top with
minced parsley, paprika to taste, and
dots of butter. Yield: 8 servings.

Oyster Stew

  1 *pint oysters*
  4 *tablespoons butter or margarine*
  4 *cups milk*
1½ *teaspoons salt*
 ⅛ *teaspoon pepper*
    Paprika

Carefully clean fresh oysters, or drain canned oysters. Melt butter or margarine; add drained oysters and cook for 3 minutes, or until edges curl. Add milk, salt, and pepper, and bring almost to boiling point. Serve hot. Garnish with paprika. Yield: 6 servings.

Kentucky Burgoo

2 *pounds foreshank soup bone*
2 *pounds pork shank*
2 *pounds veal shank*
1 *(3- to 5-pound) breast of lamb*
1 *(5- to 6-pound) hen*
8 *quarts cold water*
3 *large onions, chopped*
3 *large potatoes, chopped*
3 *raw carrots, chopped*
1 *cup diced celery*
4 *cups tomatoes, chopped*
2 *cups corn*
2 *cups butterbeans*
2 *pods red pepper*
2 *green peppers, chopped*
   Salt and cayenne pepper to taste
4 *teaspoons Worcestershire sauce*
   Small bunch parsley, finely chopped

Put the soup bone and all the meat into cold water in a 4-gallon kettle, and bring slowly to a boil. Simmer until meat is tender enough to fall from the bones. Lift meat out of stock; cool; remove from bones; chop. Add onions, potatoes, carrots, celery, tomatoes, corn, butterbeans, red and green peppers. Allow to simmer until thick. Add salt and cayenne pepper to taste.

Burgoo should be very thick, but soupy. Stir frequently during the first part of cooking and almost constantly after it thickens. Test occasionally and add more seasoning if necessary. Total cooking time should be about 10 hours. Add Worcestershire sauce 10 minutes before removing from heat. Add chopped parsley just before serving. Yield: 10 quarts.

Quick Camp Stew

6 *slices bacon*
2 *medium onions, chopped*
2 *pounds ground meat*
1 *(8-ounce) bottle catsup*
   Salt and pepper
2 *cups cooked tomatoes*
½ *pound shredded Cheddar cheese*

Cook bacon slowly until crisp. Add chopped onions, and cook until light brown. Add meat, catsup, salt and pepper, and tomatoes. Cook until meat is done, about 20 minutes. Add shredded cheese, and serve at once on rolls or bread. Yield: 6 to 8 servings.

Bake-a-Roux

8 *cups all-purpose flour*
4 *cups cooking oil*

Mix flour and oil together in a heavy ovenproof container. Place on center shelf in preheated 400° oven.

Bake at this temperature for 1½ to 2 hours. Set timer, and stir roux every 15 minutes. Roux should be a caramel color when done. Remove from oven, cool, transfer to containers with tight-fitting lids and store in refrigerator until needed. Roux may also be frozen. Yield: enough roux for 4 to 6 pots of gumbo.

South Carolina Shrimp Gumbo

½ cup bacon drippings
½ cup all-purpose flour
   Salt
1 medium onion, chopped
2 stalks celery, chopped
1 green pepper, chopped
1 cup cooked tomatoes
1 pound country sausage
3 pints water
1½ pounds shrimp
   Hot cooked rice

Heat bacon drippings in large saucepan. Add ½ cup flour, or enough to blend with drippings. Add salt. Stir until as brown as possible without burning. Add onion, celery, and pepper, and stir until wilted. Add tomatoes and cook for a minute or two, stirring constantly. Add sausage, cut into circles, and the water. Cook all together until well done; then add shrimp. Cook shrimp only a short time (about 7 minutes), or it will break into pieces. Serve over hot rice. Yield: 10 servings.

Quick Shrimp Mull

6 tablespoons butter or margarine
½ cup diced onion
2 small cloves garlic
3 teaspoons salt
2 (16-ounce) cans tomatoes
4 cups water
1 cup tomato catsup
1 teaspoon celery seed
1 cup chopped celery
3 drops Tabasco sauce
½ teaspoon Worcestershire sauce
¼ teaspoon pepper
3 teaspoons freshly squeezed lemon juice
2 pounds raw shrimp (peeled, black vein removed, and cut in two lengthwise)
½ cup fine cracker crumbs
   Hot cooked rice

Melt butter or margarine in saucepan or large, deep skillet. Add onion and cook over low heat for a few minutes. Meanwhile, peel garlic and chop fine. Add to onion with salt, tomatoes, water, catsup, celery seed, celery, Tabasco, Worcestershire, and pepper. Cover and simmer for 1 hour. Add lemon juice and shrimp and cook for 5 minutes or until shrimp are done through. Add cracker crumbs and bring to a boil, stirring constantly. Serve shrimp over hot cooked rice. Yield: 8 to 12 servings.

Modern Shrimp Gumbo

6 tablespoons salad oil
2 quarts fresh okra
1 quart raw shrimp, peeled
4 large onions, chopped
1 (16-ounce) can tomatoes (2 cups)
2 cloves garlic, minced
3 quarts hot water
2 tablespoons catsup
1 tablespoon Worcestershire sauce
2 tablespoons salt
Breadcrumbs
Hot cooked rice

Heat oil in a frying pan. When oil is hot, add chopped okra and fry for a few minutes, stirring often. Add remaining ingredients and let cook for 1 hour or more. Thicken with breadcrumbs and serve with rice. Crab gumbo or chicken gumbo can be made the same way. Yield: 10 to 12 servings.

Okra-Shrimp Gumbo

1 thin slice ham
4 cups okra, sliced thin
2 cups chopped onions
2 cloves garlic, chopped
3 teaspoons chopped parsley
1 (8-ounce) can tomato sauce
2 pounds fresh shrimp
4 cups water
1 teaspoon seafood seasoning (optional)
½ teaspoon red pepper
1 teaspoon salt
½ teaspoon pepper
Cooked rice

Cut ham into small pieces. Sauté lightly in a skillet. Add okra, and brown lightly, stirring constantly. Add onions, garlic, parsley, and tomato sauce, and let simmer for a few minutes. Add shrimp, water, seafood seasoning, red pepper, salt, and pepper. Let cook for 1 hour over very slow heat. Serve over cooked rice. Yield: 6 to 8 servings.

Country-Style Chicken Soup

1 (4-pound) stewing chicken, cut into pieces
1 cup chopped onion
1 carrot, peeled and quartered
1 bay leaf
1 teaspoon salt
8 cups water
½ cup fresh breadcrumbs
½ teaspoon salt
½ teaspoon poultry seasoning
1 egg
1 tablespoon chopped parsley
2 carrots, peeled
2 stalks celery
¼ cup chicken fat
⅓ cup all-purpose flour
1 cup milk

Place chicken in a large heavy pot with onion, quartered carrot, bay leaf, 1 teaspoon salt, and water; simmer for 2 to 3 hours, or until tender; remove chicken and chill stock. Remove chicken from bones; discard skin; reserve 1 cup chicken for soup. (Chill remainder to use for salad, casserole, or other chicken dish.)

Grind 1 cup chicken; add breadcrumbs, ½ teaspoon salt, poultry seasoning, egg, and parsley; blend. Form firmly into small balls; set aside. Remove layer of fat from chilled stock; reserve. Heat chicken stock (there should be 4 cups). Cut carrots and celery into matchstick-size pieces; add to stock; cook for 10 to 15 minutes, or until tender. Melt ¼ cup chicken fat in saucepan; blend in flour; add milk slowly, stirring constantly. Pour mixture slowly into stock; cook, stirring constantly, until mixture is thickened. Drop chicken balls into soup; heat for 5 minutes more; serve. Yield: 4 to 6 servings.

Hearty Chicken Soup

- 3 *small onions*
- 6 *stalks celery*
- ½ *cup butter or margarine*
- 1 *tablespoon all-purpose flour*
- 1½ *teaspoons salt*
- 1 *(3½- to 4-pound) tender chicken*
- ½ *tablespoon peppercorns*
- 8 *cups water*
- 1 *cup evaporated milk*
- 1 *cup cooked rice*

Chop onions and celery very fine. Sauté in butter or margarine in heavy frying pan. Stir while cooking, but do not brown. Add flour, sprinkling over all. Mix well and allow to simmer for 10 to 15 minutes. Place salt, chicken, peppercorns, and water in a large soup pot; bring to boil. Add the cooked onion mixture. Cover and cook slowly until chicken is very tender, about 1½ hours. Remove chicken and take meat from bones. Strain stock through cheesecloth. Skim

all fat from stock. Add chopped chicken and evaporated milk. Season to taste. Heat only to boiling point. Place portion of cooked rice in heated soup bowl, and add soup. Serve very hot. Yield: 8 servings.

Beef Brisket Soup

- 2 *pounds beef brisket*
- 8 *cups water*
- 1 *tablespoon salt*
- 5 *medium potatoes, peeled and diced*
  Dash celery salt
- 1 *large onion, chopped*
- ½ *cup shredded American or Cheddar cheese*
- ⅔ *cup oatmeal*
- 1 *(1-pound) can cream-style corn (optional)*

Cut brisket into pieces; simmer, covered, in salted water. When meat is tender, add potatoes, celery salt, onion, cheese, and oatmeal. Add corn, if desired. Continue to cook, covered, until vegetables are done, stirring once or twice while cooking. Remove from heat and serve in separate small bowls, allowing a piece of beef for each bowl. Yield: 8 servings.

Mushroom-Shrimp Chowder

- 3 *(10½-ounce) cans condensed cream of mushroom soup*
- 3 *soup cans milk*
  Dash cayenne pepper
- 1 *pound cleaned, cooked shrimp*

Combine soup and milk gradually, and stir until smooth. Heat to simmering, stirring constantly. Do not boil. Add cayenne and shrimp. Heat through. Yield: 6 to 8 servings.

Southern Corn Chowder

½ pound bacon, cut into 1-inch pieces
2 small onions, sliced
1 tablespoon all-purpose flour
1 cup water
2 cups finely diced raw potatoes
½ cup chopped celery
2 bay leaves
2 (1-pound) cans cream-style corn
1 cup milk
1 teaspoon salt
¼ teaspoon white pepper

Fry bacon until crisp, drain on absorbent paper, and set aside. Reserve ¼ cup bacon drippings and place in a kettle. Sauté onion in bacon drippings for about 5 minutes. Blend in flour and mix to a smooth paste. Gradually add the water and stir until smooth. Add the potatoes, celery, and bay leaves. Cover and cook over low heat for about 15 minutes or until potatoes are done. Stir occasionally. Blend in corn, milk, seasonings, and bacon. Heat for 15 minutes. Serve hot. Yield: 5 to 6 servings.

Favorite Vegetable Chowder

¼ cup butter or margarine
3 carrots, cut into 1-inch pieces
1 large potato, diced
1 onion, thinly sliced
1 (10-ounce) package frozen lima beans
1 cup green beans, cut in half lengthwise
2 cups water
1 teaspoon salt
⅛ teaspoon pepper
¼ teaspoon celery seed
⅛ teaspoon thyme
2 cups milk
¼ pound sharp cheese, shredded

Melt butter or margarine in cooker. Add carrots, potatoes, onion, lima beans, green beans, water, salt, pepper, celery seed, and thyme. Place cover on cooker and heat until steam begins to flow from vent, to release all air from cooker. Then cook according to the directions for your cooker. Reduce pressure and remove cover. Heat milk until a film forms across top. Stir in cheese and milk, continuing to stir until cheese has melted. Yield: 6 servings.

Maryland Clam Chowder

12 cups water
1 whole chicken breast
3 tablespoons chicken stock base
1 teaspoon salt
2 stalks celery, with tops
1 tablespoon freeze-dried chopped chives
2 tablespoons minced onion
½ teaspoon celery salt
¼ teaspoon thyme leaves
¼ teaspoon white pepper
1 cup sliced carrots
1 cup diced potatoes
1 (10-ounce) package frozen corn
1 (10-ounce) package frozen peas
1 whole pimiento, chopped fine
1 cup clam juice
1 teaspoon parsley flakes
1½ cups minced Chesapeake Bay soft-shell clams (about 3 dozen)

Combine water, chicken, chicken stock base, salt, and celery in a large saucepan; simmer for 1 hour. Discard celery, remove chicken, and finely chop the meat; set aside. To the stock add remaining ingredients except the clam juice, parsley flakes, clams, and chopped chicken. Simmer for 20 minutes; then add remaining ingredients. Continue cooking for 5 minutes. Yield: 4 quarts.

Meatball Chowder

½ cup breadcrumbs
½ cup milk
1 pound beef
½ pound pork
½ pound veal
1 cup diced raw potatoes
½ cup diced celery
1 egg
1 teaspoon salt
⅛ teaspoon ground nutmeg
¼ cup chopped onion
¼ teaspoon pepper
¼ teaspoon brown sugar
⅛ teaspoon ground allspice
2 tablespoons shortening
1 (10½-ounce) can tomato soup
1 cup water
1 cup diced raw potatoes
1 cup green beans
½ cup diced celery

Soak breadcrumbs in the milk. Grind beef, pork, veal, potatoes, and celery. Add soaked breadcrumbs, and mix thoroughly. Add the egg, salt, nutmeg, onion, pepper, brown sugar, and all-spice, and shape into balls no larger than 1 inch in diameter. Brown in hot short-ening. Add the soup, water, raw pota-toes, green beans, and celery. Simmer until vegetables are cooked. Yield: 6 to 8 servings.

Ham and Split Pea Soup

1½ cups dried peas
2 cups cold water
1 medium onion, sliced
1 tablespoon ham fat
Ham shank
½ teaspoon celery salt
1 teaspoon salt
¼ teaspoon pepper
7 cups cold water
White Sauce

Soak dried peas overnight in 2 cups cold water. Drain. Sauté sliced onion until tender in ham fat. Add ham shank, drained peas, celery salt, salt, pepper, and 7 cups cold water. Cover, bring to a boil, and simmer gently for 2 hours. Remove ham bone and slice meat. Combine with White Sauce, heat well, and serve. Yield: 6 to 8 servings.

White Sauce

1 tablespoon all-purpose flour
1 tablespoon shortening or drippings
2 cups cold milk

Blend flour and shortening or drippings in top of double boiler. Gradually add 2 cups milk and cook, stirring con-stantly, for about 10 minutes. Yield: 2 cups.

Curried Pea Soup

1 (10½-ounce) can green pea soup
1 (10½-ounce) can beef broth
1½ soup cans milk
½ to 1 teaspoon curry powder

Gradually combine ingredients, mixing well. Heat to serve. Yield: 4 to 6 servings.

Asparagus Soup

    4 tablespoons butter or margarine
    2 slices onion
    4 tablespoons all-purpose flour
 1½ teaspoons salt
      Few grains pepper
    3 cups milk
    2 pounds cooked asparagus
   ⅓ cup cream (optional)

Heat butter or margarine; add onion
and simmer for about 4 minutes, or until
soft. Stir in flour and seasonings. Remove from heat and slowly add milk,
stirring until well blended. Return to
low heat and cook until thick and
smooth, stirring constantly. Put asparagus through food mill, then add to soup
mixture. Reheat before serving, adding
cream if desired. Yield: 8 servings.

Black-Eyed Pea Soup

    1 cup dried black-eyed peas
    2 cups boiling water
    4 cups cold water
   ¾ teaspoon salt
      Pepper to taste
    6 slices bacon
      Lemon slices
   ½ cup cream, whipped (optional)
      Ground nutmeg (optional)

Wash peas. Pour boiling water over
them and soak for 6 hours or overnight.
Add the cold water, salt, pepper, and
1 slice bacon. Bring to a boil, cover,
and simmer for 2 hours. Mash peas to a
smooth paste (a blender is fine for this),
and heat with the liquid to the boiling
point. Cook 5 slices of bacon until crisp,
and crumble in the bottom of soup
bowls. Add a very thin slice of lemon to

each bowl. Fill bowls with soup, float
a spoonful of whipped cream on top of
each and sprinkle with nutmeg. Yield:
6 to 8 servings.

Split-Pea Soup

    1 pound (2¼ cups) green split peas
 2½ quarts water
    1 meaty ham bone
 1½ cups sliced onion
   ½ teaspoon pepper
   ¼ teaspoon garlic salt
   ¼ teaspoon marjoram
    1 cup diced celery
    1 cup sliced carrots
    1 teaspoon parsley flakes
      Salt to taste

Wash peas and put into water. Soak overnight. Or, bring water to boiling point;
add washed beans; boil for 2 minutes
only; cover; remove from heat; allow to
stand for 1 hour. (This is equal to 12 to
15 hours soaking in cold water.)

Add ham bone, onion, and seasonings.
Bring to a boil; cover; and simmer for 2
hours; stirring occasionally. Remove
bone; cut off any bits of meat. Return
meat to soup; add remaining ingredients.
Cook slowly for 45 minutes. Serve with
oyster crackers. Yield: 8 to 10 servings.

Cream of Corn Soup

   ¼ cup minced onion
    3 tablespoons melted butter or margarine
    3 tablespoons all-purpose flour
    4 cups milk
    2 cups cream-style corn

Cook onions in melted butter or margarine in top of double boiler over low

heat until tender. Add flour, and stir until smooth. Slowly add milk, and stir constantly to prevent lumping. Cook until slightly thickened, then add corn. Cook below boiling point for 5 minutes, and serve hot. Yield: 6 servings.

Cream of Cheese Soup

    2 tablespoons minced onion
    4 tablespoons butter or margarine
 4½ tablespoons all-purpose flour
    2 cups milk
    2 cups chicken stock or bouillon
  ½ pound shredded sharp cheese
  ½ cup minced cooked carrots
  ¾ cup minced cooked celery
       Chopped parsley

Fry onion in butter or margarine until tender, but not brown. Blend in flour, and heat until bubbly. Add milk and stock, and cook until sauce boils and thickens, stirring constantly. Remove from heat, and add shredded cheese. Stir until melted. Add vegetables; heat. Top with parsley. Yield: 6 servings.

Favorite Lima Bean Soup

    1 (2- to 3-pound) piece smoked ham
       shank or hocks
    1 pound dried lima beans
 2½ quarts water
  ¼ cup diced salt pork or bacon
  ¾ cup diced carrots
  ¾ cup chopped onion
  ¾ cup chopped celery
  ¾ cup diced potatoes
 1½ teaspoons salt
  ¼ teaspoon pepper
    1 tablespoon chopped parsley (optional)

Wash beans and put into water. Soak overnight. Or, bring water to boiling point; add washed beans; boil for 2 minutes only; cover; remove from heat; allow to stand for 1 hour. (This is equal to 12 to 15 hours soaking in cold water.)

Cook salt pork or bacon until lightly crisp. Add to beans in water. Add vegetables, seasonings and ham shank or hocks. Cover and simmer for about 2 hours. Remove ham shank or hocks. Remove meat from bones; dice and add to soup. Serve hot, garnished with chopped parsley. Yield: 6 to 8 servings.

Farm-Style Onion Soup

    4 cups beef stock
    1 bay leaf
       Pinch thyme
       Salt and pepper
  ¼ pound butter or margarine
    1 clove garlic, minced
    2 cups thinly sliced onions
       Toast squares
       Shredded cheese

Combine beef stock, bay leaf, thyme, salt, and pepper, and bring to a boil. Check flavor, and add more seasoning if desired. Melt butter or margarine in a deep skillet or Dutch oven. Add garlic, and simmer until garlic is browned, then discard garlic. Add onions; cover and simmer over low heat until onions are just soft and transparent. Mix the onions and hot stock. To serve, place toast squares in bottom of soup bowl, sprinkle with shredded cheese, and pour soup over them. Yield: 6 cups.

Okra Soup

- 2 pounds lean beef, cut into cubes
- 1 onion, sliced
- 4 tablespoons shortening
- 12 cups water
-   Salt
-   Pepper
- 2 cups sliced okra
- ½ cup uncooked regular rice
- 1 cup sliced tomatoes

Brown cubed beef and sliced onion in hot shortening. Add water, and salt and pepper to taste. Let cook slowly until beef is tender. Add sliced okra, rice, and sliced tomatoes. Let cook until beef is very tender and vegetables are cooked. Yield: 8 servings.

Southern Bean Soup

- 2 cups dried Northern beans
- 12 cups water
-   Meaty ham bone
- 1 cup finely chopped onion
- 2 cloves garlic, minced
- 1 small bay leaf
- 1 cup cooked mashed potatoes
- 1 cup thinly sliced celery
- 1 cup diced raw carrots
-   Salt and pepper to taste
- ½ cup cream or evaporated milk

Wash beans. Bring water to boiling point; add beans. Boil for 2 minutes only; cover; remove from heat; allow to stand for 1 hour. This is equal to 12 to 15 hours soaking in cold water.

Add ham bone, onion, garlic, and bay leaf to beans in soaking water. Bring to boiling point; reduce heat to simmer. Cover tightly and cook for about 2 hours or until beans are almost tender. Add potatoes, celery, carrots. Bring to boiling point. And salt and pepper. Cover and simmer for 1 hour longer. Remove ham bone and cut off the meat. Dice meat and return it to the soup. Reheat to just boiling, stirring carefully to avoid breaking beans. Stir heavy cream or undiluted evaporated milk into soup just before serving. Yield: 6 servings.

Cream of Peanut Butter Soup

- 6 cups peanut butter
- 24 cups milk
- 6 tablespoons all-purpose flour
-   Salt and pepper to taste
- 6 tablespoons chopped onion

Put peanut butter into a bowl and gradually add 6 cups of cold milk to thin it. Scald the remainder of the milk over hot water, then mix it with the flour. Add salt and pepper, then combine with the peanut butter and milk mixture. Add finely chopped onion and stir well. Serve very hot. Yield: 24 servings.

Cream of Peanut Soup

- ¼ cup butter or margarine
- 1 cup thinly sliced celery
- 1 medium onion, chopped fine
- 2 tablespoons all-purpose flour
- 2 quarts chicken stock or broth
- 1 cup creamy peanut butter
- 1 cup light cream

Melt butter or margarine in a large saucepan over low heat and add celery and onion. Cook until tender but not browned. Add flour and stir until mixture is smooth. Gradually add chicken broth and bring to a boil. Blend in peanut butter and simmer for about 15 minutes. Stir in cream just before serving. Yield: 8 servings.

Irish Potato Soup

- ½ cup butter or margarine
- ½ cup finely chopped onions
- 5 medium potatoes, peeled and quartered
- 1½ cups water
- 2 teaspoons salt
- 2 cups hot milk
- ½ cup cold milk
- 1 egg yolk
  Few grains cayenne pepper
- 2 tablespoons chopped parsley

Melt butter or margarine in heavy pan over low heat. Add onions, stirring until tender. Add potatoes, water, and salt. Cover pan and cook until potatoes are tender. Drain, reserving liquid. Press potatoes through sieve and add to liquid. Add hot milk and stir well. Combine cold milk and beaten egg yolk. Add slowly to warm soup, stirring constantly. Add cayenne pepper. Reheat soup slowly, but do not boil. Add parsley just before serving. Yield: 6 to 8 servings.

Potato-Tomato Soup

- 3 large potatoes
- 6 cups water
- 1 teaspoon salt
- 1 large onion, chopped
- 1 clove garlic, minced
- 4 tablespoons salad oil
- 1 (8-ounce) can tomato sauce
- ½ cup shredded cheese

Peel and dice potatoes, add water and salt, and cook until tender. Mash. Sauté onion and garlic in salad oil; add to potatoes. Stir in hot sauce and reheat. Just before serving, add cheese, blending into mixture as it melts. Yield: 6 to 8 servings.

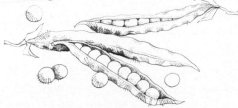

Old-Fashioned Squash Soup

- 1 medium onion, finely chopped
- ¼ cup butter or margarine
- 2 tablespoons all-purpose flour
- ¾ teaspoon salt
  Dash pepper
- ⅓ teaspoon ground nutmeg
- 1 (14-ounce) can chicken stock
- 1 cup milk
- 1½ cups cooked squash
- 2 teaspoons Worcestershire sauce
- 1 egg yolk, slightly beaten
- ½ cup light or heavy cream

Sauté the onion in butter until soft, about 5 minutes. Add the flour, salt, pepper, and nutmeg and stir until blended and bubbly. Remove from heat and gradually stir in the chicken stock and milk. Return to heat, bring to a boil, and cook, stirring, until thickened. Add the squash and Worcestershire, reduce heat to low, and cook, stirring often, until heated through. Blend together the egg yolk and cream; stir in some of the hot soup, then stir the egg mixture back into the hot soup. Cook until soup is heated through and the egg has thickened. Yield: 6 servings.

Cream of Tomato Soup

2 tablespoons butter or margarine
4 tablespoons all-purpose flour
2 cups cooked tomatoes
2 teaspoons salt
1 teaspoon pepper
1 tablespoon sugar
4 cups hot milk
   Whipped cream

Melt butter; stir in flour until well blended. Put tomatoes through sieve or food mill; add to butter-flour mixture, and cook until thick, stirring constantly. Season with salt, pepper, and sugar. Gradually add hot milk and stir until boiling point is reached. Remove from heat at once, and serve hot, with a spoonful of whipped cream on top of each serving. Yield: 4 to 6 servings.

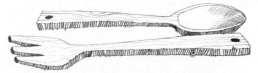

Tomato Soup Serendipity

1 (1-pound, 12-ounce) can tomatoes
½ cup cold chicken broth
2 tablespoons instant minced onion
1 tablespoon paprika
½ teaspoon garlic powder
¼ teaspoon salt
⅛ teaspoon ground black pepper
2 tablespoons olive oil
   Parsley flakes
   Thinly sliced cucumber
   Paprika

Combine tomatoes, broth, minced onion, paprika, garlic powder, salt, and pepper in container of electric blender. Blend well. Add oil; beat 1 second longer. Serve thoroughly chilled, garnished with parsley flakes and sliced cucumber rolled in paprika. Yield: 4 cups.

Vegetable Soup

1 pound lean beef, cubed
2 tablespoons butter or margarine
2 pounds marrow bone, cracked
1 bay leaf
½ cup celery leaves
4 sprigs parsley
2 teaspoons salt
6 peppercorns
1 carrot, pared and sliced
1 onion, sliced
4 quarts water
1 cup diced carrots
2 cups chopped onions
1 cup diced celery
3 stalks leek, sliced
1 cup diced potatoes
½ (10-ounce) package frozen
   peas or lima beans
2 (1-pound) cans tomatoes
1 teaspoon salt
2 tablespoons chopped parsley

Brown meat in butter or margarine in large heavy pot. Add bones, bay leaf. celery leaves, parsley, salt, peppercorns, sliced carrot, onion, and water. Cover; heat until water boils; remove film from top. Reduce heat; simmer for 1½ to 2 hours. Strain stock; reserve meat; skim fat from stock immediately or refrigerate overnight, then remove firm layer of fat. Heat soup to boiling; add diced carrots, chopped onions, celery, leek, potatoes, peas or lima beans, tomatoes, salt, and reserved meat. Reduce heat, simmer gently for 30 minutes, or until vegetables are tender; add parsley. Yield: 6 to 8 servings.

Salads & Salad Dressings

A meal is very much like the woman who prepares it, and if meat is thought of as the body of the meal, certainly the personality is the salad. Reflecting the varied moods of a meal, a salad can be as sprightly crisp as a bowl of mixed greens, as cool as a congealed aspic, or as bright as a combination of fruits.

Before the lettuce and tomato salad so popular today became a standard, vegetable greens were served as "sallet" with vinegar dressing.

One old recipe for making salad directs "where oil cannot be obtained, fresh butter, drawn or melted, is an excellent substitute and is indeed preferred to oil by some persons. . . . Always use good cider vinegar in making salads, as chemical vinegar is sometimes very unwholesome."

Today with a ready supply of oil and quality "chemical vinegar," about the only limit to what goes into a good salad is the ingenuity of the homemaker. From a first course, to the vegetable, or the main dish, or even the dessert, salads can be any part of the meal, or a meal in themselves.

Bing Cherry Salad

1 (17-ounce) can pitted bing
 cherries, drained
3 (3-ounce) packages
 cherry-flavored gelatin
1 envelope unflavored gelatin
½ cup cold water
3 (3-ounce) packages cream
 cheese, softened
1 (20-ounce) can crushed pineapple
2 (6-ounce) bottles cola beverage
 Chopped nuts (optional)

Heat cherry juice and dissolve cherry
gelatin in this. Add unflavored gelatin
to ½ cup cold water; add to hot gelatin
mixture and stir until dissolved. Mash
cream cheese and add to warm mixture.
Add 1 cup each of cherries and undrained pineapple. Chill slightly. Add
remainder of cherries and pineapple.
Add cola beverage, and nuts, if desired.
Chill in refrigerator until firm. Yield:
6 to 8 servings.

Bing Cherry Delight Salad

1 (17-ounce) can pitted bing
 cherries, drained
1 (20-ounce) can crushed
 pineapple, drained
3 (3-ounce) packages cherry-
 flavored gelatin
1½ cups boiling water
1½ cups boiling pineapple juice
1½ cups boiling cherry juice
⅔ cup freshly squeezed lemon juice
½ envelope unflavored gelatin
⅔ cup ice water

Drain cherries and pineapple. Dissolve
fruit-flavored gelatin in boiling water
and juices. Dissolve unflavored gelatin
in ice water and add to boiling mixture.

Stir to dissolve. Let chill to consistency
of unbeaten egg white. Add cherries
and pineapple just before it congeals.
Yield: 6 to 8 servings.

Cherry Salad

1 (3-ounce) package cherry-
 flavored gelatin
1 cup boiling water
1 (17-ounce) can pitted bing
 cherries, drained
1 cup commercial sour cream
¼ cup chopped pecans

Dissolve gelatin in boiling water; stir
in cherry juice. Chill until gelatin becomes syrupy. Stir in sour cream and
blend thoroughly. Add cherries and
nuts. Chill until firm. Yield: 6 servings.

Creamy Frozen Fruit Salad

¼ cup sugar
½ teaspoon salt
1½ tablespoons all-purpose flour
¾ cup syrup drained from fruit
1 egg, slightly beaten
2 tablespoons vinegar
1 cup drained, diced canned pears
¾ cup drained pineapple tidbits
2 cups mashed, medium-ripe bananas
½ cup drained, chopped,
 maraschino cherries
1 cup chopped pecans
⅔ cup evaporated milk
1 tablespoon freshly squeezed
 lemon juice

Combine sugar, salt, and flour in saucepan. Add fruit syrup, egg, and vinegar.
Cook over medium heat, stirring constantly until thickened. Cool. Add fruit
and nuts to cooled mixture. Chill evap-

orated milk in freezer until soft ice crystals form (about 10 or 15 minutes). Whip until stiff, about 1 minute. Add lemon juice; whip for 1 additional minute to make very stiff. Fold into fruit mixture. Spoon into lightly oiled 6½-cup mold. Freeze until firm, about 5 to 6 hours. Yield: 12 servings.

Creamy Fruit Salad

    1 (3-ounce) package lemon-
        flavored gelatin
    ¾ cup hot fruit cocktail syrup
    1 cup cottage cheese
1⅓ cups drained, canned fruit cocktail
    ½ cup chopped nuts
    ½ cup chopped, unpeeled apples
    ¼ cup freshly squeezed lemon juice
    1 cup undiluted evaporated milk

Dissolve gelatin in hot fruit cocktail syrup. Cool slightly. Fold in remaining ingredients and mix well. Chill in refrigerator until firm. Yield: 6 to 8 servings.

Cranberry Mold

    1 (17-ounce) can pitted bing
        cherries, drained
    1 envelope unflavored gelatin
    2 (3-ounce) packages cherry-
        flavored gelatin
    1 (1-pound) can whole-berry
        cranberry sauce
    ½ cup chopped apples
    ½ cup chopped celery
    ½ cup chopped English walnuts
    ½ teaspoon salt

Drain cherries and measure juice. Add water to make 1½ cups. Dissolve un-

flavored gelatin in ½ cup cold juice. Heat remaining juice to boiling; pour over flavored and unflavored gelatin and stir until dissolved. Add all ingredients and mix well. Pour into 8-cup mold and chill in refrigerator until firm. Yield: 8 to 10 servings.

Cranberry-Orange Congealed Salad

    1 (3-ounce) package orange-
        flavored gelatin
1½ cups boiling water
    1 cup jellied cranberry sauce
    1 cup diced celery
    2 tablespoons minced onion
    3 tablespoons white vinegar

Dissolve gelatin in boiling water. Chill until slightly thickened. Add cranberry sauce, cut in ¼-inch cubes; celery; onion; and vinegar. Mix gently. Chill until firm. Yield: 6 servings.

Cranberry Salad

    2 cups sugar
    1 cup water
2½ tablespoons unflavored gelatin
    ½ cup cold water
    4 cups raw cranberries, ground
    1 medium orange with rind, ground
    1 cup chopped celery
    1 cup chopped nuts

Cook sugar and 1 cup water to make a thin syrup. Add gelatin which has been soaked in ½ cup cold water; stir until dissolved; cool. Add other ingredients; pour into an 8-cup mold and chill. Yield: 8 to 10 servings.

Millionaire Salad

1 *(11-ounce) can mandarin*
   oranges, drained
1 *cup flaked coconut*
½ *cup miniature marshmallows*
1 *cup diced pineapple*
2 *tablespoons commercial sour cream*

Mix oranges, coconut, marshmallows, and pineapple. Moisten with sour cream and chill. Yield: 4 to 6 servings.

Orange Sherbet Salad

2 *(3-ounce) packages orange-*
   flavored gelatin
1 *cup boiling water*
1 *pint orange sherbet*
1 *(8¼-ounce) can crushed pineapple*
1 *cup miniature marshmallows*
1 *(11-ounce) can mandarin orange*
   sections, drained
½ *pint whipping cream, whipped*

Dissolve gelatin in boiling water. Add orange sherbet. When partially set, add other ingredients, folding in the whipped cream last. Chill until firm. Yield: 12 servings.

Pineapple Salad

1 *(20-ounce) can crushed pineapple,*
   drained
1 *(3-ounce) package lemon- or orange-*
   flavored gelatin
2 *(3-ounce) packages cream*
   cheese, softened
1 *cup chopped celery*
1 *cup chopped nuts*
1 *(3-ounce) can pimientos, chopped*
1 *cup mayonnaise or salad dressing*

Measure juice drained from pineapple;

add water to make 2 cups. Heat liquid to boiling and dissolve gelatin in liquid. Add other ingredients and stir well. Spoon into a 10-cup mold or pan and chill in refrigerator. Stir mixture several times. Yield: 8 to 10 servings.

Sunshine Salad

1 *(3-ounce) package lemon-*
   flavored gelatin
½ *teaspoon salt*
1½ *cups hot water*
1 *(9-ounce) can crushed pineapple*
1 *tablespoon freshly squeezed lemon*
   juice or vinegar
1 *cup grated raw carrots*
⅓ *cup chopped pecans*
   Few leaves of escarole
   Mayonnaise

Dissolve gelatin and salt in hot water. Add pineapple and lemon juice. Chill until slightly thickened. Fold carrots and pecans into gelatin-pineapple mixture. Chill until firm. Serve on escarole, and top with mayonnaise. Yield: 4 to 6 servings.

Strawberry Salad

1 *(3-ounce) package strawberry-*
   flavored gelatin
1½ *cups boiling water*
1 *(10-ounce) package*
   frozen strawberries
1 *(3-ounce) package lemon-*
   flavored gelatin
1 *cup boiling water*
½ *cup pineapple juice*
1 *(3-ounce) package cream*
   cheese, softened
½ *cup drained, crushed pineapple*
1 *cup heavy cream, whipped*

Dissolve strawberry gelatin in 1½ cups boiling water; add strawberries and stir until berries are completely thawed. Pour into a flat dish and chill until firm.

Dissolve lemon gelatin in 1 cup boiling water. Add pineapple juice, and cool. Blend in softened cream cheese and crushed pineapple; chill until slightly thickened. Fold in whipped cream and pour lemon mixture over firm strawberry mixture. Chill until firm. Yield: 10 to 12 servings.

Waldorf Salad

    2 cups diced apples
       Juice of ½ lemon
    1 cup chopped celery
    ½ cup chopped pecans
       Mayonnaise or salad dressing
       Lettuce leaves

Put diced apples into large bowl; sprinkle with lemon juice. Add celery and nuts, and toss. Add mayonnaise or salad dressing to hold together, and serve on lettuce leaves. Yield: 4 to 6 servings.

Red and White Strawberry Salad

    2 (3-ounce) packages strawberry-
       flavored gelatin
    2 cups boiling water
    2 (10-ounce) packages frozen strawberries
    2 bananas, mashed
    1 (20-ounce) can crushed
       pineapple, drained
    1 cup commercial sour cream
       Crisp greens

Dissolve gelatin in boiling water. Add partially thawed strawberries. Stir well, then add bananas and pineapple. Place half of mixture in 13- x 9- x 2-inch dish. Put into refrigerator to congeal. Allow other half to thicken slightly, but remain at pouring consistency. When refrigerated half is set, top with sour cream. Add remaining fruit mixture and return to refrigerator. Cut in squares; serve on crisp greens. Yield: 12 to 15 servings.

Sweet Relish Congealed Salad

    1 envelope unflavored gelatin
    ¼ cup cold water
    ¾ cup boiling water
    1 cup sugar
    ½ cup cider vinegar
    1 tablespoon tarragon-flavored vinegar
    1 cup sweet pickle relish
    1 (8½-ounce) can crushed
       pineapple, drained
    ½ cup finely chopped pecans
       Ripe stuffed olives

Sprinkle gelatin in cold water. Add to boiling water and stir until dissolved. Add sugar and vinegars, and set aside to cool. When gelatin begins to thicken, add relish, drained pineapple, and nuts. Pour into lightly oiled 8-cup mold and chill until firm. Garnish with ripe stuffed olives. Yield: 6 to 8 servings.

24-Hour Salad

2 eggs, well beaten
¼ cup freshly squeezed lemon juice
2 tablespoons sugar
Dash salt
3 tablespoons butter or margarine
1 cup heavy cream, whipped
2 cups miniature marshmallows
2 cups diced pineapple, drained
2 cups pitted white cherries, drained
½ cup diced oranges
1 cup halved and seeded grapes
¼ cup chopped blanched almonds

Combine eggs, lemon juice, sugar, and salt and cook over low heat until thick. Add butter and cool. Fold cream into cooled mixture. Combine this mixture lightly with marshmallows, well drained fruits, and nuts. Chill 24 hours so the delicate flavors will blend. Yield: 12 servings.

Tangy Gelatin Salad

1 (3-ounce) package lemon- or lime-flavored gelatin
1 cup boiling water
1 pound cottage cheese, sieved
1 (20-ounce) can crushed pineapple
½ cup chopped nuts
1 teaspoon horseradish
1 cup whipped cream
Green pepper or pimiento, chopped (optional)

Dissolve gelatin in boiling water. Cool. Add sieved cottage cheese and other ingredients. Spoon into 6-cup mold and chill in refrigerator until firm. Yield: 6 servings.

White Fruit Salad

4 egg yolks
1 cup milk
1 envelope unflavored gelatin
¼ cup fruit juice
4½ cups miniature marshmallows
1 (20-ounce) can crushed pineapple, drained
1 (17-ounce) can white cherries, drained and pitted
½ pound chopped blanched almonds
Juice of 1½ lemons
1 cup cream, whipped

Beat egg yolks; add milk and scald in top of double boiler. Dissolve gelatin in fruit juice and add to milk and egg mixture. Cool and add remaining ingredients. Let sit in refrigerator for several hours. Yield: 10 servings.

Chicken Salad Supreme

2½ cups diced cooked chicken
2 cups chopped celery
1 cup sliced white grapes
½ cup slivered toasted almonds
½ cup finely chopped sweet pickles
2 tablespoons minced parsley
4 hard-cooked eggs, chopped
1 teaspoon salt
1½ tablespoons unflavored gelatin
4 tablespoons water
½ cup hot chicken stock
1 cup mayonnaise
½ cup whipping cream, whipped

Combine chicken, celery, grapes, almonds, pickles, parsley, eggs, and salt. Soak gelatin in cold water for 5 minutes and dissolve in hot chicken stock. When cold, add mayonnaise and whipped cream. Stir until thick and fold in the chicken mixture. Pack into individual molds or an 8-cup ring. Yield: 8 to 10 servings.

Chicken Salad

    5 cups cooked, diced chicken
 1½ cups diced celery
    4 hard-cooked eggs, chopped
    1 (8¼-ounce) can crushed
       pineapple, drained
 2½ teaspoons salt
   ⅛ teaspoon pepper
    1 cup diced sweet pickles
    2 cups mayonnaise
       Lettuce leaves

Toss first eight ingredients together lightly and serve on lettuce leaves. Yield: 6 to 8 servings.

Molded Chicken Salad

    2 envelopes unflavored gelatin
    1 cup cold water
    1 (10½-ounce) can condensed cream
       of celery soup
   ½ teaspoon salt
    2 tablespoons freshly squeezed
       lemon juice
    1 teaspoon instant minced onion
    1 cup salad dressing
    2 tablespoons diced pimiento
    1 cup diced celery
    2 cups diced, cooked chicken
       Salad greens

Sprinkle gelatin on the water in a 2½-quart saucepan. Place over moderate heat, stirring constantly, until gelatin is dissolved (about 3 minutes). Remove from heat; stir in undiluted cream of celery soup, salt, lemon juice, instant minced onion, and salad dressing; beat until smooth. Chill, stirring occasionally, until mixture mounds when dropped from a spoon. Add pimiento, celery, and chicken. Mix well and spoon into a 6-cup loafpan or mold. Chill until firm. Unmold on salad greens. Yield: 6 servings.

Roast Beef Salad

    3 cups cubed, cooked beef
   ½ cup chopped dill pickles
   ½ cup chopped celery
   ⅓ cup finely chopped onion
   ⅓ cup mayonnaise or salad dressing
    1 teaspoon prepared mustard
    1 teaspoon Worcestershire sauce
    1 teaspoon salt

Combine first four ingredients. Blend mayonnaise or salad dressing with remaining ingredients. Mix lightly with meat mixture; chill. Yield: 4 to 6 servings.

Ham and Macaroni Salad

   ½ pound boiled or baked ham
   ½ cup diced Cheddar cheese
    2 cups cooked elbow macaroni
    1 cup chopped celery
    1 small onion, chopped
   ½ cup diced dill pickle
   ½ cup mayonnaise
    2 teaspoons prepared mustard

Cut ham into ½-inch cubes. Combine ham and cheese with macaroni, celery, onion, and pickle. Mix mayonnaise and mustard; add to macaroni mixture and mix well. Chill until ready to serve. Yield: 4 servings.

Molded Ham Salad

1 (3-ounce) package lemon-flavored gelatin
¼ teaspoon onion salt
   Dash ground cloves
1 cup boiling water
¾ cup cold water
3 tablespoons freshly squeezed lemon juice
1½ cups chopped boiled ham
1 cup small raw cauliflower flowerets
½ cup diced celery
1 tablespoon chopped pimiento

Dissolve gelatin, onion salt, and cloves in boiling water; add cold water and lemon juice. Chill until syrupy; add remaining ingredients. Put into a 1-quart mold; chill until firm. Yield: 4 to 6 servings.

Ham and Cucumber Salad

2 (3-ounce) packages lemon- or lime-flavored gelatin
1 teaspoon salt
2 cups boiling water
1½ cups cold water
¼ cup vinegar
1 cup slivered, cooked ham
1 cup sliced celery
¾ cup diced, drained pineapple
½ cup thinly sliced quartered cucumber
¾ teaspoon grated onion
1½ to 3 tablespoons prepared horseradish
   Radish roses
   Cucumber slices

Dissolve gelatin and salt in boiling water. Add cold water and vinegar. Chill until very thick. Fold in remaining ingredients except radish roses and cucumber slices. Pour into two 1-quart ring molds. Chill until firm. Unmold on platter. Garnish with radish roses and cucumber slices. Serve with your favorite dressing. Yield: 8 servings.

Ham and Celery Salad

2 cups diced, cooked ham
1 cup chopped celery
3 sweet pickles, chopped
½ green pepper, chopped
   Mayonnaise or salad dressing

Mix ham with celery, pickles, and green pepper. Add enough mayonnaise or salad dressing to moisten. Yield: 3 to 4 servings.

Molded Salmon Salad

2 envelopes unflavored gelatin
½ cup cold water
1 cup mayonnaise
½ cup light cream
1 tablespoon sugar
½ teaspoon salt
   Juice of 1 lemon
1 (1-pound) can salmon
½ cup chopped celery
2 teaspoons minced onion

Soak gelatin for 5 minutes in cold water. Place container in hot water until gelatin is dissolved. Combine mayonnaise and cream, and stir until smooth. Add sugar, salt, and lemon juice. Stir gelatin into mixture. Break salmon into small pieces and add to mayonnaise mixture with celery and onion. Pour into an 8-cup ring mold. Chill until firm. Yield: 6 servings.

Hot Turkey Salad

2 cups diced, cooked turkey
2 cups diced celery
½ cup slivered toasted almonds
½ teaspoon salt
2 teaspoons grated onion
2 tablespoons freshly squeezed lemon juice
1 cup mayonnaise
½ cup shredded American cheese
1 cup crushed potato chips

Combine turkey, celery, almonds, salt, onion, lemon juice, and mayonnaise. Toss until well mixed. Pile lightly into greased 2-quart baking dish. Sprinkle with cheese and potato chips. Bake at 450° for 10 minutes. Serve hot. Yield: 6 servings.

Congealed Salmon Salad

2 tablespoons unflavored gelatin
¼ cup cold water
1 cup boiling water
3 tablespoons freshly squeezed lemon juice
2 cups flaked salmon
¾ cup salad dressing or mayonnaise
1 cup diced celery
¼ cup chopped green pepper
1 teaspoon minced onion
½ teaspoon salt
Dash pepper

Soften gelatin in cold water; add boiling water, then chill thoroughly. Add

lemon juice, salmon, salad dressing or mayonnaise, and seasonings. Pour into greased mold and chill until firm. Yield: 6 servings.

Shrimp-Apple Salad

1½ pounds frozen shrimp, cooked and diced
1 cup diced celery
2 cups diced apples
¼ cup freshly squeezed lemon juice
2 tablespoons salad oil
1 teaspoon salt
3 hard-cooked eggs, coarsely chopped
¼ cup mayonnaise or salad dressing
Lettuce cups

Combine shrimp, celery, and apples. Mix together lemon juice, salad oil, and salt, and add to shrimp mixture. Chill. Just before serving, add eggs and mayonnaise or salad dressing. Serve in lettuce cups. Yield: 6 servings.

Tuna Salad

2 (7-ounce) cans tuna
4 cups shredded salad greens
4 medium tomatoes
3 hard-cooked eggs
Salt and pepper to taste
½ cup mayonnaise
¼ cup freshly squeezed lemon juice

Arrange salad greens in bottom of large salad bowl. Cover with tuna, and flank with quartered tomatoes and slices of hard-cooked eggs. Add seasonings and drizzle lemon juice over all. Serve with mayonnaise and garnish. Yield: 6 to 8 servings.

Tuna Fish Salad

2 (7-ounce) cans tuna fish
½ cup mayonnaise or salad dressing
1 cup chopped celery
2 tablespoons chopped sweet pickles
2 tablespoons chopped onion
2 hard-cooked eggs, chopped
½ teaspoon salt
  Lettuce

Drain tuna. Break into pieces. Combine next six ingredients and mix lightly. Serve on lettuce. Yield: 6 servings.

Beet Salad

1 (3-ounce) package lemon-
  flavored gelatin
1 cup hot water
1 cup diced, canned beets
¾ cup canned beet juice
3 tablespoons vinegar
½ teaspoon salt
2 tablespoons grated onion
½ cup diced cucumbers

Dissolve gelatin in hot water. Drain beets and set aside. Add beet juice, vinegar, salt and onion to gelatin. Partly chill, then add beets and cucumbers. Chill until firm. Yield: 6 to 8 servings.

Carrot Salad

1 (3-ounce) package orange-
  flavored gelatin
2 cups boiling water
2 cups grated carrots
½ cup flaked coconut
1 (8¼-ounce) can crushed pineapple
¼ cup chopped pecans

Dissolve gelatin in boiling water. Let sit in refrigerator until mixture begins to thicken. Stir in other ingredients and spoon into individual molds. Return to refrigerator to chill. Yield: 6 servings.

Caesar Salad

1 clove garlic, mashed
½ cup salad oil
2 quarts salad greens
1 (2-ounce) can anchovy fillets
2 tomatoes, cut in wedges
1 egg, beaten
1 teaspoon Worcestershire sauce
¼ cup freshly squeezed lemon juice
¼ teaspoon pepper
½ teaspoon salt
½ cup grated Parmesan or bleu cheese
1 cup croutons

Add garlic to oil; let stand. Break salad greens into large bowl. Add anchovies, cut into pieces, and tomatoes. Strain oil, and pour over vegetables. Combine other ingredients (except croutons) and beat well. Add to salad, along with croutons, and toss lightly. Yield: 6 servings.

To make croutons: Cut bread into ½-inch cubes. Fry in hot shortening to which garlic has been added; drain.

Carrot Congealed Salad

1 (3-ounce) package lemon-
  flavored gelatin
2 cups boiling water
2 cups shredded carrots
1 cup diced celery
1 cup drained, crushed pineapple
½ cup chopped nuts

Dissolve gelatin in boiling water. After it begins to congeal, add other ingredients. Chill. Yield: 6 servings.

Carrot-Raisin Salad

    2 cups grated carrots
    ½ cup raisins
       Mayonnaise or salad dressing
       Coconut or drained pineapple cubes
       (optional)

Combine grated carrots and raisins and add just enough salad dressing or mayonnaise to moisten. Coconut or drained pineapple cubes may also be added. Yield: 4 servings.

Congealed Spring Salad

    2 (3-ounce)packages lemon-
       flavored gelatin
1 ¾ cups boiling water
    2 cups cold water
    1 tablespoon salt
    3 tablespoons vinegar
1 ½ cups finely chopped carrots
1 ¾ cups finely chopped cabbage
1 ½ cups finely chopped spinach
    1 teaspoon finely chopped onion
       Salad greens

Dissolve gelatin in boiling water. Add cold water, salt, and vinegar. Divide mixture into three parts. Chill first part and when it begins to thicken, add carrots, and pour into an oiled loaf mold; chill until firm. Repeat with second part, adding cabbage for second layer; pour onto firm layer in mold; chill until firm. To chilled and thickened third part, add spinach and onion and pour

onto firm gelatin. Chill until firm. Unmold on salad greens. Slice and serve with mayonnaise or salad dressing. Yield: 12 servings.

Cole Slaw

    4 cups shredded cabbage
    1 to 3 tablespoons sugar
    4 tablespoons vinegar
    1 tablespoon minced onion
    ½ teaspoon salt
    ⅓ cup salad oil
       Parsley and paprika for garnish

Wash, drain, and chill cabbage. Shred. Combine sugar, vinegar, onion, salt, and salad oil. Add cabbage and mix lightly. Garnish with parsley and dash of paprika. Yield: 6 servings.

Three-Day Cole Slaw

    1 medium head cabbage, chopped or
       shredded
    1 medium onion, chopped
    1 green pepper, chopped
    1 (3-ounce) can pimiento, chopped
    ½ cup honey
    ½ cup vinegar
    ½ cup cooking oil
    2 teaspoons sugar
    2 teaspoons salt

Combine chopped cabbage, onion, pepper, and pimiento. Set aside. Combine other ingredients and bring to a hard boil. Pour hot sauce over chopped vegetables and mix well. Pack into containers and cover. Let sit in refrigerator for 3 days without removing cover. Yield: 12 servings.

Molded Avocado Ring

2 envelopes unflavored gelatin
½ cup cold water
1¼ cups boiling water
6 tablespoons freshly squeezed lemon juice
1½ teaspoons grated onion
2¼ teaspoons salt
Dash Tabasco sauce
3 cups sieved avocado
¾ cup salad dressing or mayonnaise

Soften gelatin in cold water. Dissolve in boiling water. Season with lemon juice, grated onion, salt, and Tabasco. Stir in avocado and salad dressing or mayonnaise. Pour into 8-inch ring mold and chill until firm. Yield: 6 to 8 servings.

Mixed Pea Salad

½ cup mayonnaise or salad dressing
¼ cup French dressing
1 cup canned green peas
1 cup sliced celery or carrots
½ cup diced American cheese
Salt and pepper

Mix mayonnaise or salad dressing and French dressing. Add drained peas and chill 2 hours, until flavors blend. Mix with celery and cheese. Season to taste. Yield: 6 servings.

Golden Glow Salad

1 cup water
1 cup pineapple juice
1 (3-ounce) package lemon-flavored gelatin
1 cup drained, crushed pineapple
2 cups grated carrots

Boil water and pineapple juice. Dissolve gelatin in boiling mixture. Let cool, and when it has thickened slightly, add pineapple and carrots. Pour into one large 5-cup oiled mold or six individual oiled molds. Chill in refrigerator until firm. Yield: 6 servings.

Tossed Cauliflower Salad

1 medium head of cauliflower
½ cup French dressing
1 small avocado
½ cup sliced stuffed olives
3 tomatoes, cut in eighths
½ cup crumbled Roquefort cheese
Salad greens

Separate cauliflower into flowerets; cover with ice water and chill 1 hour; drain. Chop cauliflower coarsely; pour French dressing over it and let stand for 2 hours. Just before serving, dice avocado and add to salad along with olives, tomato wedges, and cheese. Toss lightly, and serve on a bed of crisp salad greens. Yield: 8 servings.

Perfection Salad

1 (3-ounce) package orange- or lemon-flavored gelatin
1 cup boiling water
1 cup cold water
1 teaspoon salt
1 tablespoon freshly squeezed lemon juice
1 cup shredded cabbage
½ cup chopped celery
½ cup shredded carrots
1 tablespoon finely minced onion

Dissolve gelatin in boiling water; add

cold water, salt, and lemon juice; chill.
When mixture is slightly thick, add the
cabbage, celery, carrots, and onion.
Pour into mold and chill until firm.
Yield: 6 to 8 servings.

Rainbow Salad

1 cup finely chopped cabbage
1 cup finely chopped green pepper
1 cup grated carrots
1 cup chopped lettuce
½ cup finely chopped cucumber
½ cup sliced onion
1 cup sliced celery
1 cup tomato chunks
1 cup (¼ pound) shredded
   American cheese
1 cup cooked or canned green peas
½ teaspoon salt
⅛ teaspoon pepper
1 teaspoon sugar
½ cup vinegar
   Lettuce leaves

Toss all ingredients except lettuce
leaves. Chill. Serve in lettuce-lined
salad bowl. Yield: 6 to 8 servings.

Rice and Bean Salad

2 cups cooked rice
2 (1-pound) cans red kidney
   beans, drained
4 hard-cooked eggs, chopped
1 cup chopped sweet pickles
½ cup chopped onion
½ cup chopped celery
½ cup chopped green pepper
1 teaspoon salt
½ teaspoon pepper
⅔ cup mayonnaise or salad dressing
   Lettuce

Combine all ingredients except lettuce
and chill. Serve on crisp lettuce. Yield:
12 to 15 servings.

Wilted Lettuce

3 slices bacon
½ cup vinegar
½ cup water
2 tablespoons sugar
1½ teaspoons salt
1 small onion, minced
1 egg, well beaten
   Fresh leaf or head lettuce

Snip bacon into small pieces; sauté
until crisp in large skillet. Stir in vinegar, water, sugar, salt, onion, and egg.
Heat to boiling, stirring constantly.
Wash and drain lettuce. Tear into small
pieces. Toss with hot dressing in skillet.
Yield: 6 servings.

Potato Salad

½ cup mayonnaise or salad dressing
2 tablespoons prepared mustard
1 pound (4 or 5 medium) cubed,
   cooked potatoes
3 hard-cooked eggs, coarsely chopped
¼ cup chopped ripe olives or pickles
2 tablespoons slivered green pepper
1 cup thinly sliced celery
1 small onion, diced
   Salt and pepper

Combine mayonnaise or salad dressing
and mustard; add potatoes. Chill 2 to 3
hours to blend flavoring. Add eggs,
olives or pickles, green pepper, celery,
and onion. Season to taste. Chill.
Yield: 6 servings.

Hot German Potato Salad

1½ tablespoons all-purpose flour
2 tablespoons sugar
2 tablespoons bacon drippings
1 teaspoon salt
¼ teaspoon ground black pepper
½ cup water
⅓ cup cider vinegar
4 teaspoons prepared mustard
3 tablespoons minced green onion
4 cups sliced, cooked potatoes
½ teaspoon celery seed
¼ cup chopped celery
2 tablespoons diced green pepper
2 tablespoons diced pimiento
4 slices crisp bacon, crumbled

Mix flour and sugar together in a skillet. Add bacon drippings, salt, pepper, water, and vinegar. Stir and cook until thickened. Add mustard and onion. Then add potatoes, celery seed, celery, green pepper, and pimiento; mix well, but lightly. Sprinkle with bacon. Serve hot. Yield: 6 to 8 servings.

Tomato Aspic

1½ tablespoons unflavored gelatin
¼ cup cold water
2½ cups tomato juice
1 tablespoon grated onion
3 whole cloves
1 bay leaf
¼ cup chopped celery
1 teaspoon chopped parsley
½ teaspoon salt
1 teaspoon sugar
2 teaspoons freshly squeezed lemon juice

Soften gelatin in the cold water. Mix the tomato juice with the seasonings, cover, and simmer 15 minutes. Strain, add the softened gelatin, and stir until dissolved. Pour into six individual molds. Chill until firm. Yield: 6 servings.

Three-Bean Salad

⅔ cup vinegar
1 cup sugar
⅓ cup salad oil
1 fresh onion, chopped
1 (16-ounce) can green beans
1 (16-ounce) can yellow wax beans or bean sprouts
1 (16-ounce) can kidney beans

Combine all ingredients. Let sit overnight in refrigerator. Drain well before serving. Yield: 8 to 10 servings.

Tossed Garden Salad

1 head lettuce
2 large tomatoes
4 fresh green onions, including tops
1 medium cucumber
1 bunch radishes
Few leaves spinach
Bunch chives (6 to 8 spikes)
½ teaspoon salt
Commercial French dressing
Salad greens

Cut lettuce in 1-inch cubes. Chill, peel, and cut tomatoes into wedges. Cut onions into cubes. Peel and slice cucumber. Slice radishes. Chop spinach leaves and cut chives very fine. Place all on a bed of salad greens. Season with salt and French dressing. Yield: 6 to 8 servings.

The key to making successful salads is through the crisping and chilling of all ingredients. For salad dressing recipes, see Page 76.

Deviled Potato Salad

8 hard-cooked eggs
2 tablespoons vinegar
1 tablespoon prepared horseradish
2½ tablespoons prepared mustard
1 cup mayonnaise or salad dressing
1 cup commercial sour cream
½ teaspoon celery salt
1 teaspoon salt
6 medium potatoes, cooked in jackets, peeled and cubed (4½ cups)
1 cup chopped celery
¼ cup chopped onion
2 tablespoons chopped green pepper
2 tablespoons chopped pimiento
  Tomato wedges
  Cucumber slices

Cut eggs in half and remove yolks. Mash and blend yolks with vinegar, horseradish, and mustard. Add mayonnaise, sour cream, celery salt, and salt; mix well. Chop egg whites; combine with potatoes, celery, onion, green pepper, and pimiento. Fold in egg yolk mixture; chill. Garnish with tomato wedges and cucumber slices. Yield: 6 to 8 servings.

Egg Salad-Stuffed Tomatoes

6 hard-cooked eggs
1 cup sliced celery
2 tablespoons minced green pepper
1 teaspoon minced onion
¼ cup mayonnaise
  Pinch chili powder
1 tablespoon vinegar
1 teaspoon salt
⅛ teaspoon pepper
6 tomatoes
  Parsley
  Lettuce

Cut eggs into medium-sized pieces. Then add rest of ingredients except tomatoes, parsley, and lettuce, and refrigerate. Before serving, wash chilled tomatoes, and remove cores. Then fill tomato cavities with egg salad, garnish with sprigs of parsley, and serve on lettuce. Yield: 6 servings.

Celery Seed Dressing

1 teaspoon salt
1 teaspoon dry mustard
1 teaspoon paprika
1 teaspoon celery seed
½ cup light corn syrup
¼ to ⅓ cup vinegar
1 cup salad oil
1 tablespoon grated onion

Place all ingredients in a small bowl. Beat until well blended and thickened. Place in a covered container and chill for several hours. Yield: 1¾ cups.

Condensed Milk Salad Dressing

1 egg, beaten
1 tablespoon dry mustard
1 teaspoon salt
½ teaspoon pepper
½ teaspoon paprika
¾ cup vinegar
1 (15-ounce) can sweetened condensed milk
¼ cup melted butter

Beat egg until lemon colored. Add other ingredients and beat thoroughly. Chill before serving. Serve on fruit salad. Yield: 1½ to 2 cups.

Buttermilk Dressing

¼ cup buttermilk
¼ cup mayonnaise or salad dressing
1 teaspoon salt
⅛ teaspoon Worcestershire sauce
   Dash paprika

Combine all ingredients and mix well.
Serve over shredded cabbage. Yield:
6 servings.

Dressing for Fruit Salad

2 (3-ounce) packages cream cheese,
   softened
1 cup mayonnaise
1 cup cream, whipped
1½ cups chopped nuts

Cream together cream cheese and mayonnaise. Fold in whipped cream and
chopped nuts. Use over fruit salads.
Yield: 3½ cups.

Cooked Salad Dressing No. 1

2 whole eggs or 4 yolks
¼ cup vinegar
2 tablespoons butter or margarine
5 tablespoons cream cheese, softened
2 tablespoons cream
½ teaspoon sugar
½ teaspoon salt
¼ teaspoon dry mustard
   Dash paprika
⅛ teaspoon celery seed
3 drops Tabasco sauce

Beat eggs and vinegar together until
smooth. Cook mixture in top of a double
boiler, stirring constantly, until the
consistency is that of thick cream.
Remove at once from heat, add butter

or margarine and cream cheese, and
stir until mixture is smooth. Then add
cream and seasonings. Yield: 1 cup.

Cooked Salad Dressing No. 2

1½ tablespoons butter or margarine
2 tablespoons all-purpose flour
1 teaspoon sugar
1 teaspoon salt
1 teaspoon dry mustard
   Few grains cayenne pepper
1 egg, slightly beaten
¾ cup skimmed milk
¼ cup vinegar

Melt butter or margarine in top of double boiler. Mix dry ingredients; add
egg, melted butter or margarine, and
milk, then very slowly add the vinegar.
Cook until mixture thickens. Cool.
Yield: 1¼ cups.

Low-Calorie French Dressing

3 tablespoons salad oil
¾ teaspoon salt
1 teaspoon sugar
⅛ teaspoon paprika
½ teaspoon dry mustard
¼ teaspoon Tabasco sauce
1 cup grapefruit juice, divided
2 teaspoons cornstarch

Combine salad oil, salt, sugar, paprika,
mustard, and Tabasco sauce in mixing
bowl. Blend ½ cup grapefruit juice
and cornstarch in small saucepan.
Cook over low heat, stirring constantly
until mixture thickens and comes to a
boil. Add to salad oil mixture; beat
with rotary beater until smooth. Beat in
remaining ½ cup grapefruit juice.
Yield: 1½ cups.

Honey-Lime Salad Dressing

1 egg, beaten
¼ cup lime juice
1 teaspoon grated lime rind
½ cup honey
⅛ teaspoon salt
⅛ teaspoon ground mace
1 cup commercial sour cream

Combine egg, lime juice, grated lime rind, and honey in saucepan; cook over low heat until thickened, stirring constantly. Add salt and mace; cool. Fold in sour cream; chill. Yield: 1½ cups.

Mayonnaise

1 whole egg or 2 egg yolks
½ teaspoon dry mustard
1 teaspoon salt
2 tablespoons vinegar
1 cup salad oil

Put the egg, mustard, salt, vinegar, and ¼ cup of the salad oil in the container of an electric blender. Cover container and flick motor quickly on and off high speed. Remove cover, turn motor on high, and immediately add the remaining oil in a steady stream. Yield: 1½ cups.

Fruit Dressing

½ cup sugar
1 tablespoon all-purpose flour
1 egg yolk
Juice of 1 lemon
½ cup unsweetened pineapple juice
1 cup heavy cream, whipped

Combine sugar, flour, and egg yolk in top of double boiler. Add lemon and pineapple juices; cook until thick. Fold in whipped cream, and serve over fruit salad. Will keep for 3 days in refrigerator. Yield: 1½ cups.

Green Goddess Salad Dressing

1 cup mayonnaise
½ cup commercial sour cream
¼ teaspoon garlic powder
2 green onions and tops, coarsely cut
¼ cup coarsely cut green pepper
2 tablespoons freshly squeezed lemon juice
¼ cup parsley
¼ teaspoon black pepper
3 anchovy fillets
Dash Worcestershire sauce

Place all ingredients in blender; cover and blend for 10 seconds on high speed or until pale green and smooth. Yield: about 2 cups.

Garlic Cream Dressing

1 clove garlic
2 teaspoons salt
⅔ cup salad oil
⅓ cup vinegar
⅓ cup heavy cream
Pepper to taste

Cut the clove of garlic into small pieces on a chopping board and sprinkle with salt. Mash salt and garlic together with flat side of a knife blade. Continue rubbing the garlic until it is completely blended with the salt. Combine the garlic-salt mixture with salad oil, vinegar, and cream. Add pepper to taste. Shake well before serving. Yield: 1½ cups.

Guests will feel complimented when you serve them Quail with Wild Rice. See recipe on Page 105.

Tomato Soup–French Dressing

1 (10½-ounce) can condensed tomato
   soup
1 cup salad oil
1 tablespoon black pepper
1 tablespoon Worcestershire sauce
1 tablespoon prepared mustard
1 tablespoon garlic salt or 1 button
   garlic, cut fine
1 teaspoon salt
½ cup sugar
½ cup vinegar

Pour soup into mixing bowl. Stir with
spoon while adding other ingredients in
order given. Place in covered jar in the
refrigerator. Shake well each time
before using. Yield: 3 cups.

Honey-Fruit Dressing

⅔ cup sugar
1 teaspoon dry mustard
1 teaspoon paprika
¼ teaspoon salt
1 teaspoon ground celery seed
1 tablespoon poppy seed
⅓ cup strained honey
5 tablespoons cider vinegar
1 tablespoon freshly squeezed
   lemon juice
1 teaspoon grated onion
1 cup salad oil

Mix dry ingredients; add honey, vinegar, lemon juice, and onion. Slowly
pour oil into mixture, beating constantly until slightly creamy. Yield: 2 cups.

Orange Salad Dressing

¼ cup sugar
4 tablespoons all-purpose flour
½ teaspoon salt
½ teaspoon mustard
⅛ teaspoon paprika
1 cup orange juice
2 tablespoons butter or margarine
¼ cup freshly squeezed lemon juice

Mix sugar, flour, salt, mustard, and paprika in a saucepan; add orange juice
slowly and bring to the boiling point,
stirring constantly. Cook slowly for 3
minutes. Add butter or margarine, and
when melted, add lemon juice. Beat
until smooth, and cool. Yield: 1¼ cups.

Poppy Seed Dressing

1½ cups sugar
2 teaspoons dry mustard
2 teaspoons salt
⅔ cup vinegar
3 tablespoons onion juice
2 cups salad oil
3 tablespoons poppy seed

Mix sugar, mustard, salt, and vinegar.
Add onion juice and stir in thoroughly.
Use medium speed on mixer. Add oil
slowly, beating constantly, and continue to beat until thick. Add poppy
seed and beat for a few minutes. Store
in a cool place or in the refrigerator,
but not near freezing section. Yield:
2½ cups.

Fish & Seafood

From a quite literal point of view, the first Southerners were Indians, and mounds of oyster shells buried deep by time along Southern coasts testify that the taste for seafood is an old one in this part of the country.

The waters which border and wind through the South offer sport for everyone, from lovers of the surf to fishermen on small lakes. Likewise, the varied harvest of these seas and inland lakes and rivers provides enough culinary appeal to please any taste.

The variety of fish native to Southern waters is amazing — from Chesapeake Bay crabs, to North Carolina oysters, to Louisiana crawfish, to Mississippi catfish, to Texas shrimp. State festivals throughout the South proudly demonstrate this fact.

Supply is also abundant. Even for those who would rather do the cooking than the catching, seafood of all kinds is readily available. Modern packaging has made passé the old adage of oysters being available only in the "r" months, although they are more plentiful then, and grain-fed catfish are becoming the basis of a very palatable industry in the Mississippi River Valley states.

Each locale in the South has developed its own special techniques of preparing native seafood, from Maryland crab cakes to New Orleans jambalaya.

Because seafood has remained an important part of the Southern diet since settlers gained possession of the shores, seafood recipes are an integral part of our legacy. As with so many other foods, the best recipes seem to be the tried and true.

Crab Imperial

1 tablespoon butter or margarine
1 cup cream
½ teaspoon salt
  Dash red pepper
½ teaspoon dry mustard
1 tablespoon Worcestershire sauce
1 teaspoon vinegar
1 cup finely chopped red and
  green pepper
¾ cup breadcrumbs
1 pound crabmeat

Melt butter or margarine; add cream, salt, red pepper, mustard, Worcestershire sauce, and vinegar. When thoroughly mixed and heated, add red and green peppers and breadcrumbs. Mix well. Remove from heat, and very gently mix in crabmeat. Stuff shells or baking dishes, mounding high, remembering not to break the lumps of crabmeat. Sprinkle lightly with breadcrumbs, and bake at 425° until brown. Yield: 6 to 8 servings.

Crab Newburg

2 (6½-ounce) cans crabmeat
¼ cup butter or margarine
½ cup cooking sherry
4 egg yolks
1¾ cups heavy cream
½ teaspoon salt
  Paprika
  Hot cooked rice

Remove any cartilage from crabmeat, being careful not to break meat chunks too small. Place crabmeat, butter, and cooking sherry in chafing dish or top of double boiler. Cook over direct heat, stirring gently, until liquid is reduced about half. Place slightly beaten egg yolks in cup and add cream to make 2 cups. Blend thoroughly. Add salt. Stir cream mixture into crab mixture. Place over hot water. Cook, stirring gently, until mixture thickens. If too thick, add more cream or a little milk. Sprinkle with paprika. Serve over hot rice. Yield: 6 servings.

Stuffed Crabs

18 medium crabs
 4 tablespoons shortening
½ cup chopped green onions
 2 cups breadcrumbs, divided
½ cup chopped celery
¼ cup minced parsley
 1 teaspoon salt
½ teaspoon black pepper
¼ teaspoon red pepper
  Butter or margarine

Scald crabs and remove shells. Clean and place about six of the shells in boiling water, to which a bit of soda has been added. Let remain for about 10 minutes. Then remove and scrub shells, clean thoroughly, wash in clear water, and set aside to drain. Remove meat from crabs. Put shortening into deep frying pan and heat. Add onion, and cook slightly. Add 1½ cups breadcrumbs, chopped celery, parsley, crabmeat, and seasoning, mixing as added. Cook slowly over low heat for about 5 minutes; then put mixture into clean shells to bake. Put breadcrumbs on top of each, and dot with butter or margarine. Bake at 375° until top is browned. Yield: 6 servings.

Fresh Fried Fish and hot Hushpuppies are Southern go-togethers.
See recipes on Pages 95 and 197.

Crab Jambalaya

  1 **pound crabmeat**
  ½ **cup chopped bacon**
  ½ **cup chopped onion**
  ½ **cup chopped celery**
  ½ **cup chopped green pepper**
  2 **cups cooked tomatoes**
  ¼ **cup uncooked regular rice**
  1 **tablespoon Worcestershire sauce**
  ½ **teaspoon salt**
  ⅛ **teaspoon pepper**

Remove any shell or cartilage from crabmeat. Fry bacon until lightly browned. Add onion, celery, and green pepper; cook until tender. Add tomatoes, rice, and seasonings. Cover and simmer for 20 to 25 minutes or until rice is tender, stirring occasionally. Add crabmeat and heat. Yield: 6 servings.

Deviled Crabs

  1 **dozen fine, large crabs**
  ½ **pint cream**
  2 **tablespoons all-purpose flour**
  1 **tablespoon butter**
     Yolks of 4 hard-cooked eggs, mashed fine
  1 **tablespoon salt**
  1 **tablespoon chopped parsley**
  ¼ **teaspoon ground nutmeg**
  ¼ **teaspoon cayenne pepper**
  1 **egg, beaten**
     Breadcrumbs

Boil the crabs. Take out and drain after they have cooled in their own water. Break off the claws, separate the shells, remove the spongy portions of the fingers, and then pick out the meat. Put the cream on to boil, rub the flour and butter together well and add to the boiling cream. Stir and cook for 2 minutes.

Take from the heat and add the crabmeat and yolks of the hard-cooked eggs, mashed very fine. Add chopped parsley, ground nutmeg, salt, and cayenne. Clean the upper shells of the crabs, fill them with the mixture, brush over with a beaten egg, sprinkle with breadcrumbs, and brown in oven at 425°; or, better still, if you have a frying basket, plunge the crabs into the hot shortening until a nice brown. Yield: 6 servings.

Southern Manor Frog Legs

  8 **frog legs**
  ½ **cup freshly squeezed lemon juice**
     Salt and pepper
  1 **egg, beaten**
     Cracker crumbs

Only the hind legs of the frog are eaten. Skin the legs and scald in boiling salt water (1 teaspoon salt to 1 quart water) and lemon juice for about 2 minutes. Dry after boiling. Season with salt and pepper, dip in beaten egg, then in cracker crumbs. Fry for 3 minutes in deep, hot shortening. Turn and fry on other side. Yield: 4 servings.

Boiled Lobsters

  1½ **gallons water**
  ⅓ **cup salt**
  6 **(1-pound) live lobsters**
     Melted butter or margarine

Place water in large container. Add salt. Cover and bring to the boiling point over high heat. Plunge lobsters headfirst into the boiling salted water. Cover and cook for 20 minutes. Drain. Crack claws. Serve with melted butter or margarine. Yield: 6 servings.

Broiled Boiled Lobsters

2 boiled lobsters
1 tablespoon butter or margarine, melted
  Dash white pepper
  Dash paprika
¼ cup butter or margarine, melted
1 tablespoon freshly squeezed lemon juice

Lay lobsters open as flat as possible on a broiler pan. Brush lobster meat with the 1 tablespoon melted butter or margarine. Sprinkle with pepper and paprika. Broil about 4 inches from source of heat for 5 minutes, or until lightly browned. Combine the ¼ cup melted butter or margarine and the lemon juice; serve with lobsters. Yield: 2 servings.

Lobster Thermidor

2 tablespoons butter or margarine
1 teaspoon minced onion
2 cups cooked lobster meat
1 (4-ounce) can mushrooms
2 cups medium white sauce
  Shredded Cheddar cheese
  Dry toast

Heat butter in skillet or chafing dish over direct flame. Add onion and lobster. Cook for 5 minutes and add mushrooms. Cook for 5 minutes and add white sauce. Place in double boiler and heat over boiling water. Top with shred-

ded cheese. Serve hot over pieces of dry toast. Yield: 4 servings.

Oven Barbecued Mullet

1 (2-pound) mullet
2 tablespoons chopped onion
1 tablespoon shortening
¾ cup catsup
2 tablespoons vinegar
¼ cup freshly squeezed lemon juice
3 tablespoons Worcestershire sauce
2 tablespoons brown sugar
½ teaspoon salt
⅛ teaspoon pepper
  Parsley
  Lemon slices

Scale and clean fish. Bone and place in shallow baking pan. Brown onions lightly in shortening; add remaining ingredients and simmer for 5 minutes. Pour over fish and bake at 425° for 30 minutes, or until fish is tender. Garnish with chopped parsley and lemon slices. Yield: 3 to 4 servings.

Broiled Virginia Oysters On Toast

Only large, plump oysters should be broiled because small ones shrivel too much in cooking. Wipe oysters dry, dip in melted butter seasoned with salt and cayenne, then roll in crumbs. Place in narrow-mesh broiling pan. Use moderate heat to prevent burning. Brown one side, then the other. Keep hot until time to serve. Serve on toast with melted butter or margarine. Garnish with sprig of parsley and quarter of lemon. Allow at least 6 large oysters per person.

Fried Oysters

1 quart oysters
2 eggs, slightly beaten
2 tablespoons milk
1 teaspoon salt
⅛ teaspoon pepper
1 cup breadcrumbs, cracker crumbs,
   or cornmeal
   Hot shortening for frying

Drain oysters. Mix egg and milk. Dip oysters in egg mixture, then in crumb or cornmeal mixture. Fry in deep, hot shortening; when brown on one side, turn and brown on other side. Serve hot. Yield: 6 servings.

Oyster Jambalaya

3 teaspoons shortening
1 teaspoon all-purpose flour
1½ cups finely chopped onion
1 clove garlic, minced
1 cup chopped green pepper
¼ cup finely chopped celery
½ cup ground pork
½ pound ground veal
3 dozen oysters
2 teaspoons salt
¼ teaspoon black pepper
¼ teaspoon red pepper
2 cups cooked rice
1½ tablespoons finely chopped parsley
1½ tablespoons chopped onion tops

Make a golden brown roux with shortening and flour. Add onion, garlic, green pepper, and celery, and cook slowly until clear, stirring frequently. Add pork and veal and cook until brown, about 10 minutes. Drain liquid from oysters. Stir into vegetable mixture, and cook for 5 minutes. Add oysters, salt, black and red pepper. After 15 minutes, stir in rice.

Transfer to top of double boiler to keep hot for 1 hour to let flavors blend. Before serving, stir in parsley and onion tops. Yield: 8 servings.

Baked Corn and Oysters

1 (17-ounce) can cream-style corn
1 cup crackers, crushed
1 beaten egg
½ teaspoon salt
½ cup milk or cream
¼ teaspoon black pepper
1 teaspoon sugar
¼ cup melted butter
1 cup small, fresh oysters

Combine ingredients in order named. Pour the mixture into a greased 1½-quart baking dish and bake at 375° for 25 minutes. Do not overbake or oysters will become tough. Yield: 4 to 6 servings.

Oyster Pie

¼ teaspoon celery salt
1 teaspoon onion juice
1 dozen oysters
2 cups white sauce
   Pastry for 7-inch pie

Put celery, salt, onion juice and oysters in white sauce in 1-quart baking dish. Season to taste, cover with a rich piecrust, and bake at 450° for 20 minutes or until piecrust is done. Yield: 4 servings.

Baked Shad with Dressing

Dress fish, wipe dry, rub with salt and lemon juice; also oil well with butter, and add a slight sprinkling of cracker meal. Stuff with following Dressing. Place on rack, and put a little water in bottom of pan. Bake for 1 hour or longer, basting freely with butter and the water. Sprinkle with salt and pepper; and lay bacon slices in gashes.

Dressing

1 cup breadcrumbs (toasted and
   moistened with hot water)
1 tablespoon freshly squeezed lemon juice
3 stalks celery leaves, chopped
2 tablespoons butter or margarine
1 onion, chopped

Combine all ingredients. Yield: Dressing for 4-pound fish.

Fried Shad Fillets

2 pounds shad fillets
1 egg, beaten
1 tablespoon milk
1 teaspoon salt
½ cup all-purpose flour
½ cup dry breadcrumbs
  Shortening

Cut fish into serving-size portions. Combine egg, milk, and salt. Combine flour and crumbs. Dip fish in egg mixture and roll in flour and crumb mixture. Place fish in a heavy frying pan which contains about ⅛ inch of shortening, hot but not smoking. Fry. When fish is brown on one side, turn carefully and brown the other side. Cooking time: approximately 10 minutes, depending on thickness of fish. Drain on absorbent paper. Yield: 6 servings.

Salmon Croquettes

2 cups salmon
2 cups soft breadcrumbs
½ cup milk
2 eggs
1 teaspoon salt
  Few grains cayenne pepper
1 tablespoon freshly squeezed
  lemon juice
1 tablespoon chopped parsley
2 cups dry breadcrumbs
  Hot shortening

Drain the oil from the salmon; remove skin and bones; separate into fine flakes. Cook the breadcrumbs in the milk for 5 minutes; stir in the unbeaten eggs, seasonings, and salmon. Let cool before shaping croquettes. Allow 1 rounded tablespoon of the mixture for each croquette. Make into balls, and shape as desired. After shaping the croquettes, coat them on all sides with finely sifted dry breadcrumbs. Let stand to dry before frying if possible. Croquettes should be fried in deep, hot shortening until brown. Yield: 6 to 8 servings.

Salmon Loaf

2 cups (1-pound can) drained
  flaked salmon
1½ cups fine dry breadcrumbs
1 (10½-ounce) can condensed cream of
  celery soup
½ cup minced green pepper
2 eggs, slightly beaten

Combine all ingredients; pack lightly into a greased loafpan (9 x 5 x 3 inches). Bake at 350° for about 1 hour. Yield: 6 servings.

Cooked Shrimp
For Cocktails or Salad

        8 cups water
      ¼ cup sliced onion
        1 clove garlic
        1 bay leaf
        2 stalks celery with leaves
   1½ tablespoons salt
      ⅛ teaspoon cayenne pepper
        2 pounds shrimp
      ½ lemon, sliced

Simmer water, onion, garlic, bay leaf, celery, salt, and cayenne pepper for 15 minutes. Add shrimp and lemon. When water comes to a boil, cook for 5 minutes. Drain. Remove shells and make an incision down the back, then wash and remove black veins. Shrimp may then be used for cocktails, salads, or in dishes calling for cooked shrimp. Yield: 6 to 8 servings.

Shrimp Creole

      ¼ cup butter
        1 cup coarsely chopped onions
        1 cup diced celery
        1 small clove garlic, finely minced
        2 tablespoons all-purpose flour
        1 teaspoon salt
        1 teaspoon sugar
            Dash cayenne pepper
        1 teaspoon paprika
      ½ small bay leaf
        4 drops Tabasco sauce
      ½ cup diced green pepper
        1 (1-pound, 3-ounce) can tomatoes
        2 cups cooked, cleaned shrimp (1 pound fresh shrimp or 2 (7-ounce) cans
            Cheese Rice

Melt butter in fry pan. Add onion, cel-

ery, and garlic; cook slowly until tender but not brown. Add flour and seasonings; stir until blended. Stir in green pepper and tomatoes. Cook for 10 minutes over low heat, stirring occasionally. Add shrimp and heat. Serve in hot casserole lined with Cheese Rice. Yield: 6 servings.

Cheese Rice

        3 cups water
        1 tablespoon butter
        1 teaspoon salt
   1½ cups uncooked regular rice
        2 cups shredded American cheese
        2 tablespoons finely chopped onion
        1 teaspoon prepared mustard

Bring water to boiling point. Add butter, salt, and rice; bring to a boil, reduce heat to low and cook covered for 20 to 25 minutes or until tender. Stir cheese, onion, and mustard into hot rice.

French Fried Shrimp

   1½ pounds shrimp, fresh or frozen
        2 eggs, beaten
        1 teaspoon salt
      ½ cup all-purpose flour
      ½ cup dry breadcrumbs

Peel shrimp, leaving the last section of the shell on if desired. Cut almost through lengthwise and remove sand veins. Wash. Combine egg and salt. Dip each shrimp in egg, and roll in flour and crumb mixture. Fry in a basket in deep fat at 350° for 2 to 3 minutes or until golden brown. Drain on absorbent paper. Serve plain or with a sauce. Yield: 6 servings.

South Louisiana Shrimp

2 pounds shrimp
1 small onion
1 clove garlic
½ tablespoon vinegar
   Water to cover shrimp
   Sauce

Boil shrimp and other ingredients, but do not overcook. To do this, drop shrimp into boiling water and allow to return to boiling point; and cook for exactly 8 minutes. Drain, peel, and devein in ice water. Marinate the shrimp in Sauce for 2 hours before serving. Yield: 8 servings.

Sauce

1 clove garlic, mashed
   Juice of 1 freshly squeezed lemon
1 cup olive oil
½ teaspoon salt
   Dash Tabasco sauce
2 or 3 drops Worcestershire sauce
1 tablespoon mustard
   Catsup to suit taste

Combine ingredients and blend. Yield: sauce for 8 servings of shrimp.

Shrimp Addie

6 strips bacon
2 to 2¼ cups cooked tomatoes
2 large green peppers, cut into strips
1 clove garlic, finely chopped (optional)
2 cups boiled peeled shrimp (1 pound in shell)
   Hot cooked rice or grits

Cook bacon in heavy skillet until brown and crisp; remove from skillet and drain. Add tomatoes, green peppers, and garlic to skillet; simmer until peppers are tender and tomatoes are reduced to about one-half (about 40 minutes). Add shrimp, and simmer 5 minutes longer or until thoroughly hot. Serve with either hot rice or grits. Yield: 4 servings.

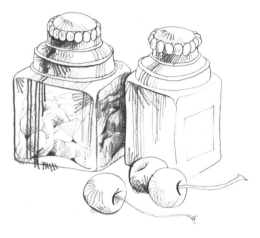

Quick Breaded Shrimp

2 (4½-ounce) cans shrimp
2 eggs
½ cup milk
1 tablespoon freshly squeezed lemon juice
1 tablespoon melted butter or margarine
1 cup all-purpose flour
½ teaspoon salt
1 teaspoon baking powder
   Breadcrumbs, plain or Italian style
   Hot shortening

Drain and rinse shrimp; blot dry and set aside. Combine all ingredients except breadcrumbs into a smooth, thick batter. Dip the shrimp in batter, drain well and dredge in crumbs. Drop into hot shortening (375°) and fry for 1 minute or until crisp and golden brown. Yield: 5 servings.

Shrimp Bisque

¾ *pound cooked shrimp*
2 *tablespoons chopped onion*
2 *tablespoons chopped celery*
¼ *cup butter or margarine*
2 *tablespoons all-purpose flour*
1 *teaspoon salt*
¼ *teaspoon paprika*
⅛ *teaspoon black pepper*
4 *cups milk*
Parsley

Grind shrimp. Cook onion and celery in butter or margarine until tender. Blend in flour and seasonings. Add milk gradually and cook until thick, stirring constantly. Add shrimp; heat. Garnish with chopped parsley sprinkled over the top. Yield: 6 servings.

Pascagoula Shrimp Boil

3 *ounces prepared shrimp boil (commercial spice mix)*
1 *small onion, sliced*
1 *lemon, sliced*
1 *clove garlic, sliced*
1 *gallon water*
½ *cup salt*
5 *pounds shrimp, fresh or frozen*
 Peppy Seafood Sauce

Tie the shrimp boil, onion, lemon, and garlic in a piece of cheesecloth. Place water in a large container. Add salt and bag of seasonings. Cover and bring to the boiling point over a hot fire. Add shrimp and return to the boiling point. Cover and cook for 5 minutes or until shrimp are tender. Drain. Serve hot with Peppy Seafood Sauce. Yield: 6 servings.

Note: If shrimp is to be used for salads or cocktails, cook as above, remove from water, chill, devein, and chill.

Peppy Seafood Sauce

½ *cup chili sauce*
½ *cup catsup*
3 *tablespoons freshly squeezed lemon juice*
1 *tablespoon horseradish*
1 *tablespoon mayonnaise or salad dressing*
1 *teaspoon Worcestershire sauce*
½ *teaspoon grated onion*
¼ *teaspoon salt*
3 *drops Tabasco sauce*
 Dash pepper

Combine all ingredients and chill thoroughly. Yield: 1½ cups or 6 generous servings.

Shrimp and Rice

1 *pound shrimp*
1 *teaspoon Worcestershire sauce*
2 *tablespoons all-purpose flour*
1 *teaspoon paprika*
¼ *cup butter or margarine*
½ *cup chopped celery*
⅓ *cup chopped green pepper*
¼ *cup minced onion*
3 *cups hot cooked rice*
4 *slices bacon*
 Salt and pepper to taste

Clean and devein shrimp; sprinkle with Worcestershire sauce. Roll in mixture of flour and paprika. Melt butter in large skillet. Add celery, green pepper, and onion, and cook over low heat for about 5 minutes. Add shrimp; increase heat and cook for about 5 minutes more, or until flour browns and shrimp turn pink. Add hot rice and a small amount of water, if needed. Fry bacon until crisp, crumble and add with bacon drippings to shrimp. Add salt and pepper to taste. Serve hot. Yield: 4 servings.

Southern Christmas dinner specialties include Holiday Turkey and Baked Country Ham. See recipes on Pages 138 and 126.

Red Snapper With Shrimp Stuffing

Select a fish weighing 3 to 4 pounds. Have fish dressed. Clean, rub salt inside and out, and stuff with Shrimp Stuffing. Fasten together with skewers, or lace with string to hold in place.

Brush fish with melted fat and place in greased baking pan. Bake at 350° for about 40 minutes, or until fish flakes easily when tested with a fork.

Shrimp Stuffing

¼ cup chopped celery
2 tablespoons chopped onion
2 tablespoons butter or margarine
3 slices cooked bacon, minced
1 cup soft breadcrumbs
½ cup chopped shrimp
1 egg
  Salt and pepper

Sauté celery and onion in butter or margarine until soft. Add remaining ingredients and mix well. Yield: stuffing for 3- to 4-pound fish.

Tuna Bake

2 (7-ounce) cans chunk-style tuna
1 medium onion, chopped
1 medium green pepper, chopped
2 (16-ounce) cans small English peas
2 (10½-ounce) cans condensed cream of celery soup
  Salt and pepper to taste
2 (10-count) cans ready-to-cook biscuits
2 cups shredded American cheese

Drain small amount of oil from tuna into a skillet. Sauté chopped onion and pepper in oil until transparent. Combine onion, pepper, tuna, peas, and soup in a 2-quart casserole. Add salt and pepper to taste.

Flatten each biscuit; add small amount of shredded cheese and fold over, pinching edges together to form a pocket. Place on top of tuna mixture. Bake at 400° for about 15 minutes, or until biscuits are browned. Yield: 10 to 12 servings.

Tuna-Egg Scallop

1 (7-ounce) can tuna
1 tablespoon freshly squeezed lemon juice
2 tablespoons butter or margarine
4 tablespoons all-purpose flour
¼ teaspoon dry mustard
2½ cups milk
3 hard-cooked eggs, chopped
1 tablespoon minced parsley
¼ teaspoon Tabasco sauce
1 cup soft buttered breadcrumbs

Drain oil from tuna. Reserve the oil. Break tuna into pieces; add lemon juice. Melt butter, add tuna oil, flour, and dry mustard; stir to a smooth paste. Add milk and cook, stirring constantly until mixture thickens and comes to a boil. Add tuna, eggs, parsley, and Tabasco. Turn into individual casseroles. Sprinkle with buttered breadcrumbs. Bake at 375° for 25 minutes or until crumbs are lightly browned. Yield: 4 to 6 servings.

Tuna Fish Croquettes

1 (10½-ounce) can condensed chicken
   with rice soup
1 tablespoon butter
1 tablespoon all-purpose flour
6 saltine crackers, crushed
1 (7-ounce) can solid light tuna, flaked
   Salt and pepper
1 cup crushed saltine crackers
   Hot oil for frying

Make cream sauce of soup, butter, and flour. Add 6 crushed crackers, tuna, and seasonings. Chill. Shape into croquettes and roll in crushed crackers. Fry in hot oil. Yield: 9 croquettes.

Bass with Oyster Stuffing

2 (3- to 4-pound) bass, split and boned
   Oyster Stuffing
¼ cup melted butter
   Salt and pepper to taste

Grease shallow pan, or line with aluminum foil. Place two halves of fish, skin-side down, in pan. Spread with Oyster Stuffing; place other halves, skin-side up, on stuffing. Fasten with skewers. Brush with melted butter; sprinkle with salt and pepper. Bake at 350° for about 1 hour. Brush occasionally with butter. Yield: 6 servings.

Oyster Stuffing

1 cup oysters, chopped
3 cups dry bread cubes
2 teaspoons salt
⅛ teaspoon pepper
⅛ teaspoon sage
3 tablespoons butter
1 small onion, minced
2 tablespoons minced parsley
½ cup minced celery

Place oysters in skillet; sauté for about 5 minutes; drain. Combine bread cubes, salt, pepper, sage, and oysters. Melt butter in another skillet, add onion, parsley, and celery, and sauté until tender. Add to oyster mixture.

Broiled Fish No. 1

Use dressed whole fish. Salt well and rub thoroughly with salad oil. Broil for 15 to 20 minutes to each side, depending on size of fish. Sprinkle with paprika.

Broiled Fish No. 2

2 pounds fillets or steaks
   (bass, trout, snapper, etc.)
1 teaspoon salt
⅛ teaspoon pepper
4 tablespoons melted butter

Cut fish into serving-size portions. Sprinkle both sides with salt and pepper. Place fish on preheated greased broiler pan about 2 inches from heat, skin-side up, unless skin has been removed. Brush with melted butter. Broil for 5 to 8 minutes or until slightly brown; baste with melted butter. Turn carefully and brush with melted butter. Cook for 5 to 8 minutes, or until fish flakes easily when tested with a fork. Remove carefully to a hot platter and serve immediately. Yield: 4 to 6 servings.

Baked Stuffed Fish

1 (3- to 4-pound) fish, dressed
1½ teaspoons salt
3 tablespoons chopped onion
¾ cup celery, chopped
6 tablespoons melted butter or margarine
⅛ teaspoon pepper
1 teaspoon thyme, sage, or savory seasoning
4 cups breadcrumbs

Clean, wash, and dry fish. Sprinkle inside and out with salt. Cook the onions and celery in melted butter or margarine for about 10 minutes, or until tender. Add cooked vegetables and seasonings to breadcrumbs, and mix thoroughly. Add water, if needed to moisten. Stuff fish loosely with dressing, and sew the opening with needle or string, or close with skewers. Place fish in a greased baking pan. Brush with melted fat and bake at 350° for 40 to 60 minutes, or until fish flakes easily when tested with a fork. Baste with melted butter or margarine occasionally during baking, if fish seems dry. Remove string or skewers and serve hot. Yield: 6 servings.

Baked Fish

Select scaled and cleaned trout, bluefish, or any other medium-size fish. Wipe the skin with a damp cloth. Cut off head, tail, and fins. The fish may be boned if desired by running a small sharp knife under the flesh close to the backbone along the four sets of bone (two long, two short).

Sprinkle inside and out with salt and pepper. Spread lightly with butter or margarine, or arrange strips of salt pork over the surface. Place in a greased pan and bake at 350°, allowing about 15 minutes per pound.

Fish 'n' Dressing

1 to 2 cups flaked fish
2 Cups cornbread and breadcrumbs
1 to 2 teaspoons chopped pimientoes
   Salt and pepper to season
2 tablespoons finely chopped green pepper
2 tablespoons finely chopped onion
2 tablespoons finely chopped celery
1 teaspoon Worcestershire sauce
1 egg
   Milk

Mix all ingredients, adding enough milk

to moisten the mixture well. Place in a well greased baking dish and bake at 350° for 15 to 20 minutes. Yield: 6 servings.

Fried Fish

2 eggs
2 tablespoons water
　Salt and pepper
3 or 4 small fish
　About ½ cup cornmeal
　Hot shortening

Beat eggs, water, and seasonings together. Dip fish first in egg mixture, then in cornmeal. Fry in hot shortening until coating is golden brown and fish is tender. Yield: 3 or 4 servings.

Planked Fish

　3 or 4 pounds fish, dressed
1½ teaspoons salt
　⅛ teaspoon pepper
　4 tablespoons butter or margarine
　Seasoned mashed potatoes
　Seasoned cooked vegetables (peas, carrots, cauliflower, tomatoes, or onions)

If hardwood plank is used, oil well and place in a cold oven and heat thoroughly as oven preheats.

Clean, wash, and dry fish. Sprinkle inside and out with salt and pepper. Brush with melted butter or margarine. Place fish on the hot, oiled plank or in ovenware or metal platter. Bake at 400° for 35 to 45 minutes or until fish flakes easily when tested with a fork. Remove from oven and quickly arrange

a border of hot mashed potatoes around fish. Place in a preheated broiler until potatoes are slightly browned, about 5 minutes. Remove and arrange two or more hot vegetables around fish. Garnish with parsley and lemon or tomato wedges. Serve immediately on the plank. Yield: 6 servings.

Pan Fried Fish

2 pounds fillets, or 6 small pan-dressed fish
1 teaspoon salt
⅛ teaspoon pepper
1 tablespoon milk or water
1 egg, slightly beaten
1 cup cornmeal
　Salad oil or melted shortening

Sprinkle both sides of fish with salt and pepper. Combine milk and beaten egg. Dip fish in this mixture, then in cornmeal. Heat ⅛-inch oil or shortening in heavy skillet or frying pan. When hot, but not smoking, fry fish at moderate heat. When brown on one side, turn carefully and brown on other side. Total cooking time will be about 10 minutes, depending on thickness of fish. Remove from pan, and drain on absorbent paper. Serve immediately. Yield: 4 to 6 servings.

Deep-Fat Fried Fish

2 pounds fillets or pan-dressed fish
  (catfish, trout, bass, etc.)
1 teaspoon salt
⅛ teaspoon pepper
1 egg
1 tablespoon milk or water
1 cup cornmeal, breadcrumbs, or
  all-purpose flour
  Shortening for deep-fat frying

Cut fish into serving-size portions.
Sprinkle both sides with salt and pepper.
Beat egg slightly, and blend in the milk.
Dip the fish in egg and roll in cornmeal
or breadcrumbs. Use a deep kettle with
a frying basket and enough hot shortening to cover the fish, but do not have
the kettle more than half full of shortening. Heat shortening to 375°.

Place a layer of fish in the frying basket
and cook to an even golden brown, for
about 3 to 5 minutes. Raise basket,
remove fish, and drain on absorbent
paper. Serve immediately. Yield: 4 to 6
servings.

Smoked Fish

Remove the entrails and slit the fish
open, leaving scales on. Place fish on
screen wire, scales down, brush with
butter and oil, and allow to smoke over
a bed of hot, green oak coals. From time
to time, mop it with vegetable oil, and
before you know it, the fish is ready to
eat.

Note: For a truly different taste, make a pan of
brown gravy and add flaked, smoked fish. It is also
delicious made into patties, if there is enough left
over.

Sauce for Fish

¾ pound butter or margarine
2 small cloves of garlic, grated
10 tablespoons meat sauce
4 tablespoons vinegar
4 tablespoons freshly squeezed
  lemon juice
  Salt to taste

Brown butter lightly. Grate garlic and
add with other ingredients to butter.
Simmer for a few minutes. Yield: sauce
for 4 or 5 fish.

Wild Game

Hunting is the most ancient form of food gathering. While today's supermarket has replaced field as the source of staple meat, wild game is a delicious change of pace.

Assuming a successful hunt, the head of the kitchen must take over, all too often unnecessarily frightened of what may be an unfamiliar meat. Keeping in mind the fact that most wild game is prepared like comparable domestic meats and poultry, there are really only a few basics to remember.

Because game is lean it may be somewhat less tender, though no less flavorful, than domestic breeds. For this reason, larding or marinating is often advisable. Young, tender game is best cooked by dry heat and older and less tender cuts by moist heat.

Unless braising or stewing, it is best to cook game without the addition of water. Parboiling is not recommended unless specifically called for in the recipe.

There is a wider taste range in wild game, and proper cooking will bring out varied flavors and aromas. For those who object to a "wild taste," which is usually the result of improper handling or cooking rather than any fault with the meat, removal of areas where fat is concentrated in older animals is usually sufficient.

As in cooking domestic cuts, the degree of doneness in game is largely a matter of personal choice. Venison is often preferred cooked rare to medium rare, while duck, according to an old test, is cooked until "the blood will follow the knife."

Accompaniments to game should be simple. The wise choice still seems to be those vegetables that were available to our ancestors who depended on wild game for all their meat.

Dove Pie

6 doves
4 cups water
1 onion, chopped
1 small bunch parsley, chopped
3 whole cloves
2 tablespoons all-purpose flour
2 tablespoons butter or margarine
 Salt and pepper
 Pastry for double crust pie

Place doves in a saucepan; cover with water; add onion, parsley, and cloves. Cook until tender. Remove doves. Skim liquid and thicken it with a paste made of flour and butter or margarine. Season to taste with salt and pepper. Line a baking dish with pastry and place birds in dish. Cover with gravy. Top with pastry. Bake at 350° for 1 hour. Yield: 4 to 6 servings.

Dove Hash à la Reith

4 cups diced, cooked breasts of doves
1 (10½-ounce) can chicken consomme
6 tablespoons butter, divided
2½ tablespoons all-purpose flour
⅔ cup cream
⅔ cup breadcrumbs
⅔ cup chopped green pepper
⅔ cup chopped onion
2 tablespoons chopped parsley
½ teaspoon ground sage
½ teaspoon salt
 Freshly ground black pepper to taste
2 ounces sherry wine

Cook whole doves in chicken consomme until tender. Remove breasts and dice meat. Measure 4 cups and set aside. Blend 3 tablespoons butter with flour and cream. Sauté breadcrumbs, green

pepper, onion, parsley, and sage in remaining 3 tablespoons butter. Mix the sautéed ingredients, flour mixture, and dove meat. Place in skillet. Add salt, pepper, and sherry, and let cook gently for 25 or 30 minutes. Before serving, put into a casserole dish and cook for a few minutes under the broiler. To keep right consistency while sautéing, add pot liquor left from cooking whole doves. Yield: 4 to 6 servings.

Braised Doves

6 doves
¼ cup all-purpose flour
1 teaspoon salt
⅛ teaspoon pepper
 Shortening

Roll doves in a dry mixture of flour, salt, and pepper. Brown birds in a skillet with a small amount of shortening added. Remove most of the drippings, add a small amount of water, and simmer birds over low heat for 1 hour. Yield: 2 to 4 servings.

Roast Doves

14 to 16 doves
 Salt and pepper to taste
 All-purpose flour
½ cup salad oil
½ cup chopped green onions
1½ cups water
1 cup sherry
¼ cup chopped parsley

Dredge doves in seasoned flour. Brown in oil in heavy roaster in a 400° oven. Add chopped onions and water. Cover. Reduce heat to 350°; cook until tender.

Add sherry and baste often during cooking. Add chopped parsley to gravy before serving. Yield: 6 to 8 servings.

Doves Brazos Valley

- 6 doves
- 1½ sticks melted butter
- 1 tablespoon Worcestershire sauce
- 1 teaspoon garlic salt
- ⅓ cup cooking sherry
- 1 cup chopped mushrooms
- ½ teaspoon ground nutmeg
- Salt and pepper to taste
- ⅓ cup all-purpose flour
- Toast

Brown doves on all sides in melted butter in a large skillet. After doves become brown, add remaining ingredients, except flour, to drippings to make sauce. Cover skillet. Allow to simmer for about 20 minutes. Remove the doves from skillet; add flour to the sauce to make a roux. Place doves on toast and top with sauce. Yield: 3 servings.

Oyster-Stuffed Dove Pie

- 16 doves
- 2 cups chopped celery
- 1 cup chopped onions
- 3 slices bacon, chopped
- Salt and pepper to taste
- 4 cups water
- 4 dozen oysters
- 4 tablespoons all-purpose flour
- ¼ cup water
- Pastry for double crust pie

Have doves picked and drawn; do not split open. Wash doves in cold water and dry. Keep in refrigerator for several days. When ready to cook, place doves in heavy pot and add celery, onions, bacon, salt and pepper; cover with water 3 inches above birds. Let come to a boil; reduce heat; stir; cover with heavy top and let simmer for about 30 minutes or until doves are tender. Remove from heat. Dip out each bird onto a flat pan, let cool enough to handle.

Drain oysters, and stuff as many as possible into each dove.

Mix flour with ¼ cup water to make paste; then add enough liquid from pot to blend well. Add this to the pot in which doves were cooked; place on low heat and stir constantly until thickened to about the consistency of cream. Add the remaining oysters and remove from heat.

Line bottom and sides of a casserole with flaky pastry and bake at 350° for about 10 minutes to set pastry. Remove from oven and let cool. Put in layer of doves; then a layer of liquid with oysters. Repeat until casserole is within ½-inch of top. Cover with pastry. Prick top of pastry and bake at 350° until pastry is golden brown. Serve hot. Yield: 8 servings.

Barbecued Duck

1 cup salad oil
½ cup vinegar
¼ cup soy sauce
6 cloves garlic, crushed
1 sprig rosemary
1 tablespoon celery seed
　Salt and pepper to taste
4 wild ducks

Combine first seven ingredients to make sauce, and simmer for about 10 minutes. Cut ducks into halves and barbecue, turning several times and basting generously with sauce until tender. Yield: 8 to 10 servings.

Braised Duck and Citrus Sauce

1 wild duck
2 tablespoons shortening
1 teaspoon salt
⅛ teaspoon pepper
½ cup hot water
1 teaspoon meat concentrate
1 teaspoon brown sugar
　Juice ½ lemon
　Juice ½ orange
¼ cup thin strips lemon peel
¼ cup thin strips orange peel
2 teaspoons raspberry jelly
2 tablespoons grape juice (optional)
2 oranges

Heat pressure cooker, add shortening. Rub duck (cut into serving-size pieces) with salt and pepper, and brown on all sides. Remove duck and prick skin in several places. Place duck on rack in cooker. Add meat concentrate dissolved in hot water. Place cover on cooker. Allow steam to flow from vent pipe to release all air from cooker. Place

indicator weight on vent pipe and cook at 10 pounds pressure or "cook" position for 15 to 20 minutes.

Cool cooker. Remove duck and keep warm. Remove excess fat from liquid in cooker. Mix sugar and duck stock in shallow pan, add lemon and orange juice, orange and lemon peel, raspberry jelly. Cook for a few minutes .

Lay pieces of duck on heatproof platter, skin-side up. Arrange sections of orange on duck. Pour the sauce over all, and run platter under hot broiler until piping hot. Yield: 4 to 5 servings.

Wild Duck

Soak cleaned birds in cold water overnight with ½ teaspoon soda to each quart water. Rinse and wipe dry, inside and out.

Place ducks breast-side down on rack in shallow baking pan. Season with salt, fresh pepper, and a small amount of curry powder. Place strips of thinly sliced bacon over breasts; roast, uncovered, at 325° for 2 hours, or until tender and crispy brown. Garnish with fresh applesauce in orange cups.

Wild Duck on Brown Rice

Dress wild ducks; cook in a pressure saucepan for 20 minutes. Split ducks down back. Fill the inside with quartered apples (or apple peelings or onions, which can be discarded later). Place ducks, back-side down, on cooked Brown Rice. Roast uncovered at 500° for 15 minutes. Then reduce the heat to 350° and cook 1 hour per pound.

Brown Rice

    1 cup brown rice
2½ cups boiling water
    3 bouillon cubes
½ teaspoon salt

Cook rice in boiling water to which bouillon cubes and salt have been added. Cook until rice is tender. If rice is too dry, add boiling water, or another bouillon cube dissolved in boiling water. Yield: Rice for 4 servings.

Wild Duck with Wild Rice

    2 wild ducks
    1 teaspoon salt
    2 cups chopped celery
    1 cup chopped onions
    2 cloves garlic, chopped
    1 cup catsup or chili sauce
    1 teaspoon salt
¼ teaspoon black pepper
    2 tablespoons vinegar
    1 tablespoon sugar
    1 teaspoon Worcestershire sauce
    2 cups water
       Hot cooked wild rice

Place cleaned ducks in cold water with 1 teaspoon salt and bring to a boil. Simmer for about 1 hour.

Place remaining ingredients in another pan and bring to a boil. Remove ducks from water, place them breast-side down in a roasting pan. Pour hot mixture over ducks. Place cover on pan and bake in 300° oven for about 2 hours. Uncover and turn ducks breast-side up to brown during the last 30 minutes of cooking. Skin may be peeled off and ducks sliced. Serve with brown or wild rice using the mixture the ducks were cooked in for sauce. Yield: 4 to 6 servings.

Roast Wild Duck No. 1

    2 wild ducks
    1 onion, quartered
    1 apple, quartered
    3 stalks celery, cut into long strips
    1 cup finely chopped celery
    1 cup finely chopped onion
    1 cup seeded raisins
    1 cup coarsely chopped pecans
    4 cups soft breadcrumbs
½ teaspoon salt
    2 eggs, beaten
½ cup scalded milk
    6 slices bacon

The day before ducks are to be roasted, stuff cavity with quartered onion and apple and celery stalks, cut into large pieces. Let stand in refrigerator overnight. Next morning combine chopped celery, onion, raisins, and pecans with breadcrumbs and salt. Add eggs and mix well. Add scalded milk and blend.

Remove stuffing and weigh ducks. Stuff with breadcrumb dressing. Sew up all openings. Place 3 strips of bacon across breast of each duck in an uncovered roasting pan. Roast at 500° for 15 minutes, then reduce heat to 300° and roast, allowing 30 minutes per pound. Yield: 4 to 6 servings.

Roast Wild Duck No. 2

2 wild ducks
  Salt and pepper to taste
1 onion, chopped
1 apple, chopped
1 stalk celery, chopped
1 clove garlic, chopped
1 (10½-ounce) can consomme
1 cup red wine
2 tablespoons Worcestershire sauce

Rub ducks with salt and pepper inside and out. Stuff cavities with onion, apple, celery, and garlic. Place breast-side down in roasting pan. Pour consomme and red wine over ducks. Sprinkle Worcestershire sauce over ducks. Roast for 3 to 4 hours at 325°, basting often. Turn breast-side up and continue roasting for 30 minutes or until brown, basting often. Add water to maintain level of sauce, if needed. Yield: 4 to 6 servings.

Duck Gumbo

2 or 3 ducks
  Salt and pepper
¼ cup all-purpose flour
¼ cup bacon drippings or cooking oil
1 large onion, chopped fine
1 large green pepper, chopped fine
4 tablespoons all-purpose flour
2 to 3 cups water
  (from cooking giblets)
  Hot cooked rice or potatoes

Cut up ducks for frying. Boil giblets in a large amount of water and set aside. Season ducks with salt and pepper and roll each piece in flour; brown in hot bacon drippings or cooking oil. Remove from oil. Add chopped onion and green pepper and cook until soft; remove from oil. Make a roux by adding 4 tablespoons flour to the oil and cooking until very dark brown. Add water from giblets. Return onion, pepper, and duck to this and cook at very low temperature for about 2 hours. Serve hot over rice or potatoes. Yield: 4 to 6 servings.

Wild Duck with Prunes

2 wild ducks
1 (1-pound) package dried prunes
  Salt and pepper to taste
  Water

Stuff ducks with uncooked prunes. Salt and pepper to taste. Place ducks in a roasting pan breast-side up. Fill pan with water to a depth of 1 inch. Place aluminum foil over ducks to cover and place lid on pan. Bake at 325° for 3½ to 4 hours. Add water as needed during cooking. After cooking, cool and carve ducks. Season broth and return ducks to liquid. Let stand overnight. Serve ducks with gravy made from broth. Yield: 4 to 6 servings.

Roast Duck

2 ducks, cut in half
  Garlic
  Salt and pepper
1 cup chopped celery
1 large onion, chopped
1 or 2 cloves garlic, chopped
1 cup chili sauce
1 tablespoon Worcestershire sauce
1 tablespoon dry mustard
½ tablespoon ground nutmeg
  Juice of 1 small lemon
2 cups water
  Paprika

Rub ducks with garlic, salt, and pepper. Place breast-side down in roaster. Combine other ingredients except paprika; pour over ducks. Bake at 325° for 3 hours. When ducks are tender, turn breast-side up and sprinkle with paprika. Bake until golden brown. Serve gravy with ducks. If a thickened gravy is desired, add a small amount of flour to drippings and cook until thickened. Yield: 4 servings.

Creole Game Stew

3 ducks (teal, butterball, or mallards are best)
4 tablespoons all-purpose flour
  Salt and pepper to taste
4 tablespoons peanut oil
½ cup chopped onion
¾ cup chopped green pepper
¼ cup all-purpose flour
3 chicken bouillon cubes
3 cups hot water

Cut ducks into serving-size pieces. Dredge with 4 tablespoons flour, salt, and pepper. Brown in peanut oil in a heavy skillet. Remove ducks. Add onion and green pepper and cook until flour is browned. Add bouillon cubes to hot water and stir until dissolved. Add to browned flour mixture in skillet, along with ducks and vegetables. Cook over low heat for 1½ to 2 hours.

Serve with hot fluffy rice tossed with chopped parsley or chopped green pepper. Yield: 3 to 6 servings.

Roast Pheasant

1 (2- to 3-pound) young pheasant
  Salt and pepper
1 bay leaf
1 clove garlic, crushed
  Few celery leaves
1 slice lemon
4 slices bacon
  Melted butter or margarine
1 large onion, sliced
2 (4-ounce) cans mushrooms
1 cup chicken broth or 1 bouillon cube and water

Sprinkle pheasant inside and out with salt and pepper. Place bay leaf, garlic, celery leaves and lemon in cavity. Tie legs together with string. Turn wings under. Cover breast with bacon slices and cheesecloth soaked in melted butter or margarine. Place pheasant breast-side up in baking pan. Arrange the onion slices and mushrooms with liquid around pheasant. Pour chicken broth over pheasant. Roast at 350° for about 30 minutes per pound, or until tender, basting frequently with liquid in pan. Remove cheesecloth and string. Yield: 3 to 4 servings.

Roast Stuffed Opossum

- 1 opossum
  Salt and pepper
- 1 chopped onion
- 1 tablespoon shortening
- 1 cup breadcrumbs
- ¼ teaspoon Worcestershire sauce
- 1 hard-cooked egg
- 1 teaspoon salt
- 1 quart water

Skin the opossum (or scald and scrape). Clean and dress; then wash it in soda water. Rub with salt and pepper. Brown onion in shortening. Add opossum liver, and cook until tender. Make stuffing by mixing breadcrumbs, Worcestershire sauce, eggs, salt, and enough water to moisten breadcrumbs. Mix thoroughly, and stuff opossum. Truss as you would a fowl. Place in roasting pan and pour 1 quart water into the pan. Roast uncovered at 350° until tender (about 2½ hours). Baste every 15 minutes. Serve with sweet potatoes. Yield: 4 to 6 servings.

Braised Quail with Bacon

- 6 quail
- 18 strips bacon
- 2 tablespoons butter or margarine
- ½ cup hot water
- 4 tablespoons all-purpose flour
- 6 slices toast

Prepare quail for cooking, cover, and let stand overnight in refrigerator. The next day, cover quail with salted water, using 1 tablespoon salt for each quart water. Let stand for 15 minutes; drain and dry inside and out with a cloth.

Place 1 strip bacon in cavity of each bird and place in shallow roasting pan. Place a strip of bacon over breast of each and a strip over the legs. Bake at 450° for 5 minutes; reduce heat to 350° and continue cooking for 40 minutes, basting frequently with a mixture of the butter and hot water. At the end of the baking time, sprinkle with flour, increase heat to 450°, and brown for about 10 minutes. Serve on toast. Yield: 6 servings.

Fried Quail

Dress and chill quail. Soak in light cream for 2 hours. Then dredge birds with flour and seasonings. Fry in ¼ inch shortening in skillet until brown, then lower heat to simmer and cook 40 to 45 minutes longer, turning occasionally. Remove birds and make cream gravy from the drippings.

Baked Quail

- 6 quail
  Water
- 4 tablespoons Worcestershire sauce
- 1 teaspoon Tabasco sauce
- 3 tablespoons olive oil
  Juice of 3 lemons
- ½ stick butter
- 2 tablespoons molasses
  Salt and pepper to taste
- 1 teaspoon prepared mustard

Place quail in roasting pan with enough water to cover bottom of the pan. Cover and place in 300° oven. Combine other ingredients and blend together over low heat. When quail have cooked for 30 minutes, remove from oven and pour sauce over birds. Return to oven, cover, and continue cooking 30 to 40 minutes longer, basting frequently. During the last 10 minutes of cooking time, remove cover to brown birds and thicken the sauce. Yield: 6 servings.

Smothered Quail

6 quail
6 tablespoons butter or margarine
3 tablespoons all-purpose flour
2 cups chicken broth
½ cup sherry wine
   Salt and pepper to taste
   Cooked rice

Prepare quail; brown in heavy skillet or Dutch oven in 6 tablespoons butter or margarine. Remove quail to baking dish. Add flour to butter in skillet and stir well. Slowly add chicken broth, sherry, and salt and pepper to taste; blend well and pour over quail. Cover baking dish and bake at 350° for about 1 hour. Serve with cooked rice. Yield: 6 servings.

Quail with Wild Rice

10 quail
 1 stick butter or margarine
1½ cups port wine
1½ pounds chicken livers
 2 large onions, chopped
 1 green pepper, chopped
 2 cloves garlic, minced
1½ sticks butter or margarine
2½ cups cooked wild rice
 2 cups chicken broth

Sew together body cavity of quail. Sauté in 1 stick butter or margarine until quail are browned. Place in baking dish. Cover dish and bake at 325° for about 30 minutes.

Sauté livers, onions, pepper, and garlic in 1½ sticks butter or margarine. Do not let vegetables brown, but cook to a clear color. Add cooked rice, chicken broth, and wine. Place mixture in 3-quart baking dish; cover and bake at 325° for about 20 minutes or until liquid is absorbed. Serve quail over rice. Yield: 8 to 10 servings.

Variations

Body cavity of quail may be sewed up and the quail lightly browned in butter and placed on top of the stuffing in baking pan. Mix chicken broth and wine and pour over quail and stuffing. Cover pan and bake at 375° for about 30 minutes.

Ranch-Style Creamed Quail

12 quail
   Salt and pepper
 1 pound butter or margarine
 4 cups sweet cream
 1 to 1½ cups toasted breadcrumbs

Salt and pepper cleaned, dressed quail; simmer slowly in butter in cooker until tender. Add cream and continue simmering until done. Remove quail to hot platter. Sift toasted breadcrumbs over quail. Pour cream gravy from cooker over quail. Yield: 12 servings.

Hunters' Sautéed Quail

6 club rolls
¾ cup butter, divided
6 quail, split
1 teaspoon salt
   Freshly ground black pepper
   Fruit Sauce

Split rolls in half and hollow out centers. Toast in a 325° oven until brown. Melt ¼ cup butter and brush the rolls with the butter. Sauté the quail over high heat in the remaining ½ cup of butter for 10 minutes or until golden brown. Sprinkle with salt and pepper. Arrange quail on rolls and serve with Fruit Sauce. Yield: 6 servings.

Fruit Sauce

1 cup seedless white grapes
1 cup water
4 tablespoons butter or margarine
½ cup port wine
⅛ teaspoon ground cloves
½ teaspoon ground ginger
2 tablespoons finely chopped mushrooms
½ cup finely chopped filberts

Put grapes into 1 cup water and bring to a boil. Cover, reduce heat, and simmer for 5 minutes. Drain off water. Add butter, wine, cloves, and ginger to grapes. Cover and simmer for 5 minutes. Stir in mushrooms and simmer for 5 minutes. Add filberts (hazelnuts), and serve immediately. Yield: 6 servings.

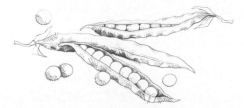

Roast Quail

4 quail
4 slices bacon
1 tablespoon butter or margarine
½ cup hot water
   Juice of half lemon
1 (3-ounce) can broiled
   mushrooms, drained

Wipe excess moisture off the quail, inside and out. Bind each bird with a slice of bacon. Place birds in a buttered pan and roast at 350° for about 30 minutes, or until tender. Baste occasionally. Remove birds; add butter or margarine, water, and lemon juice to drippings, stirring to make a gravy. Add mushrooms. Serve birds on toast with gravy poured over them. Yield: 2 to 4 servings.

Br'er Batter Rabbit

1 rabbit
½ cup vinegar
1 onion, sliced
1 clove garlic
1 small bay leaf
1 sprig parsley
   Salt and pepper
2 eggs
1 cup crushed crackers
¼ teaspoon salt
⅛ teaspoon ground nutmeg
1 tablespoon all-purpose flour
   Milk
   Hot shortening

Skin rabbit, cut into serving-size pieces and soak overnight in cold water to which ½ cup vinegar has been added. When ready to cook, rinse pieces and put into large kettle. Add just enough water to cover; add onion, garlic, bay leaf, parsley, and salt and pepper. Cover, and simmer slowly until tender. Do not boil. Remove rabbit onto paper towel to drain.

Beat eggs slightly. Add crushed crackers, salt, and nutmeg. Stir in flour and thin with milk, if necessary, to right dipping consistency. Dip pieces of rabbit into this batter and fry in hot shortening slowly on both sides until crisp and golden brown. Yield: 4 servings.

Southern Squirrel Pie

6 *squirrels*
2 *cups chopped onions*
2 *cups chopped celery*
1 *cup coarsely chopped salt pork*
4 *cups water*
  Red and black pepper to taste
  Salt to taste
2 *hard-cooked eggs*
2 *tablespoons shortening*
2 *tablespoons all-purpose flour*
1 *cup hot water*
1 *cup liquid from squirrel pot*
2 *tablespoons all-purpose flour*
½ *cup liquid from squirrel pot*
¼ *cup water*
  Pastry for double crust pie

Cut squirrels into pieces; put into heavy pot and add onions, celery, salt pork, peppers, and salt. Cover with water 3 inches above squirrels and bring to a boil; turn to low heat and simmer for about 1 hour or until squirrels are tender.

Brown 2 tablespoons flour in 2 tablespoons shortening in a skillet. Add 1 cup hot water and 1 cup liquid from squirrel pot. Stir well and remove from heat.

Remove squirrels from pot, add the flour mixture and the browned flour mixture to liquid in the pot; mix well and cook for about 2 minutes until it has started to slightly thicken. Line a casserole with pastry. Bake at 350° for 10 minutes to set pastry. Remove pastry from oven and let cool slightly; then put in layer of squirrel, layer of 4 to 6 slices of hard-cooked egg and 1 cup of liquid. Repeat layers until casserole is within ½ inch of the top. Use as much as possible of all liquid to avoid a dry pie. Cover with pastry top. Slit top of pastry and bake at 350° until crusts are brown. Yield: 6 servings.

Squirrel Stew

3 *squirrels*
2 *onions, chopped*
1 *green pepper, chopped*
2 *medium potatoes, diced*
¼ *cup diced celery*
4 *tablespoons chili powder*
  Salt and pepper to taste
  Dash Louisiana hot sauce
1 *cup cooked rice*

Cover squirrels with water and cook until tender. Remove from water and cool; reserve broth. Remove meat from bones and put back into broth. Bring to a boil and add all other ingredients except rice. Cook for about 45 minutes or until vegetables are tender. Add cooked rice. Serve hot. Yield: 6 servings.

Rabbit in Barbecue Sauce

1 rabbit (about 3 pounds ready-to-cook)
   cut into serving pieces
   Flour, salt, and pepper
3 tablespoons cooking oil
   Barbecue Sauce

Roll rabbit in mixture of flour, salt, and pepper. Heat the oil and brown rabbit on all sides over moderate heat (about 20 minutes). Pour Barbecue Sauce over rabbit; cover pan.

Bake at 325° for about 45 minutes, or until meat is tender. Uncover the pan and place under broiler. Broil for 15 minutes, or until meat is brown. Yield: 6 servings.

Barbecue Sauce

2 tablespoons brown sugar
1 tablespoon paprika
1 teaspoon salt
1 teaspoon dry mustard
¼ teaspoon chili powder
   Few grains cayenne pepper
2 tablespoons Worcestershire sauce
1 cup tomato juice
¼ cup chili sauce or catsup
¼ cup vinegar
½ cup chopped onion

Combine ingredients and cook over low heat for 15 minutes. Yield: 2½ cups.

Country-Style Squirrel

2 squirrels
   Salt and pepper to taste
   All-purpose flour
3 tablespoons shortening
2 cups water

Cut squirrels into serving-size pieces and shake in a paper bag containing salt, pepper, and flour to dredge well. Fry in skillet until golden brown. Remove squirrel from skillet and pour off all drippings except 2 teaspoonfuls. Add water and bring to a boil. Return squirrel to skillet; cover, and cook over low heat for about 1 hour, until meat almost leaves bone. Turn squirrel occasionally and baste often. Yield: 3 to 4 servings.

Coon and Sweet Potatoes

1 coon
   Vinegar
   Salt and black pepper to taste
   Water to cover
   Cayenne pepper to taste
3 cloves garlic, chopped
1 cup chopped celery
1 large onion, chopped
1 medium green pepper, chopped
   Shortening
   All-purpose flour
6 medium sweet potatoes

Dress coon and soak for 1 hour in a mild vinegar solution. Drain. Cut coon into serving-size pieces. Salt and pepper coon and cover with water. Add cayenne pepper, chopped garlic, celery, onion, and green pepper, and boil until partially tender. Remove from heat and drain. Brown coon in a small amount of shortening, then place in roasting pan. Make a thin brown gravy with the flour and drippings; pour over coon in roasting pan. Place peeled sweet potatoes around coon and bake at 350° until potatoes are done. Yield: 3 to 4 servings.

Venison Meatballs

- 1 *pound ground venison*
- ½ *pound ground pork*
- ½ *cup fine, dry breadcrumbs*
- 1 *egg, beaten*
- ½ *cup cooked mashed potatoes*
- 1 *teaspoon seasoned salt*
- ½ *teaspoon brown sugar*
- ¼ *teaspoon pepper*
- ¼ *teaspoon ground allspice*
- ¼ *teaspoon ground nutmeg*
- ⅛ *teaspoon ground cloves*
- ⅛ *teaspoon ground ginger*
- 3 *tablespoons butter or margarine*

Combine all ingredients except butter. Mix well and shape into balls about 1 inch in diameter. Melt butter in skillet over low heat. Add meatballs and brown on all sides, shaking pan now and then. Cover with tightly fitting lid and cook over low heat for 15 minutes. Yield: 6 to 8 servings.

Venison, Hunter's Style

- 3 *pounds venison*
  Salt and pepper
- 2 *tablespoons butter or margarine*
- 1 *onion, chopped*
- 1 *(1-inch) cube ham, minced*
- 1 *clove garlic, minced*
- 2 *bay leaves*
- 2 *sprigs thyme, crushed*
- 1 *tablespoon all-purpose flour*
- 2 *cups warm water*
- 4 *cups consomme*
- ½ *pound fresh mushrooms, chopped*
  Grated rind of 1 lemon

Cut venison into pieces 2 inches square. Salt and pepper generously. Heat butter in skillet and brown vension slowly.

When almost brown, add onion; brown slightly. Then add ham, garlic, bay leaves, and thyme. Stir and simmer for 2 minutes. Add the flour and cook a few minutes longer.

Add warm water and let cool to a good simmer. Add consomme and cook slowly for 1 hour. Season again according to taste; then add mushrooms and grated lemon rind. Let cook for 30 minutes longer. Serve on a very hot plate. Yield: 8 servings.

Venison, Greer Style

Slice venison steaks and fry until about half-done; then pour off drippings, leaving just enough to make gravy. Add potatoes, onions, and water. Cook slowly until meat is tender. Season with salt and pepper. Thicken gravy with flour.

Venison Burgers

- 2½ *pounds ground venison*
- ½ *cup minced onion*
- 1 *clove garlic, minced*
- 4 *tablespoons chopped parsley*
- ⅔ *cup dry red wine*
- 2 *tablespoons soy sauce*
  Salt and pepper to taste
  Hamburger buns

Mix all ingredients; form into thick patties. Cook on barbecue grill, 4 inches from coals, or broil in oven, 10 minutes on each side (less for rare burgers). Serve immediately in hot hamburger buns. Yield: 8 to 10 servings.

Venison Chili

½ pound suet
2 large onions, chopped
1 large garlic clove, minced
5 tablespoons all-purpose flour
¼ cup chili powder
1 teaspoon cumin
  Cubes of venison for 8 to 10 servings
½ teaspoon oregano
1 bay leaf
3 (8-ounce) cans tomato paste
2 cups canned tomatoes
1 tablespoon salt
1 teaspoon pepper
6 chili peppers, chopped

Cook suet in skillet, then remove cracklings. Add onions and garlic and cook until soft, but not brown.

Mix flour, chili powder, and cumin in a paper bag. Add cubes of venison and shake until each piece is coated. Add to onion and cook until brown. Add other ingredients and simmer for 4 to 5 hours, stirring occasionally and adding hot water as needed. Yield: 8 to 10 servings.

Venison Rump Roast

Tuck halves of one garlic clove into two slits in meat. Season generously with salt, freshly ground pepper, onion salt, and celery salt. Rub with flour. Cover roast with thick slices of fresh side pork, skewering them in place so they will remain on top of meat during entire cooking period. Fat from the pork helps prevent meat from drying out during long, slow roasting time. Roast uncovered at 300° until tender and no red juices run. Allow about 25 minutes per pound. Garnish with broiled, jellied peaches; fill centers of canned peach halves with currant jelly. Place under broiler until jelly bubbles and edges of peaches are slightly brown.

Rehrbraten

4 to 5 (½- to 1-inch) venison steaks
1 (1½-ounce) box pickling spices
1 (8-ounce) bottle Italian dressing
1 to 2 cups tart red wine
  Meat tenderizer
  All-purpose flour
  Margarine

Trim all cartilage from steaks (shoulder, round, or rump roasts may be used); cut steaks into "teriyaki" strips.

Make a marinade of the pickling spices, Italian dressing, and red wine. Lay venison strips in a flat shallow dish with enough marinade to cover the meat. Cover the dish with plastic wrap or aluminum foil and place in the refrigerator. The marinating process must be at cold temperature and the meat must be completely covered with the marinade at all times.

After 3 or 4 days, take the meat out of the marinade, drain well, and wipe with a paper towel. Sprinkle both sides with a meat tenderizer. Flour the meat on both sides and brown in margarine in an iron skillet or Dutch oven.

Strain the marinade into a shallow baking dish. Add to meat and when it is simmering briskly, cover and continue cooking until meat is tender, about 3 hours. Peek at it occasionally and, if the gravy cooks down, add more wine so that the meat is completely covered at all times. Yield: 6 to 8 servings.

Note: Onions, small potatoes, scallions, carrots, and celery sticks may be added if desired. These vegetables add a special zest to the other vegetable you will have with the meal. With this dish serve a steamed green vegetable such as broccoli, asparagus, or brussels sprouts served with hollandaise sauce or hot slaw dressing.

Venison Pot Roast

3 to 4 pounds venison (shoulder, rump, round)
  All-purpose flour
  Salt and pepper
  Shortening
5 whole carrots
5 whole potatoes
5 whole onions
  Turnips or celery, if desired

Dredge meat with flour, add salt and pepper, and brown in hot shortening. Braise the meat for 2 to 3 hours over low heat (small amount of water in covered skillet). When meat is tender, add the vegetables, and more hot water if necessary, and cook until vegetables are done. Make a gravy of the liquid in the pan and pour over the meat and vegetables. Yield: 6 to 8 servings.

Broiled Venison

Have steaks cut ¾ inch thick. Brush with salad oil, and place under hot broiler about 2 to 3 inches below heat. Sear on both sides. Lower rack and continuing broiling until done, turning occasionally. Allow at least 15 minutes for broiling. Add salt and pepper to taste just before serving. If preferred, marinate steaks in French dressing for 1 hour and pan broil.

Note: If preferred, marinate steaks in French dressing for 1 hour and pan broil.

Braised Venison

Dredge well with flour and sear on all sides in shortening. Add enough water to cover the bottom of pan; add 1 tablespoon vinegar. Cover tightly and cook very slowly for about 2 hours, adding a little more liquid as necessary. About 30 minutes before meat is tender, add ½ cup each of chopped celery, apple, carrot, and onion. This mixture will flavor the gravy and add flavor to meat, absorbing some of the gamy flavor. It may be strained from the gravy before serving, if desired.

Smoked Wild Turkey

Rub 10- to 15-pound wild turkey with curing salt. Refrigerate for 5 days in a plastic bag. Then wash turkey thoroughly inside and out being careful to remove all the salt. The turkey must be smoked in a covered barbecue pit using dampened hickory sawdust. Add sawdust to the fire from time to time to keep the smoke going. Smoke for 36 hours, turning every now and then. Baste every hour during the daytime with a mixture containing equal parts of cola beverage, vinegar, and white wine.

Barbecued Wild Turkey

1 (8- to 10-pound) wild turkey
Salt and pepper
Celery leaves from 1 bunch celery
2 onions, coarsely chopped
½ to ¾ cup salad oil
Barbecue Sauce

Remove turkey neck if still attached, but leave skin. Rub cavity of bird with salt. Stuff with celery leaves and onion. Truss by folding over neck skin and skewering it to the back, sewing shut body cavity, and tying drumsticks to tail. Brush salad oil on bird. Sprinkle liberally with salt and pepper. Put on outdoor barbecue grill and cook slowly for about 4 hours, or until tender and done. Brush bird with salad oil several times during cooking. Thirty minutes before cooking is completed, add remaining salad oil to hot Barbecue Sauce and brush bird with this mixture about every 10 minutes. Yield: 12 to 14 servings.

Barbecue Sauce

3 sticks margarine
½ teaspoon Worcestershire sauce
½ teaspoon rosemary
½ cup finely chopped onion
1 (8-ounce) can tomato sauce or 1 cup catsup
1 teaspoon black pepper
1 teaspoon salt
½ cup freshly squeezed lemon juice
½ teaspoon oregano
½ teaspoon garlic salt
½ teaspoon thyme

Melt margarine in a saucepan; add remaining ingredients and bring to full boil. Simmer for 30 minutes. Yield: sauce for 8- to 10-pound turkey.

Wild Turkey

Dry pick and singe wild turkey. Wash with warm water (4 teaspoons soda to the gallon). Remove tendons. Soak the fowl in salt water (4 tablespoons salt to the gallon of water) for 3 to 3½ hours. Pour off salt water, wash turkey, and rub well with lemon juice. Make a paste of butter and flour — 8 to 10 tablespoons butter to 1 cup flour. Spread paste over the turkey. Place bird in 475° to 500° oven and brown quickly to set the paste. Stuff bird with dressing.

Dressing for Wild Turkey

4 cups breadcrumbs (half cornbread and half biscuit and light bread)
2 cups diced celery
1 cup chopped onion
2 tablespoons freshly squeezed lemon juice
1 teaspoon salt
¼ teaspoon red pepper
½ teaspoon Worcestershire sauce
½ teaspoon steak sauce
1 to 1½ cups butter
1 cup hot water

Combine breadcrumbs, celery, onion, lemon juice, salt and pepper. Blend Worcestershire sauce and steak sauce with butter and add to mixture. Stuff turkey and place in roaster with 1 cup hot water. Cover and bake at 325° for 30 minutes to the pound. When turkey is almost tender, remove cover and brown. Make gravy from drippings when bird is done. Yield: 6 to 8 servings.

Meats

Southern homemakers would consider the calendar year incomplete if it included many days without at least one lingering, plate-filling, eye-appealing hot meal.

Meat, of course, is the mainstay and basis for any such meal, and luckily in the South we have a wide variety from which to choose. Not only does the choice of local meat range from chicken to turkey to pork to beef to lamb, but woman's (and man's) ingenuity has devised so many ways of preparing each of these that it would be fairly easy to serve a different meat dish every night for years without exact duplication.

Barbecuing is a favorite Southern method of preparation, and many cooks feel that any meat not worth barbecuing is hardly worth eating. From deep pits in the rich Texas soil, to small grills on apartment patios in the cities of the South, we all love that distinctive spicy taste, and rare is the cook of any standing who doesn't claim at least one personal favorite barbecue sauce.

Of course, Texans rave about their beef, and Virginians their ham, but undoubtedly the common denominator of Southern meat cookery is chicken. From the traditional fried, to smothered, to broiled, chicken belongs to the South.

Many meat dishes are old family favorites, and it's not unusual for a roast to conjure up memories of Grandmother's table on Sunday; fried chicken, those picnics by the river; or fried ham, the breakfasts that got you off to a good start on cold winter mornings. Family reunions and holiday dinners weren't, and aren't, complete without at least three and sometimes as many as seven different meats. And who wouldn't sympathize with the young bride whose husband told her very bluntly after her first dinner that anyone who couldn't fry chicken shouldn't be allowed to marry.

We agree with him. Meat is indeed the mainstay and rightly so.

Roasting Chart For Beef
Roasting at 300° to 325°

Cut	Approximate Weight (Pounds)	Meat Thermometer Reading (Degrees)	Approximate Cooking Time* (Minutes Per Pound)
Standing Rib[1]	6 to 8	140 (rare) 160 (medium) 170 (well)	23 to 25 27 to 30 32 to 35
Standing Rib[1]	4 to 6	140 (rare) 160 (medium) 170 (well)	26 to 30 34 to 38 40 to 42
Rolled Rib	5 to 7	140 (rare) 160 (medium) 170 (well)	32 38 48
Rib Eye[2] (Delmonico)	4 to 6	140 (rare) 160 (medium) 170 (well)	18 to 20 20 to 22 22 to 24
Tenderloin, whole[3]	4 to 6	140 (rare)	45 to 60 (total)
Tenderloin, half[3]	2 to 3	140 (rare)	45 to 50 (total)
Rolled rump (high quality)	4 to 6	150 to 170	25 to 30
Sirloin tip (high quality)	3½ to 4 6 to 8	140 to 170 140 to 170	35 to 40 30 to 35
Beef loaf (9 x 5 inches)	1½ to 2½	160 to 170	1 to 1½ hrs.

*Based on meat taken directly from the refrigerator.
[1]Ribs which measure 6 to 7 inches from chine bone to tip of rib.
[2]Roast at 350° oven temperature.
[3]Roast at 425° oven temperature.

Roasting Chart For Beef
Cooking in Liquid

Cut	Approximate Weight (Pounds)	Approximate Total Cooking Time (Hours)
Fresh or corned beef	4 to 6	3½ to 4½
Cross-cut shanks	¾ to 1¼	2½ to 3
Beef for stew		2½ to 3½

Picnic Burgers

1½ pounds ground beef
¾ cup uncooked oatmeal
¼ cup chopped onion
2 teaspoons salt
⅛ teaspoon pepper
1 cup tomato juice

Combine all ingredients thoroughly. Shape into nine flat hamburgers. Pan-fry only until meat is browned. (Do not cook completely.) Chill thoroughly. Wrap each hamburger in aluminum foil. Keep in refrigerator until packing lunch. Cook these foil-wrapped hamburgers by placing them directly on the grill over fire. Cook for about 5 minutes on one side, then turn and cook on other side. Yield: 9 servings.

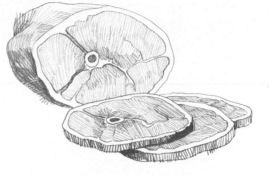

Southern Baked Hash

1 large onion, sliced thin
1 green pepper, sliced thin
2 tablespoons butter or margarine
1 pound ground beef
¼ cup regular rice, uncooked
1 cup canned tomatoes
½ teaspoon salt
½ teaspoon chili powder
¼ teaspoon pepper

Fry onion and pepper in butter or margarine until brown. Remove from skillet. Put ground meat into skillet and cook until meat is browned; add onion and pepper. Stir rice, tomatoes, salt, chili powder, and pepper into the meat. Bake uncovered in a greased 2-quart casserole at 350° for 1 hour. Yield: 3 to 4 servings.

Italian Spaghetti

1 pound ground beef
2 medium onions, chopped
½ large green pepper, chopped
1 tablespoon butter
1 (20-ounce) can tomatoes
1 (6-ounce) can tomato paste
1 (4-ounce) can mushrooms
1 clove garlic, chopped
1 tablespoon Worcestershire sauce
1 tablespoon (or more) chili powder
   Salt and pepper to taste
1 (7-ounce) package spaghetti
   Parmesan cheese

Fry ground beef, chopped onions, and pepper in butter until slightly browned. Add canned tomatoes, tomato paste, mushrooms, chopped garlic, Worcestershire sauce, chili powder, and salt and pepper to taste. Simmer over low heat for 3 to 4 hours. If desired, cook, package, and freeze.

Cook spaghetti according to directions on box. Serve by pouring meat sauce over spaghetti, then sprinkling with Parmesan cheese. Yield: 6 to 8 servings.

Braised Short Ribs of Beef

Place short ribs of beef in a roasting pan. Season with salt and pepper. Brown in a 400° oven for 20 minutes. Add ½ cup water and cover closely. Reduce temperature to 300° and cook slowly until tender, about 1½ hours.

Brisket of Beef

1 (4- to 5-pound) brisket of beef
2 medium onions, sliced
1 bay leaf
5 carrots
  Salt and pepper
  Boiling water
1 stalk celery
  Horseradish Sauce

Place meat in a heavy kettle, add seasonings and vegetables, and enough boiling water to cover. Bring to a boil, then reduce heat. Cook slowly until tender, about 3 to 4 hours. Slice meat and serve in Horseradish Sauce. Yield: 4 to 6 servings.

Horseradish Sauce

1 large onion, chopped
4 tablespoons butter or margarine
2 tablespoons all-purpose flour
2 cups soup stock
1 cup fresh horseradish
1 cup vinegar
2 cloves
2 bay leaves
1 teaspoon salt
  Pepper
½ cup sugar

Sauté onion in melted butter or margarine until brown. Add flour and soup stock gradually, then add remaining ingredients. Heat the sliced meat in the sauce.

Beef Stroganoff

2 pounds beef for stew, cut in pieces ½ inch wide
6 tablespoons all-purpose flour
1½ teaspoons salt
¼ teaspoon pepper
3 tablespoons shortening
1 cup chopped onions
1 cup tomato juice
2 cups liquid (water and liquid from mushrooms)
1 (4-ounce) can button mushrooms
3 tablespoons all-purpose flour
1 cup commercial sour cream
  Cooked noodles or rice

Dredge meat with flour seasoned with salt and pepper; brown in shortening. Add chopped onions and brown. Pour off drippings. Add tomato juice and 1½ cups liquid. Cover and cook slowly for 1½ hours. Add mushrooms. Thicken with flour added to the remaining ½ cup liquid, stirring constantly. Fold in sour cream. Serve over cooked noodles or rice. Yield: 6 to 8 servings.

Braised Stuffed Beef Heart

1 beef heart
¼ cup shortening
¼ cup chopped celery
2 tablespoons chopped onion
2 tablespoons chopped parsley
3 to 4 cups breadcrumbs
½ teaspoon salt
½ teaspoon savory
  Pepper to taste
2 cups water

Wash the heart and remove fat. Make a slit in the center of the heart and remove veins, arteries, and gristle. Set aside to prepare the stuffing. Melt shortening and add celery, onion, and parsley. Cook for a few minutes and add breadcrumbs. Add salt, savory, and pepper. Fill the heart cavity with the stuffing, and fasten together with metal skewers and string, or by sewing. Brown the heart in a small amount of shortening. Place in a Dutch oven, add water, and cover. Bake at 300° for about 4 hours. Use liquid for gravy. Yield: 8 servings.

Pot Roast with Vegetables

1 (4- to 5-pound) beef chuck roast
   Salt and pepper
   All-purpose flour
3 tablespoons shortening
¼ teaspoon thyme or marjoram
½ cup chopped onions
½ cup water
8 medium carrots
8 small onions
4 medium potatoes, quartered

Sprinkle roast with salt and pepper and dredge in flour. Melt shortening in heavy skillet, and brown roast slowly and thoroughly. Sprinkle meat with thyme and chopped onions. Add water, cover tightly, and cook slowly over low heat for 2½ hours, or until meat is almost tender. Turn meat two or three times during cooking, and add small amounts of water when necessary. Add vegetables, and sprinkle with salt and pepper. Cover, and cook until meat and vegetables are tender — about 20 minutes. To make gravy, dilute drippings with water, and thicken with a flour and water paste. Season. Yield: 6 to 8 servings.

Electric Skillet Dinner

1 (1-pound) round steak
   Bacon drippings
1 large green pepper
3 fresh tomatoes
3 medium onions
3 or 4 potatoes
1 (1-pound) can beef gravy

Cut the steak into small cubes. Sear and brown in bacon drippings. Add pepper, tomatoes, onions, and potatoes, all cut into wedges. Pour the beef gravy or stock made from bouillon cubes over steak. Cover skillet and steam at 325° for 30 to 40 minutes. Yield: 4 to 6 servings.

Swiss Steak with Vegetables

2 pounds round or chuck steak
½ cup all-purpose flour
2 teaspoons salt
⅛ teaspoon pepper
1 small onion, chopped
3 tablespoons shortening
1 cup tomatoes
1½ cups sliced carrots
1½ cups chopped celery

Cut steak at least 1½ inches thick. Mix flour, salt, and pepper, and thoroughly pound into steak. Brown meat and onion in hot shortening. Add tomatoes. Cover and bake at 350° for about 1 hour and 45 minutes. Add carrots and celery 45 minutes before removing from oven. Yield: 6 servings.

Curry of Beef

1 medium onion, chopped
1 clove garlic, chopped
¼ teaspoon mustard seed
1 small cinnamon stick
2 tablespoons shortening
1 pound top round or sirloin steak, cubed
1 tablespoon curry powder
1 teaspoon paprika
¼ teaspoon thyme
½ (6-ounce) can tomato paste
Salt to taste
Water

Sauté onion, garlic, mustard seed, and cinnamon in shortening; add beef, curry powder, paprika, and thyme. Brown for about 10 minutes, stirring occasionally. Scrape brown from pan; add tomato paste and salt. Cover with water, and simmer until meat is tender, about 20 minutes. Taste, and add more seasoning if needed. Serve hot over rice, or refrigerate for later use. Yield: 4 to 6 servings.

Stuffed Flank Steak

1 (1½- to 2-pound) flank steak
1 teaspoon salt
1 cup breadcrumbs
¼ cup chopped onion
1 teaspoon poultry seasoning
½ cup chopped celery
¼ cup shortening, melted
1 cup water

Select a flank steak weighing 1½ to 2 pounds. Sprinkle salt on steak. Make a stuffing by combining breadcrumbs, onion, poultry seasoning, celery, and melted shortening. Spread over the steak. Roll steak crosswise and fasten edges with metal skewers to hold in the stuffing. Brown the steak on all sides in a small amount of shortening, in heavy skillet. Add 1 cup water and cover skillet. Bake at 350° for 2 hours. To serve, cut across the roll in 1-inch slices. Yield: 3 servings.

Hamburger Steak

1 egg
¼ cup breadcrumbs
½ cup tomato soup or puree
1½ teaspoons salt
⅛ teaspoon pepper
2 pounds round steak, ground
2 tablespoons shortening

Beat egg, mix with crumbs, tomato soup, and seasoning. Add meat, and mix thoroughly. Form into patties, and pan broil in hot shortening until brown. Reduce heat, and cook covered for about 10 minutes longer. Yield: 8 servings.

Meat Loaf

1½ pounds ground beef
½ (10½-ounce) can condensed tomato soup
1 cup cracker crumbs
2 stalks celery, chopped
1 egg
½ cup cubed American cheese
1 large onion, chopped
½ medium green pepper, chopped
1½ teaspoons salt
¼ teaspoon pepper
American cheese slices
¼ cup water
½ (10½-ounce) can condensed tomato soup

Combine first 10 ingredients. Mix well and form into one large or two small meat loaves. Freeze if desired, and bake without thawing. Just unwrap, place in greased baking dish, and top with slices of American cheese. Combine water and tomato soup and pour over cheese slices. Bake at 350° for 45 minutes. Yield: 8 to 10 servings.

Creole Meat Loaf

1½   pounds ground beef
 ½   pound ground pork
  1   small green pepper, grated
  2   eggs, beaten
  1   small onion, grated
  1   cup milk
  1   cup toasted breadcrumbs
     Salt and pepper
  1   tablespoon Worcestershire sauce
     Creole Sauce

Mix ingredients thoroughly in the order given and shape into a loaf. Pack into a greased 9- x 5- x 4-inch loafpan; cover with Creole Sauce, and bake at 350° for 1 hour. Yield: 6 to 8 servings.

Creole Sauce

  2   tablespoons shortening
  2   tablespoons all-purpose flour
 ½   green pepper, chopped
 ½   small onion, chopped
  1   clove garlic, chopped
  1   cup milk
  2   cups canned tomatoes
     Salt and pepper
  1   tablespoon Worcestershire sauce

Melt shortening; add flour, and cook over medium heat until a rich brown, stirring constantly. Add chopped pepper, onion, and garlic. Let simmer until wilted; add milk. Add tomatoes, salt, pepper, and Worcestershire sauce. Let come to a boil and cook for 4 to 5 minutes. Yield: 2½ cups.

Pizza Meat Loaf

  1   (20-ounce) can tomatoes
 ½   teaspoon Tabasco sauce
  1   egg
1½   cups soft breadcrumbs
 ¼   cup finely chopped onion
  2   tablespoons finely chopped parsley
 ¼   teaspoon thyme
  2   teaspoons salt
1½   pounds ground beef
  8   (¾-inch) strips American cheese

Drain tomatoes; measure ¾ cup of the liquid. Reserve remaining tomatoes and liquid for your own tomato sauce recipe. Add Tabasco sauce to egg and tomato liquid in large mixing bowl; blend. Stir in breadcrumbs. Add seasonings and ground beef. Mix until blended. Form into loaf in shallow baking pan. Bake at 350° for 45 minutes, then spoon one-third of the tomato sauce over meat loaf. Place cheese strips across top. Bake 15 minutes longer. Yield: 8 servings.

Roasting Chart For Fresh Pork
Roasting at 300° to 350°

Cut	Approximate Weight (Pounds)	Meat Thermometer Reading (Degrees)	Approximate Cooking Time (Minutes Per Pound)
Loin			
Center	3 to 5	170	30 to 35
Half	5 to 7	170	35 to 40
End	3 to 4	170	40 to 45
Roll	3 to 5	170	35 to 40
Boneless Top	2 to 4	170	30 to 35
Crown	4 to 6	170	35 to 40
Picnic Shoulder			
Bone-In	5 to 8	170	30 to 35
Rolled	3 to 5	170	35 to 40
Boston Shoulder	4 to 6	170	40 to 45
Leg (fresh ham)			
Whole (bone-in)	12 to 16	170	22 to 26
Whole (boneless)	10 to 14	170	24 to 28
Half (bone-in)	5 to 8	170	35 to 40
Tenderloin	½ to 1		45 to 60
Country-style backbones		Well Done	Hours 1½ to 2½
Spareribs			1½ to 2½

Roast Suckling Pig

1 (6-pound) pig
1 tablespoon salt
16 cups dressing
1 cup water
2 tablespoons melted butter or margarine

Clean pig and scrub inside thoroughly, especially feet, ears, and mouth. Wipe with a damp cloth. Rub inside and out with salt. Fill cavity loosely with dress-ing, draw edges of opening together with skewers and lace with a strong cord. Press forefeet and hind feet forward and skewer or tie in place. Force a block of wood in the mouth to hold it open. Cover ears and tail with aluminum foil to keep from burning. Cut several small gashes through the skin along back of neck to allow excess fat to escape. Place in upright position in open roasting pan and add 1 cup water. Add melted butter or margarine. Roast at 350° for 3 to 3½ hours, basting occasionally. Yield: 16 servings.

Dixie Pork Chops

    8 pork chops
       About 3 tablespoons shortening
    ½ teaspoon salt
    ½ teaspoon sage
    4 apples, cored and cut in rings
    ¼ cup brown sugar
    2 tablespoons all-purpose flour
    1 cup hot water
       Few drops vinegar
    ½ cup seedless raisins

Brown chops in hot shortening. Remove chops and save fat. Put chops in baking dish; sprinkle with salt and sage. Top with apple rings and sprinkle with sugar. In skillet blend fat, flour, water, and vinegar and cook until thick. Add raisins; pour over the chops. Bake in uncovered baking dish at 350° for 1 hour. Yield: 8 servings.

Pork Hock Dinner

    4 pork hocks
       Hot water
    2 teaspoons salt
    4 medium carrots
    4 medium onions
    4 medium potatoes
    1 small head cabbage
       Salt
       Pepper
       Paprika

Wash hocks and place in Dutch oven or large, deep pan. Cover with hot water, add 2 teaspoons salt (if fresh hocks are used), and simmer, covered, until meat is nearly tender (about 1½ hours). Add whole carrots, peeled onions, and pared potatoes, cut in half. Cover and cook for 15 minutes. Add cabbage, cut in wedges, and cook, covered, for 15 minutes longer, or until vegetables are tender. Sprinkle vegetables with salt, pepper, and paprika. Yield: 4 servings.

Braised Pork Chops

    4 to 6 chops (½- to 1-inch)
       Salt
       Pepper
       All-purpose flour
       Shortening

Sprinkle the chops with salt, pepper, and flour. Brown in a small amount of shortening. When browned on both sides, add a small amount of water. Cover the pan closely and cook over low heat for 30 to 45 minutes or in a 325° oven for 45 minutes to 1 hour, or until tender and thoroughly done. Yield: 4 to 6 servings.

Baked Pork Chops

    4 pork chops
       Salt and pepper
    4 tablespoons cooked rice
    2 cups cooked tomatoes

Brown pork chops, which have been sprinkled with salt and pepper, on both sides. Place in baking dish and put 1 tablespoon rice on each chop. Pour the cooked tomatoes over the chops. Bake at 350° for 1 hour. When ready to serve, lift chops carefully with rice and baked tomatoes intact. Yield: 4 servings.

Favorite Pork and Dumplings

6 pork steaks or chops, bones removed
½ cup water
1 medium onion, thinly sliced
1½ to 3 cups water
    Dumplings

Brown meat in heavy, deep skillet. Add ½ cup water and sliced onion. Cover and simmer until meat is tender, about 45 to 50 minutes. Drain off excess fat and add additional water. Make Dumplings.

Dumplings

¾ cup milk
1½ cups instant-blending, self-rising flour

Add milk to flour and stir only until blended. Drop by spoonfuls onto hot meat (not in the liquid). Cook for 10 minutes, uncovered, then cover skillet and cook 10 minutes longer. Liquid can be thickened for gravy or served without the thickening. Yield: 6 servings.

Baked Stuffed Pork Chops

4 rib pork chops (1 to 1½ inches thick)
3 tablespoons minced onion
2 tablespoons butter or margarine
1¼ cups dry bread cubes
¾ cup drained whole-kernel corn
¼ teaspoon salt
⅛ teaspoon pepper
⅛ teaspoon sage
¼ cup all-purpose flour
½ cup water

Cut slit from the bone side of chops almost to fat side, to make pocket. Cook onion in butter or margarine until tender, then add bread cubes, corn, and seasonings. Mix lightly, and moisten with 1 tablespoon water. Stuff the pocket of each chop with one-fourth of the dressing. Cut a little fat from edges of chops and fry out in skillet. Flour the chops and brown in the hot fat. Transfer to a large casserole, sprinkle with salt and pepper, and add ½ cup water. Cover and bake at 325° for 1 hour; uncover and bake for 15 minutes more to brown meat. Yield: 4 servings.

Pork Crown Roast

1 (6- to 10-pound) crown roast of pork loin (14 to 16 ribs)
    Salt
    Pepper

Have your butcher fashion a pork crown roast at the market. He will tie the roast to form a circle with ends of rib bones exposed. Be sure the backbone is removed for easy carving. Season with salt and pepper. Place crown roast, rib ends down, on rack in open roasting pan. Do not add water and do not cover. Roast at 325° for 2 hours. Remove from oven.

Invert roast so that rib ends are up. Insert roast meat thermometer into center of the thickest part of roast, making certain that it does not rest in fat or on bone. Continue roasting until meat thermometer registers 170°. Remove roast to heated platter; garnish.

Allow roast to "rest" at room temperature for 15 minutes before carving. Slice between ribs. One rib section will make a serving for one person. Yield: 14 to 16 servings.

Roast Pork with Apples And Potatoes

1 (3-pound) boned pork loin
2 to 3 teaspoons salt
½ teaspoon pepper
½ teaspoon thyme
½ teaspoon rosemary
  Pinch allspice
½ clove garlic, mashed
4 to 8 small potatoes
2 tart apples

Remove most of fat from roast. Combine salt and spices and rub over surface of roast. Cover and refrigerate for 12 hours before roasting. Wipe off seasonings. Roll and tie roast. Bake at 325° for about 35 to 40 minutes per pound, or until meat thermometer registers 185°. Add a small amount of hot water to the pan juices and baste from time to time.

Peel potatoes and slice lengthwise; add to roast when roast is about half-cooked. Fifteen minutes later add the apples which have been peeled and quartered. Skim fat from juices; serve juices with roast. Yield: 8 servings.

Georgia Hot Sausage Pie

1 pound hot pork sausage
2 cups canned tomatoes
2 cups whole-kernel corn, drained
2 tablespoons minced onion
2 tablespoons bacon drippings
3 tablespoons all-purpose flour
1 teaspoon sugar
1 teaspoon salt
  Breadcrumbs

Cook sausage slowly in heavy skillet until brown, crumbly, and well done. Add tomatoes and drained corn; simmer for 10 minutes. Sauté onion in bacon drippings; mix flour, sugar, and salt; blend with bacon drippings and onion. Add to sausage and vegetables; heat to boiling point. Spoon into 2-quart baking dish; top with breadcrumbs, slices of buttered bread cut in triangles, biscuit dough, or pastry. Bake at 425° for 20 minutes, or until topping is browned. Serve hot. Yield: 6 to 8 servings.

Fried Sausage

To cook bulk sausage, mold cakes about ½ inch thick and fry. In an uncovered pan, cook the cakes slowly and thoroughly until brown and crisp on both sides. Remove the cakes, drain on paper to remove excess fat, and serve hot.

Before cooking link or cased sausage, prick the casing in several places with a fork. Lay the pieces in a cold skillet, add 1 or 2 tablespoons water, cover and steam for a few minutes. Remove lid and finish cooking at moderate heat until thoroughly done, turning frequently.

Roasting Chart For Ham

Follow label instructions. If none is available the following method may be used:

Place ham on a rack in a shallow roasting pan. Insert meat thermometer with the bulb in thickest part. The bulb should not rest in fat or touch bone. Do not add water or cover. Bake at 325° according to the time and temperature chart below. If a glaze is desired, brush it on the ham 30 minutes before the end of the cooking time.

Fully-cooked hams should be heated to an internal temperature of 140°. Cook-before-eating hams should be cooked to an internal temperature of 160°.

Fully-Cooked Ham Roasting Chart

Type Ham	Weight (Pounds)	Approximate Baking Time at 325° (Hours)
Boneless, half	3 to 5	1½ to 1¾
Fully-Cooked	7 to 10	2½ to 3
	10 to 12	3 to 3½
	12 to 14	3½ to 4
Bone-In	10 to 13	3 to 3½
Fully-Cooked	13 to 16	3½ to 4
Semi-Boneless, half	4 to 6	1¾ to 2½
Fully-Cooked	10 to 12	3 to 3½
Canned Hams	1½ to 3	1 to 1½
	3 to 7	1½ to 2
	7 to 10	2 to 2½
	10 to 13	2½ to 3
Picnic, Fully-Cooked	4 to 8	1¾ to 2¾

Cook-Before-Eating Ham Roasting Chart

Type Ham	Weight (Pounds)	Approximate Baking Time at 325° (Hours)
Boneless,	8 to 11	2½ to 3¼
Cook-Before-Eating	11 to 14	3¼ to 4
Bone-In, half	5 to 7	3 to 3¼
Cook-Before-Eating	10 to 12	3½ to 4
	12 to 15	4 to 4½
	15 to 18	4½ to 5
	18 to 22	5 to 6
Picnic, Cook-Before-Eating	4 to 8	2½ to 4*
Shoulder Roll, Cook-Before-Eating	2 to 3	1½ to 2*

*Cook to an internal temperature of 170°.

Candied Ham Loaf

2 cups whole wheat breadcrumbs
1 cup milk
2 eggs, slightly beaten
2 pounds ground ham
1 pound ground pork
1 teaspoon dry mustard
½ teaspoon salt
½ cup brown sugar
½ teaspoon ground cloves

Soak breadcrumbs in milk; add eggs. Combine ham, pork, mustard, and salt; add to crumb mixture and mix well. Combine brown sugar and cloves; spread in bottom of 9- x 5- x 4-inch loaf-pan. Pack meat mixture in pan. Bake at 350° for 1½ hours. Yield: 6 servings.

Cider Jelly Glazed Ham

1 (about 14-pound) whole ham cooked and ready to eat
1⅓ cups Cinnamon-Cider Jelly
Whole cloves
Watercress or other greens
Spiced whole red crabapples

Place ham with fat side up in a shallow baking pan. Bake at 325° for 2½ to 3 hours. One-half hour before ham is done, remove from oven. Remove drippings. Cut away rind. Score ham with a sharp knife, making diagonal cuts across entire fat surface. Stud top of ham with whole cloves. To glaze the ham, spoon ⅔ cup jelly onto the ham. Return ham to oven for 10 minutes. Spoon remaining jelly onto ham and return to oven for 20 to 25 minutes. Garnish with watercress or other greens and serve hot or cold with spiced crab-apples and Cider-Cinnamon Sauce. Yield: About 8 servings.

Cider-Cinnamon Sauce

6 tablespoons Cinnamon-Cider Jelly
1 tablespoon cornstarch
¼ cup orange juice
2 tablespoons lemon juice
Dash salt
2 tablespoons raisins or currants

Melt jelly over low heat. Mix cornstarch with orange and lemon juices; add to jelly with remaining ingredients. Bring to a boil and cook for 2 to 3 minutes, stirring constantly, until thickened. Serve warm or cold with glazed ham. (This recipe may be doubled to make 12 servings.) Yield: 6 servings.

Cinnamon-Cider Jelly

4½ cups (2 pounds) sugar
4 cups sweet apple cider
1 box powdered fruit pectin
1 to 2 tablespoons red cinnamon candies

Measure sugar and set aside. Measure cider into a large saucepan. Add powdered fruit pectin and cinnamon candies and mix well. Place over high heat and stir until mixture comes to a hard boil. At once stir in sugar. Bring to a full rolling boil and boil hard for 1 minute, stirring constantly. Remove from heat, skim off foam with metal spoon, and pour quickly into glasses. Cover jelly at once with ⅛ inch hot paraffin. Yield: About 8 medium glasses (4 pounds jelly).

Baked Country Ham

1 (10-pound) country-cured ham
1 cup ginger ale
1 cup brown sugar or ½ cup molasses
4 tablespoons all-purpose flour
1 tablespoon dry mustard
2 tablespoons water
  Whole cloves

Wash ham. Cover with boiling water and boil for 10 minutes. Then simmer for 3 hours. Remove skin, place in roaster, fat-side up. Bake at 325° for 1½ hours, basting frequently with a mixture of ginger ale and ham stock. Remove from oven. Cover with a paste made of brown sugar or molasses, flour, mustard, and water. Dot with cloves. Return to oven in uncovered roaster and bake for 30 minutes. Yield: 10 to 12 servings.

Baked Ham Slice

1 ham slice, 1-inch thick
1 teaspoon dry mustard
2 tablespoons brown sugar
2 cups milk

Rub ham with mustard and brown sugar, put into baking dish, and cover with the milk. Bake at 300° for 1 hour. Yield: 2 servings.

Boiled Ham

To boil an old Kentucky or Virginia ham, put washed ham into a large boiler and completely cover with boiling water. Simmer until tender, but do not boil. Cook for 25 to 30 minutes to the pound.

When ham is about half-done, add 1 cup vinegar and 1 cup brown sugar. Let ham remain in liquid until it is cold.

Broiled Ham Slice

Have ham slice cut ¾ to 1 inch thick. Score fat around edge of ham to prevent curling. Place on broiler rack in broiler pan. When inserting broiler pan in oven, allow 2 inches between surface of meat and heat. When brown, turn and brown second side. Broil 8 to 10 minutes on each side. Yield: 4 to 6 servings.

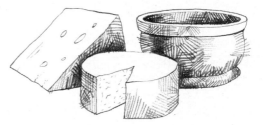

Maryland Stuffed Ham

Cover an 8- to 10-pound ham with cold water and bring to a boil. Turn ham and boil for 10 minutes. Skin ham and set aside to cool.

Scald 5 pounds mixed kale and watercress. Chop 1 dozen spring onions, 1 large bunch parsley, and 1 entire stalk celery. Mix scalded greens, chopped greens, and add 2 teaspoons salt, ½ teaspoon pepper, 2 teaspoons celery seed, and 2 teaspoons mustard seed.

With a wide knife, gash ham deeply with blade held the long way of ham (not over 12 gashes for whole ham). Stuff gashes well with mixed greens and seasonings. Place ham in prepared cloth sack and pack extra greens around it. Sew tightly, cover with water, and boil for 3 hours, then cool in kettle. When quite cold, remove and drain. Take off sack and place ham on platter with extra stuffing all over it. Slice and serve cold. Yield: 10 to 12 servings.

Boiled Country Ham

Scrub the ham with a brush and scrape it well. Let soak in cold water overnight or longer if the ham is very old and large. Put in a large kettle and cover with water. Add 2 cups molasses or sugar, 1 teaspoon whole cloves, 2 teaspoons peppercorns (unground pepper), 1 cup vinegar (sweet pickle juice may be used for vinegar), and 2 sticks cinnamon. Cook slowly until tender when pierced with a fork, allowing 20 to 30 minutes cooking time per pound.

When done, let stand in the water until cold. Then remove from the water and remove the rind. Score the surface fat and spread with a mixture of brown sugar, breadcrumbs, and prepared mustard. Insert a whole clove in the center of each section and bake at 325° for about 35 minutes, or until brown.

Sugar-cured ham may be cooked by the same method, but does not need soaking before cooking, and it does not take as long to cook.

Mississippi Stuffed Ham And Dressing

Bake ham half-done. Skin, remove excessive fat (½ inch). Turn over and insert small vegetable knife at the hock and split, following the bone carefully. Cut bone out of the meat, leaving as little meat on it as possible. When bone is removed, fill cavity with a highly seasoned Dressing made of breadcrumbs, pressing it well into all cut places. Pour in a little melted butter. Sew up the ham with a cord. Make enough Dressing to cover entire ham (½ inch). Moisten with juice of ham, and wrap in cheesecloth. Bake at 275°. Leave cheesecloth on until ham is cold.

Dressing

1 pound breadcrumbs
3 cups crumbled cornbread
1 teaspoon ground cloves
1 teaspoon ground allspice
1 teaspoon ground ginger
1 teaspoon ground mace
1 teaspoon onion salt
1 teaspoon garlic salt
1 teaspoon black pepper
½ cup molasses
2 tablespoons mustard
3 eggs, well beaten

Mix the crumbs, cornbread, and all spices well. Add molasses, mustard, and eggs. Moisten with juice of ham, and fill cavity.

Fried Ham with Red-Eye Gravy

Slice ham about ¼ to ½ inch thick. Cut gashes in fat to keep ham from curling. Place slices in a heavy skillet and cook slowly. Turn several times, and cook until ham is brown. Remove from pan and keep warm. To the drippings in the skillet, add about ½ cup hot water; cook until gravy turns red. A little strong coffee might be added to deepen the color. Serve hot with fried ham and biscuits.

Roasting Chart For Whole Chickens

Approximate Weight (Pounds)	Oven Temperature (Degrees)	Approximate Cooking Time (Hours)
3½ to 4	350	2 to 2¾
4 to 5	350	2½ to 3
over 5	325	3 to 3½

Roast Chicken

Rub cavity lightly with salt. Place enough dressing in neck end to fill. Fasten neck skin down to back with skewer. Stuff body cavity with dressing. Cover chicken with a tent of aluminum foil or a cloth dipped in melted fat.

Place bird in a shallow pan on a rack on its side, or place bird breast down in V-shaped rack and leave in this position throughout the roasting. Roast at 325° or 350° until tender, turning bird on other side when half-done. Baste with drippings occasionally.

Arkansas Petit Jean (Chicken 'n' Rice)

2 frying-size chickens
2 teaspoons salt
  Juice from ½ lemon
1 cup all-purpose flour
1 teaspoon paprika
¼ teaspoon white pepper
½ cup salad oil
½ cup water
¼ teaspoon rosemary leaves, crushed
1 cup uncooked regular rice
1 (10½-ounce) can mushroom soup
1 cup commercial sour cream

Cut chicken into frying-size pieces. Sprinkle with salt and lemon juice. Set aside for 15 minutes. Mix flour, paprika, and white pepper in a bag. Shake a few pieces of chicken in the bag at a time to coat evenly. Fry chicken in salad oil, one half at a time, until golden brown.

Return all the chicken to the skillet, add the water and rosemary leaves, and cover with a heavy lid. Turn heat low and let simmer for about 35 to 40 minutes, or until chicken is tender.

While chicken is simmering, cook rice according to directions on package. Spoon rice onto warm serving platter and surround with the chicken. Make sauce by adding mushroom soup to skillet in which chickens were cooked.

Gradually add sour cream, stirring constantly. Heat thoroughly (do not boil). Spoon over chicken and rice. Yield: 8 to 10 servings.

Chicken Supreme

4 chicken breasts, cut in half
¼ pound butter or margarine
¼ cup all-purpose flour
½ teaspoon salt
1 teaspoon paprika
8 slices ham (country cured preferred)
2 cups diced celery
1 cup orange juice
1 cup commercial sour cream

Lightly salt chicken breasts. Melt butter or margarine. Mix flour, salt, and paprika in bag. Add chicken and shake to coat each piece evenly. Brown lightly in butter or margarine.

Grease an 8- x 12-inch baking dish. Place slices of ham in dish, cover with diced celery. Place browned chicken breasts, skin-side up, on the ham slices. Add flour left in bag to melted butter or margarine; blend well, then add orange juice. Remove from heat and add sour cream. Pour this gravy over chicken. Cover baking dish and bake at 350° for 1 hour and 15 minutes. Yield: 4 servings.

Fried Chicken

1 (1½- to 2½-pound) fryer
1 cup all-purpose flour
½ teaspoon salt
¼ teaspoon fresh ground pepper
  Shortening

Dress and disjoint fryer. Chill overnight. Combine flour, salt, and pepper. Put flour mixture into paper bag and drop in several pieces of chicken at a time. Shake bag to coat chicken with flour. Melt 1½ to 2 inches shortening in a large, hot frying pan. When all chicken is in, cover for 5 to 7 minutes. Uncover, and turn chicken when underside is golden brown. Cover again for 5 to 10 minutes; then remove top, and cook until other side is brown. Reduce heat, cover, and cook 20 to 25 minutes longer. Turn chicken only once. Yield: 4 servings.

Variations

Add one or more of the following to the flour — ¼ teaspoon paprika, monosodium glutamate, chili powder, or curry powder. Some cooks insist that chicken be left in sweet milk for an hour or so (this milk may be used later in gravy). Others dip the pieces of chicken into buttermilk before coating with flour.

Chicken Cacciatore

   1 large onion, chopped
   1 large green pepper, chopped
   1 clove garlic, minced
   4 tablespoons salad oil, divided
   1 (3-pound) frying chicken
   ½ cup all-purpose flour
1¾ cups cooked, drained tomatoes
   ½ cup tomato sauce
   2 teaspoons salt
   ¼ teaspoon pepper
   ¼ teaspoon ground allspice
   1 bay leaf
   ¼ teaspoon thyme
   ¾ teaspoon oregano
   1 pimiento, chopped
   1 (4-ounce) can sliced mushrooms

Brown chopped onion, green pepper strips, and minced garlic in 2 tablespoons salad oil. Remove these and set aside for later use. Place pieces of chicken in paper bag with flour, and shake. Remove chicken and place in skillet. Add remaining salad oil and fry until golden brown. Return browned onion, pepper, and garlic to the skillet. Mix tomatoes, tomato sauce, salt, pepper, spices, pimiento, and mushrooms. Add to chicken. Simmer covered, for 30 to 40 minutes, or until chicken is tender. Yield: 4 to 5 servings.

Chicken Maryland

Use either broilers or roasters (about 3½ pounds). Cut into serving pieces. Shake pieces in mixture of flour, salt, and pepper. Remove pieces, and dip into mixture of 1 beaten egg diluted with 2 tablespoons milk or water. Now dip pieces in breadcrumbs. Let pieces dry for about 30 to 40 minutes. Brown chicken at high heat in about 1 to 1½ inches hot shortening. Reduce heat, and continue cooking for 30 to 45 minutes. Serve with Cream Gravy. Yield: 6 servings.

Cream Gravy

To every 2 tablespoons shortening in the skillet, add 2 tablespoons flour. Brown for a few minutes, stirring constantly to prevent lumping. Add 1½ cups milk, or part milk and part water, and cook until thickened. Season to taste and serve hot.

Chicken Pie Superb

   1 (4- to 5-pound) chicken
   1 carrot, diced
   1 onion, diced
   1 stalk celery, chopped
   1 sprig parsley, chopped
   1 teaspoon rosemary
   ½ teaspoon salt
   ⅛ teaspoon pepper
   5 tablespoons all-purpose flour
1½ cups chicken stock
   1 cup cream
   1 teaspoon salt
   ¼ teaspoon pepper
   ¼ pound butter or margarine
   1 (4-ounce) can mushroom slices
      Pastry

Clean and disjoint chicken. Place on rack in container half-filled with hot water. Add carrot, onion, celery, parsley, rosemary, ½ teaspoon salt, and pepper. Partly cover with a lid and simmer for 3 to 4 hours or until tender, turning occasionally. Cool chicken in broth, breast-side down. Skim off excess fat from stock.

Make a sauce by blending flour with
¼ cup of the strained stock in a saucepan. Stir in slowly the remaining stock
and cream. Cook until thick, stirring
constantly to avoid lumps. Season with
salt and pepper. Place the chicken in a
baking dish, discarding the breastbone
and cutting white meat into pieces, as for
serving. The two pieces of back in the
center support the crust. Add the sauce.
Dot butter or margarine over sauce and
chicken. Add mushrooms, or put them
into the sauce. Cover sauce and chicken
with a pastry, ⅓ inch thick.

Press pastry against sides of dish and cut
gashes across the top. Bake at 425°
for 12 to 15 minutes. Yield: 6 servings.

Chicken Hash

1 (3½- to 4-pound) hen
1 bunch carrots
   Salt and pepper
1 small bay leaf
1 bunch celery
4 cups hot water
4 tablespoons butter or margarine
4 tablespoons all-purpose flour
2 cups chicken stock
1 cup cream
1 (4-ounce) can mushrooms, sliced

Place the first six ingredients in a large
pot and cover. Bring to boiling, then
reduce heat and simmer until done (3 to
4 hours). Remove chicken from bones
and cube meat. Drain off stock. Make a
cream sauce using butter or margarine,
flour, and chicken stock, in the top of a
double boiler. Add the cream and sliced
mushrooms. Then stir cream sauce into

chicken. Serve hot. Yield: 6 to 8
servings.

Sour Dough Chicken Pie

2 recipes plain biscuit dough
2 (3-pound) chickens, cooked, boned,
   and cut in bite-size pieces
1 pound butter
1 recipe sour dough *
   Pepper
10 eggs
2½ to 3 cups chicken stock
2 tablespoons all-purpose flour
2 cups milk

Line bottom and sides of large baking
pan with one-half of the plain biscuit
dough, rolled thin. Place about one-
third of the cooked and boned chicken
over the pastry and dot with butter. Roll
sour dough very thin and cut into dumplings; place layer over chicken and
sprinkle with pepper. Over this break 6
whole raw eggs to make a layer; dot
with butter. Cover with another layer of
sour dough dumplings. Repeat layer of
chicken, butter, and dumplings. Add the
remaining 4 whole raw eggs and remainder of chicken. Dot with butter and
cover with chicken stock seasoned to
taste. Sprinkle 2 tablespoons flour over
top and add 2 cups milk.

Roll out remainder of biscuit dough and
cut into four equal pieces. Place on top
of pie, trim off excess, and press edges of
dough together to seal. Dot with butter.
Bake at 300° for about 2 hours. Yield:
15 servings.

*Sour dough as the term applies here
refers to a recipe of biscuit dough (2
cups flour) covered and left in the refrigerator for 3 days.

Country Captain

2 large hens
4 medium green peppers
2 small onions
2 cloves garlic
2 tablespoons butter or margarine
3 teaspoons curry powder
2 teaspoons thyme
   Salt and pepper to taste
3 (4-ounce) can mushrooms
½ pound blanched almonds
½ pound currants or raisins
   Cooked rice

Cut up chicken and steam until tender. While chicken is steaming, cut up peppers, onions, garlic, and sauté in a frying pan until slightly brown, not done. Add to this, curry powder, thyme, salt, pepper, tomatoes, and mushrooms. When this is well blended, add cooked chicken and half of blanched and toasted almonds, and half of raisins; cook together for 1 hour. (Do not thicken gravy.) When ready to serve, pour mixture over cooked rice, or place rice around it, and sprinkle remaining almonds and raisins over the whole. Yield: 6 to 8 servings.

Fried Chicken
(Electric Skillet-Style)

1 (3-pound) frying-size chicken
½ cup all-purpose flour
1 teaspoon salt
¼ teaspoon pepper
½ cup butter or vegetable oil
¾ cup water

Preheat electric skillet to 375° (for crisp chicken, preheat to 425°). Cut chicken into serving-size pieces. Combine flour, salt, and pepper. Melt butter or vegetable oil in skillet. Dip chicken into seasoned flour. Place in skillet, and cook until chicken is golden brown on all sides. Add the water. Cover skillet, lower temperature to 250° and continue cooking for about 45 minutes longer, or until chicken is tender. Yield: 6 servings.

Chicken Pie with
Sweet Potato Crust

3 cups diced, cooked chicken
1 cup diced, cooked carrots
6 cooked small white onions
1 tablespoon chopped parsley
1 cup evaporated milk
1 cup chicken broth
2 tablespoons all-purpose flour
1 teaspoon salt
⅛ teaspoon pepper
   Sweet Potato Crust

Arrange chicken, carrots, onions, and parsley in layers in casserole. Combine milk and chicken broth. Add slowly to flour, blending well. Cook until thickened, stirring constantly. Pour over chicken and vegetables in casserole. Cover with Sweet Potato Crust. Bake at 350° for about 40 minutes. Yield: 6 to 8 servings.

Sweet Potato Crust

1 cup sifted all-purpose flour
1 teaspoon baking powder
½ teaspoon salt
1 cup mashed sweet potatoes
⅓ cup melted butter or margarine
1 egg, well beaten

Combine flour, baking powder and salt; sift once. Work in mashed sweet potatoes, melted butter or margarine, and egg. Roll ¼ inch thick and use as cover for chicken or meat deep-dish pie.

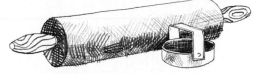

Chicken à la King

  1 tablespoon butter or margarine
  ¼ cup sliced mushrooms
  ¼ cup chopped green pepper
  3 tablespoons butter or margarine
  3 tablespoons all-purpose flour
  1 teaspoon salt
    Dash pepper
1½ cups milk
  ¼ cup light cream
  2 tablespoons chopped pimiento
1½ cups diced, cooked chicken
  1 egg yolk, slightly beaten

Melt butter or margarine in 2-quart saucepan over medium heat. Add mushrooms and green pepper. Cook until mushrooms are browned. Remove mushrooms and green peppers from saucepan. Add butter or margarine to saucepan and melt. Add flour, salt, pepper, and blend well. Add milk, and stir constantly until mixture thickens. Cook for 5 minutes, stirring occasionally. Add mushrooms, green pepper, cream, pimiento, and chicken to mixture in saucepan; heat thoroughly.

Gradually add small amount of sauce to egg yolk while stirring. Return to saucepan and heat, stirring constantly for 1 minute, or until mixture has thickened. Yield: 6 servings.

Chicken Tetrazzini

1½ to 2 cups diced, cooked chicken
1½ cups noodles
1½ cups diced celery
  1 tablespoon diced green pepper
  ½ cup chopped onion
  1 clove garlic, minced
  1 tablespoon chopped parsley
  3 cups chicken broth
  ½ (10½-ounce) can mushroom soup
  ¾ cup cooked tomatoes
    Salt and pepper
  ¾ cup shredded sharp cheese
  2 tablespoons breadcrumbs

Dice cooked chicken. Cook noodles, diced celery, green pepper, chopped onion, minced garlic, and chopped parsley in chicken broth. Combine chicken, noodles, vegetable mixture, mushroom soup, drained tomatoes, salt and pepper. Add shredded cheese and breadcrumbs. Bake at 300° until lightly browned. Yield: 8 servings.

Chinese Chicken

  ¼ cup flour
  3 tablespoons butter or margarine
  1 (20-ounce) can crushed pineapple
  1 cup chicken stock
  2 cups diced, cooked chicken
  1 green pepper, chopped
  2 cups diced celery
    Salt and pepper to taste

Combine flour, butter or margarine, and undrained pineapple. Cook until thick and smooth, stirring constantly. Add chicken, chicken stock, fresh green pepper, and celery. Season to taste. Cook slowly for 5 minutes. Yield: 4 to 6 servings.

Chicken Pilau

1   (2-pound) chicken, dressed
1   teaspoon salt
6   to 8 slices of fat side-meat
5   cups liquid stock
4   cups uncooked regular rice
4   or 5 hard-cooked eggs
    Pepper to taste

Cook salted chicken and fat meat in water to cover. When chicken is thoroughly done and meat is dropping from the bones, remove bones from chicken and set chicken aside. Remove fat meat. Add rice to the liquid in which the chicken and fat meat have been boiled. Add hard-cooked eggs cut fine, and pepper. Cook rice tender and dry, without stirring. Add chicken and heat. Yield: 12 servings.

Chicken and Rolled Dumplings

Disjoint chicken, barely cover with water, and add 1½ teaspoons salt. Simmer until meat is tender, 2 to 4 hours, depending on age and size of chicken. Add Dumplings.

Rolled Dumplings

2   cups all-purpose flour
2   teaspoons baking powder
1   teaspoon salt
⅓   cup shortening
½   cup milk

Combine flour, baking powder, and salt. Cut in shortening. Add milk to make a stiff dough. Roll out to about ⅛-inch thickness, and cut into 1-inch squares, 1- to 1½-inch strips, or diamonds. Sprinkle lightly with flour and drop into boiling chicken stock. Cover closely and boil gently for 8 to 10 minutes. Yield: 6 to 8 servings.

Drop Dumplings

2   cups all-purpose flour
1   teaspoon salt
4   teaspoons baking powder
¼   teaspoon pepper
1   egg, well beaten
3   tablespoons shortening
⅔   cup milk (about)

Combine dry ingredients. Add egg, melted shortening, and enough milk to make a moist, stiff batter. Drop by teaspoonfuls into boiling stock. Cover very closely and cook for 10 to 15 minutes, or until dumplings are done. Yield: 6 to 8 servings.

Chicken and "Slick" Dumplings

1   (5-pound) hen
    Boiling salted water
2   cups self-rising flour
¼   cup vegetable shortening
¾   cup boiling water
    Salt and pepper to taste

Cook hen in boiling salted water until tender; remove from broth. Cool chicken, cut from bone and set aside. Measure 1 quart broth into large saucepan. Bring to a boil and add chicken.

Put flour in large bowl; cut in shortening

with pastry blender or forks. Add boiling water, a small amount at a time. Shape mixture into a ball and roll to a thickness of ⅛ inch on a lightly floured board. Cut into strips. Drop strips into boiling broth, cover, and cook for about 8 to 10 minutes. Add salt and pepper to taste. Yield: 6 servings.

Roast Cornish Game Hen

1 *individual-size Cornish hen*
4 *tablespoons melted butter or margarine*
    Herb Gravy

Place bird, breast-side down, in baking pan which has a tight-fitting cover. Brush back with butter or margarine. Roast uncovered at 400° until hen begins to brown, about 20 minutes. Reduce heat to 350°. Cover closely and roast until thoroughly tender — the entire time will be about 1 hour — but hen must be tested for tenderness.
Use drippings to make Herb Gravy.
Yield: 1 to 2 servings.

Herb Gravy

¼ *cup drippings*
½ *cup instant nonfat dry milk powder*
2 *tablespoons all-purpose flour*
½ *teaspoon whole basil, crushed*
¼ *teaspoon powdered marjoram*
1½ *cups water*

Pour drippings into roasting pan or saucepan. In another container, sprinkle dry milk powder, flour, and seasonings over water, beat until just blended. Pour into drippings. Blend well, cook over low heat, stirring constantly until thickened. Serve hot over Cornish Game Hen.

Glorified Lamb Chops

1 *teaspoon dry mustard*
2 *teaspoons butter or margarine*
6 *thick lamb chops*
2 *cups buttered cracker crumbs*
2 *teaspoons salt*
⅛ *teaspoon pepper*

Mix mustard and butter or margarine until well blended, and spread over each lamb chop. Roll the chops in buttered cracker crumbs, season with salt and pepper, and broil until tender. Yield: 6 servings.

Roast Lamb Shoulder Stuffed

1 *(4- to 5-pound) lamb shoulder, boned*
¼ *cup butter or margarine*
2 *tablespoons finely chopped onions*
3 *cups soft breadcrumbs*
½ *cup finely diced celery*
2 *tablespoons chopped parsley*
2 *teaspoons powdered sage*
1 *teaspoon salt*
⅛ *teaspoon pepper*
¼ *cup water*

Have butcher bone the shoulder, leaving a roomy pocket in which to place the stuffing. Melt the butter or margarine, add onion, and cook over medium heat until onion is yellow, but not brown. Add breadcrumbs, celery, parsley, and seasonings. Cook for about 5 minutes over medium heat, stirring constantly. Add water. Dust lamb with salt and pepper. Fill cavity with stuffing and sew or skewer the edges together. Place on rack in an uncovered roasting pan and roast at 325°, allowing 45 minutes per pound. Yield: 6 servings.

Roasting Chart For Lamb
Roasting at 300° to 325°

Cut	Approximate Weight (Pounds)	Meat Thermometer Reading (Degrees)	Approximate Cooking Time (Minutes Per Pound)
Leg	5 to 8	175-180	30 to 35
Boneless Leg	3 to 5	175-180	35 to 40
Crown Roast	4 to 6	175-180	40 to 45
Rib (Rack)	4 to 5	175-180	40 to 45
Shoulder (bone-in)	4 to 6	175-180	30 to 35
Shoulder (cushion-style)	3 to 5	175-180	30 to 35
Shoulder (rolled)	3 to 5	175-180	40 to 45

Broiled Lamb Patties

1 pound ground lamb
1 teaspoon salt
⅛ teaspoon pepper
2 tablespoons chopped parsley

Mix all ingredients well. Shape into patties. Arrange on broiler rack, leaving 2 inches between the surface of the patties and the heat. Broil on one side until brown (about 10 minutes). Season, turn and brown other side. Yield: 4 to 6 servings.

Roast Lamb

Wipe leg of lamb with a clean, damp cloth. Season with salt and pepper. Place roast, fat side up, on a rack in an open roasting pan. Do not add water; do not cover; and do not baste. Roast at 325°. To determine doneness accurately, use a meat thermometer. For medium done, roast for 30 to 35 minutes per pound, or until meat thermometer registers 175°. For well done, roast for 35 to 40 minutes per pound, or until meat thermometer registers 182°.

Turkey Creole

1 tablespoon shortening
1 tablespoon all-purpose flour
2 small onions,
   Chopped garlic (optional)
1 green pepper, chopped
2 teaspoons chopped parsley
2 cups canned tomatoes
¾ cup chopped celery
1 (3-ounce) can mushrooms
2 cups diced, cooked turkey
2 teaspoons Worcestershire sauce
   Salt and pepper

Put shortening, flour, onions, green pepper, and parsley into skillet and cook until onions are brown. Add tomatoes, chopped celery, and mushrooms. Season with salt and pepper. Add cooked turkey and cover. Let cook very slowly for 1 hour. One-half hour before serving, add Worcestershire sauce. Serve over cooked rice and sprinkle with chow mein noodles, or serve rice and creole separately. Yield: 6 servings.

Roast Turkey

Start preparing the stuffing a day or so ahead of time if you like, but refrigerate dry ingredients and broth separately until time to use the dressing. Do not stuff the turkey until time to roast it.

For each generous serving of roasted whole turkey, allow ¾ to 1 pound of ready-to-cook weight for birds weighing less than 12 pounds; ½ to ¾ pound for birds weighing 12 pounds and over. Clean bird thoroughly. Salt inside of bird. Fill the neck cavity loosely with dressing. Fold the neck skin to back, fastening to backbone with a poultry pin. Fold wingtip over neck skin. Spoon the dressing into body cavity, shaking the bird to settle dressing. Do not pack it. Place skewers across opening and lace shut with cord. Tie drumsticks securely to tail. Brush skin with soft fat.

Cover the turkey with a tent of aluminum foil or a piece of thin cloth moistened with fat. Baste the turkey with pan drippings or melted fat several times during roasting. When the roasting is about half-done, cut the string or skin to release the legs; the bird cooks better and looks better.

Turkey is done when the leg joints move easily and the flesh on the legs is soft and pliable when pressed with the fingers. When a meat thermometer is used, it should register 185° placed in the center of the inside thigh muscle or in the center of the thickest meaty part.

Use the chart to determine how long to roast turkey. It gives the approximate time required to cook chilled turkeys of various weights. Stuffed turkeys require approximately 5 minutes per pound more time.

Roasting Chart For Whole Turkeys

Approximate Weight (Pounds)	Oven Temperature (Degrees)	Approximate Cooking Time (Hours)
4 to 8	325	3 to 4
8 to 12	325	4 to 4½
12 to 16	325	4½ to 5
16 to 20	325	5½ to 7
20 to 24	325	7 to 8½

Fried Turkey

3 pounds turkey
½ cup all-purpose flour
2 teaspoons paprika
2 teaspoons salt
¼ teaspoon pepper
¼ teaspoon poultry seasoning (optional)
1 cup shortening (for frying)

Cut turkey into serving-size pieces. Combine flour and seasoning in a paper bag. Shake turkey, two or three pieces at a time, in the bag to coat evenly. Use any leftover flour for gravy. Cook to a uniform golden brown in about ½ inch of moderately hot shortening in a heavy skillet. Start pieces skin-side down. Browning requires 15 to 20 minutes.

Reduce heat, cover tightly, and cook until tender, about 50 minutes. If skillet cannot be covered tightly, add 1 to 2 tablespoons water. The turkey is done when the thickest pieces are fork-tender. Uncover the last 10 minutes of cooking to crisp skin. Gravy may be prepared with the pan drippings.

Holiday Turkey

For safety's sake, cook your holiday turkey correctly. Some recipes for overnight cooking of turkeys are unsafe. In these recipes, usually the temperature is set at 450° or 500° for about an hour. At the end of 1 hour the oven is turned off and the oven door kept closed until the next morning. Another method recommends baking at 250° overnight.

Both of these methods are dangerous. In the first one, the temperature in the center of the turkey has not had a chance to reach the 300° recommended for safety, and any cooking of turkey under 300° is dangerous. Scientific data, including bacterial counts, show that at these low oven temperatures, the temperature of the turkey meat remains in the danger zone so long that salmonella can multiply at a fantastic rate. Here's how you can see that your family is protected:

Thawing Methods

1) Place turkey in its original wrap on a tray in the refrigerator and allow 2 to 4 days to thaw. This keeps juice loss to a minimum.

2) Leave bird in original wrap and place under cold running water. Allow 6 to 12 hours to thaw.

3) Thaw bird in original wrap in a closed paper bag at room temperature. Allow 12 hours for an 8- to 10-pound bird; 16 hours for a 20- to 25-pound bird.

Baking the Turkey

Thaw turkey completely. Remove giblets, rinse them, and place in a pan with seasonings and water. Let simmer 2 hours or longer. Use the broth in the dressing; add chopped giblets to the gravy.

Rinse turkey quickly in cool water and pat dry. Rub inside with salt. The cavity may be loosely filled with dressing or the dressing cooked in a separate pan. Fold neck skin under back and fasten with a skewer. Tie drumsticks to tail. Twist wing tips onto back, if desired.

Place turkey, breast-side up, on a rack in a shallow pan that has been lined with aluminum foil. Brush the skin with butter. Insert meat thermometer so that the bulb is in the center of the inside thigh muscle. Be sure that the bulb does not touch bone.

Place a loose tent of aluminum foil over the legs and breast to prevent excessive browning. Cook in a preheated 325° oven until the skin is a light golden brown. When the turkey is two-thirds done, cut cord to release the legs and permit heat to reach heavy-meated part.

Roast until thermometer reaches 180° to 185°. An 8- to 12-pound turkey will take approximately 3½ to 4½ hours to cook to this temperature. The traditional "doneness" test when a thermometer is not used is a "feel" test. Turkey is done when the thickest part of the drumstick feels very soft when pressed between protected fingers.

When the turkey is done, remove to a warm platter and keep hot. Cover tightly with foil and allow to stand for 30 minutes. This will let the juices be absorbed into the meat and makes carving easier.

Care of Leftovers

If the turkey has been stuffed for baking, remove all dressing from the cavity before storing. Remove meat from the bones, and cool the dressing, meat, and gravy thoroughly. After meat and dressing have cooled, wrap in aluminum foil and store in the refrigerator. Use within 3 or 4 days after baking. Sliced turkey, wrapped in moistureproof and vapor-proof paper or aluminum foil, may be frozen for later use.

Puffy Turkey Casserole

    1   cup milk
    1   cup turkey broth
 1½   tablespoons butter or margarine
 1¾   cups soft breadcrumbs
   ½   teaspoon salt
   ⅛   teaspoon black pepper
   ¾   cup diced turkey
    5   eggs, separated
         Mushroom Sauce

Heat milk and turkey broth. Add butter or margarine, breadcrumbs, seasonings, and turkey. Beat egg yolks and stir into the mixture. Heat for about 5 minutes, or until the mixture thickens, over low heat. Fold in stiffly beaten egg whites. Turn mixture into a 1½-quart casserole. Place in a pan of hot water. Bake at 325° for 1 hour and 15 minutes, or until a knife inserted in the center comes out clean. Serve with Mushroom Sauce. Yield: 6 to 8 servings.

Mushroom Sauce

    1   cup sliced mushrooms
   ⅓   cup butter or margarine
   ¼   cup flour
 2¼   cups turkey broth
   ½   cup milk
   ½   teaspoon salt
 ¹⁄₁₆ teaspoon black pepper

Sauté mushrooms in butter or margarine. Blend in flour. Gradually add turkey broth and milk. Add salt and pepper. Cook until of medium thickness, stirring constantly. Yield: 3½ cups.

Turkey Pies

1½ cups chopped, cooked turkey
1½ cups diced, cooked potatoes
 ½ cup diced, cooked carrots
  2 tablespoons chopped, raw onion
 ½ cup shredded Parmesan cheese
1½ cups medium cream sauce
   Salt
   Pepper
   Pastry

Combine turkey, potatoes, carrots, and onion. Add shredded cheese and cream sauce. Season to taste with salt and pepper. Place in individual baking dishes. Roll out pastry; cut slightly larger than baking dishes, and place on top of turkey mixture. Cut slits in pastry. Bake at 400° until pastry is brown. Yield: 4 small pies.

Turkey Rolls

2 tablespoons butter or margarine
2 tablespoons all-purpose flour
1 cup hot milk or chicken broth
2 egg yolks
2 cups diced, cooked turkey
1 tablespoon minced parsley
1 tablespoon grated onion
¼ teaspoon ground ginger
½ teaspoon salt and pepper
  Pastry squares

Melt butter or margarine, add flour, and then add liquid. Cook until thick, and then blend with egg yolks. Add this to turkey with seasonings. Cook over hot water for 10 minutes. Remove from heat and cool, then place in 5-inch pastry squares. Seal squares and bake at 350° for 45 minutes. Yield: 6 to 8 servings.

Rice Dressing

2 cups cooked rice
2 tablespoons chopped onion
1 teaspoon chopped parsley
1 cup diced celery
2 tablespoons shortening
2 teaspoons Worcestershire sauce
  Salt and pepper
2 hard-cooked eggs (optional)

Cook rice and set aside. Brown the onion, parsley, and celery in the shortening. Combine all the ingredients and blend thoroughly. One cup of breadcrumbs moistened with 1 cup of milk may be added. Yield: 3 cups.

Cornbread Dressing

6 cups crumbled cornbread
4 cups loaf bread or biscuits, crumbled
1 cup chopped celery
¾ cup finely chopped onion
½ cup butter or margarine, or
   chicken stock
1 tablespoon salt
⅛ teaspoon pepper
¼ teaspoon marjoram, or sage (optional)
1 cup water
4 eggs, beaten
2 cups broth or milk

Prepare bread for dressing. Cook celery and onions in 1 cup water on low heat until tender. Add to the crumbs and seasoning. Stir in beaten eggs and enough broth or milk to make a moist dressing. Pour into greased pan and bake at 400° for about 30 minutes, or until browned. Or, stuff the crop and body cavity of a bird weighing about 4 to 8 pounds. The Dressing will swell during roasting, so pack it loosely. Yield: 6 to 8 servings.

Favorite Bread Dressing

1 cup minced onion
1 quart diced celery
1 cup shortening
1 tablespoon salt
½ teaspoon pepper
2 teaspoons poultry seasoning
4 quarts breadcrumbs
1½ to 2 cups broth or water

Cook onion and celery in shortening over low heat until onion is soft but not browned, stirring occasionally. Meanwhile blend seasonings with bread, which has been crumbled. Add the onion, celery, and fat and blend. Pour the broth gradually over surface, stirring lightly. Add more seasoning as desired. Yield: Dressing for a 14- to 18-pound turkey.

Variations

Cornbread Dressing: Reduce bread to 2 quarts. Add 2 quarts cornbread or cornmeal muffins, crumbled.

Egg Dressing: Add 3 or 4 well beaten eggs to bread mixture.

Oyster Dressing: Cook 1 to 2 pints oysters in the oyster liquid until edges curl. Add to bread with seasoning. Include oyster liquor as part or all of the liquor in Dressing. Chop oysters if they are large.

Chestnut Dressing: Add 1 cup chestnuts.

Cooking Giblets, Neck Pieces

Separate the neck from the back and break into pieces. Cut liver and gizzard in half. Cook gently in salted water to cover. Necks and gizzards take at least 1½ hours; livers, ½ to 1 hour.
To make gravy, remove meat from neck and add to broth. Chop liver and gizzard fine. Add seasonings, and a small amount of flour to thicken, if desired.

Barbecue Shredded Beef

3 pounds chuck roast
   Water
3 teaspoons salt
2 tablespoons shortening
1 cup chopped onions
2 teaspoons paprika
1 teaspoon pepper
1 teaspoon dry mustard
   Dash cayenne pepper
½ teaspoon salt
3 tablespoons sugar
3 tablespoons Worcestershire sauce
1 clove garlic, minced
1 (6-ounce) can tomato paste
   Hamburger buns

Cook meat until very tender in a small amount of water to which 3 teaspoons salt have been added. While meat is cooking, make sauce: Melt shortening and add onions; cook until tender, but not browned. Add remaining ingredients and cook over low heat for 20 minutes. When meat is done, shred it fine. Add meat and liquid to the sauce and mix well. Cover and cook very slowly for 30 minutes. If necessary, add a little water if mixture becomes too thick. Serve on hamburger buns. Yield: 10 to 12 servings or 1½ quarts.

Oven-Barbecued Chicken

- 1 frying chicken
- ½ cup all-purpose flour
- 1 teaspoon salt
- ⅛ teaspoon pepper
- 6 tablespoons butter or margarine
- ¼ cup shortening
- ½ cup sliced onion
- ½ cup chopped celery
- ½ cup sliced green pepper
- 1 cup catsup
- 1 cup water
- 2 tablespoons Worcestershire sauce
- 2 tablespoons brown sugar
- ⅛ teaspoon pepper

Cut the chicken in serving pieces and dredge with a mixture of flour, salt, and pepper. Fry in 4 tablespoons of the butter or margarine and the shortening until golden brown. Transfer into a 3-quart casserole. Cook onion in remaining butter until clear. Add other ingredients, and bring to boil. Pour sauce over chicken, cover, and bake at 325° for about 1 hour. Yield: 4 servings.

Barbecued Spareribs

- 4 pounds spareribs
  Instant seasoned meat tenderizer
- 2 medium onions, sliced
  Western Barbecue Sauce

Allow about 1 pound of spareribs per person. Prepare all surfaces of the meat, one side at a time, as follows: Thoroughly moisten surface of meat with water. Sprinkle seasoned meat tenderizer evenly, like salt, over entire surface of the meat, about ½ teaspoon per pound. Do not use salt.

To insure penetration and retain juices, pierce meat deeply with a kitchen fork at approximately ½-inch intervals. Meat is ready for cooking immediately.

Place ribs in shallow roasting pan, meat side up; place sliced onions around ribs. Roast at 350° for 45 minutes. Remove from pan and transfer to barbecue or broiler.

Coals are ready when gray, shot with a ruddy glow. Place ribs, meaty side down, on grill set 6 inches above coals; barbecue for 15 minutes; turn, brush with Western Barbecue Sauce. Continue to cook until crispy brown and well done, about 30 to 45 minutes, frequently turning and brushing with sauce. To serve, cut into one- or two-rib pieces with kitchen scissors. Yield: 4 servings.

Pit Barbecue Pig (Georgia)

Barbecue (means from beard to tail) is a deft blending of Old World and New World cookery. The feast is usually held in summer when the weather is blistering hot. (We don't know why early spring and fall are passed up.) It is the custom in the Southeast to serve Brunswick Stew right along with the barbecue . . . sweet potatoes; boiled corn; slaw; garden salads; lemonade, barrels of it; watermelon, and boiled coffee.

To be greeted by the aroma of roasting meat and fragrant campfire coffee is a rare experience! We happily pass on the method for Georgia Barbecue Pig.

Select first-class meat, weighing from 35 to 50 pounds. Remove head near shoulders and feet just above the first joint. Cut or saw smoothly, longitudinally, through the center of the backbone so the pig will open perfectly flat. Cut out the thin flanks on each side of the carcass in a circular cut and throw away. Now it is ready for the pit. Run sharpened iron rods (or oak sticks) longitudinally through hams and shoulders, allowing extensions of both sides to catch the banks of the pit. This makes it convenient to hold carcass up and furnishes hand holds to turn.

These rods should be inserted near the skin and under the ribs in order that the neck, shoulders, and hams may go down lower into the pit for better cooking, and the rods under the ribs prevent their falling out when tender.

Laterally insert three or four small rods (iron or oak) which must be stuck through at proper intervals at sides extending through the carcass. This prevents meat from dropping off when done. The rods are strapped in place by using hay wire.

The pit should be 16 inches deep and as long as needed. Small green oak wood is best to use for making the red coals. The heat must not be too great when the cooking is first begun. When the meat is warm, baste with a strong solution of warm salt water containing a little cayenne pepper. This is continued at intervals until meat is nearly done. The moisture from the water prevents the meat from scorching. As often as the meat becomes dry, turn meat side up and baste with this salt solution. Never salt before cooking.

As the meat cooks more heat may be applied. Keep the coals bunched under the shoulders and hams, allowing the thin part of the pig to have less heat. When meat is nearly done, baste two or three times with plain warm water. This drives the salt in and washes off the outside salt. Always use warm water, never cold. Place carcass over pit, meat side down and cook this way, turning only long enough to baste the inside and allowing the skin to become hot from time to time. Meat must not burn and should be carefully watched.

When nearly done, place skin side down and begin basting with the barbecue sauce. When done and very tender, remove some of the coals from pit, turn skin down to brown and crisp. At this time it should be watched closely. The skin should be brown and crisp, not gummy. During this last cooking, the meat side is up and the basting done frequently.

The sauce, as well as the salt water, must be kept warm. Remember the cooking is slow and takes a long time. When ready to serve, cut up, putting the skin into one pan, meat into another. If the meat must wait for time to serve, baste frequently with butter sauce. Do not put any sauce over the skin, as this will make it soft and gummy. To be good it must be crisp and brittle.

Western Barbecue Sauce

- 1 teaspoon oregano
- 1 teaspoon garlic powder
- 3 teaspoons paprika
- 1 teaspoon seasoning salt
- 3 teaspoons chili powder
- 1 teaspoon ground cloves
- 2 teaspoons ground mustard
- 2 teaspoons onion salt
- 1 teaspoon smoke salt
- 4 bay leaves
- ½ teaspoon ground red pepper
- 1 teaspoon crushed red pepper
- 1 teaspoon salt
- 2 teaspoons brown sugar
- 1 cup garlic vinegar
- 1 cup tarragon vinegar
- 1 cup catsup
- 2 teaspoons Worcestershire sauce
- 1 cup shallot vinegar
- 1 cup grated onion
- 1 cup olive oil
- 1 cup tomato juice

Blend all ingredients and mix well. Bring to a boil, reduce heat, and simmer for 30 minutes. Yield: about 1½ to 2 quarts.

Tomato Creole Sauce (Open Kettle)

Mix together 1 quart sliced white onions and 12 finely chopped green peppers. Simmer until soft. Add about twice this bulk in tomatoes and cook together over a low heat until tender. Season to taste. Pack into clean, hot jars and seal immediately. Yield: 4 to 6 quarts.

South Carolina Barbecue Sauce

- 13 ounces salt
- 1 pint tomato juice
- 1 cup vinegar
- 2 (14-ounce) bottles catsup
  Juice of 4 lemons
- 2½ ounces ground red pepper
- 1¼ ounces black pepper

Place salt in mixing bowl, add tomato juice, vinegar, catsup, lemon juice, and pepper. Stir continually until thoroughly mixed. Yield: enough for an 80-pound pig.

Barbecue Sauce (Bayou Bengal Style)

- 4 pounds butter
- 1 gallon cooking oil
  Juice of 4 to 6 lemons (leave rinds of lemons in sauce)
- 1 bottle hot red pepper sauce
- 1 gallon catsup
- 2 quarts to 1 gallon rich meat stock rendered from bones of pork, lamb, beef or veal
- 2 pounds fresh or frozen okra, finely chopped
- 12 tablespoons prepared mustard
- 4 pounds finely chopped or ground onions
- 4 large sour pickles, finely chopped
- 4 (5-ounce) bottles Worcestershire sauce
- 2 cloves garlic, finely chopped
- 2 large green peppers, finely chopped
  Salt and pepper
  Spices to taste

Combine ingredients and heat. (If you use 1 gallon of broth, you may reduce the amount of butter. Reduce recipe proportionately for smaller quantities of meat.) Yield: 2 gallons.

Casseroles

Becoming more and more popular as a convenient cooking method, the casserole is actually a very old form of food preparation, taking its name from the first primitive pieces of shallow pottery which were referred to as casseroles.

But saying only that a casserole can be convenient and a good use of whatever happens to be handy is like saying beef makes good hamburgers — a perfectly true, but terribly inadequate, description.

The French have long considered casserole cookery a gourmet specialty of considerable import to be assembled with care and served with pride. However, all too often the American casserole doesn't get the credit it deserves.

Preparing a meal or a sizeable portion of a meal in one dish offers decided advantages. A one-dish meal cuts time spent in the kitchen and eliminates the worry of coordinating times and temperatures. Also, many casserole dishes are attractive enough to go from oven to table with no additional serving pieces necessary.

A casserole is based on much the same principle as soup, combining a variety of foods from bread to meat to vegetables sealed with spices, cheese, or milk. Most casseroles are ideal for advance preparation and many are suitable for freezer storage.

A casserole offers an excellent opportunity for variety and creativity from the simplest to the most lavish foods. With a chioce of recipes, and the most basic foods, a casserole can be anything from Monday night supper from Sunday's leftovers to Sunday dinner itself.

Call a casserole convenient, or by its middle name practical, but don't forget that its surname is appetizing.

Beef and Rice Casserole

2 pounds ground beef
1 teaspoon garlic salt
  Salt and pepper to taste
1 cup chopped onion
1 cup uncooked regular rice
1½ cups tomato juice
½ cup shredded American cheese

Season ground beef with garlic salt, salt, and pepper; brown. Sauté onion lightly; add to meat. Cook rice according to package directions and add with tomato juice to hot meat mixture. Place in a greased 2-quart casserole, cover with shredded cheese, and bake at 450° until bubbling. Yield: 8 servings.

Beef-Biscuit Pie

1½ teaspoons salt, divided
⅛ teaspoon pepper
3 tablespoons all-purpose flour
1½ pounds beef stew meat, cut in 1½-inch cubes
3 tablespoons shortening
3½ cups water
2 celery stalks with leaves, finely chopped
1 bay leaf
6 whole cloves
12 small white onions
6 medium carrots, sliced
3 medium potatoes, peeled and cut in halves

Blend together ½ teaspoon of the salt, the pepper, and flour, and toss lightly over meat to coat. Reserve leftover flour. Put shortening in a heavy skillet; add beef, and brown. Add water, ½ teaspoon of the salt, celery, bay leaf, and cloves. Cover; simmer 2 to 2½ hours, or until meat is almost tender. Add remaining salt and vegetables. Cover, and cook until vegetables are tender. Measure reserved flour, add enough to make 2 tablespoons. Add 3 tablespoons water; stir to a smooth paste. Gradually add to stew, stirring until thickened. Place in a 3-quart casserole and arrange biscuits around edge. Bake at 425° for 10 to 15 minutes, or until biscuits are well done. Yield: 6 to 8 servings.

Beef-Corn Casserole

1 pound ground chuck beef
3 tablespoons butter or margarine
  Seasoned salt to taste
1 cup uncooked regular rice
1 cup whole-kernel corn
½ cup chopped onion
½ cup minced green pepper
1 tablespoon Worcestershire sauce
1 teaspoon prepared mustard
1 teaspoon sugar
½ teaspoon paprika
2 cups tomatoes
½ cup buttered breadcrumbs
½ cup pimiento
3 strips breakfast bacon

Lightly brown beef by stirring and crumbling meat in butter; add seasoned salt to taste while cooking. Remove from pan and place in buttered 2-quart casserole; add rice, corn, onion, and green pepper. Then mix Worcestershire sauce, mustard, sugar, paprika, and tomatoes. Add more salt if needed. Pour tomato mixture over beef-corn mixture in casserole. Top with breadcrumbs, strips of pimiento, and bacon. Bake at 350° for 30 to 40 minutes. Yield: 6 servings.

Canned Meat Casserole

1 (12-ounce) can luncheon meat
1 cup fine breadcrumbs
¾ cup evaporated milk
2 medium onions
4 tablespoons all-purpose flour
3 tablespoons butter or margarine
1 (8½-ounce) can green peas
2½ cups sliced potatoes
   Liquid from peas plus water to
   make 1 cup
¼ teaspoon salt
   Dash pepper

Shred or chop luncheon meat. Add breadcrumbs and milk; blend well. Chop 1 onion very fine and blend into meat mixture. Shape mixture into 12 balls and coat well with flour.

Melt butter or margarine, add other onion, sliced thin, and cook gently until transparent. Remove onion and save. Brown meat balls. Grease a 2-quart casserole. Arrange meat balls, cooked onion, peas, and potatoes in two layers each. Add onions and drippings from frying meat. Add liquid and seasonings. Bake at 375° about 10 minutes. Yield: 6 servings.

Cheese and Beef Casserole

2 eggs, slightly beaten
1 cup milk
2 tablespoons Worcestershire sauce
2 teaspoons salt
   Pepper to taste
1 teaspoon dried mustard
2 cups dry breadcrumbs
2 pounds ground beef
4 tablespoons minced onion
¼ pound sharp Cheddar cheese, sliced

Combine eggs, milk, Worcestershire sauce, salt, pepper, mustard, and breadcrumbs. Allow to stand 5 minutes. Then add ground beef and onion and mix well. Place half the mixture in bottom of greased 8- x 8-inch baking dish. Arrange slices of cheese evenly on top. Cover with remainder of meat mixture. Bake at 350° for 40 to 50 minutes. Yield: 9 servings.

Company Beef Casserole

1 pound ground beef
2 tablespoons shortening
1 medium onion, chopped
2 cups canned tomatoes
1 tablespoon catsup
1 tablespoon steak sauce
¼ cup chopped green pepper
2 tablespoons chopped parsley
1 (5-ounce) package elbow macaroni
   Salt and pepper
1 (10½-ounce) can cream of
   mushroom soup
1 cup shredded Cheddar cheese

Brown ground beef in shortening in heavy skillet until all red color disappears. Add onion, tomatoes, catsup, steak sauce, green pepper, and parsley. Simmer for 30 minutes. Cook macaroni according to package directions. Combine macaroni and ground beef mixture in a 2-quart baking dish. Season to taste. Gently spoon mushroom soup into mixture. Mix lightly, lifting from the bottom. Sprinkle shredded cheese over the top. Bake at 350° for 30 minutes, or until top is bubbly and browned. Yield: 6 servings.

Corned Beef Casserole

1 (8-ounce) package macaroni
1 (10½-ounce) can cream of chicken soup
1 (12-ounce) can corned beef, cut into small pieces
1 cup milk
¼ pound Cheddar cheese, shredded
1 small onion, chopped
Buttered breadcrumbs

Cook macaroni according to package directions. Drain. Combine with soup, corned beef, milk, cheese, and onion. Put into a greased 1½-quart casserole dish and top with breadcrumbs. Bake at 350° about 30 minutes or until crumbs are browned. Yield: 6 to 8 servings.

Beef-Macaroni Casserole

1½ cups cut macaroni
2 teaspoons shortening
½ cup chopped onion
1 pound ground beef
1 teaspoon salt
1 teaspoon steak sauce
¼ teaspoon pepper
½ cup catsup
1½ cups shredded cheese
1 egg
1½ cups milk
½ cup catsup

Cook macaroni according to package directions. Drain, and place in a large mixing bowl. Place shortening in a skillet and cook the chopped onion until browned. Add ground beef and cook until all color is removed. Drain off excess fat. Add salt, steak sauce, pepper, and ½ cup catsup. Mix the meat and macaroni and let cool. When mix-ture is cool, add shredded cheese and mix well. Place mixture in two 1-quart casserole dishes.

To bake: Mix together egg, milk, and ½ cup catsup and additional shredded cheese, if desired. Pour over the cas-serole mixture and bake in a covered casserole dish at 350° about 25 to 30 minutes, or until it heats through and starts to bubble. Yield: 8 servings.

Note: This is an excellent dish to make ahead of time and freeze.

Skillet Dinner with Squash

1 pound ground beef
Bacon drippings
4 or 5 yellow crookneck squash, sliced
1 small green pepper, chopped
1 (16-ounce) can tomatoes
1 teaspoon salt
½ teaspoon pepper

Sear ground beef in bacon drippings in electric skillet. Add vegetables, salt and pepper. Cover and let simmer for 40 minutes. Yield: 4 to 6 servings.

Spanish Casserole

1 large onion, chopped
1 large green pepper, chopped
Shortening
1 pound ground beef
2 cups corn
1 (10½-ounce) can condensed tomato soup
2 (3-ounce) cans mushroom slices
1 teaspoon chili powder
1 (5-ounce) package noodles
½ cup shredded cheese

Sauté the onion and green pepper in small amount of shortening. Add ground beef and brown. Then add corn, soup, mushrooms, and chili powder. Cook the noodles for 5 minutes. Drain and add to meat mixture. Put in a 2-quart baking dish and bake at 350° for 30 minutes. Yield: 8 servings.

Hamburger-Baked Beans Casserole

    2 strips bacon
    1 medium onion, chopped
    1 pound ground hamburger meat
    2 (1-pound) cans pork and beans
  ½ cup molasses
  ½ cup catsup
  ½ teaspoon dry mustard
    1 teaspoon salt
    1 tablespoon Worcestershire sauce

Cut bacon into small pieces. Cook in frying pan with onion until onion has partially cooked. Add hamburger meat and cook until meat is white. Add other ingredients and mix well. Spoon mixture into a 2-quart baking dish and bake at 375° for 30 minutes. Yield: 6 to 8 servings.

Ranch Casserole

1 ½ pounds ground beef
    2 tablespoons shortening
    1 teaspoon salt
    1 package onion soup mix
  ½ cup water
    1 cup catsup
    2 tablespoons prepared mustard
    2 tablespoons vinegar
  ½ cup piccalilli relish

Sauté meat in shortening. Add other ingredients and cook in covered skillet about 30 minutes, or bake in covered casserole at 325° for 30 to 40 minutes. Serve over rice or on buns. Yield: 6 to 8 servings.

Simply Delicious Skillet Dinner

    1 tablespoon shortening
  ½ pound ground beef
    1 medium onion, chopped
    1 small clove garlic, minced
    2 tablespoons minced parsley
    1 (6-ounce) can tomato paste
2 ¼ cups water
    1 teaspoon sugar
    1 teaspoon salt
       Dash pepper
    1 (5-ounce) package noodles
       Parmesan cheese

Melt shortening in heavy skillet; add ground beef, onion, garlic, and parsley. Brown lightly. Combine tomato paste with water, sugar, salt, and pepper, mixing until smooth. Add to meat mixture, mixing well. Cover, reduce heat, and simmer for 10 minutes. Add noodles, cover, and cook until noodles are tender, stirring occasionally. Serve with grated Parmesan cheese. Yield: 4 servings.

Easy Chicken Soufflé

       3 tablespoons butter or margarine
       3 tablespoons all-purpose flour
       1 cup milk
          Pinch salt
       2 well beaten egg yolks
  1⅓ cups boned, diced, cooked chicken
       1 teaspoon onion juice
       2 well beaten egg whites
       ¼ teaspoon cornstarch
       ¼ teaspoon sugar

Make a cream sauce of the butter or margarine, flour, milk, and salt. Add beaten egg yolks, diced chicken, and onion juice. When cool, add beaten egg whites into which ¼ teaspoon each of cornstarch and sugar have been added when half beaten.

Place mixture into a 1-quart buttered casserole. Place in a pan of hot water and bake at 325° for 1 hour. Yield: 6 servings.

Chicken Paprika Casserole

       1 (10½-ounce) can cream of
          mushroom soup
       ¼ cup milk
  1⅓ cups diced, cooked chicken
       1 teaspoon paprika
       ½ teaspoon Worcestershire sauce
     14 salted crackers
          Butter or margarine
          Sliced mushrooms
          Pimiento

Combine soup and milk. Add chicken and seasonings. Pour into greased 1½-quart casserole. Cover with cracker crumbs and dot with butter or margarine. Bake at 350° about 20 minutes. Garnish with sliced mushrooms and pimiento, if desired. Yield: 4 servings.

Chicken and Rice Casserole

       1 (10½-ounce) can cream of
          chicken soup
       ½ cup milk
       ½ cup cubed, cooked chicken
       3 cups cooked rice
       1 cup shredded American cheese
       1 cup cooked green peas
       ¼ cup chopped pimientos

Blend chicken soup and milk in a 1½-quart greased casserole. Then stir in cubed chicken, cooked rice, cheese, peas, and pimientos. Bake at 375° about 25 minutes. Yield: 8 servings.

Cheese-Rice Casserole

       3 cups cooked rice
  1½ cups cooked green peas
       ½ pound American cheese, shredded
       1 egg, beaten
  2½ cups white sauce
       2 tablespoons butter or margarine

Place rice, peas, and cheese in alternating layers in a greased casserole, ending with the cheese layer. Combine egg and white sauce. Pour into casserole. Dot with butter or margarine. Bake at 375° about 25 minutes. Yield: 6 servings.

Macaroni and Cheese

       2 tablespoons butter or margarine
       2 tablespoons all-purpose flour
  1½ cups milk
       2 eggs
       1 cup shredded Cheddar cheese
       ½ teaspoon Worcestershire sauce
       3 drops Tabasco sauce
  1½ cups cooked macaroni

Melt butter or margarine in top of double boiler; add flour, and stir until well blended. Reserve 2 tablespoons of the milk to mix with eggs. Pour remaining milk gradually into butter-flour mixture, stirring constantly. Cook until smooth. Pour gradually into slightly beaten eggs mixed with milk. Add cheese, and stir until melted. Add Worcestershire sauce and Tabasco and pour over macaroni in a 1½-quart baking dish. Bake at 350° for 35 minutes. Yield: 6 servings.

Cheese Soufflé

    1 tablespoon butter
    1 clove garlic
    5 slices white bread (buttered and
       cut into cubes)
    ½ pound cheese, shredded
    4 eggs
    2 cups milk
       Tabasco sauce to taste
    1 teaspoon Worcestershire sauce
    1 teaspoon dry mustard
       Salt and pepper

Rub 1-quart casserole dish with butter and garlic. Then make alternate layers of cubed bread and shredded cheese. Beat eggs, milk, Tabasco sauce, Worcestershire sauce, dry mustard, salt, and pepper together. Pour over layered bread and cheese in the prepared casserole dish. Let stand for 6

hours or more. Place casserole dish in a pan of water and bake at 300° for 1½ hours. Yield: 4 to 6 servings.

Cheese Pudding

    8 slices white bread
    ⅓ cup butter or margarine
    2 cups shredded cheese
    3 cups milk
    4 eggs
 1 ⅓ teaspoons salt
    ⅓ teaspoon dry mustard

Spread the bread with butter or margarine and cut each slice into four pieces. Alternate layers of cheese and bread in greased, flat baking dish so that cheese is on top. Combine milk, eggs, salt, and mustard. Pour mixture over cheese and bread. Let stand in refrigerator overnight. Bake at 325° for about 40 minutes. Yield: 8 servings.

Green Rice

    ¾ cup shredded cheese
    6 tablespoons minced parsley
    ¼ teaspoon salt
    2 tablespoons chopped onion
    3 tablespoons melted butter or
       margarine
 2 ¼ cups cooked rice
    ¾ cup milk
    1 egg, beaten

Combine cheese, parsley, salt, onion, butter or margarine, and rice. Combine milk and egg and add to rice mixture. Blend thoroughly; turn into an oiled ring mold or 2-quart baking dish. Cover, and bake at 350° for 1 hour. Yield: 6 servings.

Grits Casserole

1 cup regular grits
3 cups boiling water
½ teaspoon salt
½ stick butter or margarine
4 eggs
1 cup milk
¼ cup shredded Cheddar cheese

Pour the grits into boiling water to which salt has been added. Mix well, and cook until thickened. Add the butter or margarine, beaten eggs, milk, and cheese. Stir thoroughly and place in a greased 2-quart casserole. Bake at 350° about 30 minutes. Yield: 4 to 6 servings.

Mexican Rice Casserole

4 slices bacon and drippings
½ cup chopped onion
½ cup chopped green pepper
1 cup uncooked regular rice
1 pound ground beef
1 small clove garlic
1¾ cups water
1 (8-ounce) can tomato sauce
¾ cup raisins
2 teaspoons salt
1 tablespoon chili powder
2½ cups shredded cheese

Fry bacon until crisp. Remove from pan and drain. Add onion and pepper to drippings and cook until tender. Add rice and cook until golden. Stir in beef and garlic; cook until meat is almost done. Stir in water, tomato sauce, raisins, and seasonings. Heat to boiling. Reduce heat, cover and simmer for 20 minutes. Spoon half of mixture into a greased 2-quart casserole. Sprinkle

with half of cheese and half of crumbled bacon. Add remainder of meat mixture and top with remaining cheese and bacon. Bake at 450° about 15 minutes or until cheese is bubbly. Yield: 8 servings.

Corn and Sausage Casserole

4 eggs
1 (1-pound) can cream-style corn
1 teaspoon salt
¼ teaspoon pepper
1 cup soft breadcrumbs
1 pound pork sausage
½ cup cracker crumbs

Beat eggs; add corn, salt, pepper, breadcrumbs, and sausage. Put in greased 2- to 3-quart casserole. Add cracker crumbs on top. Bake uncovered at 350° for 50 minutes. Yield: 6 to 8 servings.

Hot Sausage Pie

1 pound pork sausage
2 cups canned tomatoes
2 cups whole-kernel corn
2 tablespoons minced onion
2 tablespoons bacon drippings
3 tablespoons all-purpose flour
1 teaspoon sugar
1 teaspoon salt
  Buttered breadcrumbs

Cook sausage slowly in skillet until brown, crumbly, and well done. Add tomatoes and drained corn; simmer for 10 minutes. Sauté onion in bacon drippings; mix flour, sugar, and salt; blend with bacon drippings and onion. Add to sausage and vegetables and heat to boiling point. Spoon into 2-quart baking dish; top with buttered breadcrumbs and bake at 425° for 20 minutes, or until topping is browned. Serve hot. Yield: 6 to 8 servings.

Pork and Celery Pie

1 *pound ground lean pork shoulder*
1¼ *teaspoons salt*
  Dash pepper
1 *cup thinly sliced carrots*
1 *cup diced potatoes*
1 *tablespoon shortening*
1 *(10½-ounce) can condensed cream of celery soup*
¾ *cup water*
  Pastry for four individual pies

Combine meat, seasonings, carrots, and potatoes. Cook in melted shortening in heavy skillet until lightly brown. Blend in soup and water. Pour into four greased individual casseroles. Top with piecrust. Bake at 400° about 30 minutes, or until piecrust is done. Yield: 4 servings.

Pork Chop-Vegetable Casserole

8 *pork chops*
½ *cup chopped onion*
½ *cup chopped green pepper*
1 *(10½-ounce) can cream of mushroom soup*
1 *cup water*
3 *cups cooked regular rice*
2 *cups cooked green peas*
1 *teaspoon salt*
⅛ *teaspoon pepper*

Place pork chops in a skillet and brown on both sides. Lift chops out of skillet. Place onion and green pepper in the skillet and cook until tender. Add a small amount of shortening if needed to cook the onion and pepper. Add mushroom soup, water, rice, peas, salt, and pepper. Mix well. Pour half the rice and pea mixture into a greased 2-quart baking dish. Arrange half the pork chops over the rice and peas. Add the rest of the rice and peas, and top with the remaining pork chops. Bake at 350° for 30 minutes. Yield: 8 servings.

Skillet Sausage and Sweets

1 *(10½-ounce) can condensed consommé*
1 *tablespoon cornstarch*
2 *tablespoons brown sugar*
1 *tablespoon orange juice*
1 *teaspoon grated lemon rind*
1 *(1-pound, 7-ounce) can sweet potatoes, drained*
1 *pound sausage links, cooked*
8 *apple slices (about 1 medium cooking apple)*
  Chopped pecans (optional)

Gradually blend consommé into cornstarch; add sugar, juice, and lemon rind. Heat; stir until thickened. Add potatoes, sausage, and apple slices. Cook over low heat about 20 minutes, spooning glaze over ingredients. Garnish with pecans, if desired. Yield: 4 servings.

Supper Sausage Casserole

        1 pound sausage
        6 cooked potatoes, sliced
        1 cup cooked lima beans
        1 teaspoon salt
      ½ cup milk
      ¼ cup butter or margarine
      ½ cup dry breadcrumbs

Brown sausage in skillet. Place alternate layers of potatoes, sausage, and lima beans in a well greased 1½-quart baking dish. Add 2 tablespoons liquid from skillet to salt and milk, and pour over casserole. Mix melted butter or margarine with breadcrumbs and toss lightly with fork. Sprinkle over casserole. Bake at 350° for 30 minutes. Yield: 6 servings.

Sausage-Bean Bake

      ¼ cup molasses
        3 tablespoons prepared mustard
        2 tablespoons vinegar or freshly
            squeezed lemon juice
        2 teaspoons Worcestershire sauce
      ¼ teaspoon Tabasco sauce
        2 (1-pound) cans baked beans
        2 cups cooked apple slices
        1 pound pork link sausage

Combine molasses and mustard; stir in vinegar or lemon juice, Worcestershire sauce, and Tabasco. Turn baked beans and apple slices into 1½-quart casserole; stir in molasses mixture. Bake at 450° for 30 minutes. While beans are cooking, place sausage links in cold skillet. Cook over low heat for 12 to 15 minutes, turning often until browned. Pour off fat as it accumulates. To serve, place sausage on top of beans. Yield: 8 to 10 servings.

Applesauce-Sweet Potato-Ham Scallop

        4 medium sweet potatoes
        2 cups canned applesauce
      ¼ cup brown sugar
      ½ teaspoon ground nutmeg
    1¼ pound ham slice
        1 teaspoon dry mustard
        3 tablespoons brown sugar
      ½ teaspoon ground nutmeg
        3 tablespoons vinegar

Pare sweet potatoes; halve lengthwise. Combine applesauce, sugar, and ½ teaspoon nutmeg. Arrange alternate layers of sweet potatoes and applesauce mixture in flat casserole dish; place ham slice on top. Cover and bake at 350° for 1 hour, or until sweet potatoes and ham are tender. About 20 minutes before casserole is done, make a topping for the ham by combining the dry mustard, brown sugar, ½ teaspoon nutmeg, and vinegar. Spread on top of ham. Yield: 4 to 6 servings.

Deep Dish Oyster Pie

           Pastry for double crust pie
        1 pint oysters, drained
        1 cup chopped celery
        1 teaspoon salt
      ½ teaspoon pepper
      ½ cup butter or margarine
        3 cups medium white sauce

Make pastry and line a shallow baking dish with half of it. Pick over oysters to remove any bits of shell. Place half of oysters on the pastry, add half the celery, salt, pepper, butter or margarine, and white sauce. Then add second layer of oysters and other ingredients. Top with pastry. Bake at 375° for 45 minutes. Yield: 4 to 6 servings.

Oyster Cream Casserole

- 2 cups oysters, drained
- 1 cup soft breadcrumbs
- 2 eggs, beaten
- 1 cup commercial sour cream
- 1 teaspoon salt
- 1 tablespoon freshly squeezed lemon juice
- 1 tablespoon chopped parsley
- ¼ teaspoon pepper

Combine all ingredients and pour into a well buttered 1½-quart casserole. Bake at 350° for 35 to 40 minutes. Serve with cheese biscuits and green salad with celery seed dressing. For dessert, serve luscious pineapple cake. Yield: 4 servings.

Crab Casserole

- 1 pound crabmeat
- ½ cup chopped celery
- 2 tablespoons chopped green pepper
- ¼ cup melted butter or margarine
- 2 tablespoons all-purpose flour
- 1 cup milk
- 1 egg yolk, beaten
- 2 tablespoons freshly squeezed lemon juice
- ½ teaspoon salt
- ⅛ teaspoon pepper
- 1 tablespoon melted butter or margarine
- ¼ cup dry breadcrumbs

Remove all shell or cartilage from crabmeat. Cook celery and green pepper in butter or margarine until tender. Blend in flour. Add milk gradually and cook until thick, stirring constantly. Stir a little of the hot sauce into egg yolk; add to remaining sauce, stirring constantly. Add lemon juice, seasonings, and crabmeat. Combine butter or margarine and breadcrumbs; sprinkle over casserole. Place in a well greased 1-quart casserole. Bake at 350° for 20 to 25 minutes, or until brown. Yield: 6 servings.

Jambalaya Casserole

- 1 (5-ounce) package elbow spaghetti
- 2 strips bacon, chopped
- ½ cup chopped onion
- ½ cup chopped green pepper
- ½ clove garlic, minced
- 2 tablespoons all-purpose flour
- 2¼ cups canned tomatoes
- ½ pound cubed boiled ham
- 1 cup cooked cleaned shrimp
- ¼ cup breadcrumbs
- 2 tablespoons grated Parmesan cheese
- 2 tablespoons melted butter or margarine

Cook spaghetti in boiling, salted water until tender. Drain and rinse. Brown chopped bacon in skillet. Add onion, green pepper, and garlic. Brown and stir in flour. Add tomatoes, and cook until thickened, stirring constantly. Add spaghetti, ham, and shrimp. Pour into 1½-quart casserole. Combine breadcrumbs, cheese, and butter or margarine, and sprinkle over casserole. Bake at 350° about 30 minutes. Yield: 4 servings.

Salmon Casserole

    1 (8-ounce) package elbow macaroni
    ½ cup minced onion
    2 tablespoons butter
    1 can cream of celery soup
    ⅔ cup milk
    ½ pound sharp shredded cheese
    1 teaspoon salt
      Dash pepper
    ½ teaspoon dry mustard
    1 (1-pound) can salmon
    1 package frozen green peas
    2 tablespoons grated Parmesan cheese

Cook macaroni according to package directions; drain. Sauté onion in butter; add soup, milk, shredded cheese, and seasonings. Stir until cheese melts. Remove bones from salmon and thaw peas slightly to separate. Combine macaroni with sauce and add salmon and peas. Pour into a greased 2-quart casserole. Sprinkle with cheese and bake at 350° for 30 to 40 minutes. Yield: 6 servings.

Shrimp Thermidor

    ¾ pound cooked, peeled, cleaned shrimp
    1 (4-ounce) can mushroom stems and
      pieces, drained
    ¼ cup butter or margarine, melted
    ¼ cup all-purpose flour
    1 teaspoon Worcestershire sauce
    ½ teaspoon dry mustard
    ¼ teaspoon salt
      Dash cayenne pepper
    2 cups milk
    ½ cup pitted ripe olives, sliced crosswise
      Grated Parmesan cheese
      Paprika

Cut large shrimp in half. Sauté mushrooms in butter or margarine for 5 minutes. Blend in flour and seasonings. Add milk gradually and cook until thick, stirring constantly. Add olives and shrimp. Place in six well greased, individual shells or 5-ounce custard cups. Sprinkle with cheese and paprika. Bake at 400° for 10 to 15 minutes or until cheese browns. Yield: 6 servings.

Shrimp and Corn au Gratin

    ¼ package (2 ounces) medium noodles
    2 teaspoons salt
    3 tablespoons margarine
    3 tablespoons all-purpose flour
      About 1 cup milk
    ½ teaspoon salt
    ¾ cup shredded Cheddar cheese
    1 (12-ounce) can whole-kernel corn
    1 (4-ounce) can chopped mushrooms
    1 (5-ounce) can shrimp, deveined

Cook noodles in 2 quarts boiling water until just tender (8 to 10 minutes). While noodles cook, make sauce. Drain liquid from corn and mushrooms into measuring cup. Add enough milk to make 1½ cups. Melt margarine in saucepan and stir in flour, mixing until smooth. Gradually add milk mixture, stirring constantly until thickened. Remove from heat and add ½ teaspoon salt and ½ cup shredded cheese. Stir until cheese is melted. Drain noodles and rinse with hot water. Return drained noodles to cooking pan. Add corn, mushrooms, and shrimp. Pour cheese sauce over all and mix lightly with a fork. Turn into well greased 1½-quart baking dish. Sprinkle remaining ¼ cup cheese over top. Bake casserole at 400° for 30 minutes. Yield: 6 servings.

Shrimp Casserole

¾ *pound cooked, peeled, cleaned shrimp*
½ *cup chopped celery*
¼ *cup chopped green pepper*
3 *tablespoons chopped onion*
¼ *cup melted butter or margarine*
6 *tablespoons all-purpose flour*
1 *teaspoon salt*
1 *(10½-ounce) can cream of mushroom soup*
1½ *cups milk*
1 *tablespoon melted butter or margarine*
¼ *cup dry breadcrumbs*

Cut large shrimp in half. Cook vegetables in butter or margarine until tender; blend in flour and salt. Combine soup and milk; add to vegetable mixture and cook until thick, stirring constantly. Add shrimp and pour into a well greased 1-quart casserole. Combine melted butter or margarine and breadcrumbs; sprinkle over top of casserole. Bake at 400° about 10 minutes. Yield: 6 servings.

Tuna-Noodle Casserole

1 *(5.5-ounce) package egg noodles with sour cream cheese sauce mix*
2 *tablespoons butter or margarine*
⅔ *cup milk*
1 *tablespoon chopped chives*
2 *tablespoons chopped pimiento*
1 *(6½-ounce) can tuna, drained*
 Salt
 Pepper
 Paprika

Cook noodles according to package directions. Add butter, milk, sauce mix, chives, and pimiento. Mix well. Stir in tuna; season to taste with salt and pepper. Pour into 1-quart casserole; sprinkle top with paprika. Cover. Bake at 350° about 25 minutes. Yield: 4 servings.

Tuna-Rice Casserole

3 *cups hot cooked rice*
1 *cup flaked tuna*
½ *cup sliced stuffed olives*
2 *hard-cooked eggs, sliced*
¼ *teaspoon salt*
 Dash pepper
¾ *cup salad dressing or mayonnaise*
½ *cup water*
 Buttered breadcrumbs

Place alternate layers of rice, tuna, olives, and eggs in a greased 1½-quart casserole. Place in pan of hot water. Bake, covered, at 400° for 15 minutes. Add salt and pepper to salad dressing or mayonnaise. Gradually add water, stirring after each addition until smooth. Pour over contents of casserole and top with buttered breadcrumbs. Bake, uncovered, about 15 minutes longer. If overcooked, sauce will curdle. Serve hot. Yield: 6 to 8 servings.

Tuna Quickie Casserole

1 (4-ounce) package broad noodles
2 teaspoons salt
3 cups boiling water
1 (10½-ounce) can condensed cream
   of mushroom soup
⅓ cup milk
1 (7-ounce) can tuna
1 cup cooked green peas
   Buttered breadcrumbs

Cook noodles in boiling salted water for about 2 minutes. Cover, remove from heat, and let stand for about 10 minutes. Meanwhile, combine mushroom soup, milk, tuna, and peas. Rinse noodles with warm water and drain well. Fold noodles into tuna mixture; pour into a greased 1-quart casserole. Sprinkle with breadcrumbs and bake at 350° for about 30 minutes. Yield: 4 servings.

Tuna au Gratin

1 tablespoon butter or margarine
⅓ cup minced green pepper
3 tablespoons minced onion
2 tablespoons butter or margarine
2 tablespoons all-purpose flour
1 cup milk
1 (7-ounce) can tuna, drained
½ teaspoon salt
⅛ teaspoon freshly ground pepper
½ teaspoon Worcestershire sauce
1½ tablespoons chopped pimiento

Melt 1 tablespoon butter or margarine in heavy skillet over low heat. Add green pepper and onion; sauté for 5 minutes. Melt 2 tablespoons butter or margarine in a saucepan over low heat; add flour, and blend. Add milk and cook until thick, stirring constantly. Break tuna into large chunks. Add salt, pepper, Worcestershire sauce, pimiento, tuna, sautéed green pepper and onion. Pour into four greased individual casseroles. Bake at 375° for 15 minutes, or until bubbly. Serve hot. Yield: 4 servings.

Tuna Casserole

3 cups hot cooked rice
1 cup flaked tuna
½ cup sliced stuffed olives
2 hard-cooked eggs, sliced
¼ teaspoon salt
   Dash pepper
1 cup salad dressing
½ cup milk

Divide rice and reserve 1 cup for topping; also save 1 slice of stuffed olive and 3 slices hard-cooked eggs for garnish.

Place alternate layers of rice, tuna, olives, and eggs in a 1¾-quart greased casserole. Place in a pan of hot water, and bake, covered, at 400° about 15 minutes. Add salt and pepper to salad dressing. Gradually add milk, stirring until smooth. Pour over contents of casserole and top with the reserved 1 cup cooked rice. Bake, uncovered, about 15 minutes longer; do not overcook. If overcooked, sauce will curdle. Serve hot. Yield: 6 to 8 servings.

Note: All of the rice may be used in the layers and buttered breadcrumbs may be used for a topping.

Seafood Medley Casserole

1 pound fish fillets (sole, haddock, flounder)
1 pound sea scallops
½ pound cooked, cleaned shrimp (optional)
1 (7½-ounce) can crab or lobster meat
1 green pepper, diced
4 tablespoons butter or margarine
4 tablespoons all-purpose flour
¼ teaspoon dry mustard
1 teaspoon salt
1 cup heavy cream
2 tablespoons finely chopped onion
½ teaspoon Tabasco sauce
4 tablespoons freshly grated Parmesan cheese, divided
2 cups toasted bread cubes

Poach fillets in water seasoned with a little parsley, onion, carrot, celery leaves, salt, and Tabasco. Drain; reserve 1 cup of liquid for cream sauce. With a fork, gently break fillets into pieces and place in buttered 2-quart casserole. Cut scallops into bite-size pieces and add to fillets in casserole with shrimp, crabmeat and green pepper. Toss lightly. To make cream sauce, melt butter in heavy saucepan; blend in flour, dry mustard, and salt. Gradually add reserved 1 cup fish liquid and heavy cream, stirring constantly until mixture thickens and comes to a boil. Remove from heat and stir in onion, Tabasco, and 2 tablespoons Parmesan cheese. Mix with fish in casserole. Top with bread cubes and sprinkle on cheese. Bake at 350° for 30 minutes. Yield: 8 main dish servings.

Asparagus Casserole

2 tablespoons butter or margarine
2 tablespoons all-purpose flour
2 tablespoons asparagus liquid
1 cup cream
½ teaspoon salt
½ teaspoon pepper
 Dash paprika
½ cup shredded cheese
1 (3-ounce) can mushrooms
2 (14½-ounce) cans asparagus
 Cracker crumbs

Melt butter or margarine and gradually add flour, stirring constantly. Add asparagus liquid, and mix well. Add cream, stirring constantly until thick. Season with salt, pepper, and paprika. Add cheese, and stir until melted. Add mushrooms. Line bottom of 1½-quart casserole with one can of the drained asparagus. Cover with sauce. Add second can of asparagus and cracker crumbs. Bake at 350° for about 25 minutes. Yield: 6 servings.

Asparagus-Almond Casserole

1 (14½-ounce) can asparagus
½ to 1 cup crushed potato chips
⅓ cup chopped almonds
1 (10½-ounce) can cream of mushroom soup

Place a layer of asparagus in a 1-quart casserole, then a layer of potato chips, then chopped almonds. Repeat. Pour mushroom soup over this. If soup is very thick, add small amount of milk. Bake 15 minutes at 375°. Yield: 4 to 6 servings.

Asparagus Casserole with Ham

>   2   tablespoons butter
>   1   tablespoon all-purpose flour
>   1   can cream of mushroom soup
> ¼   teaspoon prepared mustard
>   1   (14½-ounce) can asparagus
>   1   (17-ounce) can green peas
>   4   hard-cooked eggs, sliced
>   1   cup chopped cooked ham
> ½   cup buttered breadcrumbs
> ¼   cup shredded cheese

Blend butter and flour in a saucepan. Add mushroom soup and cook until thick; stir in mustard. Combine the asparagus, peas, eggs, and ham in a 2-quart casserole; pour mushroom sauce over all. Mix breadcrumbs with cheese. Spread over top of casserole. Bake at 300° for 30 minutes, or until brown and bubbly. Yield: 4 to 6 servings.

Asparagus-Egg Casserole

>   2   cups cooked, fresh or canned,
>   asparagus
>   2   tablespoons butter or margarine
>   2   tablespoons all-purpose flour
> ½   teaspoon salt
>   Dash pepper
>   1   cup milk
>   1   cup shredded American cheese
>   1   cup buttered breadcrumbs
>   4   hard-cooked eggs, sliced

Prepare asparagus (drain canned asparagus). Make white sauce of butter or margarine, flour, salt, pepper, and milk. Stir in cheese. Place half of buttered breadcrumbs in greased 1½-quart casserole. Place alternate layers of eggs, asparagus, and cheese sauce on the breadcrumbs. Cover top with remaining breadcrumbs. Bake at 350° for 15 minutes. Yield: 8 servings.

Lima Bean Casserole

> ½   pound dried lima beans
>   4   slices bacon, diced
>   2   medium onions, sliced
> ⅔   teaspoon salt
> ¼   teaspoon pepper
> ½   teaspoon poultry seasoning
>   1   cup milk
>   1   cup buttered breadcrumbs

Soak beans overnight in water to cover. In morning, bring slowly to boiling point. Simmer until tender but not broken, and drain. Cook bacon, remove from pan, and cook onions in drippings. Grease deep baking dish, put into it a layer of beans, then a layer of onions, seasonings, and diced bacon. Repeat until all ingredients are used. Pour in milk, sprinkle buttered breadcrumbs over all, and bake at 375° for 25 to 30 minutes. Yield: 4 servings.

Vegetable Medley Casserole

> 1½   cups cubed potatoes
>   2   cups shredded cabbage
> 1½   cups sliced small carrots
> ¾   cup sliced onions
>   1   cup shredded cheese
>   1   cup medium white sauce
> 1½   cups shredded corn cereal
>   2   tablespoons melted butter or
>   margarine

Cook potatoes in small amount of boiling salted water about 10 minutes. Add cabbage, carrots, and onions. Cover and cook until tender, about 15 minutes. Drain. Arrange in 1½-quart casserole or individual casseroles. Melt cheese in white sauce. Pour over vegetables. Sprinkle with crumbled cereal mixed with melted butter. Bake at 375° about 15 minutes. Yield: 4 to 6 servings.

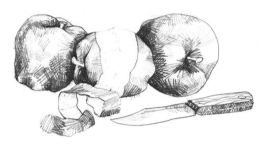

Glazed Sweet Potato Casserole

1 cup white corn syrup
¼ cup butter or margarine
⅓ cup pineapple juice
8 to 10 canned or cooked sweet potatoes, halved
¾ cup (9-ounce can) pineapple tidbits, drained
⅓ cup pecan halves

Combine corn syrup, butter or margarine, and pineapple juice in a saucepan. Place over medium heat and simmer for 5 minutes. Place potatoes in greased 13- x 9- x 2-inch baking dish. Sprinkle with pineapple tidbits and pecans. Add syrup mixture. Bake at 375° for 40 minutes. Baste every 10 minutes with

syrup mixture. Serve hot. Yield: 6 to 8 servings.

Broccoli Casserole

3 (10-ounce) packages frozen broccoli
1 (6-ounce) package cream cheese with chives
2 (10-ounce) cans frozen cream of shrimp soup
Juice of 1 lemon
Paprika

Cook broccoli as directed on package; drain. Mix cream of shrimp soup, cream cheese, and lemon juice. In a greased 2-quart casserole, alternate layers of broccoli and soup mixture. Sprinkle top with paprika. Bake at 350° for 30 minutes. Yield: 8 servings.

Zucchini-Cheese Bake

3 medium zucchini
1 (4¾-ounce) can chicken spread
1 (10½-ounce) can condensed cheese soup
¼ cup milk
½ teaspoon dry mustard
½ cup combination grain cereal flakes

Trim zucchini and cut each in half lengthwise. Parboil for 10 minutes in salted water in a large frying pan. Drain and arrange in a shallow 2-quart baking dish.

Spread top of each zucchini half with chicken spread, dividing evenly. Mix soup, milk, and mustard. Pour mixture over zucchini and sprinkle with cereal. Bake at 350° for 30 minutes or until tender. Yield: 6 servings.

Eggplant Casserole

2 cups diced eggplant
½ cup diced celery
¼ cup chopped onion
1 egg, slightly beaten
⅓ cup milk or cream
2 tablespoons butter or margarine
1 cup breadcrumbs
½ cup shredded cheese

Peel, dice, and measure eggplant. Cook until tender in a small amount of boiling salted water. Sauté celery and onion until tender. Drain eggplant; add to celery and onions, and sauté slightly. Remove from heat, and add beaten egg and milk or cream. Pour in a 1-quart baking dish. Dot with butter or margarine, sprinkle with breadcrumbs, and cover with shredded cheese. Bake at 350° for 30 minutes. Yield: 6 servings.

Note: You may add ½ to 1 cup of finely diced ham, roast, or other leftover meat to this recipe.

Squash Casserole

1½ pounds yellow squash
1 small onion, minced
1 tablespoon minced parsley
1 egg, slightly beaten
¼ cup milk
½ cup cottage cheese, sieved
½ teaspoon salt
½ teaspoon pepper
1 teaspoon sugar
¼ cup finely chopped pecans

Parboil squash, mash, and add all other ingredients except nuts. Place in 1-quart casserole, and sprinkle pecans over the top. Bake at 350° about 30 to 45 minutes, or until top is browned. Yield: 6 to 8 servings.

Hominy Casserole

4 slices bacon
6 tablespoons all-purpose flour
1 teaspoon sugar
1 teaspoon salt
1 teaspoon chili powder
2¼ cups tomatoes
3 cups cooked hominy
2 cups onion rings
1 cup shredded American cheese

Sauté bacon in large frying pan until crisp; set aside; add enough shortening to bacon drippings in pan to make 4 tablespoons. Blend in flour, sugar, salt, and chili powder; stir in tomatoes and cook, stirring constantly, until mixture is thick. Layer hominy, onion rings, and tomato mixture in a 2-quart baking dish. Sprinkle with cheese and top with bacon slices. Bake at 325° about 25 minutes. Yield: 6 servings.

Corn and Tomato Scallop

¼ cup butter or margarine
¼ cup all-purpose flour
1 cup milk
1 tablespoon sugar
½ teaspoon salt
2 cups canned whole-kernel corn, drained
1 cup canned tomatoes, drained
¾ cup dry breadcrumbs
2 tablespoons butter, melted

Make white sauce with ¼ cup butter, flour, and milk. Add sugar, salt, corn, and tomatoes. Pour into a buttered 8-inch square baking dish and cover with buttered crumbs. Bake at 350° for 45 minutes. Yield: 6 to 8 servings .

Vegetables

As is the case with so many of our Southern foods and foodways, the earliest cultivation and cooking of vegetables in this region came from the Indians. They gave us, among other vegetables, sweet potatoes and corn, which were to become the basis for a variety of dishes from bread to dessert.

The word vegetable comes from a Latin root which means "to enliven." In hard times, it was the vegetables which so readily sprang from the rich Southern soil that not only enlivened meals but kept many a family going. Toward the end of winter, as the vegetables stored from the preceding summer ran out, people often suffered from "the six-weeks-want" and doctored themselves with sulphur and molasses.

In addition to the cultivated vegetables so important in pioneer times of want or plenty, there were always the wild greens which are thought of as so intrinsically Southern. Dandelion, burdock, mustard, and, of course, turnip greens were delicacies as well as staples.

With modern refrigeration and marketing, it is no longer necessary to gather our vegetables the night before they are to be cooked or to suffer from "the six-weeks-want" of our great-grandmother's day, but their recipes for preparing vegetables will do any modern table proud.

Fresh Asparagus with Brown Butter

2 pounds fresh asparagus
  Boiling salted water
¼ pound butter

Break off the woody base of asparagus spears. Wash stalks well in cold water, then trim off the scales with a small knife. Wash again. Tie the stalks in serving-size bundles (allowing 1 pound for 3 persons). Stand bundles upright in an asparagus cooker or a deep saucepan. Pour in boiling salted water to a depth of about 1 inch, salt lightly, and cover. Cook for 15 minutes. Drain.

While asparagus is cooking, melt butter in heavy pan over low heat, stirring occasionally and watching carefully until butter browns. Serve over hot cooked and drained asparagus. Yield: 6 servings.

Fresh Asparagus with Butter And Egg Sauce on Toast

2 pounds fresh asparagus
1 teaspoon salt
  Boiling water
6 slices whole wheat toast
⅓ cup butter or margarine
1 tablespoon freshly squeezed lemon juice
¼ teaspoon ground nutmeg
⅛ teaspoon ground white pepper
3 hard-cooked eggs

Wash asparagus, remove scales from stalks, break off tough ends and wash again. Place in a saucepan with salt and ½ inch boiling water. Bring to boiling point and cook, uncovered, for 5 min-

utes. Cover and continue cooking until asparagus is crisp-tender, about 10 minutes. In the meantime, soften butter or margarine and mix with lemon juice, nutmeg, and white pepper. Peel eggs and separate the yolks from whites. Put yolks through a sieve or chop fine and blend with the sauce. Arrange toast on warm platter. Place asparagus on toast. Spoon sauce over the asparagus. Sprinkle with finely chopped hard-cooked egg whites. Yield: 6 servings.

Marinated Asparagus

2 (14½-ounce) cans white asparagus, drained
1 cup dill pickle liquid
½ cup sliced dill pickles
  Salt and pepper
  Pimiento strips

Combine asparagus and pickle liquid. Chill for 2 hours, then drain. Arrange asparagus and pickles on serving plate. Sprinkle with salt and pepper. Garnish with pimiento strips. Yield: 6 servings.

Asparagus Vinaigrette

2 (10½-ounce) cans asparagus
1 teaspoon salt
⅛ teaspoon black pepper
½ teaspoon dry mustard
  Dash cayenne pepper
1 tablespoon capers
¼ teaspoon paprika
3 tablespoons wine vinegar
½ cup salad oil
1 tablespoon finely chopped pimiento
1 tablespoon finely chopped parsley
½ tablespoon finely chopped chives

Drain asparagus and set aside. Boil liquid until about two-thirds of amount has evaporated. Reduce temperature to simmer and add asparagus. Combine remaining ingredients in a separate saucepan and heat to make sauce. When ready to serve, place asparagus in serving bowl and add sauce. Yield: 8 servings.

Creole String Beans

4 cups canned or frozen string beans
1 onion, sliced
2 cups canned tomatoes
1 teaspoon dried mixed herbs
½ cup salad oil
6 strips bacon

Chop string beans and cook in salted water until tender. Add onion rings, canned tomatoes, herbs, salad oil, and bacon, cut in 1-inch strips. Simmer for 20 to 25 minutes, and serve hot. Yield: 6 servings.

Goldenrod Beans

1½ pounds fresh, whole green beans
2 cups boiling water
2¼ teaspoons salt
3 hard-cooked eggs
1½ tablespoons butter or margarine
2 tablespoons all-purpose flour
½ teaspoon salt
Few grains black pepper
¾ cup evaporated milk
¾ cup mayonnaise

Cook beans, covered, in boiling water to which 2¼ teaspoons salt has been added for 15 to 30 minutes. Drain off ½ cup liquid and set aside; keep beans hot. Chop egg whites and set aside. Press yolks through a sieve.

Melt butter or margarine; blend in flour, ½ teaspoon salt, and pepper. Stir in the ½ cup liquid from the beans and boil for 2 minutes, stirring constantly. Add chopped egg whites and evaporated milk and heat thoroughly. Remove from heat and stir in mayonnaise. Drain beans and place in hot serving dish. Cover beans with cooked sauce and sprinkle top with sieved egg yolks. Yield: 4 to 6 servings.

Green Beans au Gratin

4 tablespoons butter or margarine
4 tablespoons all-purpose flour
1 teaspoon salt
⅛ teaspoon dry mustard
1½ cups milk
½ cup diced processed cheese
3 cups green beans (fresh, frozen, or canned)
Parmesan cheese
Paprika
Slivered almonds

Melt butter; add flour, salt, and mustard; cook over low heat until bubbly. Add milk slowly and cook until thick and smooth. Add cheese and stir until melted. Add beans cooked in salted water until just underdone. Pour into buttered 1½-quart casserole dish; sprinkle with Parmesan cheese and paprika. Bake at 350° for 30 minutes. Add slivered almonds, if desired. Yield: 6 servings.

Barbecued Lima Beans

   3 *slices bacon*
   1 *onion, sliced*
   1 *clove garlic, halved*
   2 *tablespoons all-purpose flour*
   3 *tablespoons vinegar*
1½ *cups tomato juice*
 ¾ *teaspoon dry mustard*
 ½ *teaspoon salt*
     Dash pepper
   3 *tablespoons sugar*
   3 *cups cooked green lima beans*

Cut bacon slices in halves and fry until crisp. Remove bacon from pan, and cook onion and garlic in the drippings until lightly browned. Remove garlic, and add the remaining ingredients except the lima beans. Cook 5 minutes longer, stirring until slightly thickened and smooth. Add lima beans, and pour into a 1½-quart baking dish. Top with crisp bacon, and bake at 350° for 35 minutes. Yield: 6 servings.

Red Beans and Rice

 ½ *cup chopped onions*
   2 *tablespoons butter or margarine*
1⅓ *cups packaged precooked rice*
   1 *teaspoon salt*
 ⅛ *teaspoon pepper*
   2 *cups liquid (bean liquid plus tomato juice)*
   2 *cups drained red kidney beans*
 ½ *cup shredded sharp cheese*

Sauté onions in the butter or margarine in saucepan over medium heat until tender, but not brown. Stir occasionally. Add precooked rice, salt, pepper, and liquid. Bring quickly to a boil over high heat, uncovered, fluffing rice gently once or twice with a fork. Do not stir. Cover, and simmer gently for 3 minutes. Remove from heat, and let stand for 10 minutes. Add beans to rice mixture. Reheat, mixing lightly with a fork. Arrange in serving dish. Serve with shredded sharp cheese on top. Yield: 4 to 6 servings.

Savory Baked Beans

   1 *medium onion, chopped*
   1 *green pepper, chopped*
 ⅓ *cup sweet pickle relish*
 ¼ *cup vinegar*
   1 *cup chili sauce*
 ½ *cup molasses*
   1 *tablespoon prepared mustard*
 ¼ *teaspoon hot pepper sauce*
   4 *(1-pound) cans baked beans*
   1 *onion, sliced*

Combine chopped onion, pepper, pickle relish, vinegar, chili sauce, molasses, mustard, and hot pepper sauce in skillet or saucepan; simmer for 10 minutes. Stir in beans and onion slices. Heat thoroughly and serve at once or turn into greased casserole and bake at 350° for 45 minutes. Yield: 12 servings.

Sweet-Sour Beans

   2 *strips bacon*
   1 *cup minced onion*
   1 *tablespoon all-purpose flour*
 ¾ *cup vegetable liquid*
 ¼ *cup vinegar*
   2 *tablespoons sugar*
   1 *teaspoon salt*
 ¼ *teaspoon black pepper*
   2 *cups cooked green beans*

Brown the bacon until crisp; set aside. Cook onion in bacon drippings until it turns yellow. Stir in the flour. Add vegetable liquid, vinegar, sugar, salt, and pepper, and bring to a boil. Stir in the beans. Stir gently until heated through. Serve with crisp bacon sprinkled over the top. Yield: 4 servings.

Butterbeans, Spanish-Style

    1 tablespoon bacon drippings
    1 onion, chopped
 ½ dry red pepper, cut fine
    1 cup cooked tomatoes
    1 tablespoon all-purpose flour
    2 cups cooked or canned butterbeans

Put bacon drippings in a frying pan. Add onion and pepper and cook until softened. Add tomatoes and stir in flour; cook 3 minutes. Add beans and more salt if necessary. Heat slowly to boiling point. Yield: 4 to 6 servings.

Dried Butterbeans

Soak dried butterbeans overnight in soft water to cover. Drain; cook until tender in fresh boiling salted water with a slice of diced salt pork.

Green Beans with Mushrooms

    4 cups cooked green beans
    1 (4-ounce) can mushrooms
    3 tablespoons butter or margarine

Drain bean and mushroom liquid into saucepan. Boil liquid rapidly until reduced to about ½ cup. Add drained beans, mushrooms, and butter or margarine; heat to serve. Yield: 6 to 8 servings.

Beets in Orange Sauce

    2 cups sliced, cooked beets
    2 tablespoons butter or margarine
    1 tablespoon sugar
    1 tablespoon cornstarch
 ½ teaspoon salt
 ⅛ teaspoon paprika
 ½ cup reserved beet juice
 ½ cup orange juice
    1 teaspoon freshly squeezed lemon juice

Drain beets, reserving juice. Place drained beets in a 1-quart casserole and set aside. Melt butter or margarine in saucepan. Remove from heat and stir in sugar, cornstarch, salt, and paprika. Cook over low heat until mixture bubbles. Remove from heat and gradually stir in beet juice. Cook rapidly, stirring constantly, until mixture thickens. Blend in orange and lemon juice. Pour over beets. Bake at 350° for 15 to 20 minutes. Yield: 4 to 6 servings.

Harvard Beets

 ½ cup sugar
    2 teaspoons cornstarch
 ½ cup vinegar
  12 small cooked beets or
        1 (16-ounce) can, drained
    2 tablespoons butter

Mix sugar, cornstarch, and vinegar together. Stir over low heat until thickened. Add butter and pour over prepared beets in saucepan and let stand on back of range for 30 minutes. If not warm enough, heat before serving. Yield: 4 servings.

Celebrity Broccoli

2 (10-ounce) packages frozen broccoli
2 tablespoons butter
2 tablespoons minced onion
1½ cups commercial sour cream
2 teaspoons sugar
2 teaspoons vinegar
1 teaspoon poppy seed
1 teaspoon paprika
½ teaspoon salt
⅛ teaspoon cayenne pepper
¼ cup chopped pecans

Cook broccoli according to package directions until tender; drain. Melt the butter in a small saucepan; add onion and sauté lightly. Remove from heat and stir in the sour cream, sugar, vinegar, poppy seed, paprika, salt, and cayenne pepper. Arrange the broccoli on a heated platter, and pour the sour cream sauce over it. Sprinkle with pecans. Yield: 6 to 8 servings.

Southern Broccoli

1½ pounds fresh broccoli
¼ cup vegetable shortening
1 teaspoon salt
2 tablespoons water
Freshly squeezed lemon juice

Wash broccoli. Cut off tough ends, split stalks lengthwise into fourths, then chop stalks and flowerets coarsely with knife on board. Melt shortening in heavy skillet or saucepan. Add broccoli, salt, water, and mix lightly. Cover, cook over medium heat for 13 minutes, or until tender-crisp (with bright green color), stirring occasionally. Sprinkle with lemon juice and serve. Yield: 5 servings.

Bavarian Cabbage

2 tablespoons butter or margarine
1 medium head cabbage, coarsely shredded
2 tablespoons chopped onion
½ teaspoon salt
Dash ground nutmeg
¼ cup water
1½ teaspoons sugar
2 tablespoons vinegar

Melt butter or margarine. Add cabbage, onion, salt, nutmeg, and water. Cook until just barely done, about 5 minutes. Add sugar and vinegar and blend thoroughly. Cook 3 minutes longer. Yield: 6 servings.

Cabbage Medley

2 tablespoons bacon drippings
1 medium cabbage, shredded
2 green peppers, chopped
1 cup chopped celery
1 cup chopped onion
¼ cup water
3 cups chopped cooked meat
Salt and pepper

Heat drippings in large iron skillet. When hot, add all vegetables and ¼ cup water. Let simmer for 15 to 20 minutes. Add meat, and salt and pepper to taste. Cover and let cook 15 to 20 minutes longer. Yield: 6 to 8 servings.

Five-Minute Cabbage

3 cups milk
8 cups chopped cabbage
3 tablespoons all-purpose flour
½ teaspoon salt
3 tablespoons bacon drippings

Heat milk to simmering. Add cabbage, and simmer for 2 minutes. Mix flour, salt, and bacon drippings. Add ½ cup of the hot milk to the flour mixture, and blend. Stir this into the cabbage and cook 3 minutes longer, stirring constantly. Serve hot. Yield: 8 servings.

Fried Cabbage

    3   tablespoons bacon drippings
    5   cups coarsely chopped cabbage
    1   medium onion, chopped
    1   teaspoon salt
        Dash ground nutmeg
 1 ½   teaspoons sugar
        Cayenne pepper
    2   tablespoons vinegar

Heat bacon drippings in deep saucepan. Add cabbage, onion, salt, and nutmeg. Cover, cook slowly for about 20 minutes, stirring often. Add sugar and cayenne pepper to vinegar and mix well. Pour over cabbage and cook for 5 minutes longer. Yield: 2 to 3 servings.

Skillet Vegetable Curry

    4   cups shredded cabbage
    1   green pepper, shredded
    2   cups diced celery
    2   large onions, sliced
    2   tomatoes, chopped
  ¼   cup bacon drippings
    2   teaspoons sugar
  ¾   teaspoon salt
  ¼   teaspoon pepper
  ¼   teaspoon curry powder

Combine ingredients in large skillet. Cover. Cook over medium heat 5 minutes. Yield: 8 servings.

Stuffed Whole Cabbage

    1   (2-pound) head cabbage
        Boiling water to cover cabbage
    1   cup finely chopped luncheon meat
    1   cup shredded American cheese
  ¼   cup finely chopped onion
  ½   cup soft breadcrumbs
    1   tablespoon milk
  ½   teaspoon salt
  ¼   teaspoon black pepper
 1 ½   cups diced fresh tomatoes
  ¾   cup boiling water
  ¾   teaspoon salt
  ¾   cup bread cubes
 1 ½   tablespoons melted butter or
        margarine

Remove outer leaves from cabbage and save them for salad or soup. Place cabbage head in a saucepan with 1 teaspoon salt and enough boiling water to cover. Boil, uncovered, until almost tender, about 30 minutes. Remove from water. Drain well. Cut off top and carefully scoop out inside leaving a 1½-inch shell. Place cabbage in a deep casserole. Finely shred enough of the cabbage center to make 1 cup. Combine with luncheon meat, cheese, onion, ½ cup breadcrumbs, milk, and salt. Mix well and spoon into the cabbage shell.

Combine tomatoes, water, salt. Pour into casserole around cabbage. Cover with aluminum foil or casserole top. Bake at 350° for 1 hour. Remove from oven and sprinkle with ¾ cup bread cubes mixed with melted butter or margarine. Bake for 15 minutes or until cubes have browned. Serve with some of the tomato sauce spooned over each portion. Yield: 6 servings.

Glazed Carrots

15 small carrots
 6 tablespoons butter or margarine
    Juice of ½ lemon
 3 tablespoons brown sugar

Scrape carrots and cut in half length-wise. Boil carrots in salted water until tender. Drain well. Melt the butter or margarine in a heavy skillet; add the lemon juice and brown sugar, and heat, stirring until mixture becomes thick. Add the carrots and heat, spooning syrup over them until they are well glazed. Yield: 6 servings.

Sautéed Carrots and Apples

12 medium carrots
 2 large cooking apples
 3 tablespoons butter or margarine
 1 tablespoon sugar
¼ teaspoon salt

Wash and scrape carrots and cut into thin, crosswise slices. Core unpeeled apples and cut into ¼-inch thick cross-wise slices. Melt butter or margarine in a large skillet. Add apple slices, and brown on one side. Turn, add carrots and sprinkle with sugar and salt. Cover and cook until tender. Yield: 6 servings.

Cauliflower Polonaise

 1 head cauliflower, cooked
½ cup soft breadcrumbs
¼ cup butter or margarine
    Juice of ½ lemon
 1 teaspoon salt
¼ teaspoon pepper

Lightly brown crumbs in butter or margarine. Add lemon juice, salt and pepper. Stir mixture; sprinkle over cooked cauliflower just before serving. Both the cauliflower and the sauce should be hot when served. Yield: 4 servings.

Creamed Cauliflower and Peas

 3 (10-ounce) packages frozen
    cauliflower
 1 (10-ounce) package frozen peas
¼ cup water
¼ teaspoon salt
    Milk
¾ cup finely chopped onion
¼ cup butter or margarine
 3 tablespoons all-purpose flour
½ teaspoon salt
¼ teaspoon pepper
¼ teaspoon ground nutmeg
 1 cup light cream
¼ cup buttered breadcrumbs

Cook cauliflower as directed on package; drain. Put peas, water, and ¼ teaspoon salt in saucepan; bring to boiling, reduce heat, cover, and simmer for 5 minutes. Drain peas, reserving liquid. Add enough milk to liquid to make 1 cup. Set aside.

Sauté onion in butter until golden. Remove from heat; stir in flour, ½ teaspoon salt, pepper, and nutmeg. Gradually stir in reserved liquid and cream; bring to boiling, stirring constantly.

Combine cauliflower, peas, and sauce in a 2-quart casserole. Top with bread-crumbs. Cover and refrigerate over-night. Bake, covered, at 400° for 30 minutes; uncover and bake an additional 20 minutes or until bubbly. Yield: 8 to 10 servings.

Corn Pudding

2 cups fresh corn, cut from cob
1 cup milk
2 tablespoons butter or margarine
2 tablespoons all-purpose flour
1 teaspoon salt
1 tablespoon sugar
   Red or white pepper to taste
3 eggs

Cut corn from cob, or use leftover stewed corn. Add milk, butter or margarine, flour, and seasonings. Beat eggs together until light; add to the mixture. Pour into a buttered 1-quart baking dish, and bake at 350° for 1 hour, or until firm like a custard. Preferred method: Place dish with pudding in a pan of boiling water for better custard-like texture. Bake at 350° for 1 hour and 15 minutes, or until custard is set. Yield: 4 to 6 servings.

Corn Soufflé

4 tablespoons butter or margarine
4 tablespoons all-purpose flour
1½ cups milk
1 teaspoon salt
⅛ teaspoon cayenne pepper
1 cup whole-kernel corn
2 tablespoons chopped pimiento
1½ teaspoons Worcestershire sauce
½ teaspoon prepared mustard
1 teaspoon onion juice
6 eggs, separated

Melt butter or margarine in saucepan.

Add flour and blend. Gradually add milk, salt, and cayenne. Cook over low heat, stirring occasionally until thickened and smooth. Remove from heat; add remaining ingredients except eggs. Mix lightly. Add beaten egg yolks, blend, and allow to cool. Fold in stiffly beaten egg whites and pour into 2-quart ungreased casserole. Cut around the mixture with a knife (about 2 inches from edge), and bake at 350° for 1½ hours. Serve at once. Yield: 6 servings.

Fried Corn

8 ears fresh corn
½ cup milk
½ teaspoon salt
¼ teaspoon pepper
4 tablespoons butter or margarine
2 eggs, beaten

Cut corn from cob and add milk, salt, and pepper. Put butter or margarine in heavy skillet. When skillet is hot, add corn. Cook until tender, stirring occasionally. Just before ready to take up, add beaten eggs and blend in well. Serve hot. Yield: 6 servings.

Southern Fried Hominy

3 slices bacon
2 cups hominy, drained
⅛ teaspoon salt
⅛ teaspoon pepper

Cut bacon in small pieces and fry until bacon is about half-done. Add drained hominy, salt, and pepper, and continue to fry for 5 minutes, turning occasionally. Yield: 4 to 5 servings.

Baked Corn

2 cups cream-style canned corn or 3 cups
  fresh corn, cut cream-style
1 cup milk
3 tablespoons all-purpose flour
2 eggs
1 tablespoon sugar
  Salt to taste

Mix ingredients well in order given and
pour into shallow, buttered 1-quart
baking dish. Bake at 350° until slightly
brown. Yield: 6 servings.

Carolina Corn

6 strips bacon
3 to 4 eggs, slightly beaten
½ cup milk
2 cups fresh or canned whole-kernel corn
2 tablespoons bacon drippings
⅛ teaspoon pepper
½ teaspoon salt

Cook bacon to delicate brown in heavy
skillet. Remove from drippings, and cut
in small pieces. To slightly beaten eggs,
add milk, corn, bacon, and drippings.
Return to skillet and cook over medium
heat, stirring constantly until set. Add
pepper and salt. Yield: 6 servings.

Cheese-Corn-Tomato Dish

3 tablespoons all-purpose flour
3 tablespoons melted shortening
1 onion, sliced
2 cups cooked tomatoes
2 cups cooked corn
2 teaspoons salt
¼ to ½ pound Cheddar cheese cut
  in thin slices

Brown the flour in a heavy skillet. Take
flour from the skillet and blend with 2
tablespoons of the melted shortening.
Brown onion slices in the remaining
shortening. Add tomatoes, corn, salt,
and flour-shortening mixture, and cook
for about 10 minutes. Stir in the cheese.
When it has melted, serve on waffles or
thin, crisp toast. Yield: 6 servings.

Corn Fritters

½ cup all-purpose flour
2 teaspoons baking powder
½ teaspoon salt
  Dash black pepper
1 tablespoon melted shortening
2 eggs, beaten
½ cup milk
2 cups corn, cut from cob

Combine dry ingredients. Cut in shortening and add beaten eggs, milk, and
corn. Beat well and drop by tablespoonfuls into deep, hot fat, and fry until
brown. Yield: 4 to 6 servings.

Corn-on-the-Cob

1 to 2 ears for each serving
  Butter or margarine
  Pepper
  Salt

Corn to be cooked on the cob should be
fresh. The longer it stands after pick-
ing, the less flavor it has. Have salted
water boiling rapidly. Place shucked
and cleaned corn in the water and cook
below boiling for 8 to 12 minutes. Cook
only a few ears in each boiler. Serve hot
with plenty of butter or margarine,
freshly ground pepper, and salt.

Corn Savory

1 medium green pepper, minced
3 tablespoons bacon drippings
2 tablespoons all-purpose flour
1 cup milk
½ teaspoon salt
    Dash paprika
2 cups fresh corn, cut from cob
2 tablespoons shredded cheese
½ cup buttered breadcrumbs

Sauté the pepper in drippings for about 5 minutes. Add flour and blend smoothly. Stir in the milk and cook until it boils and thickens. Add seasonings, then the corn. Turn into greased 1½-quart casserole. Combine cheese and breadcrumbs. Spread over the top and bake at 350° for 20 to 30 minutes. Yield: 10 to 12 servings.

Note: For canned corn, decrease the amount of milk.

Eggplant Stuffed with Oysters

1 (2-pound) eggplant
¼ cup minced onion
1 clove garlic, minced
2 tablespoons minced celery
½ cup butter
1 pint oysters, drained and chopped
¼ cup soft breadcrumbs
¼ cup minced parsley
½ teaspoon thyme

Cut eggplant in half lengthwise; scoop out centers, leaving wall about ½ inch thick. Chop eggplant cut from centers. Sauté chopped eggplant, onion, garlic, and celery in butter until onion is golden.

Combine oysters and remaining ingredients and add to hot eggplant mixture. Spoon into eggplant shells and place in buttered baking dish. Cover and bake at 375° for 30 minutes. Yield: 6 servings.

Roast Corn-on-the-Cob

Select two full ears of corn per person. Pull husks part of the way down and remove as much silk as possible, then re-cover corn. Drop ears of corn in a pan of water for about 30 minutes to absorb moisture. When fire has burned down to glowing coals, place corn on a low grill just over the fire, and turn ears frequently as they cook. This will take about 30 to 45 minutes. If you have no grill, wrap corn in paper, soak in water, and cook directly on the coals. When corn is done, strip off husks, dip into melted butter or margarine, and season with salt and pepper.

Corn and Tomato Soufflé

1½ cups canned corn
1½ cups canned tomatoes
3 eggs, separated
½ teaspoon salt
1 cup milk
2 tablespoons butter, melted

Mix the corn and tomatoes together; add beaten egg yolks, salt, milk, and butter. Beat egg whites until stiff; fold into mixture. Pour into a greased 1-quart casserole and bake at 350° for 20 minutes, or until firm. Yield: 6 servings.

Stuffed Eggplant

- 2 small eggplants
- ¼ cup diced green pepper
- ¼ cup diced onion
- ¼ cup diced celery
- 1 tablespoon vegetable oil
- 1 (10½-ounce) can condensed tomato soup
- 1 cup cooked regular rice
- ½ teaspoon salt
- Dash pepper
- Dash thyme
- 1½ cups cracker crumbs

Cut eggplants in half lengthwise and simmer in salted boiling water until almost tender (about 10 minutes). Brown the green pepper, onion, and celery in vegetable oil. Combine the soup, rice, salt, pepper, and thyme. Scoop out center of eggplants; leave ½ inch of pulp around edges (save pulp scooped out of eggplants and add to spaghetti sauce another day). Sprinkle 2 tablespoons cracker crumbs over bottom of each shell. Fill with rice mixture. Spread remaining crumbs over top; dot with butter or margarine. Bake at 375° for about 30 minutes. Yield: 4 servings.

Eggplant Soufflé

- 1 medium eggplant
- Salt and pepper
- ¼ cup butter or margarine
- 1½ to 2 cups milk
- 2 eggs
- 1 cup cracker crumbs

Peel, slice, and cook eggplant until it mashes easily; season with salt and pepper, and add other ingredients. This mixture should be the consistency of a pudding. Pour into buttered 1-quart baking dish about 1½ inches deep. Bake at 350° for 20 to 30 minutes until it is set like a custard, but not dry and stiff. It will fall if not served immediately. Yield: 6 servings.

Scalloped Eggplant

- 1 large eggplant
- 1 small onion, chopped fine
- 2 tablespoons butter or margarine
- 1 teaspoon sugar
- 1 (10½-ounce) can cream of mushroom soup
- 1 egg, beaten
- ⅓ cup breadcrumbs
- 3 tablespoons shredded cheese

Peel and slice eggplant and soak about 30 minutes in salt water; drain and drop into boiling water. Cook until tender. Sauté onion in butter or margarine until tender, but not brown. Combine eggplant, onion, sugar, mushroom soup, and egg. Pour into 1-quart baking dish; sprinkle top with breadcrumbs and cheese. Bake at 350° for 45 minutes, or until cheese is bubbly. Yield: 6 servings.

Creole Eggplant

- 2 medium onions, chopped
- 2 tablespoons shortening
- 1 green pepper, chopped
- 4 ribs celery, chopped
- 2 cups canned tomatoes
- 2 medium eggplants cooked in salted water, drained, and mashed (be sure to get all water out)
- 1 cup breadcrumbs
- 1 cup shredded Cheddar cheese

Brown onions in shortening. Add pepper, celery, and tomatoes and cook until vegetables are tender. Add cooked, mashed eggplant and mix well. Add half the breadcrumbs and cheese. Place in greased 1½-quart casserole. Top with remainder of breadcrumbs and cheese. Bake at 375° until cheese is melted. Yield: 6 to 8 servings.

French Fried Eggplant

Peel eggplant by sections, cut into strips, and drop cut pieces quickly into salted ice water. Allow to stand in ice water for about ½ hour. Drain and dry between paper towels. Dip into beaten eggs, then in cracker crumbs, and chill before frying in deep shortening.

Buttered Okra

- 1 pound fresh okra
- 1½ cups boiling water
- 1 teaspoon salt
- 2 tablespoons butter or margarine
  Pepper

Wash okra, but do not cut off stems. Add okra to boiling salted water. Cover, bring back to boiling and boil for 3 to 5 minutes. Remove from heat; drain. Add butter or margarine, and white or black pepper as desired. Yield: 4 servings.

Fried Okra

- 2 pounds fresh okra
- ½ teaspoon salt
- ⅛ teaspoon pepper
- ½ cup cornmeal
- 4 tablespoons bacon drippings or salad oil

Wash okra well; drain. Larger pods of okra may need to be boiled in salted water until tender. Cut off tip and stem ends; slice okra across in ¼-inch rounds. Season slices with salt and pepper; roll in cornmeal. Sauté well coated okra in hot bacon drippings or salad oil until tender and golden brown on both sides. Yield: 8 servings.

Onions au Gratin

- 2 cups cooked, small, white onions
- 1 (10¾-ounce) can cream of mushroom soup
- ½ cup shredded American cheese
- ½ cup fine, dry breadcrumbs
- 2 tablespoons melted butter or margarine

Place cooked and drained onions in a 1½-quart casserole. Blend mushroom soup with cheese; pour over the onions. Top with buttered crumbs. Bake at 325° for 20 minutes, or until sauce is bubbling. Yield: 4 to 6 servings.

French Fried Onion Rings

- 4 large onions, peeled
- ⅔ cup milk
- ½ cup all-purpose flour
  Shortening for frying

Cut cleaned onions into ¼-inch slices and separate into rings. Soak onion rings in milk for 10 to 15 minutes. Dredge rings in flour, then fry in deep fat heated to 365°, a few at a time, until well browned (about 2 to 3 minutes). Drain on paper toweling. Season and serve immediately. Yield: 4 to 6 servings.

Sweet–Sour Onions

 4 large onions, peeled
¼ cup cider vinegar
¼ cup melted butter or margarine
¼ cup boiling water
¼ cup sugar

Slice the onions, and arrange in a 1-quart baking dish. Mix the rest of the ingredients and pour over the onions. Bake at 300° for 1 hour. Yield: 4 to 6 servings.

Fried Green Onions

Chop enough green onions and tops to make 2 cups. Put 1 tablespoon bacon drippings in heavy skillet. Heat drippings and add onions. Add ½ teaspoon salt, ⅛ teaspoon pepper, and 1 teaspoon sugar. Add ½ cup hot water and simmer for 20 to 25 minutes. Serve hot. Yield: 4 servings.

Scalloped Green Peas and Onions

¼ cup butter
¼ cup all-purpose flour
 1 teaspoon salt
 1 teaspoon seasoned salt
¼ teaspoon pepper
 2 cups milk
 1 (10-ounce) package frozen peas, partially defrosted and broken apart
 1 pound small, white onions (1 to 1¼ inch), peeled, or 2 (8-ounce) cans onions, drained
 2 medium baking potatoes, peeled and thinly sliced
 1 cup shredded Swiss cheese

Melt butter in saucepan over low heat; blend in flour, salts, and pepper. Add milk, stirring constantly. Cook and stir until sauce is smooth and thick. Arrange half of the peas, onions, and potatoes in a buttered 1½-quart shallow casserole. Spoon half of the sauce over vegetables; sprinkle half of cheese over sauce. Repeat. Cover dish and bake at 375° until vegetables are tender, about 1 hour. Yield: 6 servings.

Creamed Onions

 3 to 4 cups peeled, small, white pearl onions
 3 tablespoons butter or margarine
 3 tablespoons all-purpose flour
 2 cups cream
 1 cup shredded mild Cheddar cheese
½ teaspoon salt
¼ teaspoon ground nutmeg
¼ teaspoon paprika
 1 teaspoon curry powder
 2 dashes Tabasco sauce

Cook onions in boiling, salted water for 8 to 10 minutes. Drain and set aside. Make cream sauce of butter, flour, cream, and shredded cheese. Add seasonings and onions. Heat and serve. Yield: 6 to 8 servings.

Field Peas with Bacon

 2 slices bacon
 4 green onions, chopped
 2 tablespoons all-purpose flour
 1 chicken bouillon cube
1½ cups boiling water
½ teaspoon salt
    Dash pepper
 2 cups shelled peas (about 2 pounds)

Cook bacon until crisp; remove from pan and crumble. Brown onion in bacon drippings. Add flour, and brown. Dissolve bouillon cube in boiling water and blend into flour mixture. Season with salt and pepper. Add peas; cover and cook until tender, about 20 minutes. Top with crumbled bacon before serving. Yield: 4 servings.

French Peas

    2 pounds fresh English peas
    3 to 6 lettuce leaves
    ⅓ cup green onion slices
    1 teaspoon sugar
    ½ teaspoon salt
      Dash pepper
      Dash thyme
    3 tablespoons butter or margarine

Shell and wash peas. Cover bottom of skillet with lettuce; top with peas and onions. Sprinkle sugar and seasonings over peas, and dot with butter or margarine. Cover tightly and cook over low heat for 10 to 15 minutes, or until peas are done. Yield: 4 servings.

Black-Eyed Peas with Ham Hock

    1 pound dry black-eyed peas
    5 to 6 cups water
    1 small ham hock
    1 to 3 teaspoons salt
    1 large onion, whole

Put dry peas into a colander in sink partially filled with cold water or wash under cold running water; wash well and remove faulty peas. Drain and put into a heavy 6- to 8-quart kettle. Cover and soak for 12 hours or overnight.

The next day, add ham hock to kettle (add more water if water does not cover peas) and bring to a boil. Reduce heat and add 1 teaspoon or more salt (it is better to start with a smaller amount if salty ham hock is used). Add whole onion. Cover kettle and simmer for about 1 hour or until peas are tender. To avoid excessive breaking of peas, do not stir during cooking. Add more salt if needed. Yield: 6 servings.

Fresh Black-Eyed Peas

    ¼ pound thinly sliced fat pork
      Boiling water
    4 cups shelled, washed, fresh
      black-eyed peas
    1 teaspoon salt
    ¼ teaspoon black pepper
    ¼ teaspoon cayenne pepper
    1 whole medium onion

Cover sliced pork with boiling water; cover pan and boil for 15 minutes. Add peas, salt, pepper, and onion; add enough water to cover peas. Cover pan and cook for about 45 minutes, or until peas are tender. Add more seasoning to taste. Yield: 6 to 8 servings.

English Peas

1½ tablespoons butter or margarine
2 tablespoons water
⅓ cup green onion slices
½ cup thinly sliced mushrooms
1½ cups English peas
1 small onion, thinly sliced
½ teaspoon salt

Melt butter or margarine in saucepan; add other ingredients. Cover pan tightly and cook over moderate heat until peas are tender, shaking the pan occasionally to prevent sticking. Yield: 4 servings.

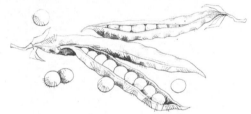

Stuffed Green Peppers

8 to 10 green peppers, fresh or frozen
1 cup uncooked regular rice
1 tablespoon shortening
1 pound ground beef
¼ cup chopped onion
¼ cup chopped green pepper
1½ teaspoons salt
½ teaspoon black pepper, if desired

Cut stem ends from peppers and remove seed. Put peppers into boiling water and cook for 2 or 3 minutes. Remove from water and drain. Cook rice as directed on package. Melt shortening in heavy skillet; add ground beef, onion, chopped pepper, salt and black pepper. Brown, add to rice, and mix. Stuff peppers with mixture. Place in baking dish and bake at 350° for 30 minutes. Yield: 8 to 10 servings.

Saucy Stuffed Peppers

6 medium green peppers
Boiling water
1 pound sausage
½ pound ground veal
1 teaspoon salt
¼ teaspoon pepper
1 cup uncooked oats, regular or quick-cooking
⅔ cup tomato juice
1 (10½-ounce) can condensed tomato soup
¼ cup milk

Cut about ¼-inch slice from top of each green pepper; remove seed. Cook peppers for about 5 minutes in enough boiling water to cover; drain. Pan-fry pork sausage and veal until lightly browned. Drain on absorbent paper. Combine meats, salt, pepper, oats, and tomato juice. Fill green peppers with this mixture.

Place peppers upright in shallow baking pan; add small amount of water. Bake at 350° for 45 to 50 minutes. Serve hot with a sauce made of tomato soup and milk. Yield: 6 servings.

Potatoes au Gratin

4 tablespoons butter or margarine
4 tablespoons all-purpose flour
1 cup potato water
1 cup milk
¼ teaspoon salt
4 cups diced cooked potatoes
1 cup shredded cheese
½ cup buttered breadcrumbs

Melt butter or margarine in saucepan over low heat. Gradually stir in flour, potato water, milk, and salt; cook until slightly thickened. Remove sauce from heat; add potatoes and shredded cheese. Pour mixture into 1½-quart baking dish, cover with buttered bread-crumbs, and bake at 350° until crumbs are brown. Yield: 6 to 8 servings.

Creamed Potatoes

2 cups diced, raw potatoes
   Salted water
2 tablespoons butter or margarine
1 cup hot milk or cream
   Salt and pepper

Cook potatoes in small amount of salted water until tender. Drain. Whip the potatoes until smooth and fluffy. Add butter or margarine, milk or cream, and blend well. Add salt and pepper to taste. Set over hot water until ready to serve. Yield: 4 to 6 servings.

French Fried Potatoes

Pare medium-sized potatoes; cut lengthwise into eights. Let stand in cold water for 1 hour; drain potatoes, and dry. Fry, a few at a time, in deep, hot shortening about 1½ minutes. Drain thoroughly and sprinkle with salt. Serve hot.

Hash Browned Potatoes

2 cups diced, cooked potatoes
2 tablespoons finely chopped onion
4 teaspoons all-purpose flour
1½ teaspoons salt
   Pepper
2 tablespoons milk
2 to 3 tablespoons melted shortening

Combine potatoes and onion. Mix flour, salt, and pepper, and slowly blend in the milk. Combine with potato-onion mixture. Heat shortening in a heavy skillet. Add potatoes, and cook over medium heat until the under side is brown. Turn to brown the other side. Yield: 4 servings.

Scalloped Potatoes

6 medium potatoes, peeled and sliced thin
6 slices mild cheese, cut in small pieces
1 medium onion, peeled and sliced
1 teaspoon salt
¼ teaspoon pepper
1 cup evaporated milk

Place alternate layers of potatoes, cheese, and onions in a greased 1½-quart casserole. Add salt and pepper. Pour milk over mixture. Bake at 350° for 1 hour, or until potatoes are tender and brown. Serve hot. Yield: 6 servings.

Stuffed Baked Potatoes

3 baked potatoes
1½ tablespoons butter or margarine
1 tablespoon finely chopped onion
¼ to ½ cup hot milk
¼ teaspoon salt
   Dash pepper
   Shredded cheese

Cut baked potatoes in half and scoop out center; mash thoroughly. Add other ingredients, except cheese, and beat un-til light and fluffy. Pile lightly into shells, and sprinkle shredded cheese over top. Bake at 425° for 5 minutes. Yield: 6 servings.

Boiled New Potatoes with Lemon Butter Sauce

1½ pounds new potatoes
    Boiling water
1 teaspoon salt
    Lemon Butter Sauce

Wash potatoes, scrape or pare; or, if desired, cook in the jackets. Place in saucepan with ½-inch boiling water and salt. Cover and bring to the boiling point. Boil until tender, about 25 to 40 minutes. Drain. Serve with Lemon Butter Sauce. Yield: 6 servings.

Lemon Butter Sauce

2 tablespoons butter or margarine
1 tablespoon freshly squeezed lemon juice
¼ teaspoon salt
⅛ teaspoon black pepper

Melt the butter or margarine and add the lemon juice, salt, and black pepper. Serve hot.

Texas Potatoes

4 cups diced potatoes
1 cup minced onion
1 teaspoon salt
⅓ cup chopped pimientos
1 teaspoon pepper
2 cups shredded American cheese
2 cups medium white sauce
½ cup cracker crumbs
2 teaspoons butter or margarine

Cook diced potatoes for 5 minutes with minced onion and salt in a small amount of boiling water. Drain. Add pimientos and place in greased 1½-quart casserole. Add pepper and cheese to white sauce and pour over potatoes.

Top with crumbs and dot with butter or margarine. Bake at 350° until brown, about 30 minutes. Yield: 4 to 6 servings.

Baked Potatoes

Choose firm, smooth potatoes of the baking type. Scrub potatoes thoroughly and dry. If you like a crunchy crust, bake without any coating or covering. If you like the skin soft, rub with shortening or cover with aluminum foil. Bake at 425° for 40 to 60 minutes, depending on size. When potatoes are done, roll gently under the hand to make the inside mealy. Make a crisscross slash on top and gently push up. Add salt, pepper, and butter.

Spinach Soufflé

3 egg yolks
⅔ cup milk
2 tablespoons butter or margarine
½ pound shredded cheese
½ teaspoon salt
    Pepper to taste
2 cups cooked, drained, spinach
3 egg whites

Beat egg yolks slightly. Add milk, butter or margarine, cheese, salt, and pepper. Cook until smooth, stirring constantly. Add spinach. Fold in stiffly beaten egg whites. Place mixture in buttered 3-cup mold, place in pan of hot water, and bake at 350° for about 40 minutes, or until firm. Yield: 4 to 6 servings.

Buttered Spinach

1½ pounds fresh spinach
    Boiling water
½ teaspoon salt
1 tablespoon butter or margarine

Remove roots and discolored leaves. Wash at least five times to remove all sand. Lift out of water into another pan; do not bruise. Place spinach in large saucepan and add ½ inch boiling water. Cook uncovered for first few minutes of cooking. Turn with fork until all leaves are wilted. Cover and cook for 8 to 10 minutes. Drain, and add salt and butter or margarine. Yield: 4 servings.

Squash au Gratin

2 cups cooked squash
2 tablespoons butter or
   margarine, melted
   Salt and pepper
2 eggs, beaten
1 cup buttered breadcrumbs
⅓ cup shredded cheese

Combine squash, melted butter or margarine, seasonings, and beaten eggs. Alternate layers of squash, breadcrumbs, and cheese in 1-quart casserole; bake at 375° for 10 minutes. Yield: 4 servings.

Candied Squash

2 medium butternut or acorn squash
1 stick butter or margarine
½ cup brown sugar, firmly packed
½ cup water
2 tablespoons white corn syrup
¼ teaspoon ground cinnamon

Cut squash in large slices and cook just until tender when pierced with a fork (do not overcook; squash should retain its shape). Drain and cut into cubes (you should have about 6 cups prepared squash).

Melt butter and brown sugar in large skillet; add water, corn syrup, and cinnamon and stir until blended. Add squash; toss until cubes are coated. Cover and cook over low heat for 10 minutes. Uncover and cook about 5 minutes longer. Yield: 8 servings.

Baked Acorn Squash

3 acorn squash
3 tablespoons honey
1 teaspoon salt
¼ teaspoon pepper
1 teaspoon ground ginger
¼ teaspoon ground nutmeg
2 tablespoons butter or margarine

Cut squash in half crosswise, and scoop out seed. Arrange squash, cut side down, in shallow baking dish. Bake at 375° for 30 minutes. Turn squash cut side up, and spoon mixture of honey, salt, pepper, ginger, nutmeg, and butter or margarine into cavities. Continue baking for 30 to 40 minutes, or until squash are tender when tested with a fork. Serve hot. Yield: 6 servings.

Baked Squash

   6 medium squash
   ½ medium onion, chopped
   ½ cup diced cooked ham
   3 tablespoons butter or margarine
   ½ cup milk
   1 egg
   ½ cup breadcrumbs
      Salt and pepper to taste

Cut squash in pieces and cook in small amount of water until tender. Drain thoroughly and mash. Add all other ingredients, mix, and bake in a 1-quart casserole at 325° for 30 minutes. Yield: 4 servings.

Squash Fritters

   2 cups grated raw summer squash
   ¼ teaspoon grated onion
      Few grains pepper
   2 teaspoons sugar
   1 teaspoon salt
   6 tablespoons all-purpose flour
   2 eggs
   2 teaspoons melted butter or margarine

Combine squash, onion, pepper, sugar, salt, and flour. Beat eggs and add to squash. Add butter or margarine. Drop by tablespoonfuls onto oiled griddle. Cook until delicate brown; turn and brown other side. Serve immediately. Yield: 6 servings.

Tips for Cooking Rice

One cup raw rice will make 3 cups when cooked.

One cup precooked rice will make 2 cups when cooked.

It is neither necessary nor desirable to wash rice before cooking.

Avoid blanching rice after cooking. The water removes the vitamins in fortified rice.

Cumin Rice

   1 (10½-ounce) can cream of
      mushroom soup
   1 (10½-ounce) can cream of
      celery soup
   1 (10½-ounce) can cream of
      chicken soup
   1½ cups uncooked regular rice
   1½ cups water
   ½ to 1 teaspoon cumin

Combine all ingredients and place in oiled 1½-quart baking dish and bake, uncovered, at 350° for 2 hours. Yield: 6 servings.

Hopping John

   1 cup black-eyed peas
   1 medium ham hock
   1 medium onion, diced
   2 stalks celery, chopped
   1 small bay leaf
   2 to 3 cups water
   ½ teaspoon salt
   ¼ teaspoon pepper
   1 cup uncooked regular rice

Put peas, ham hock, onion, celery, and bay leaf in saucepan and add water and seasoning. Simmer, covered, until peas are tender. Cook rice according to package directions. Combine peas, rice, ham cut from the bone and minced, and liquid from peas. Simmer for a few minutes to combine flavors. Yield: 8 servings.

Red Rice

- 3 tablespoons shortening
- 1 onion, chopped
- 1 green pepper, chopped
- 1 (1-pound) can tomatoes
- 1 (4-ounce) can tomato paste
- Dash hot sauce
- Dash black pepper
- 3 tablespoons catsup
- 1 teaspoon salt
- 1¼ cups uncooked regular rice

Melt shortening; add onion and green pepper, and brown slightly. Add all other ingredients except rice and bring to a full boil. Add rice and stir once; cover pan and cook over low heat for 30 minutes. Yield: 4 servings.

Sweet Potato Pudding

- 1 cup butter or margarine
- 1 cup sugar
- 6 egg yolks
- 2 teaspoons brandy flavoring
- 2 teaspoons sherry flavoring
- 1 teaspoon ground allspice
- 1 teaspoon ground cinnamon
- 1 teaspoon ground ginger
- Ground nutmeg to taste
- 1 lemon
- 2 cups cooked sweet potatoes
- 6 egg whites, stiffly beaten

Cream together the butter or margarine and sugar; add egg yolks and beat well. Add flavorings, spices, lemon

juice, and grated lemon rind. Combine with the sieved or finely mashed sweet potatoes. Fold stiffly beaten egg whites into the potato mixture. Place in a 2-quart buttered baking dish and bake at 350° for 45 minutes. Yield: 6 servings.

Orange Candied Sweet Potatoes

- 6 medium sweet potatoes
- 1 cup orange juice
- ½ teaspoon grated orange rind
- 1 cup water
- 2 cups sugar
- ¼ cup butter or margarine
- ½ teaspoon salt

Peel and slice uncooked potatoes in ¼-inch slices; arrange in buttered 1½-quart baking dish. Make syrup of other ingredients and pour over potatoes. Cover and bake at 350° for about 30 minutes or until tender. Baste occasionally. Remove lid the last 10 minutes to brown. Yield: 6 servings.

Sweet Potatoes in Orange Baskets

Boil sweet potatoes until tender, remove skins, mash, and season with milk and butter or margarine. Add a few broken pecans and mix well. Cut oranges in half crosswise, remove all juice and pulp, but keep the rind whole. Fill orange halves with potato mixture. Bake uncovered at 350° until lightly browned. Decorate with pecans or marshmallows.

Sweet Potato Surprise

    2 cups cooked sweet potatoes
    1 egg, beaten
    ½ teaspoon salt
    ⅛ teaspoon pepper
    8 marshmallows
    ½ cup crushed corn flakes
       Hot shortening

Combine warm, mashed potatoes with beaten egg, salt and pepper. Add a little milk if mixture is too dry to form into balls. Shape into eight balls with a marshmallow inside each. Roll in crushed corn flakes. Fry in deep hot shortening until golden brown. Yield: 6 to 8 servings.

Scalloped Sweet Potatoes And Apples

    2 cups sliced boiled sweet potatoes
  1½ cups sliced tart apples
    ½ cup brown sugar
    4 tablespoons butter or margarine
    1 teaspoon salt

Put half the sliced potatoes in a buttered 1-quart baking dish and cover with half of the sliced apples. Sprinkle with half the sugar, dot with butter or margarine, and sprinkle with half of the salt. Repeat layers. Bake at 350° for 1 hour. Yield: 6 to 8 servings.

Yams on Half-Shell

    4 medium sweet potatoes
    ⅓ cup seedless raisins
    1 teaspoon salt
    1 tablespoon sugar
    1 tablespoon butter or margarine

Bake sweet potatoes in moderate oven until soft. When done, cut lengthwise and scoop out pulp, being careful not to break the shells. Mash the pulp; add raisins, salt, sugar, and butter or margarine. Mix well and pile lightly into potato shells. Brown at 425°. Serve hot. Yield: 6 to 8 servings.

Glazed Sweet Potatoes

  5 or 6 medium sweet potatoes
    2 tablespoons water
    1 cup sugar (brown or granulated)
    ½ teaspoon salt
    2 tablespoons butter or margarine

Wash sweet potatoes and boil until nearly done. Drain; remove skins; cut lengthwise into slices and arrange in a baking dish. Make a syrup of boiling water, sugar, and salt. Add butter or margarine. Pour syrup over sweet potatoes. Bake at 350° about 35 minutes or until potatoes are glazed. Baste with syrup two or three times during baking. Yield: 4 servings.

Note: Other vegetables, such as carrots and butternut or acorn squash may be glazed in the same manner.

Candied Sweet Potatoes

    3 large sweet potatoes
    1 cup brown sugar
       Ground cinnamon
    4 tablespoons melted butter
    6 pieces orange peel
    ½ cup water

Boil whole potatoes until tender. Remove skins and slice thin. Put a layer of potatoes into buttered 1½-quart baking dish and sprinkle with sugar, cinnamon, and butter. Repeat until all potatoes are used. When dish is filled, sprinkle top with sugar, cinnamon, butter, and orange peel. Add water and bake at 350° about 30 minutes, or until brown and well candied. Yield: 4 servings.

Sweet Potato Puffs

 2 tablespoons butter
 2 tablespoons all-purpose flour
½ cup milk
   Salt
 2 cups cooked, mashed sweet potatoes
¼ cup chopped peanuts or pecans
 1 egg
   Cornflake crumbs

Cream butter and flour in saucepan; when well mixed, add milk and salt and cook until thickened. Add mashed potatoes and nuts. Set aside until cool. When cool enough to handle, shape into 6 rolls. Dip in beaten egg, then crumbs, and back into egg mixture. Drop into hot shortening, 350° to 375°, and cook until well browned. Drain. Yield: 6 servings.

Hawaiian Sweet Potatoes

 2 (1-pound, 7-ounce) cans sweet potatoes, drained
 1 (9-ounce) can crushed pineapple, not drained
 6 tablespoons melted butter or margarine
¾ teaspoon salt
½ cup packed dry breadcrumbs
 2 tablespoons brown sugar
   Dash ground cloves

Mash sweet potatoes in a medium bowl;

measure 4 cups. Stir in pineapple, 2 tablespoons butter or margarine, and salt. Turn into 1-quart ungreased casserole. Combine the remaining butter or margarine with breadcrumbs, brown sugar, and cloves. Sprinkle over potatoes. Bake at 375° for 30 minutes. Yield: 6 large servings.

Whipped Sweet Potatoes

 8 medium sweet potatoes
½ cup cream
½ cup brown sugar
 1 teaspoon ground nutmeg
 2 tablespoons grated orange rind
⅛ teaspoon ground cloves
 3 eggs
⅔ cup roasted peanuts

Boil potatoes in salted water until tender. Remove skins, mash, and add remaining ingredients. Whip until light and fluffy. Turn into a buttered 1½-quart casserole. Dust with additional brown sugar, and sprinkle with finely chopped roasted peanuts. Bake at 450° until brown. Yield: 10 servings.

Broiled Tomatoes

 3 large tomatoes
 1 teaspoon salt
   Dash pepper
⅓ cup finely chopped onion
½ teaspoon basil
 1 tablespoon butter or margarine

Cut tomatoes in half. Sprinkle with salt and pepper. Combine onion and basil, and top tomatoes with mixture. Dot with butter or margarine and broil for 10 minutes. Yield: 6 servings.

Creamed Tomatoes

½ cup thick sweet cream
4 tablespoons all-purpose flour
2 tablespoons crushed celery leaves
2 cups cooked tomatoes
½ teaspoon salt
6 slices toast
¼ cup shredded Cheddar cheese

Mix cream and flour and stir until smooth. Add celery leaves to cooked tomatoes and heat to boiling. Remove from heat and add cream mixture, stirring constantly. Return to heat and cook about 2 minutes. Add salt, pour mixture over toast, and sprinkle with shredded Cheddar cheese. Serve hot. Yield: 6 servings.

Curried Tomatoes

3 pounds firm, ripe tomatoes
3 tablespoons salad oil
2 cups thinly sliced onions
1 clove garlic, minced
1 teaspoon salt
2 teaspoons curry powder
¼ cup water

Wash, dry, and quarter the tomatoes. Heat oil in skillet, add onions and sauté for 5 minutes. Mix in garlic, salt, and curry powder; add tomatoes and water. Cover, and cook over low heat for 15 minutes. Yield: 8 servings.

Fried Green Tomatoes

4 large, firm, green tomatoes
½ cup all-purpose flour or cornmeal
1 teaspoon salt
¼ teaspoon pepper
  Bacon drippings or shortening

Cut tomatoes in ¼-inch slices. Mix flour or cornmeal with salt and pepper. Coat tomatoes with this mixture. Place in heavy skillet containing hot bacon drippings or shortening. Fry slowly until brown, turning once. Yield: 6 servings.

Scalloped Tomatoes with Corn

1 (16-ounce) can tomatoes
  or 2 cups stewed fresh tomatoes
1½ cups fresh or cream-style canned corn
1 teaspoon salt
½ tablespoon sugar
⅛ teaspoon pepper
3 tablespoons melted butter
2 cups dry bread cubes

Combine tomatoes, corn, salt, sugar, and pepper. Spoon into a buttered 2-quart casserole. Pour melted butter over bread cubes and put on top of mixture. Cover and bake at 350° for 30 minutes. Yield: 6 servings.

Mashed Turnips

Peel and cube turnips. Put into rapidly boiling salted water and add ½ teaspoon sugar and a peeled and diced white potato for every pound of turnips. Boil until just tender, about 10 minutes; drain and mash. Season with salt, pepper, and butter, or margarine. Add hot milk, and continue beating until mixture is the consistency of mashed potatoes. Beat until light and serve hot.

It's hard to improve on the simplest way to serve cooked vegetables. Just cook properly, season with salt, pepper, and butter. Vegetable recipes begin on Page 164.

Tomatoes Stuffed with Corn

    6 medium tomatoes (firm and ripe)
    ¼ cup minced onion
    ¼ cup butter or margarine
    2 cups fresh corn kernels or canned
       niblets
    ¼ cup shredded Cheddar cheese
    2 tablespoons chopped parsley
    1 teaspoon salt
    ¼ teaspoons pepper

Scoop pulp and juice out of tomatoes; arrange tomato shells in a shallow baking pan; save pulp and juice for soup. Sauté onion in butter or margarine until golden. Add corn to onions and stir in cheese, parsley, salt, and pepper. Spoon mixture into tomato cups. Bake at 350° for 15 to 20 minutes, or until heated through. Yield: 6 servings.

Succotash

    2 cups canned tomatoes
    ½ medium onion, minced
    1 whole clove
    1 teaspoon sugar
    1 teaspoon salt
    ½ teaspoon pepper
    2 cups canned corn
    2 cups butterbeans
    1 tablespoon bacon drippings
    1 tablespoon butter or margarine

Put canned tomatoes into saucepan and add minced onion, clove, sugar, salt and pepper. Cook for 15 minutes, stirring frequently. Then add canned corn and butterbeans. Simmer for 10 minutes and add bacon drippings and butter or margarine. Serve hot, as the main dish of the meal.

Variation

Pour the vegetables, after cooking, into a greased 1½-quart baking dish, cover with ½ cup shredded cheese or with buttered breadcrumbs and bake at 375° for 10 to 15 minutes. Yield: 6 to 8 servings.

Scalloped Tomatoes Supreme

    6 slices bacon, chopped
    1 small onion, chopped
    2 tablespoons chopped green pepper
    3 cups cooked tomatoes
       Salt and pepper
 1½ cups cooked rice
    6 hard-cooked eggs
       Shredded cheese

Chop bacon and fry until crisp. Remove bacon, and brown onions and green pepper in drippings. Add tomatoes and bacon; season with salt and pepper. Arrange layers of rice, sliced hard-cooked eggs, tomatoes, and cheese in a buttered 1½-quart casserole. Bake at 325° until hot and cheese is melted. Yield: 6 servings.

Pot Likker

Southern "pot likker" is the liquid, or liquor, in which greens are cooked. Those who like to have a quantity of liquid will need to add additional boiling water as the greens are cooking. A favorite way of serving the "pot likker" is over cornbread squares.

Sautéed Fresh Turnip Greens

1 pound fresh turnip greens
2 strips bacon
⅓ cup chopped onion
⅓ cup minced green pepper
1 teaspoon salt
¼ teaspoon black pepper
½ teaspoon sugar
2 teaspoons freshly squeezed lemon juice
1 hard-cooked egg

Wash turnip greens thoroughly. Trim off coarse stems. Fry bacon in heavy skillet until crisp; remove it from the drippings and set aside. Add onion and green pepper to bacon drippings and sauté until limp. Add coarsely chopped turnip greens to onions and green pepper. Stir to mix well. Cover tightly and cook for 10 to 15 minutes, or until tender. Add salt, black pepper, sugar, and lemon juice. Toss lightly. Turn into serving dish and garnish with crisp, crumbled bacon and slices of hard-cooked egg. Yield: 4 servings.

Rutabaga Pudding

2 cups mashed, cooked rutabagas, or turnips (about 1¼ pounds)
2 tablespoons butter or margarine
1 cup soft breadcrumbs
¼ teaspoon ground mace
⅛ teaspoon black pepper
1 teaspoon salt
1 tablespoon sugar
⅛ teaspoon ground ginger
½ cup milk
1 egg, beaten
1 tablespoon melted butter or margarine

Combine mashed rutabagas, butter or margarine, breadcrumbs, mace, pepper, salt, sugar, ginger, and milk. Add beaten egg, and spoon into buttered 1-quart casserole; brush top with melted butter or margarine. Bake at 350° for 45 minutes, or until browned. Yield: 6 servings.

Fresh Turnip, Mustard, or Collard Greens

1 large bunch greens (about 2 to 2½ pounds)
¼ pound salt pork, diced
  About ½ cup boiling water
  Salt to taste

Check leaves of fresh greens carefully; remove pulpy stems and discolored spots on leaves. Wash thoroughly in several changes of warm water; add a little salt to the last water. Put greens into colander to drain.

Cook diced salt pork for about 10 minutes in boiling water in covered saucepan. Add washed greens a few at a time, cover pot, and cook slowly until greens are tender. Do not overcook. Add additional salt, if needed.

An alternate method is to wash greens carefully and put into large cooking pot with only the water that clings to leaves. Chopped turnip roots may be added when the greens are almost done. Add salt and bacon drippings after greens have cooked tender. Serve with vinegar or hot pepper sauce.

Breads

Cornbreads probably belong to the South more than they do to any other region. The Indians were found growing corn when settlers first reached our Eastern shores.

In time of hardship and poverty, the colonial homemaker learned to "make do" with supplies on hand. Since corn was readily available, it was made into ash cakes — cornmeal and water mixed, shaped by hand, and cooked in the ashes of a campfire. Hoe cake, essentially the same mixture, was baked on the blade of a hoe over a roaring campfire.

Corn pone gets its name from its shape rather than from the cooking method. It, too, was often a mixture of boiling water and cornmeal, shaped by hand, and cooked in a heavy skillet — with a bit of homemade lard if it happened to be available.

It is not known just when biscuits became a popular Southern food, but once introduced, this delicacy was here to stay. Even today, young brides are judged by the lightness of the biscuits they make. In colonial times sweet potato biscuits were popular because this root vegetable could be easily grown throughout the South.

The younger generation questions the seldom-used term "light bread," for bakery bread has in most cases supplanted the making of yeast breads in the home. But farm homemakers still make hot loaf breads and rolls. Colonial cooks made their own leavening, or yeast, from hops.

Another favorite risen bread is the true salt-rising bread. A mixture of unbolted cornmeal and water is allowed to stand for 24 hours or longer and yeast from the air forms the leavening. To hasten the process, some modern-day cooks use a commercial yeast to start salt-rising bread.

Hot Buttermilk Biscuits, served with plenty of butter and homemade preserves, bring compliments to the cook. See recipe on Page 192.

Baking Powder Biscuits

    2 cups all-purpose flour
    3 teaspoons baking powder
    1 teaspoon salt
    ¼ cup shortening
    ¾ cup milk

Combine the dry ingredients, and cut in the shortening. Add milk, stirring until all flour is moistened. Turn out on lightly floured board. Work the biscuits for about 20 seconds, then roll out to ½-inch thickness. Cut out biscuits and place on ungreased baking sheet. Bake at 450° for about 8 to 10 minutes. Yield: 12 (2-inch) biscuits.

Beaten Biscuits (Maryland)

    8 cups all-purpose flour, unsifted
    1 teaspoon baking powder
    1 teaspoon salt
    1 cup lard
    2 cups milk

Combine dry ingredients. Work in the lard with fingers, then stir in the milk. Turn onto pastry board and beat with a wooden mallet; fold over, and beat again. Continue folding dough and beating for about 30 minutes, or until blisters appear on the dough. Pinch off pieces about the size of small walnuts, work round in hand, and press flat. Stick four times with silver fork. Bake on ungreased baking sheet at 450° for about 20 minutes. Yield: 36 biscuits.

Biscuits from Mix

    ½ cup water
    2½ cups Biscuit Mix

Stir water into Mix. Turn onto a lightly floured surface and knead for 30 seconds. Pat to ½-inch thickness and cut into biscuits. Bake on ungreased baking sheet at 450° for 12 to 15 minutes. Yield: 10 to 12 biscuits.

Biscuit Mix

     8 cups all-purpose flour
     4 tablespoons baking powder
    10 tablespoons nonfat dry milk solids
     4 teaspoons salt
     1 cup lard

Combine flour, baking powder, dry milk solids, and salt. Cut in lard until the mixture has a fine, even crumb. Cover tightly and store until ready for use. Yield: about five batches of 10 to 12 biscuits each.

Buttermilk Biscuits

    2 cups all-purpose flour
    ½ teaspoon soda
    ⅔ teaspoon salt
    3 tablespoons shortening
    ¾ cup buttermilk

Combine dry ingredients. Cut in shortening. Add milk all at once. Knead lightly and roll out to ½-inch thickness. Cut out and place on ungreased baking sheet. Bake at 450° for 12 to 15 minutes. Yield: 12 (2-inch) biscuits.

Butter Rolls

Make a rich biscuit dough. Roll thin; spread well with butter and molasses, or sprinkle with either white or brown sugar and ground cinnamon; and you may add raisins, currants, or nuts. Roll tightly and cut roll at end into rings ½-inch thick. Place in greased pan and bake at 400° until done, about 15 to 20 minutes.

Note: Meat Rolls may be made like the Butter Rolls. Brush with butter, spread with seasoned ground meat. Roll and bake at 375° for 30 to 35 minutes.

Cheese Biscuits

    2 cups sifted all-purpose flour
    3 teaspoons baking powder
    1 teaspoon salt
    6 tablespoons butter or margarine
    1 cup shredded American cheese
   ⅔ cup milk

Combine dry ingredients. Cut in butter or margarine, add cheese and milk, and mix until all dry ingredients are just moistened. Turn out on a lightly floured board and knead for a few seconds. Roll or pat to ½-inch thickness. Cut with floured biscuit cutter and place on a greased baking sheet. Brush the tops with milk. Bake at 450° for 12 to 15 minutes. Yield: 12 medium or 20 small biscuits.

Jam Windmills

    2 cups all-purpose flour
    3 teaspoons baking powder
   ½ teaspoon salt
    2 tablespoons sugar
    4 tablespoons shortening
    1 egg
   ½ to ⅔ cup milk

Combine flour, baking powder, salt, and sugar. Cut in shortening. Beat egg and add milk. Add to dry ingredients to make a soft dough. Turn out on floured board and knead gently for ½ minute. Roll ⅛-inch thick, and cut into 3-inch squares. Cut diagonally from each corner to the center. Fold corners toward center, pinwheel fashion. Bake on ungreased baking sheet at 450° for 10 to 12 minutes. Yield: 18 windmills.

Monkey Biscuits

    2 tablespoons butter
   ½ cup molasses
       Day-old biscuits

Put 2 tablespoons butter and ½ cup molasses into a skillet. Heat slightly, drop in split, day-old biscuits. Fry both sides. Serve hot.

Tea Biscuits

    1 cup butter
    3 tablespoons sugar
    2 eggs
   ¾ cup milk
    4 cups all-purpose flour
    4 teaspoons baking powder
    1 teaspoon salt
       Melted butter

Cream butter and sugar; add well beaten eggs, then milk, then dry ingredients sifted together. Turn out on lightly floured board and roll ¼ inch thick. Cut with biscuit cutter, grease with melted butter, and fold over and press edges together. Slightly grease the top of each biscuit. Bake on greased baking sheet at 400° about 10 to 15 minutes. Yield: 30 biscuits.

Sourdough Biscuits

Starter

1 peeled, grated, medium potato
1 cup sugar
3 cups water
3 cups all-purpose flour

Combine all ingredients and let stand in gallon jar or crock, lightly covered with a cloth, for 3 days. After a cup of starter is taken out to make biscuits, add 1 cup water, ½ cup flour, and 1 table-spoon sugar to the starter so that there will be a supply for the next batch of biscuits.

Biscuits

1 cup starter
¼ cup melted shortening
½ teaspoon salt
About 1 cup all-purpose flour

Mix all ingredients, adding enough flour to make dough easy to handle. Roll to about ½-inch thickness on floured board. Cut out and place on greased baking sheet. Bake at 425° for 20 minutes. Serve hot. Yield: 12 biscuits.

Stir 'n' Roll Biscuits

2 cups all-purpose flour
1 teaspoon salt
3 teaspoons baking powder
⅔ cup milk
⅓ cup salad oil

Combine dry ingredients in a mixing bowl. Pour milk and salad oil into mea-suring cup. Do not stir, but pour all at once into flour. Mix dough with a fork until mixture leaves sides of bowl and forms a ball. Turn onto a large square of

waxed paper and with ends of paper in hands, press dough, kneading lightly over and over eight to ten times. Do not add extra flour when turning onto paper. Top with another square of waxed paper and roll to thickness desired, ½ inch or less. Cut as desired. Bake on ungreased baking sheet at 475° for 10 to 12 minutes. Yield: 12 biscuits.

Note: For buttermilk biscuits, use 2 cups flour, 2 teaspoons baking powder, 1 teaspoon salt, ¼ teaspoon soda, ⅓ cup salad oil, and ⅔ cup buttermilk.

Sweet Potato Biscuits

1 cup all-purpose flour
3 teaspoons baking powder
½ teaspoon salt
4 tablespoons shortening
1 cup cooked, mashed sweet potatoes
½ to ¾ cup milk

Combine flour, baking powder, and salt. Cut in shortening and add sweet pota-toes. Add enough milk to make dough stiff enough to roll. Cut and place on greased baking sheet. Bake at 400° for 20 to 30 minutes. Yield: 12 biscuits.

Note: This dough may be rolled a bit thinner and used as a "roof" for cobblers and pies.

Prize Biscuits

2 cups sifted self-rising flour
¼ teaspoon soda
4 tablespoons shortening
¾ to 1 cup buttermilk

Sift flour, measure, add soda, and sift again. Cut in shortening, using fork or pastry blender, until particles of mixture are the size of a pea. Add milk enough to make a soft dough. Knead until ingredients are well blended. Roll on floured board, cut, bake on a baking sheet in a hot oven until golden brown. Yield: 12 (2-inch) biscuits.

Sesame Seed Biscuits

Use recipe for Buttermilk Biscuits and sprinkle 2 teaspoons sesame seed on top of biscuits. Yield: 12 biscuits.

Sour Cream Biscuits

  2 cups all-purpose flour
  ¾ teaspoon salt
  ½ teaspoon soda
  1 cup commercial sour cream

Combine dry ingredients. Add cream; blend; and knead lightly. Pat or roll out and cut. Bake on ungreased baking sheet at 450° for 10 minutes. Yield: 16 biscuits.

Ham Biscuits

Use large, crusty biscuits. Split, and insert a generous slice of fried or baked ham. On the other hand, for a tea or a party nothing can surpass a tiny, crunchy biscuit with a filling of tasty minced ham, or slivers of baked ham.

Quick Cheese Biscuits

Roll biscuit dough thin. Cut biscuits and cover each with paste of shredded cheese and butter. Pinch 2 biscuits (covered sides in) together and bake. Yield: 10 to 12 biscuits.

Buttermilk Cornbread

  1 cup cornmeal
  4 tablespoons all-purpose flour
  ½ teaspoon soda
  1 teaspoon salt
  1 tablespoon melted shortening
  1 egg
  1 cup buttermilk

Sift together cornmeal, flour, soda, and salt. Melt shortening in pan in which cornbread is to be baked. Beat egg and add to buttermilk. Then pour this mixture into the sifted dry ingredients and stir only until well mixed. Add the melted shortening; stir well. Pour batter into hot, greased 10-inch pan. Bake at 425° for about 30 to 35 minutes or until brown. Yield: 6 servings.

Country Cornbread

  1½ cups cornmeal
   ¾ cup all-purpose flour
    1 teaspoon salt
  2½ teaspoons baking powder
    2 eggs, beaten
  1½ cups milk
    6 tablespoons shortening

Combine cornmeal, flour, salt, and baking powder. Combine beaten eggs and milk and stir into cornmeal mixture. Mix well. Put shortening into a 10-inch skillet and put into preheated 400° oven. As soon as shortening is very hot, coat sides of skillet and stir remaining shortening into cornbread mixture. Spoon mixture into hot skillet and bake for about 20 to 25 minutes or until golden brown. Yield: 6 to 8 servings.

Corn Crisps

2½ to 3 cups boiling water
1½ cups cornmeal
1½ teaspoons salt
4 tablespoons shortening

Pour boiling water over cornmeal, stirring vigorously. Stir in salt and shortening. Drop by tablespoonfuls onto well greased baking sheet and bake at 425° for 20 minutes or until brown and crisp. The mixture must be very thin to spread in even, round, thin cakes, 3 inches in diameter. The amount of water needed will vary with the coarseness of the cornmeal. Yield: 6 to 8 servings.

Cornmeal Muffins

⅓ cup shortening
⅓ cup sugar
1 egg, beaten
1¼ cups milk
1 cup sifted all-purpose flour
4 teaspoons baking powder
½ teaspoon salt
1 cup cornmeal

Cream shortening and sugar; add egg and milk. Combine flour, baking powder, and salt and add to shortening mixture. Add cornmeal, stirring only enough to mix. Fill greased muffin pans two-thirds full. Bake at 425° for 25 minutes. Yield: 1 dozen muffins.

Corn Pone

1 tablespoon shortening
¾ cup boiling water
1 cup cornmeal
1 teaspoon salt

Melt shortening in pan or heavy 10-inch skillet in which pone is to be cooked. Pour boiling water over cornmeal and salt. Add melted shortening. Stir to blend well. As soon as mixture is cool enough to handle, divide into four equal portions. Form each into a pone about ¾-inch thick by patting between hands. Place in greased pan, and bake at 450° for about 50 minutes, or until a light crust is formed. Yield: 6 to 8 servings.

Crackling Bread

¼ cup all-purpose flour
1½ cups cornmeal
½ teaspoon soda
¼ teaspoon salt
1 cup sour milk
1 cup diced cracklings

Mix all dry ingredients. Add the milk, and stir in the cracklings. Form into oblong cakes and place in a greased 12-inch baking pan. Bake at 400° for about 30 minutes. Yield: 6 to 8 servings.

Hot Water Cornbread

1 cup cornmeal
1 cup boiling water
1 teaspoon salt
1 tablespoon shortening
1 teaspoon sugar
1 egg
1⅛ cups milk
1 teaspoon baking powder

Heat a greased 10-inch heavy skillet in oven. Combine cornmeal, water, salt, shortening, and sugar. Stir until mixed. Beat egg and combine with milk. Mix, and stir gradually into cornmeal mixture.

Beat in baking powder. Pour into hot, greased skillet. Bake at 425° for 20 minutes. Reduce heat to 350° and bake for 30 minutes, or until firm and light brown. Yield: 6 servings.

Sweet Milk Cornbread

- 1 cup yellow cornmeal
- 1 cup sifted all-purpose flour
- ¼ cup sugar (optional)
- ½ teaspoon salt
- 3 teaspoons baking powder
- 1 egg
- 1 cup milk
- ¼ cup melted shortening

Sift together cornmeal, flour, sugar, salt, and baking powder. Beat egg, add milk, and combine with dry ingredients. Add shortening. Pour into hot, greased 10-inch skillet or pan, muffin pan, or corn stick pan. Bake at 375° to 400° for 25 to 30 minutes, or until golden brown. Yield: 6 servings.

Hush Puppies with Onions

- 1¾ cups cornmeal
- 4 tablespoons all-purpose flour
- 1 teaspoon baking powder
- 1 teaspoon salt
- 6 tablespoons chopped onion
- 1 egg, beaten
- 2 cups boiling water

Combine dry ingredients. Add chopped onion and beaten egg. Pour boiling water over this mixture, stirring constantly until mixture is smooth. Add more water if necessary. Drop by spoonfuls into deep, hot fat. Yield: 8 to 10 servings.

Hush Puppies No. 1

- 1 cup all-purpose flour
- 2 cups sifted cornmeal
- 2 tablespoons sugar
- 1 teaspoon salt
- 3 teaspoons baking powder
- 2 eggs
- 2 cups milk

Combine dry ingredients. Beat eggs and milk together and add to dry ingredients. Drop by spoonfuls into deep, hot shortening. Fry until browned. Yield: 8 to 10 servings.

Hush Puppies No. 2

- 2 cups cornmeal
- 1 tablespoon all-purpose flour
- 1 teaspoon soda
- 1 teaspoon salt
- 6 tablespoons chopped onion
- ½ pound Cheddar cheese, grated
- 1 egg, beaten
- 1½ cups buttermilk

Mix all dry ingredients; add chopped onion, grated cheese, then the beaten egg, and buttermilk. Stir well. Drop by spoonfuls into deep, hot fat where fish are cooking. When done, they will float. Drain on paper. Yield: 6 servings.

Oklahoma Prize Cornbread

1½ cups cornmeal
  3 teaspoons baking powder
½ teaspoon soda
½ cup all-purpose flour
  1 teaspoon salt
  1 tablespoon sugar
¼ cup soft shortening
1½ cups buttermilk
  1 egg, well beaten

Sift together all dry ingredients. Add soft shortening, and mix well. Add milk and beaten egg, and continue stirring until well blended. Pour into hot, 10-inch square greased pan and bake at 500° for 20 to 25 minutes. Yield: 6 to 8 servings.

Superb Spoonbread

½ cup cornmeal
  2 cups hot milk (not boiling)
½ teaspoon salt
  4 egg yolks, beaten
  4 egg whites, beaten

Make a mush of the cornmeal, hot milk, and salt. Cook until thick. Add beaten egg yolks, then fold in beaten egg whites. Pour into buttered 1½-quart casserole. Bake at 325° for 45 minutes to 1 hour. Yield: 6 servings.

Alabama Mush Bread

  2 cups cornmeal
  2 cups boiling water
  1 cup milk
  1 egg
½ teaspoon salt
  2 tablespoons butter or margarine
  2 cups all-purpose flour

Cook cornmeal and water to make a good mush. Blend in the remaining ingredients, and turn into a well greased 10-inch skillet that has cornmeal sprinkled in it. Let it cook on top of range until bread is brown on the bottom. Put in oven and bake at 400° until bread is brown on top. Turn out on large platter and cut in wedge-shaped pieces. Yield: 10 servings.

Basic Pancakes

1½ cups sifted all-purpose flour
  2 teaspoons baking powder
  1 tablespoon sugar
  1 teaspoon salt
  1 egg, slightly beaten
1¼ cups milk
  2 tablespoons melted butter or margarine

Combine dry ingredients. Break egg in a large mixing bowl and beat slightly. Stir in the milk and melted butter or margarine. Add sifted dry ingredients all at once; stir only until flour is moistened. Do not beat. Cook on greased, hot griddle. Yield: 8 servings.

Variations

Bacon Pancakes — Break 6 slices crisp, cooked bacon into small bits and add to batter.

Pecan Pancakes — Fold ½ cup chopped pecans into batter, or sprinkle pecans on batter in the griddle.

Cheese Pancakes — Add ½ cup coarsely shredded Cheddar cheese to the milk and egg mixture.

Barbecuing makes for tender, juicy, well seasoned meats. The secret of the art lies in the bright, spicy sauces. See recipes on Page 144.

Buckwheat Cakes

 1 *package dry yeast*
 2 *tablespoons light brown sugar*
 2 *cups very warm water*
 2 *cups buckwheat flour*
 1 *cup all-purpose flour*
1½ *teaspoons salt*
 1 *cup milk, scalded and cooled*

Dissolve yeast and sugar in very warm water. Add buckwheat flour, white flour, and salt. Add milk and beat until smooth. Cover and set aside in warm place for 1 hour before using.

If you are making up batter to use the following day, use ¼ package of yeast instead of 1 full package and add an extra half-teaspoon salt.

Cook on greased, hot griddle. Yield: 8 to 10 servings.

Dessert Pancakes

2½ *cups sifted all-purpose flour*
 4 *teaspoons baking powder*
 4 *tablespoons sugar*
 1 *teaspoon salt*
 2 *eggs*
 2 *cups milk*
5½ *tablespoons melted shortening*
 2 *teaspoons grated orange rind*
    Powdered sugar

Combine dry ingredients and add all at once to liquid (beaten eggs, milk, melted shortening). Add orange rind, stir, and bake on ungreased griddle. Sprinkle with powdered sugar. Serve hot with orange wedges and honey. Yield: 6 servings.

Cornmeal Pancakes

 2 *cups cornmeal*
¾ *teaspoon salt*
¾ *teaspoon soda*
1½ *cups buttermilk*
 1 *egg*
 2 *tablespoons melted shortening*
    Powdered sugar

Mix the dry ingredients; add milk, beaten egg, and melted shortening. Stir, and cook on a well greased griddle. Yield: 6 servings.

Rice Pancakes

2½ *cups all-purpose flour*
½ *cup sugar*
 3 *teaspoons baking powder*
½ *teaspoon salt*
½ *cup cold cooked rice*
 2 *cups milk*
 1 *egg, beaten*
 2 *tablespoons melted shortening*

Mix and sift dry ingredients. Work in rice with tips of fingers. Add milk, well beaten egg, and melted shortening. Cook on hot, greased griddle. Yield: 6 to 8 servings.

Buttermilk Waffles

 2 *cups sifted all-purpose flour*
 3 *teaspoons baking powder*
 1 *teaspoon soda*
 1 *teaspoon salt*
 2 *cups buttermilk*
 4 *eggs, well beaten*
½ *cup melted butter or margarine*

Heat waffle iron while mixing batter. Combine flour, baking powder, soda, and salt. Combine buttermilk and eggs and add to flour mixture. Beat until smooth. Stir in melted butter or margarine. Pour batter from a pitcher or cup onto waffle iron. Close waffle iron at once. Serve hot. Yield: 8 servings.

Cornmeal Waffles

    2 cups cornmeal
    ½ teaspoon soda
    1 teaspoon baking powder
    1 teaspoon salt
    2 teaspoons sugar
    ½ cup all-purpose flour
    2 cups sour milk
    ½ cup salad oil
    2 eggs

Combine dry ingredients and mix well. Add milk, salad oil, and beaten eggs. Beat well. Bake in hot waffle iron until crisp and brown. Yield: 6 servings.

Potato Waffles

    2 eggs, separated
    1 cup sour milk
 1 ½ cups cooked, mashed potatoes
    ⅓ cup melted butter or margarine
    1 cup all-purpose flour
    ½ teaspoon soda
    1 teaspoon salt

Separate eggs, putting whites in one bowl and yolks in large bowl. Beat yolks and add milk, potatoes, and butter or

margarine. Sift dry ingredients and add to egg-milk mixture. Beat gently until smooth. Fold in stiffly beaten egg whites and bake in hot waffle iron. Yield: about 4 small or 3 large waffles.

Cornbread Waffles No. 1

    2 cups cornmeal
    ½ teaspoon soda
    1 teaspoon baking powder
    1 teaspoon salt
    2 teaspoons sugar
    ½ cup all-purpose flour
    2 eggs
    2 cups buttermilk
    ½ cup salad oil

Combine dry ingredients and mix well. Beat eggs in mixer. Add milk, salad oil, and dry ingredients. Beat until thoroughly mixed. Bake in waffle iron until brown and crisp. Yield: 12 waffles.

Cornbread Waffles No. 2

 1 ½ cups cornmeal
    ¾ cup all-purpose flour
    2 teaspoons baking powder
    ½ teaspoon soda
    1 teaspoon salt
    2 tablespoons sugar
    2 egg yolks
 1 ½ cups buttermilk
    4 tablespoons melted butter
    2 egg whites

Sift dry ingredients together three times. Beat egg yolks and add to dry ingredients alternately with milk. Stir in melted butter and then fold in stiffly beaten egg whites. Bake in preheated waffle iron. Serve hot. Yield: 8 waffles.

Sweet Milk Waffles

  2 cups all-purpose flour
  3 teaspoons baking powder
½ teaspoon salt
  2 eggs
1½ cups milk
  3 tablespoons melted shortening

Combine flour, baking powder, and salt. Beat eggs into milk. Stir liquid into dry mixture. Add melted shortening, and beat until smooth. Pour onto hot waffle iron and cook until brown and crisp. Yield: 8 servings.

Variations

Coconut Waffles — Add ½ cup coconut just before pouring batter on waffle iron.

Pecan Waffles — Add ½ cup finely chopped pecans and 1 teaspoon sugar to batter, or add sugar to batter and sprinkle pecans on top of batter on waffle iron before baking.

Gingerbread Dessert Waffles

  2 eggs
½ cup sour milk
  1 cup molasses
⅓ cup melted butter or margarine
  2 cups all-purpose flour
1½ teaspoons soda
1½ teaspoons ground ginger
½ teaspoon ground cinnamon
  1 teaspoon salt

Separate eggs, putting whites in one bowl and yolks in a large bowl. Beat yolks, add milk, molasses, and melted butter or margarine. Beat well.

Combine dry ingredients and add to egg-milk mixture. Blend well, then fold in stiffly beaten egg whites. Bake in hot waffle iron and serve with Easy Lemon Sauce or Fluffy Sauce. Yield: about 3 or 4 waffles.

Easy Lemon Sauce

  2 egg yolks
  3 cups water
½ cup sugar
  1 (3¼-ounce) package lemon pudding and pie filling mix

Mix slightly beaten egg yolks with ¼ cup water in saucepan. Add sugar and pudding mix; mix well. Then add remaining water gradually, stirring constantly. Cook and stir over medium heat until mixture comes to full boil. Cool, stirring occasionally. Yield: 3¼ cups sauce.

Fluffy Sauce

Make a meringue of 2 egg whites and ¼ cup sugar. Slowly fold hot Easy Lemon Sauce, as it is removed from heat, into meringue until all is blended. Yield: about 4 cups sauce.

Molasses Butter Cream

½ cup molasses
½ cup butter
½ cup evaporated milk

Combine ingredients. Cook slowly for about 10 minutes, to make a smooth syrup. Cool before serving. Yield: 1¼ cups.

Note: Honey or maple syrup may be used in place of molasses to make equally delicious spreads. They are splendid, too, for griddle cakes or French toast.

Sour Cream Waffles

2 eggs, separated
1 cup thick commercial sour cream
1 cup self-rising flour

Beat egg yolks, add cream, and beat
again. Fold in stiffly beaten egg whites
and flour. Batter should be fairly stiff
and fluffy. (If plain flour is used, add 2
to 3 teaspoons baking powder and a
little salt.) Beat gently until smooth.
Bake in hot waffle iron until crisp and
brown. Yield: 4 servings.

Cheese Waffles

2 eggs
1¼ cups milk
6 tablespoons melted shortening
2 cups sifted cake flour
2 teaspoons baking powder
¼ teaspoon salt
1 cup shredded American cheese

Beat whole eggs well, add milk, and
continue beating. Add shortening, and
beat until mixture is thoroughly
blended. Combine dry ingredients and
mix in shredded cheese. Bake in preheated waffle iron. Yield: 6 servings.

Banana-Nut Bread

½ cup shortening
1 cup sugar
2 eggs
1 cup mashed ripe bananas
¼ cup chopped nuts
2 cups all-purpose flour
1 teaspoon soda
¼ teaspoon salt

Cream shortening and sugar until light
and fluffy. Add eggs and beat well. Stir
in mashed bananas and mix well. Stir in
nuts. Sift dry ingredients and stir in.
Pour into greased loafpan and bake at
350° for 40 minutes. Yield: 1 loaf.

Apricot-Nut Bread

½ cup dried apricots
1 egg, beaten
¾ cup white corn syrup
¼ cup sugar
2 tablespoons shortening
2 cups all-purpose flour
¼ teaspoon salt
3 teaspoons baking powder
¼ teaspoon soda
½ cup orange juice
¼ cup water
½ cup chopped nuts

Soak apricots for ½ hour; drain, and cut
fine. Combine egg, corn syrup, and
sugar; beat well. Add shortening. Add
flour combined with salt, baking powder, and soda, alternately with orange
juice and water mixed. Add nuts. Pour
into greased 9- x 5-inch loafpan. Bake at
350° for 1 hour. Yield: 1 loaf.

Biscuit Coffeecake

12 uncooked biscuits
¼ cup melted butter or margarine
½ cup sugar
½ cup chopped pecans
1½ teaspoons ground cinnamon

Cut biscuits desired size. Dip biscuits in
melted butter or margarine, then in mixture of sugar, chopped pecans, and cinnamon. Put biscuits in a 9-inch piepan

and bake at 450° for about 8 minutes or until golden brown. Yield: 12 servings.

Buttermilk-Nut Bread

1¼ cups all-purpose flour
1 teaspoon salt
½ teaspoon soda
2 teaspoons baking powder
1 cup whole wheat flour
1 cup chopped nuts
2 eggs, beaten
⅔ cup honey
2 tablespoons salad oil or melted shortening
1 cup buttermilk

Grease bottom of a 9- x 5- x 3-inch loaf-pan and line with waxed paper, then grease paper. Combine flour, salt, soda, and baking powder. Add whole wheat flour and nuts. Beat eggs. Fold in honey, oil, and buttermilk. Add dry ingredients, blending only until well mixed. Bake at 325° for 50 to 60 minutes, or until bread is done in center. Cool for 10 minutes before removing from pan. Cool before slicing. Yield: 1 loaf.

Cinnamon Crunch

⅓ cup butter or margarine
½ cup sugar
¼ teaspoon salt
1 cup all-purpose flour
¼ teaspoon ground cinnamon
1 egg yolk, slightly beaten
2 tablespoons milk
¼ teaspoon almond extract
1 egg white, slightly beaten
3 tablespoons sugar
1 teaspoon ground cinnamon

Cut butter or margarine into combined ½ cup sugar, salt, flour, and ¼ teaspoon cinnamon. Add egg yolk, milk, and flavoring. Mix thoroughly. Spread mixture in an ungreased 13- x 9- x 2-inch pan. Spread egg white over top. Sprinkle 3 tablespoons sugar mixed with 1 teaspoon cinnamon over all. Bake at 350° for 25 minutes. Cut while warm, and serve with coffee or fruit for a simple dessert. Yield: 12 servings.

Klejner (Danish Fried Bread)

6 egg yolks
1 egg white
½ cup heavy cream
1 cup sugar
4 cups all-purpose flour

Combine egg yolks and egg white and beat well. Add remaining ingredients. Roll out thin and cut into diamond-shaped pieces. Make a slit in the center of each piece and pull one end through. Fry in deep, hot shortening. Yield: 36.

French Toast

2 eggs
6 tablespoons milk
⅛ teaspoon salt
6 slices bread
Hot shortening for frying

Beat eggs slightly. Stir in milk and salt. Dip the bread, one slice at a time, into the mixture. Melt shortening in heavy frying pan. When hot, place the bread slices in the pan. Turn to brown both sides. Yield: 3 to 6 servings.

Fluffy French Toast

1⅓ cups milk, divided
2 eggs, beaten
½ cup all-purpose flour
½ teaspoon salt
½ teaspoon baking powder
½ cup shortening
6 slices bread

Place 1 cup milk in a shallow dish.
Combine beaten eggs, flour, salt, and
baking powder in another shallow dish;
add ⅓ cup milk and blend. Melt shortening in skillet. Dip bread, one slice at a
time, into milk, then into egg mixture.
Turn to coat both sides of bread. Place
bread in skillet, cover, and cook over
low heat until bread is golden brown on
one side. Turn, cover, and cook until
other side is golden brown. Serve immediately. Yield: 6 servings.

Orange French Toast

⅔ cup orange juice
1 tablespoon grated orange rind
1 tablespoon sugar
¼ teaspoon ground cinnamon
2 eggs
6 slices bread
¼ cup butter or margarine

Combine orange juice, grated rind, and
sugar. Add cinnamon to eggs, and beat
until light and frothy. Whip sweetened fruit juice into beaten egg with a
fork. Dip each slice of bread into egg and
fruit mixture and fry slices slowly in
butter on moderately hot grill. Turn, to
brown lightly on both sides. Serve with
honey. For luncheon, change the shape
to suit the occasion. Yield: 3 to 6
servings.

Quick Coffeecake with Topping

1½ cups all-purpose flour
½ cup sugar
2 teaspoons baking powder
½ teaspoon salt
1 egg
⅔ cup milk
3 tablespoons melted shortening
   Topping

Combine flour, sugar, baking powder,
and salt. Beat egg, milk, and melted
shortening together. Stir liquid into dry
ingredients, mixing only enough to
moisten. Pour into greased 9- x 9-inch
pan and add Topping. Bake at 425° for
25 minutes. Yield: 1 coffeecake.

Topping

2 tablespoons butter or margarine
2 tablespoons sugar
¼ cup all-purpose flour
¼ cup dry breadcrumbs
½ teaspoon ground cinnamon

Cream butter or margarine and sugar.
Add flour, breadcrumbs, and cinnamon.
Mix to consistency of coarse crumbs and
sprinkle over Coffeecake batter before
baking. Yield: about ½ cup.

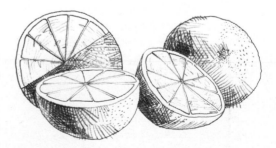

Cotty's Brown Bread

    1 egg
    ½ cup molasses
    2 cups whole wheat flour
    1 cup all-purpose flour
    2 teaspoons soda
    1 tablespoon salt
    ½ cup sugar
    2 cups sour milk

Beat egg; add molasses, and mix well.
Stir in whole wheat flour. Sift together
flour, soda, salt, and sugar. Add alternately with sour milk. Bake in greased
9- x 5- x 3-inch loafpan at 375° for about
45 minutes or until done. Yield: 1 loaf.

Fruit-Nut Bread

    ½ cup dried apricots
    ½ cup seedless raisins
    ¾ cup hot water
    ½ teaspoon grated orange rind
    ¼ cup orange juice
    ¾ cup sugar
    2 tablespoons melted margarine
       or butter
    1 teaspoon vanilla extract
    1 egg
 2 ½ cups all-purpose flour
    ¼ teaspoon salt
    4 teaspoons baking powder
    1 teaspoon soda
    ½ cup finely chopped nuts

Cover apricots and raisins with hot
water and soak for 30 minutes. Drain,
and save ¾ cup of the water; grind
fruit in food chopper until fine. Add
grated orange rind, orange juice, and
¾ cup water to the ground fruit. Stir
in sugar, melted butter or margarine,
and vanilla. Beat egg and blend in.

Combine the flour, salt, baking powder,
and soda. Combine with the fruit mixture. Add nuts, and blend well. Pour
into a greased loafpan, and bake at
350° for 1 hour. Cool and slice ¼ inch
thick. Yield: 1 loaf.

Peanut Butter Bread

    2 cups all-purpose flour
    ½ cup sugar
    2 teaspoons baking powder
    1 teaspoon salt
    ¾ cup peanut butter
    1 egg
    1 cup milk

Combine flour, sugar, baking powder,
and salt. Cut in the peanut butter with
a fork. Add well beaten egg and milk.
Stir just enough to moisten all the dry
ingredients. Bake in a greased loafpan
at 350° for about 1 hour. Yield: 1 loaf.

Potato Doughnuts

    3 tablespoons shortening
    ¾ cup sugar
    3 eggs
    1 cup mashed cooked potatoes
 2 ¼ cups all-purpose flour
    4 teaspoons baking powder
    1 teaspoon salt
    ⅛ teaspoon ground nutmeg
    ½ cup milk

Cream shortening and sugar; add well
beaten eggs and mashed potatoes. Sift
dry ingredients together and add alternately with milk. Roll out and cut as
plain doughnuts. Fry in deep, hot shortening. Yield: 3 dozen.

Date-Nut Bread

2½ cups sifted all-purpose flour
2 teaspoons baking powder
1 teaspoon soda
1 teaspoon salt
½ cup sugar (white or brown)
1 cup whole wheat flour, unsifted
2 cups chopped, pitted dates
½ cup chopped nuts
1 egg, well beaten
2 cups sour milk or buttermilk
3 tablespoons melted shortening

Combine flour, baking powder, soda, salt, and sugar. Add the unsifted whole wheat flour, then the dates and nuts. Combine egg with milk and melted shortening. Combine liquid and dry ingredients, stirring only enough to moisten dry ingredients. Pour into well greased loafpan and bake at 350° for 1 hour. Cool thoroughly. Yield: 1 loaf.

Orange Bread

⅔ cup orange juice
3 tablespoons grated orange rind
3 tablespoons melted butter or
   margarine
½ cup finely cut dates
1 cup sugar
1 egg, slightly beaten
½ cup coarsely chopped pecans
2 cups all-purpose flour
½ teaspoon soda
1 teaspoon baking powder
½ teaspoon salt

Combine orange juice, orange rind, melted butter or margarine, dates, sugar, egg, and pecans. Sift together dry ingredients; combine with other ingredients. Mix well, and pour into a greased loafpan. Bake at 350° for 50 minutes, or until done. Yield: 1 loaf.

Hominy Muffins

1 cup cooked grits
1 cup buttermilk
1 cup cornmeal
¼ cup all-purpose flour
1 teaspoon soda
1 teaspoon salt
4 tablespoons melted shortening
1 egg

Moisten cooked grits with buttermilk. Add other ingredients, and pour into greased muffin pans. Bake at 400° for about 20 minutes. Yield: 12 large muffins.

Yam Muffins

1½ cups sifted all-purpose flour
3 teaspoons baking powder
½ teaspoon salt
¼ teaspoon ground nutmeg
¼ teaspoon ground cinnamon
¼ cup soft butter or margarine
⅓ cup creamy peanut butter
¼ cup brown sugar, firmly packed
2 eggs, slightly beaten
1¼ cups mashed, cooked sweet potatoes

Combine dry ingredients. Blend butter or margarine, peanut butter, and sugar; mix well. Add eggs and sweet potatoes to blended ingredients; add dry ingredients, and mix until just blended. Spoon into greased muffin tins and bake at 400° for 35 to 40 minutes. Yield: 12 to 16 muffins.

Berry Muffins

2 cups all-purpose flour
3 teaspoons baking powder
3 tablespoons sugar
½ teaspoon salt
1 egg, well beaten
1 cup milk
3 tablespoons melted shortening
¾ cup drained berries or cherries

Sift dry ingredients together. Combine egg, milk, and melted shortening. Add this to dry ingredients, together with drained fruit, and stir until just mixed. Fill greased muffin pans two-thirds full and bake at 425° for 20 to 30 minutes. Yield: 18 muffins.

Squaw Bread

4 cups all-purpose flour
1 tablespoon sugar
1 tablespoon baking powder
2 teaspoons salt
1 tablespoon shortening
2 cups lukewarm milk
   Syrup

Combine dry ingredients, and cut in shortening. Add milk, and beat. This makes a very soft dough. Roll on floured board and cut into squares. Fry in deep, hot shortening. Serve hot with Syrup. Yield: 6 servings.

Syrup

2 cups dark corn syrup
2 cups brown sugar
½ cup bacon drippings

Heat until thoroughly mixed. Serve hot. Syrup may be made ahead of time and reheated at time it is needed. Yield: 4 cups.

Yorkshire Pudding

½ cup all-purpose flour
¼ teaspoon salt
½ cup milk
1 egg

Combine ingredients and beat together just until smooth. Pour into deep, well greased muffin pans. Bake at 425° for 30 to 40 minutes, or until golden brown. Yield: 6 servings, or 12 muffins.

Note: To bake in a roasting pan, remove beef roast from pan when done. Pour off most of the fat in pan. Pour in batter and bake for 35 to 45 minutes, or until golden brown. Cut in squares and serve with roast.

Quick Nut Bread

½ cup sugar
1 egg
1¼ cups milk
3 cups biscuit mix
1½ cups chopped nuts

Blend first four ingredients. Beat hard for 30 seconds. Stir in nuts. Bake in a greased loafpan at 350° for 45 to 50 minutes. Yield: 1 loaf.

Rice Bread

2 cups rice, boiled soft
6 eggs, lightly beaten
2 cups milk
1 cup cornmeal
1 tablespoon shortening
1 tablespoon butter
1 teaspoon salt

Combine ingredients, and mix together well. Bake in muffin pans at 350° for 20 to 25 minutes or until golden brown. Yield: 12 to 16 muffins.

Molasses Bread

    1 egg
    ¼ cup sugar
    ½ cup molasses
    ¼ cup melted shortening
    2½ cups sifted all-purpose flour
    1 teaspoon soda
    2 teaspoons baking powder
    ½ to ¾ cup buttermilk or sour milk

Beat egg until light. Add sugar, molasses, and melted shortening. Combine flour, soda, baking powder, and salt. Add to egg mixture alternately with buttermilk. Bake in greased loafpan at 350° for 1 hour. Yield: 1 loaf.

Stickies

    ½ cup syrup
    ¼ cup butter or margarine
    6 cold, sliced biscuits

Combine syrup and butter or margarine in a large skillet. Bring to a boil and boil until slightly thick. Turn heat down and add biscuits. Cook slowly, turning biscuits once. Serve hot. Yield: 6 servings.

Rolled Oats Bread

    2 cups rolled oats, regular or
       quick-cooking
    2 teaspoons salt
    ⅓ cup molasses
    1 tablespoon shortening
    2 cups boiling water
    1 package dry yeast
    ¼ cup very warm water
    4 or 5 cups all-purpose flour

Mix oats, salt, molasses, and shortening; add boiling water. Cool to lukewarm. Dissolve yeast in ¼ cup very warm water and add to lukewarm mixture. Add flour, and knead to a soft dough. Cover; let rise until double in size. Bake in two 9- x 5- x 2-inch loafpans at 375° for 50 to 60 minutes. Yield: 2 loaves.

Savannah Bread

    1¾ cups all-purpose flour
    2 teaspoons baking powder
    ½ teaspoon salt
    ¼ teaspoon soda
    ⅓ cup shortening
    ¾ cup crunchy peanut butter
    ⅔ cup sugar
    2 eggs, slightly beaten
    1 cup mashed ripe bananas

Combine flour, baking powder, salt, and soda. Cream shortening and peanut butter. Add sugar gradually while creaming; cream until light and fluffy. Add eggs, and beat well. Stir in dry ingredients alternately with mashed bananas. Mix well, but do not beat. Spoon batter into well greased loafpan. Bake at 350° for 1 hour, or until center tests done and loaf pulls slightly from sides of pan. Yield: 1 loaf.

Steamed Brown Bread

    1   cup cornmeal
1 ½   teaspoons soda
1 ½   teaspoons salt
    2   cups whole wheat flour
    1   cup raisins
    2   cups buttermilk
    ¾   cup dark molasses

Sift together the cornmeal, soda, and salt. Add to whole wheat flour and raisins, and mix well. Mix the buttermilk and molasses and add to the dry ingredients. Stir only enough to moisten the dry ingredients. Fill greased cans to within 1 inch of top. Cover the cans with waxed paper or aluminum foil and steam for 2 hours. The water in the container should be at least halfway up the sides of the cans during the steaming. Yield: about 3 or 4 pounds.

Sourdough Rolls

    1   cup (1 medium) diced potato
    ½   cup boiling water
    2   tablespoons sugar
    ½   teaspoon salt
    ¾   teaspoon dry yeast
    2   tablespoons very warm water
    ½   cup undiluted evaporated milk
    ½   cup water
    1   tablespoon sugar
    1   tablespoon salt
    2   tablespoons melted butter or margarine
    4   cups all-purpose flour

Combine potato and ½ cup boiling water. Cover and cook over low heat until potato is tender. Mash undrained potato. Add 2 tablespoons sugar and ½ teaspoon salt; blend. Cool to lukewarm. Meanwhile, dissolve yeast in 2 table-spoons very warm water. Add to potato mixture and blend. Cover, and let stand in warm place for about 24 hours.

Scald evaporated milk and ½ cup water. Add 1 tablespoon sugar, 1 tablespoon salt, and 2 tablespoons melted butter or margarine; stir until sugar dissolves. Cool to lukewarm. Add potato-yeast mixture; blend. Gradually add 3 ¼ cups flour, mixing until smooth. Turn into greased bowl. Cover and let rise in warm place overnight, or until double in bulk. Add remaining ¾ cup flour; mix well. Knead on floured surface until smooth. Shape into 36 rolls. Place on greased baking sheets and brush with melted shortening. Cover with damp towel. Let rise until double in size. Bake at 400° for 15 to 18 minutes. Yield: 36 rolls.

Christmas Stollen

   1 *package dry yeast*
  ¼ *cup very warm water*
  ½ *cup milk*
  ¼ *cup sugar*
  1 *teaspoon salt*
  2 *tablespoons melted shortening*
2¾ *to 3 cups all-purpose flour*
  1 *egg*
  ½ *cup chopped blanched almonds*
  ¼ *cup finely cut candied citron*
  ¼ *cup finely cut candied cherries*
  1 *teaspoon grated lemon rind*
  1 *tablespoon soft butter or margarine*
  2 *tablespoons sugar*
  ½ *teaspoon ground cinnamon*

Sprinkle dry yeast into very warm water. Stir until dissolved. Scald milk. Pour into large bowl. Add sugar, salt, and shortening. Cool until just warm. Stir in 1 cup flour. Mix in dissolved yeast and egg, and beat hard. Sprinkle 1 cup flour over almonds, chopped fruit, and grated lemon rind. Add to batter, and stir well. Add remainder of flour and knead. Shape into a smooth ball and place in greased bowl. Cover and let rise until doubled in bulk. Punch down. Cover and let rest for 10 to 15 minutes. With palms of hands press dough into oval shape a scant ½ inch thick. Spread half of oval with soft butter or margarine. Mix sugar and cinnamon and sprinkle over butter or margarine. Fold unspread half lengthwise over sugar and cinnamon, making edges even. Lift onto lightly greased baking sheet. Curve the ends slightly. Press down the folded edge (not the open edge). Cover, and let rise until doubled (about 1 hour and 15 minutes). Bake at 350° for about 30 to 35 minutes.

When cool, frost and decorate. Combine ¾ cup sifted powdered sugar, and 1 tablespoon cream or top milk. Pour it over loaf, letting frosting drip down the sides. Decorate with sliced candied cherries and slivered almonds. Yield: 1 loaf.

High Milk-Protein Bread

   1 *package dry yeast*
  ¼ *cup very warm water*
  2 *cups boiling water*
  3 *cups nonfat dry milk solids*
  2 *tablespoons shortening*
  2 *tablespoons sugar*
  1 *tablespoon salt*
6½ *cups all-purpose flour*

Dissolve yeast in very warm water. Measure boiling water into mixing bowl and gradually stir in milk powder, beating with egg beater, if necessary. Then stir in shortening, sugar, and salt, mixing well. Let cool to lukewarm. Stir 2 cups flour into liquid and mix thoroughly. Add yeast mixture to dough and stir well. Add enough of remaining flour to make a smooth, soft dough that handles easily. Lightly flour pastry board and place dough on it. Cover with bowl and let rest for 10 minutes. Knead bread until outside is smooth and elastic. Round up dough into two portions, cover with bowls and let rest for 10 minutes. Shape into loaves. Place in pans which have been greased in the bottom only. Do not press corners of loaves into corners of pans. Grease top of loaves. Cover with waxed paper and cloth and let rise in warm place until double in volume. Bake at 350° for about 50 to 55 minutes. Yield: 2 loaves.

Variations

Egg Bread — Add 2 beaten eggs to the lukewarm milk mixture. This will make a softer dough and a bread of lighter texture.

Raisin Bread — To the standard recipe, add 2 cups raisins or chopped prunes.

Rapidmix CoolRise White Bread

7¾ to 8¾ cups all-purpose flour
  3 tablespoons sugar
4½ teaspoons salt
  3 packages dry yeast
 ⅓ cup softened margarine
2⅔ cups very warm water (120° to 130°)
    Peanut oil

Thoroughly mix 3 cups flour, sugar, salt, and undissolved yeast in a large bowl. Add margarine. Gradually add very warm water to dry ingredients and beat for 2 minutes at medium speed with electric mixer, scraping bowl occasionally. Add ½ cup flour. Beat at high speed for 2 minutes, scraping bowl occasionally. Stir in enough additional flour to make a stiff dough. Turn out onto lightly floured board; knead until smooth and elastic, about 10 to 12 minutes. Cover with plastic wrap, then a towel. Let rest for 20 minutes.

Divide dough in half. Roll each half to a 14- x 9-inch rectangle. Shape into loaves. Place in two greased 9- x 5- x 3-inch loafpans. Brush with peanut oil. Cover loosely with plastic wrap. Refrigerate for 2 to 12 hours.

When ready to bake, remove from refrigerator. Uncover dough carefully. Let stand at room temperature for 10 minutes. Puncture any gas bubbles which may have formed with a greased toothpick or metal skewer.

Bake at 400° for 35 to 40 minutes, or until done. Remove from baking pans and cool on wire racks. Yield: 2 loaves.

Old Virginia Sally Lunn

½ cup scalded milk
6 tablespoons shortening
1 package dry yeast
¼ cup very warm water
2 cups all-purpose flour
2 tablespoons sugar
½ teaspoon salt
2 eggs

Combine milk and shortening; cool until lukewarm. Meanwhile, dissolve yeast in very warm water. Combine flour, sugar, and salt in a large bowl; make a well in the center. Stir in yeast, then milk mixture. Let rise in a warm place for about 20 minutes. Stir in beaten eggs, and mix well. Cover with a clean towel and let rise until double in bulk (about 2 hours). Then beat well and turn into greased tubepan. Cover with a clean towel and let rise in warm place until doubled in bulk. Bake in two greased loafpans or a 10-inch tubepan at 425° for 15 to 20 minutes, or until done. Split across and butter, then cut into wedges. Serve hot. Or next day, toast wedges. Yield: 1 large Sally Lunn or 2 loaves.

Raised Bread Doughnuts

¼ cup very warm water
1 package dry yeast
1 cup milk, scalded and cooked to
 lukewarm
½ teaspoon salt
4¼ cups all-purpose flour
¼ cup butter or margarine
½ cup light brown sugar
2 eggs, well beaten
½ teaspoon ground nutmeg

Measure very warm water into mixing bowl. Sprinkle in yeast; stir until dissolved. Add lukewarm milk and salt. Stir in enough flour to make a stiff batter. Cover and let rise overnight. In the morning, cream together butter or margarine and sugar; stir in eggs and nutmeg. Add creamed mixture to the batter. Add remaining flour to make a soft dough. Turn out on floured board; knead lightly until dough is smooth and elastic. Form into a ball and place in a well greased bowl. Grease top of dough; cover and set in a warm place and let rise until doubled, about 1 hour and 30 minutes. Pat out on floured board to about ¾-inch thickness. Cut into 1½-inch squares and shape into balls. Cover and let rise in a warm place until doubled, about 1 hour. Drop several at a time into deep hot shortening (375°). Fry until golden, turning once. Yield: 24 doughnuts.

Salt Rising Bread

Starter

1 cup milk
1 tablespoon sugar
7 tablespoons white cornmeal
1 teaspoon salt
2 cups lukewarm water
2 tablespoons sugar
3 tablespoons shortening
2 cups all-purpose flour

Scald 1 cup milk and stir in 1 tablespoon sugar, 7 tablespoons cornmeal, and 1 teaspoon salt. Place mixture in a jar, and cover with cheesecloth; set jar in water as hot as the hand can stand. Allow to stand for 6 to 7 hours in a warm place (115°) until it shows fermentation. The gas can be heard to escape when it has sufficiently fermented.

At the end of fermentation period, add 2 cups lukewarm water, 2 tablespoons sugar, 3 tablespoons shortening, and 2 cups all-purpose flour to make a sponge. Beat well; put in a container and set in a water bath canner; maintain heat at 115° until sponge is very light and full of bubbles.

To Make Bread

To this light sponge add about 8½ cups all-purpose flour, or enough to give a stiff dough. Knead for 10 minutes. Mold into about 4 loaves and place in greased loafpans. Cover and let rise to 2½ times the original bulk. Bake at 375° for 10 minutes, lower temperature to 350° and bake 25 minutes longer, or until loaves test done. Yield: about 4 loaves.

Sourdough Bread

Starter

1 package dry yeast
½ cup very warm water
1 tablespoon sugar
1 tablespoon salt
2 cups warm water
2 cups all-purpose flour

Sprinkle the dry yeast in ½ cup very warm water and let stand until dissolved. Stir well. Put the yeast into a large bowl or pan with a cover and add the other ingredients. Mix well. Cover, and let stand for 3 days at room temperature (78°). Stir the mixture down daily.

To Make Bread

1 cup Starter
½ cup milk
2 tablespoons sugar
2 tablespoons soft shortening
½ teaspoon salt
3 to 4 cups all-purpose flour

Put the Starter in a large mixing bowl. Scald the milk and add the sugar, shortening, and salt. When cool, add to the Starter. Stir in the flour, and turn the dough out on a lightly floured board. Knead for a minute or two.

Place dough in a greased bowl, and brush the top with melted shortening. Cover with a cloth and let rise until doubled in bulk (about 1 hour and 20 minutes). Punch down, and let rise to double in bulk again. Punch down and shape into a round ball. Let rest for 10 minutes. Shape into loaf and put into a greased loafpan. Let rise to double in bulk. Bake at 400° for about 50 minutes, or until crust is well browned. Yield: 1 loaf.

To Use Starter Again

After the 1 cup of Starter has been removed, add 1 cup warm water, ½ cup flour, and 1 teaspoon sugar to the remaining Starter. Cover and let stand until ready to use. Stir down daily.

Sweet Dough

½ cup milk
½ cup sugar
1½ teaspoons salt
¼ cup shortening
2 packages dry yeast
½ cup very warm water
2 eggs, beaten
5 cups all-purpose flour

Scald milk and stir in sugar, salt, and shortening. Cool to lukewarm. Dissolve yeast in very warm water. Stir until dissolved, then stir into the lukewarm milk mixture. Add beaten eggs and 3 cups flour. Beat until smooth, and stir in an additional 2 cups flour. Turn dough out onto lightly floured board and knead until smooth and elastic. Place in a greased bowl and brush top with soft shortening. Cover and let rise in a warm place, free from draft, until double in bulk (about 1 hour). Punch down and turn out onto lightly floured board. Use as desired to make any of the following sweet breads.

Cinnamon Buns

    1 recipe Sweet Dough
1½ cups sugar
    2 teaspoons ground cinnamon
⅔ cup raisins

Divide Sweet Dough in half. Roll out each half into an oblong 14 x 9 inches. Brush lightly with melted butter or margarine. Sprinkle each oblong with a mixture of sugar, cinnamon, and raisins. Roll up as for jellyroll to make roll 9 inches long. Seal edges firmly.

Cut into nine equal pieces. Place cut side up about 1 inch apart in greased pan. Cover, and let rise until doubled in bulk. Bake at 350° for about 35 minutes. Yield: about 2 dozen.

Kolaches

1 recipe Sweet Dough
   Filling (Choose one from list below.)

Prepare any of the fillings below. After dough rises, shape the Kolaches into ovals, or fold dough ½ inch thick and cut with a 2-inch biscuit cutter. Place about 1½ inches apart on greased baking sheet. Cover and let rise for 20 to 30 minutes. Make a depression in center of each and fill with 2 or 3 teaspoons filling. Pinch edges together tightly. Let rise for about 10 minutes, then bake at 400° for about 15 minutes. Yield: about 2 dozen.

Variations

Poppy Seed-Fruit Filling — Mix ½ cup cooked mashed apricots or prunes, ½ teaspoon cinnamon, ¼ cup sugar, and 2 tablespoons poppy seed.

Prune-Nut Filling — Mix together 1 cup cooked, mashed prunes, ¼ cup sugar, and ¼ cup chopped nuts.

Jam or Jelly Filling — Use any flavored jam or jelly; add spices or chopped nuts if desired.

Date-Nut Filling — Cook one 8-ounce package dates in small amount of water, mash, add sugar as desired, and beat until smooth. Nuts may be added if desired.

Swedish Tea Ring

    1 recipe Sweet Dough
¾ cup chopped raisins
    1 teaspoon ground cinnamon
½ cup coarsely chopped pecans
½ cup brown sugar

Roll Sweet Dough into a rectangle ¼ inch thick. Brush with melted butter or margarine, then spread with a mixture of chopped fruit, cinnamon, chopped pecans, and brown sugar. Roll as a jellyroll. Place on greased baking sheet. Draw the ends together, making a ring. With scissors, cut almost through the ring at 1-inch intervals, turning each piece with the cut side down. Brush lightly with egg white or melted butter or margarine. Let rise until double in bulk and bake in greased pan at 400° for about 25 minutes.

While still hot, glaze with thin icing made from ½ cup powdered sugar and 2 or 3 teaspoons water.

Other fruits which might be used include cooked, mashed peaches or apricots, or prune pulp. Yield: 1 ring.

Basic Yeast Rolls

  1 *package dry yeast*
  ¼ *cup very warm water*
  ½ *cup scalded milk*
  2 *tablespoons sugar*
  ¾ *teaspoon salt*
  2 *tablespoons melted butter or margarine*
  1 *egg, slightly beaten*
2½ *cups all-purpose flour*

Dissolve dry yeast in very warm water according to directions on the package. Add milk which has been cooled to lukewarm, sugar, and salt. Allow to stand for 5 minutes. Add butter or margarine and egg, and mix well. Stir in flour and beat with spoon until dough forms a ball and follows spoon around the bowl. Brush top of dough with melted butter or margarine and cover with waxed paper or towel. Set bowl in warm water until dough is light and spongy, about 20 to 25 minutes. Turn out onto floured cloth or board, knead ½ minute. Shape, let rise, and bake at 400° for 10 to 12 minutes.

All the various rolls can be shaped from the same dough. A basic yeast dough can yield a variety of well shaped rolls.

1. One of the simplest of the rolls to shape is the Cloverleaf Roll. For this roll, form dough into small balls. Dip each into melted butter or margarine and place three balls in each section of a greased muffin pan. A nice, golden brown, crusty roll is the result. Split the hot roll three ways and drop a pat of butter or margarine in the center — simply good eating!

2. The Crescent-Shaped Roll is simple but elegant. Roll a ball of dough into circular shape about ¼ inch thick. Cut into pie-shaped pieces. Brush with melted butter or margarine and roll up, beginning at the wide end. Curve into crescents on greased baking sheet. Feature these attractive hot rolls at one of your special dinners and hear your guests ask for more.

3. Bowknot Rolls are just as the name implies, and just as simple to make. Roll a portion of dough under hands to form a rope about ½ inch in thickness. Cut into pieces about 6 inches long. Tie in knots. Place on greased baking sheet. Longer pieces of dough may be tied in double knots or coiled into "snails."

4. Fan Tan Rolls are attractive in their simplicity. To make these, roll dough into a very thin rectangular sheet. Brush with melted butter or margarine. Cut into strips about 1 inch wide. Stack six or seven strips on top of each other. Cut stacked strips into 1½-inch long pieces and place on end in greased muffin pans.

5. Parker House Rolls are easily made and are always favorites. Roll out dough and cut into rounds. Crease with dull edge of knife to one side of center. Brush lightly with melted butter or margarine. Fold larger side over smaller so edges meet. Seal. Put on greased baking sheet 1 inch apart.

White Bread
(Straight-Dough Method)

- 1 cup milk
- 3 tablespoons sugar
- 2½ teaspoons salt
- 6 tablespoons shortening
- 1 cup very warm water
- 1 package dry yeast
- 6 cups all-purpose flour

Scald milk, then stir in sugar, salt, and shortening. Cool to lukewarm. Measure very warm water into a bowl and dissolve yeast in it. Stir in lukewarm milk mixture. Add 3 cups flour and beat until smooth. Add additional 3 cups flour. Turn out on lightly floured board and knead until smooth and elastic. Place in greased bowl, cover, and let rise until double in bulk. Punch down, turn out onto board and divide in half. Let rest for 15 to 20 minutes, then shape into loaves. Place in greased loafpans, cover, and let rise until double in bulk (about 1 hour). Bake at 400° for about 50 minutes. Yield: 2 loaves.

White Bread
(Sponge Method)

- 1½ cups warm water
- 2 tablespoons sugar
- 1 package dry yeast
- 2 cups all-purpose flour
- 1 cup milk
- 2 tablespoons sugar
- 1 tablespoon salt
- 3 tablespoons shortening
  About 5 cups all-purpose flour.

Measure the warm water and the sugar into a bowl. Add the yeast, and stir until dissolved. Add 2 cups flour and beat until smooth. Cover and let rise until light and spongy, about 1 hour. Scald the 1 cup milk, stir in sugar, salt, and shortening, and cool to lukewarm. Stir the sponge down and add to the lukewarm milk mixture. Stir in additional flour. Turn out onto lightly floured board and knead until smooth and elastic. Place in greased bowl, and brush with shortening. Cover and let rise until double in bulk, about 45 minutes. Punch down and turn out onto lightly floured board. Divide in half and let rest for 15 to 20 minutes. Shape into loaves and place in greased loafpans. Cover, and let rise until center is slightly higher than edge of pan, about 1 hour. Bake at 400° for about 50 minutes. Yield: 2 loaves.

Slow-Bake Rolls

- ¼ cup sugar
- ¼ cup shortening
- 2 cups milk
- 1 package dry yeast
- ¼ cup very warm water
- 8 cups all-purpose flour
- ½ teaspoon baking powder
- ½ teaspoon soda
- 3 teaspoons salt

Combine sugar, shortening, and milk and heat to boiling. Soften yeast in ¼ cup very warm water. Add softened yeast and 4 cups flour to lukewarm milk mixture. The batter should be thin. Beat.

Let rise in a warm place until batter is double in bulk (about 2 hours). Combine baking powder, soda, salt, and 2 cups flour. Add to dough, and knead in an additional 2 cups flour until dough leaves bowl. Form into smooth ball, grease lightly all over, and place in refrigerator or shape into rolls. Place rolls in a greased pan, rub surface with melted shortening, and set in a warm place. Let rolls double in size. Bake at 275° for 30 minutes, or until done but not brown. Cool on rack.

Wrap in freezer paper and freeze. To prepare for serving, bake at 400° for 10 minutes, or until brown. Yield: 36 rolls.

Coffeecake

1½ *packages dry yeast*
1 *tablespoon sugar*
¼ *cup very warm water*
¾ *cup milk, scalded and cooled*
4½ *cups all-purpose flour*
¼ *cup butter or margarine*
⅔ *cup sugar*
¼ *teaspoon salt*
2 *eggs, beaten*

Dissolve yeast and sugar in the warm water. Add the milk and 1½ cups of the flour. Beat until smooth. Cover, and let rise until light (about 45 minutes). Cream the butter or margarine; add sugar, salt, and beaten eggs. Add to yeast mixture, along with the remaining 3 cups of flour, and knead lightly. Cover and let rise in a warm place until light (about 2 hours). Yield: 2 coffeecakes.

To make two long coffeecakes, divide the dough in half and roll each into an oblong shape, 12 x 15 inches. Spread with Cinnamon or Poppy Seed Filling. Fold over twice, and place on a greased baking sheet. Let rise until light (about 1½ hours). Bake at 400° for about 20 minutes. Glaze with a mixture of powdered sugar and water.

Cinnamon Filling

6 *tablespoons butter or margarine*
¾ *cup sugar*
6 *tablespoons all-purpose flour*
⅛ *teaspoon salt*
1½ *teaspoons ground cinnamon*
½ *cup chopped pecans*

Cream butter or margarine and add sugar; mix well. Add remaining ingredients, and stir until well mixed and crumbly. Yield: about 1 cup.

Poppy Seed Filling

½ *cup poppy seed*
1 *tablespoon butter or margarine*
2 *tablespoons honey*
½ *cup sugar*

Mix together in a saucepan and cook over low heat for 5 minutes, stirring constantly. Yield: about 1 cup.

Butterhorns

 1 package dry yeast
 1 cup very warm water
 1/3 cup sugar
 1/2 cup melted butter or margarine
 3 eggs, well beaten
 5 to 6 cups all-purpose flour
 1/4 teaspoon salt

Dissolve yeast in very warm water; add sugar, melted butter or margarine, and beaten eggs. Combine flour and salt and beat gradually into yeast mixture. When dough is stiff enough to handle, turn out onto floured board and knead until elastic, air bubbles appear, and the dough is smooth. Place dough in a greased bowl, cover, and keep in a warm place and let rise until triple in bulk, for about 3 hours.

To make Butterhorns, divide dough into three parts. Roll about 1/4 inch thick on a floured board. Brush with melted butter or margarine. Cut into triangles about 3 inches long. Roll up to the point, place in a greased pan with point side down so they will not unroll while rising. When double in bulk, bake at 425° for 10 minutes. Yield: 5 dozen.

Refrigerator Rolls

 1 package dry yeast
 1/2 cup very warm water
 1/2 cup shortening
 1/2 cup sugar
 1 egg, beaten
 2 cups warm water
 1 1/2 teaspoons salt
    About 8 cups all-purpose flour

Dissolve yeast in 1/2 cup very warm water. Cream shortening and sugar. Add beaten egg, water, salt, and softened yeast. Add flour, and mix well. Put in large greased bowl and grease the top. Cover and put in refrigerator.

When ready to use, shape the rolls and put in a greased pan. Let rise for about 3 hours and bake at 400° for 12 to 15 minutes. Yield: 4 to 5 dozen rolls.

Sweet Potato Rolls

 1 cup cooked sweet potatoes
 3 tablespoons butter or margarine
 1 package dry yeast
 1/2 cup very warm water
 1 egg
 1 teaspoon salt
 3 tablespoons sugar
 5 cups all-purpose flour
 3/4 cup warm water

Blend together the mashed sweet potatoes and melted butter or margarine. Dissolve the yeast in 1/2 cup very warm water, then add to the mashed potatoes. Add egg, salt, and sugar; blend together. Add flour alternately with the 3/4 cup warm water. Turn onto well floured board and knead. Place in greased bowl and cover. Allow to rise for 2 hours. Place on board, roll to desired thickness, and cut into shapes desired. Brush tops of rolls with melted butter or margarine. Place on greased baking sheet and allow to rise for 1 hour. Bake at 425° for 15 to 20 minutes. Yield: 30 medium rolls.

Cakes & Frostings

The cake cover is as standard on the country kitchen counter as the flour canister, but cakes more than any other food are associated with special occasions.

Birthdays, weddings, and holidays all have their particular cakes rooted in tradition and personal preference. Cake decoration is an art requiring the talent and tools of a painter.

Starting from the basic sweetening, eggs, shortening, flour, milk, leavening, and flavoring, the variety of cakes is as endless as the imaginations of generations of homemakers.

Cakemaking today is a breeze compared to the efforts once required, when it took strong arm muscles — for beating with a wooden paddle — and uncanny judgment to determine the difference between a pinch and a smattering.

Sugar and eggs were ingredients of particular importance to early Southern homemakers. Pulverized sugar might have plaster of paris in it, and the homemaker who could not afford sugar at all substituted molasses and produced gingerbread.

Some advance preparation was essential when a cake called for 40 eggs, and there was no convenient carton of a graded dozen available for the original Robert E. Lee cake using "12 eggs, their full weight in sugar, a half weight in flour."

We've come a long way from that to packaged mixes and electric mixers to act as our muscles, but grating fresh coconut is still the surest sign of holidays to come.

Angel Custard Cake

6 egg yolks, beaten
¾ cup sugar
¾ cup freshly squeezed lemon juice
½ teaspoon grated lemon rind
1 tablespoon unflavored gelatin
¼ cup water
6 egg whites, beaten
¾ cup sugar
1 large angel food cake

Make a custard of egg yolks, ¾ cup sugar, lemon juice, and lemon rind. Cook over hot, not boiling water, until mixture coats a spoon. Remove from heat; add gelatin, softened in ¼ cup water, and stir until gelatin is dissolved. Fold in egg whites, beaten with the remaining ¾ cup sugar. Tear angel food cake into bite-size pieces; place in tubepan, oiled with salad oil. Pour custard over cake. Chill until firm; unmold. Fill center with whipped cream. Garnish with fresh cherries or maraschino cherries and green gumdrops. Yield: 8 servings.

Angel Food Cake

1½ cups cake flour
2 teaspoons cream of tartar
2¼ cups sugar
12 large egg whites
¼ teaspoon salt
1 tablespoon freshly squeezed lemon juice
1 teaspoon vanilla extract

Sift flour and measure. Add 1 teaspoon cream of tartar, and sift five times. Sift sugar and measure. Set aside. Beat egg whites until they hold up in peaks. Add salt and 1 teaspoon cream of

tartar. Add sugar, 2 tablespoonfuls at a time. Add lemon juice and vanilla. Fold in flour, 2 tablespoonfuls at a time. Bake in a tubepan at 375° for 30 minutes and then reduce temperature to 325° and bake for 30 minutes longer.

Cherry Angel Cake

1 package angel food cake mix
¼ cup boiling water
1 package white frosting mix
¼ cup maraschino cherry juice
   Maraschino cherries, quartered

Prepare cake according to package directions. Cool. Combine water and egg whites section of package frosting mix. Beat until foamy. Gradually add cherry juice and the sugar package of frosting mix, adding 1 tablespoon at a time, beating constantly until stiff and glossy. Frost top and sides of cake with this frosting. Garnish with cherries. Yield: 12 servings.

Cocoa Chiffon Cake

¾ cup boiling water
½ cup cocoa
1¾ cups cake flour
1¾ cups sugar
3 teaspoons baking powder
1 teaspoon salt
½ cup cooking oil
7 unbeaten egg yolks
1 teaspoon vanilla extract
¼ teaspoon red food coloring
1 cup egg whites (7 to 8 eggs)
½ teaspoon cream of tartar

Mix boiling water and cocoa; stir until smooth. Cool. Sift dry ingredients into bowl. Make a well and add oil, egg yolks, cooled cocoa mixture, vanilla, and coloring. Beat with spoon until smooth or with electric mixer on medium speed for 1 minute.

Beat egg whites and cream of tartar in large mixing bowl until whites form stiff peaks. Add to first mixture. Pour into ungreased tubepan. Bake at 325° for 55 minutes, then at 350° for 10 to 15 minutes. Invert pan over neck of funnel or bottle. When cold, loosen sides with spatula and remove cake.

No-Bake Cheesecake

- 2 envelopes unflavored gelatin
- 1 cup sugar, divided
- ¼ teaspoon salt
- 2 eggs, separated
- 1 cup milk
- 1 teaspoon grated lemon rind
- 1 tablespoon freshly squeezed lemon juice
- 1 teaspoon vanilla extract
- 3 cups creamed cottage cheese
- 1 cup heavy cream, whipped
  Crumb Topping

Mix gelatin, ¾ cup sugar, and salt in top of double boiler. Beat together egg yolks and milk; add to gelatin mixture. Cook over boiling water, stirring until gelatin dissolves and mixture thickens slightly, about 10 minutes. Remove from heat; add lemon rind, lemon juice, and vanilla. Cool. Sieve cottage cheese into large mixing bowl. Stir in cooled gelatin mixture. Chill, stirring occasionally, until mixture mounds slightly when dropped from a spoon. Prepare Crumb Topping

and set aside. Beat egg whites until stiff. Fold into gelatin-cheese mixture. Fold in whipped cream. Turn into pan and chill.

Crumb Topping

- 2 tablespoons melted butter or margarine
- 1 tablespoon sugar
- ¼ teaspoon ground cinnamon
- ¼ teaspoon ground nutmeg
- ¼ cup chocolate cookie crumbs
- ¼ cup graham cracker crumbs

Mix butter or margarine, sugar, and spices together. Add half the spiced mixture to chocolate crumbs, mix well; add remaining half to graham cracker crumbs; mix well. Sprinkle bottom of 8-inch springform pan with crumb mixtures in wedgeshape patterns, alternating chocolate and graham cracker crumbs. Turn in cheesecake mixture. Chill until set. Yield: 10 to 12 servings.

Butter Sponge Cake

- 11 egg yolks
- 2 cups sifted sugar
- 1 cup scalded milk
- 1 teaspoon vanilla extract
- 2¼ cups sifted cake flour
- 2 teaspoons baking powder
- ½ cup melted butter or margarine

Beat egg yolks and sugar until light colored and very fluffy. Add scalded milk and vanilla, beating constantly. Add flour and baking powder sifted together. Fold in melted butter or margarine. Batter will be very thin. Pour into two 9-inch well greased layer cakepans. Bake at 350° for 30 to 40 minutes. Invert pans and cool before removing.

Deluxe Chocolate Cheesecake

¾ cup finely crushed graham cracker
   or zwieback crumbs
1 tablespoon sugar
2 tablespoons melted butter
1 (3¾-ounce) package chocolate or
   chocolate fudge pudding and
   pie filling
¾ cup sugar
1 cup milk
1 square unsweetened chocolate
3 (8-ounce) packages cream
   cheese, softened
3 egg yolks
2 teaspoons vanilla extract
¼ teaspoon salt
⅛ teaspoon ground cinnamon (optional)
3 egg whites
   Sour Cream Topping

To prepare crust, combine crumbs, sugar, and butter; mix well. Grease sides of a 9-inch springform pan and coat with 2 tablespoons crumb mixture. Press remaining crumbs on bottom of pan.

To prepare chocolate filling, combine pudding mix, sugar, and milk in saucepan. Add chocolate. Cook and stir over medium heat until chocolate is melted and mixture comes to a full boil. Remove from heat. Cover. Beat cream cheese until fluffy in a large bowl. Add egg yolks and beat well. Blend in vanilla extract, salt, cinnamon, and cooked pudding. Beat egg whites until they form soft rounded peaks; fold into cream cheese mixture. Pour over crumb mixture in pan. Place on lowest rack of oven. Bake at 425° for 35 minutes, or until center is set when lightly touched. Spread Sour Cream Topping over hot cheesecake. Bake for 2 minutes longer. Yield: 10 to 12 servings.

Sour Cream Topping

1 cup commercial sour cream
¼ cup powdered sugar

Blend sour cream and powdered sugar, and spread on cheesecake.

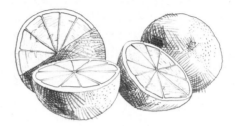

Hot Milk Sponge Cake

1 cup sifted cake flour
1 teaspoon baking powder
3 eggs
1 cup sugar
2 teaspoons freshly squeezed lemon juice
6 tablespoons hot milk

Sift flour once, measure, add baking powder, and sift together three times. Beat eggs until very thick and light and nearly white (about 10 minutes). Add lemon juice. Fold in flour, a small amount at a time. Add milk, mixing quickly until batter is smooth. Pour at once into ungreased tubepan and bake at 350° for 35 minutes, or until done. Remove from oven and invert pan for 1 hour, or until cake is thoroughly cold.

This mixture may be baked in two lightly greased 8- x 8- x 2-inch pans at 350° for 25 minutes; or in a 12- x 8- x 3-inch loafpan for 30 minutes.

Famous Old Fruitcake

- 1   pound candied grapefruit peel or citron
- 1   pound candied pineapple
- 1   pound candied red watermelon rind or cherries
- 3   pounds seeded raisins or currants
- 1½ pounds figs, dates, or apricots
- 4   cups all-purpose flour
- 1   teaspoon ground cinnamon
- ½   teaspoon ground cloves
- 1   teaspoon ground nutmeg
- ¼   teaspoon ground allspice
- ½   teaspoon salt
- ½   pound butter or margarine
- 1   cup firmly packed brown sugar
- 6   eggs, separated
- ½   cup fruit juice or sweet pickle syrup
- ½   pound almonds
- 1   pound pecans or black walnuts

Cut grapefruit peel, candied pineapple, and other fruits, except cherries and raisins, into ½-inch cubes. Leave cherries, raisins, and nuts whole. Sift flour, spices and salt. Cream butter or margarine and sugar in another bowl. Add beaten egg yolks to creamed mixture. Mix a small amount of the flour mixture with raisins and dates to keep them from sticking together. Add flour mixture alternately with fruit juice to the creamed mixture. Add fruits and nuts. Mix thoroughly. Fold in beaten egg whites.

Grease pans. Line with brown paper, and extend 1 inch above pans. Grease paper. Pack batter firmly into pans with hands to ½ inch below top of pans. Cover tops with waxed paper and place pan of water in oven under cakes. Bake at 250° for the following lengths of time: for 1-pound cakes, 2 to 2½ hours; 2-pound cakes, 3½ hours; 3-pound cakes, 4 hours. Remove waxed paper from top of cakes during last 15 minutes of baking. Yield: 11 pounds.

Light Fruitcake

- 2   cups all-purpose flour
- 2   teaspoons baking powder
- ½   teaspoon salt
- 1   pound coarsely chopped candied pineapple
- 1   pound candied cherries, whole
- 1½ pounds coarsely chopped pitted dates
- 4   eggs
- 1   cup sugar
- 2   pounds pecan halves (8 cups)

Combine flour, baking powder, and salt. Add fruits and mix well to coat with flour. Beat eggs until light and fluffy. Gradually beat in sugar. Add fruit-flour mixture and nuts; mix well with hands. Grease pans (two 9-inch springform pans or angel food pan and assorted molds as desired). Line pans with greased brown paper. Divide mixture between pans and press firmly into pans. Bake at 275° about 1 hour and 15 minutes or until cakes test done. Let cakes stand in pans about 10 minutes; turn out on racks and remove brown paper. Cool well before wrapping for storage. Yield: about 6 pounds.

Boiled Fruitcake

- 2 cups firmly packed brown sugar
- ¾ cup shortening
- 1 pound seeded raisins, cut into pieces
- 1 pound pitted dates
- 1 pound currants
- 1 cup shredded blanched almonds
- 2 eggs
- ½ cup molasses (or syrup)
- 2 teaspoons ground cinnamon
- 4 teaspoons cocoa
- 2 cups strong hot coffee
- 4 cups all-purpose flour
- 2 teaspoons soda

Mix together all ingredients except flour and soda, and boil for 10 minutes. Cool, and add the flour with which the soda has been sifted. Turn into a well greased large pan (or use several smaller pans). If baked in one pan, bake at 325° for 1 hour and 45 minutes; in several smaller pans, about 1 hour. Yield: 7 to 7½ pounds.

White Fruitcake

- 1 pound candied cherries
- 1 pound candied pineapple
- ½ pound citron
- 2 pounds white raisins
- 1 pound chopped nuts
- 2 (7-ounce) packages coconut
- 4 cups all-purpose flour
- 2 teaspoons baking powder
- 1 teaspoon soda
- 1 pound butter
- 2 cups sugar
- 10 eggs

Cut fruit into small pieces and mix with nuts and coconut. Combine flour, baking powder, and soda and add to fruit.

Cream butter and sugar until light and fluffy. Add eggs, one at a time, beating after each addition. Add first mixture and mix well. Bake in two greased tubepans at 250° for 3 hours. Yield: about 10 pounds.

Sweet Potato Fruitcake

- ¾ cup butter
- 1¾ cups sugar
- 2 eggs
- ½ cup milk
- 2 cups all-purpose flour
- 2 teaspoons baking powder
- 1 teaspoon ground cloves
- 2 teaspoons ground cinnamon
- 1 cup nuts
- 1 (5-ounce) bottle maraschino cherries
- 2 cups flaked coconut
- 1 cup cooked, mashed sweet potatoes
- 1 tablespoon peanut butter

Cream butter and sugar; add eggs, milk, and dry ingredients and mix well. Add other ingredients and mix well. This makes a very stiff dough. Put into a greased loafpan or tubepan. Bake at 375° for 3 to 4 hours.

Refrigerator Fruitcake

- ¾ pound butter or margarine
- 1 pound marshmallows
- 1 pound graham crackers, crushed
- 1 pound pecans
- 4 tablespoons firmly packed brown sugar
- 2 (7¼-ounce) boxes pitted dates
- 2 teaspoons vanilla extract
- ½ pound crystallized cherries
- ¼ pound crystallized citron, cut fine
- ½ pound crystallized pineapple

Melt the butter or margarine and the marshmallows in the top of a double boiler Put other ingredients in a large bowl; add melted mixture and mix well. Mold or shape into rolls or loaves. Wrap in waxed paper and store in refrigerator.

Kraut-Chocolate Cake

⅔ *cup softened butter or margarine*
1½ *cups sugar*
3 *eggs*
1½ *teaspoons vanilla extract*
2¼ *cups all-purpose flour*
½ *cup cocoa*
1 *teaspoon baking powder*
1 *teaspoon soda*
¼ *teaspoon salt*
1 *cup water*
⅔ *cup rinsed, drained and chopped sauerkraut*

Cream butter and sugar until light and fluffy. Add eggs, one at a time, beating well after each addition. Combine dry ingredients and add to creamed mixture alternately with water. Beat well, then stir in kraut.

Bake in two greased and floured 8-inch layer pans at 350° for 30 minutes or until cake tests done. Cool and frost with Mocha Whipped Cream Frosting or Chocolate Cream Cheese Frosting. Yield: 8 servings.

Mocha Whipped Cream Frosting

1½ *cups heavy cream*
3 *tablespoons sugar*
1 *tablespoon dry instant coffee*
2 *teaspoons cocoa*
1½ *teaspoons vanilla extract*

Combine all ingredients and beat until soft peaks form. Yield: enough for 2 (8-inch) layers.

Chocolate Cream Cheese Frosting

2 *(4-ounce) packages sweet chocolate*
2 *(3-ounce) packages cream cheese, softened*
2 *tablespoons light cream*
2 *cups sifted powdered sugar*
¼ *teaspoon salt*
1 *teaspoon vanilla extract*

Melt chocolate over hot water; cool slightly, then blend in cream cheese and cream. Add sugar gradually. Then add salt and vanilla. Yield: enough for 2 (8-inch) layers.

Devil's Food Cake

1 *cup butter or vegetable shortening*
2 *cups sugar*
4 *eggs*
2 *cups all-purpose flour*
¾ *cup cocoa*
1 *teaspoon soda*
1 *cup strong cold coffee*
1 *teaspoon vanilla extract*

Cream butter or shortening until soft and creamy. Add sugar gradually, beating until light and fluffy. Add eggs and beat thoroughly. Measure flour and cocoa and sift together. Dissolve soda in 2 tablespoons coffee, and add to rest of the coffee. Add dry ingredients alternately with coffee. Beat until well blended. Add vanilla. Pour into two 9-inch greased layer pans. Bake at 350° for about 30 minutes.

German's Sweet Chocolate Cake

- 1 cup shortening
- 2 cups sugar
- 4 egg yolks, unbeaten
- 1 teaspoon vanilla extract
- 1 (¼-pound) package German's Sweet Chocolate
- ½ cup boiling water
- 2½ cups cake flour
- ½ teaspoon salt
- 1 teaspoon soda
- 1 cup buttermilk
- 4 egg whites, stiffly beaten

Cream shortening; add sugar, then egg yolks, one at a time. Add vanilla and chocolate which has been melted in boiling water, then cooled. Mix well. Combine dry ingredients and add alternately with buttermilk to creamed mixture. Beat egg whites until stiff and fold into batter. Pour into three 8- or 9-inch layer pans which have been lined on bottom with waxed paper. Bake at 350° for 35 to 40 minutes. Cool. Frost with Coconut-Pecan Frosting.

Coconut-Pecan Frosting

- 3 egg yolks
- 1 cup evaporated milk
- 1 cup sugar
- 1 tablespoon butter or margarine
- 1½ cups flaked coconut
- 1 cup chopped pecans
- 1 teaspoon vanilla extract

Beat eggs and add milk, sugar, and butter or margarine. Cook over medium heat for about 12 minutes, stirring constantly, until mixture thickens. Remove from heat and add coconut, pecans, and vanilla. Beat until cool and of spreading consistency. Yield: enough to cover tops of 3 (8- or 9-inch) layers.

Double Fudge Cake

- 4 squares unsweetened chocolate
- 1¼ cups milks
- ¾ cup firmly packed brown sugar
- 2¼ cups all-purpose flour
- 1 teaspoon soda
- ½ teaspoon salt
- ⅔ cup shortening
- 1 cup sugar
- 3 eggs
- 1 teaspoon vanilla extract
  Fudge Frosting

Cut chocolate into small pieces and melt in milk in top of double boiler. Blend with a rotary beater. Add brown sugar and stir until smooth. Set aside to cool. Sift together flour, soda, and salt.

Cream shortening; gradually add sugar and continue to cream until light and fluffy. Add eggs, one at a time, beating well after each addition. Add vanilla and blend. Add flour and chocolate mixture slowly; blend well. Bake in three greased 8-inch layer pans for 25 to 30 minutes or until cake tests done. Cool and frost with Fudge Frosting.

Fudge Frosting

- 2 cups sugar
- ⅛ teaspoon salt
- 2 squares unsweetened chocolate, cut into small pieces
- 1 cup evaporated milk
- 2 tablespoons butter or margarine
- 1 teaspoon vanilla extract

Combine sugar, salt, chocolate, and milk in a saucepan. Cook until a few drops will form a soft ball when dropped into cool water. Remove from heat and add butter and vanilla. Let cool to lukewarm, then beat to spreading consistency. Yield: enough for 3 (8-inch) layers.

Tilden Cake

1 cup butter
2 cups sugar
4 eggs
3 cups all-purpose flour
½ cup cornstarch
2 teaspoons baking powder
½ teaspoon salt
1 cup milk
2 teaspoons lemon extract

Cream butter and sugar. Add eggs, one at a time, and beat well after each addition. Sift dry ingredients together, and add alternately with the milk. Add the lemon extract. Bake in two 9-inch layer cakepans at 350° for 30 to 40 minutes.

Burnt Sugar Cake

½ cup sugar
¼ cup hot water
½ cup shortening
1½ cups sugar
3 eggs, separated
3 cups all-purpose flour
3 teaspoons baking powder
½ teaspoon salt
1 cup water
1 teaspoon vanilla extract

Place the ½ cup sugar in a heavy skillet over low heat and stir constantly until it is melted and dark in color. Add hot water gradually, stirring until sugar is dissolved. Cool. Cream shortening. Add

sugar gradually, creaming until light and fluffy. Add well beaten egg yolks and mix thoroughly. Sift flour, baking powder, and salt together. Add alternately with water to creamed mixture. Add vanilla and browned sugar syrup, and mix to a smooth batter. Fold in stiffly beaten egg whites. Pour into two 8- or 9-inch greased paper-lined layer cakepans. Bake at 375° for 30 minutes.

White Cake No. 1

1 cup butter
2 cups sugar
3½ cups sifted cake flour
1 teaspoon salt
2 teaspoons baking powder
1 cup milk
1 teaspoon vanilla extract
8 egg whites

Cream butter and sugar together until light. Sift dry ingredients together two times; add to creamed mixture alternately with milk. Add vanilla extract. Fold in egg whites which have been beaten stiff but not dry. Pour batter into three 9-inch cakepans which have been greased and floured. Bake at 350° for 20 to 25 minutes.

White Cake No. 2

- 1 cup shortening
- 2 cups sugar
- 3 cups all-purpose flour
- ½ teaspoon salt
- 3 teaspoons baking powder
- 1 cup milk
- 1½ teaspoons flavoring
- 6 egg whites

Cream shortening. Add sugar gradually, creaming until very light and fluffy. Sift flour, salt, and baking powder together. Add flour and milk alternately to creamed mixture. Add flavoring. Fold in stiffly beaten egg whites, and mix to a smooth batter. Pour into greased, paper-lined layer cakepans. Bake at 350° for 35 minutes.

Applesauce Cake

- ⅔ cup butter
- 2 cups sugar
- 4 egg yolks
- ¾ cup unsweetened applesauce
- 2½ cups all-purpose flour
- 3 teaspoons baking powder
- 1 teaspoon ground cloves
- 1 teaspoon ground cinnamon
- ½ teaspoon ground nutmeg
- ½ teaspoon ground allspice
- 2 tablespoons cocoa
- ½ cup milk
- 2 teaspoons vanilla extract
- ⅔ cup raisins
- 4 egg whites

Cream butter; add sugar and beat until well blended. Add beaten yolks and applesauce and beat until mixture is smooth. Sift flour with baking powder and spices five times. Add to creamed

mixture alternately with milk. When well mixed add vanilla, nuts, raisins, and fold in stiffly beaten egg whites. Turn into two 9-inch greased layer cakepans and bake at 350° for about 40 minutes. Put together with a caramel frosting.

Banapple Sauce Cake

- 36 graham crackers
- 2 cups applesauce
- 3 or 4 bananas, sliced thin

Make a layer of 6 graham crackers in a loafpan, 2 crackers wide. Cover with ¾ cup applesauce. Add another layer of graham crackers, and cover with sliced bananas. Alternate layers, having applesauce layers on top and bottom. Top with graham crackers, and allow to "set" for 1 to 1½ hours. Cover with whipped cream or low-calorie topping. Yield: 6 servings.

Grape Cake

- ½ cup vegetable shortening
- ¾ teaspoon salt
- 1½ teaspoons vanilla extract
- 1½ cups sugar
- 2¾ cups sifted flour
- 3 teaspoons baking powder
- ½ cup milk
- ½ cup water
- 4 egg whites, stiffly beaten
  Grape filling
  Grape frosting

Blend shortening, salt, and vanilla. Add sugar and cream well. Sift dry ingredients and add to creamed mixture alternately with milk and water. Mix after each addition until smooth. Fold in beaten egg whites. Bake in two 9-inch greased and floured cakepans at 350° for 25 minutes.

Grape Filling

½ cup grape juice
½ cup water
3 tablespoons cornstarch
¼ teaspoon salt
½ cup sugar
4 tablespoons freshly squeezed lemon juice
1 tablespoon butter or margarine

Scald grape juice and water in top of double boiler. Combine dry ingredients and add to grape juice mixture. Cook over direct heat until thick. Return to double boiler and cook for 15 minutes, stirring occasionally. Add lemon juice and butter or margarine and blend. Cool. Spread between layers of cake. Reserve ½ cup to decorate top of cake.

Grape Frosting

1 egg white
¾ cup sugar
3 tablespoons grape juice
½ teaspoon light corn syrup

Mix all ingredients in top of double boiler and beat constantly until mixture holds a peak. Remove, and beat until thick enough to spread.

Cake Delight

1 (8-ounce) can fruit cocktail
½ pint whipping cream
2 tablespoons sugar

Drain fruit cocktail. Whip cream, and add fruit and sugar to it. Serve the mixture over sliced cake; pound and angel food are especially nice, but any cake will do. Yield: 8 servings.

Kentucky Jam Cake No. 1

¾ cup butter or margarine
1 cup sugar
3 eggs
3 cups all-purpose flour
2 teaspoons baking powder
1 teaspoon soda
¼ teaspoon salt
1 teaspoon ground cinnamon
1 teaspoon ground allspice
½ cup buttermilk
1 cup thick jam (blackberry, dewberry, etc.)
Fruit frosting

Cream the butter or margarine and sugar. Add unbeaten eggs and beat again. Sift dry ingredients together three times, then add to the creamed mixture alternately with sour milk. Fold in the jam. Pour into two well greased layer cakepans. Bake at 350° for about 45 minutes or until golden brown.

Fruit Frosting

1 cup dates
1 cup figs
1 cup raisins
1 orange
1 lemon
⅓ cup sugar

Grind dates, figs, and raisins. Then cut orange and lemon into quarters, remove seeds, and grind. Add to first mixture, and add sugar. Cook until mixture thickens, stirring constantly. Spread on cake while hot.

Kentucky Jam Cake No. 2

½ cup butter
2 cups sugar
3 eggs
3 cups all-purpose flour
1 teaspoon soda
¼ teaspoon each ground cloves, cinnamon, and allspice, if desired
⅓ cup cocoa
½ cup buttermilk
About ⅓ cup coffee
2 cups strawberry jam

Cream butter and sugar until light and fluffy. Add eggs one at a time, beating well after each addition. Combine dry ingredients; add alternately to creamed mixture with milk and coffee. Stir in jam. Bake in three greased 8-inch layer pans at 325° for 25 minutes or until cake tests done. Do not overbake. Cool and frost.

Kentucky Jam Frosting

½ cup butter
2⅓ cups sugar
4 eggs
1 cup milk
1½ cups seedless raisins
1½ cups flaked coconut
2 cups chopped pecans
2 cups candied cherries

Cream butter and sugar until light and fluffy; add eggs and beat well. Add milk and cook in top of double boiler until thick, stirring constantly. Add all fruits, nuts, and coconut and cook a few minutes longer. Spread this mixture between layers and on top and sides of cake. Yield: enough filling for 3 (8-inch) layers.

Orange Layer Cake

2½ cups sifted cake flour
1½ cups sugar
2 teaspoons baking powder
¼ teaspoon soda
1 teaspoon salt
½ cup shortening
Grated rind of 1 orange
¼ cup freshly squeezed orange juice
¾ cup milk
2 eggs

Sift together in a large bowl the flour, sugar, baking powder, soda, and salt. Add shortening, orange rind, and ⅔ cup of the liquid. Beat for 2 minutes, scraping sides of the bowl often. Add remaining liquid and eggs and beat for 2 minutes longer. Bake in layers at 350° for 25 to 30 minutes.

Prune Cake

½ cup butter or margarine
1½ cups sugar
3 eggs
2¼ cups sifted cake flour
¾ teaspoon salt
1 teaspoon baking powder
2 teaspoons ground cinnamon
1 teaspoon ground nutmeg
¾ teaspoon ground cloves
¾ teaspoon ground allspice
1 teaspoon soda
1 cup buttermilk
1¼ cups chopped, cooked prunes

Cream butter or margarine and sugar until well blended. Add eggs one at a time and beat well. Sift dry ingredients and add alternately with the buttermilk. Fold in prunes. Bake in two layer cake-pans at 350° for 35 to 40 minutes.

Hickory Nut Cake

½ cup butter or margarine
1¼ cups sugar
  2 eggs, separated
  2 teaspoons vanilla extract
  2 cups sifted cake flour
  3 teaspoons baking powder
¼ teaspoon salt
¾ cup milk

Cream butter or margarine with wooden spoon. Slowly beat in sugar and cream well. Add beaten egg yolks and vanilla. Add sifted dry ingredients alternately with milk. Fold in beaten egg whites. Pour into two greased 8-inch cakepans. Bake at 375° for 25 minutes. Fill and frost with your favorite frosting to which hickory nuts are added.

Festive Walnut Cake

  2 cups cake flour
½ teaspoon salt
2½ teaspoons baking powder
½ cup shortening
1¼ cups sugar
  2 eggs, separated
⅓ cup milk
  1 teaspoon freshly squeezed lemon juice
⅓ cup maraschino cherry syrup
    (drained from cherries)
  1 (5-ounce) bottle maraschino cherries
    (chop all but 5)
½ cup chopped walnuts
⅛ teaspoon salt
    Walnut halves
    Boiled icing

Sift flour, salt, and baking powder twice. Cream shortening and sugar and stir in egg yolks and mix well. Add liquids and dry ingredients alternately to creamed mixture. Fold in stiffly beaten egg whites. Add chopped cherries (floured) to half the batter; add chopped walnuts (floured) and ⅛ teaspoon extra salt to the other half of the batter. Bake in two greased 8-inch square pans at 375° for about 25 minutes. Frost with a boiled icing and decorate with walnut halves and 5 cherries.

Robert E. Lee Cake

  9 egg yolks
  2 cups sugar
  9 egg whites
  2 cups all-purpose flour
½ teaspoon salt
  1 tablespoon freshly squeezed
    lemon juice
    Filling

Beat egg yolks very lightly, then slowly beat in sugar. Fold in well beaten egg whites. Sift in flour with salt and mix lightly together, stir in lemon juice. Pour into three ungreased layer pans. Bake at 300° for 25 to 30 minutes.

Filling

  Juice of 2 lemons
  Juice of 3 oranges
2 cups sugar
  Grated rinds of lemon and orange
1 cup grated coconut
  Grated Coconut

Squeeze the juice of 2 lemons and 3 oranges over 2 cups sugar, and flavor with a little of the grated rinds. Add 1 cup grated coconut, blend, and put between layers and on top. Sprinkle cake with grated coconut.

Pineapple Cake

½ cup shortening
1¾ cups sugar
2 eggs
2 cups all-purpose flour
¼ teaspoon soda
2 teaspoons baking powder
1 cup buttermilk
1 teaspoon vanilla extract

Cream shortening and sugar; stir in eggs. Sift flour, soda, and baking powder together and add alternately with buttermilk to shortening mixture. Add vanilla extract. Pour into two 8-inch greased and floured cakepans. Bake at 350° for 35 minutes. Cool and put layers together with Pineapple Frosting.

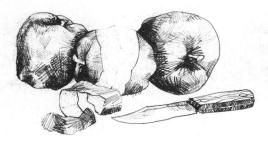

Pineapple Frosting

1 cup evaporated milk
1 cup sugar
3 egg yolks
½ cup margarine
1 teaspoon vanilla extract
1 (20-ounce) can crushed
    pineapple, drained

Combine milk, sugar, egg yolks, margarine, and vanilla extract in a saucepan. Cook over medium heat, stirring constantly until mixture thickens (about 12 minutes). Add drained pineapple. Spread between layers of cake.

Southern Coconut Cake

4 cups sifted cake flour
5 teaspoons baking powder
1½ teaspoons salt
6 egg whites
½ cup sugar
1 cup all-vegetable shortening
2 cups sugar
2 cups milk
1 teaspoon vanilla extract
1 teaspoon almond extract
    Zesty Lemon Filling (see Index)
    Coconut-Marshmallow Frosting
    (see Index)
    Flaked coconut

Combine flour, baking powder, and salt. Beat egg whites until foamy and gradually add ½ cup sugar; set aside. Continue beating until meringue will hold up in stiff peaks. Cream shortening and gradually add the 2 cups sugar; cream until light and fluffy. Add flour mixture alternately with milk, a small amount at a time, beating well after each addition. Add vanilla and almond extracts. Add beaten egg whites and fold thoroughly into batter.

Line bottom of three 9-inch cakepans with waxed paper. Lightly grease and flour pans. Pour in batter. Bake at 375° for 20 to 25 minutes, or until cake tests done. Spread Zesty Lemon Filling (see

Index) between the layers and ice cake with Coconut-Marshmallow Frosting (see Index). Sprinkle cake with flaked coconut.

Banana Delight Cake

2½ cups sifted cake flour
1⅔ cups sugar
1¼ teaspoons baking powder
1¼ teaspoons soda
1 teaspoon salt
1 teaspoon ground cinnamon
⅔ cup vegetable shortening
⅔ cup buttermilk
1¼ cups mashed ripe bananas
2 eggs

Sift dry ingredients into large mixing bowl; add shortening, buttermilk, and bananas. Mix until all dry ingredients are dampened; then beat at low speed for 2 minutes. Add eggs and beat for 1 minute. Bake in three 8-inch or two 9-inch greased and floured layer pans at 350° for 25 to 30 minutes. Cool and frost with Banana-Nut Frosting.

Banana-Nut Frosting

⅓ cup butter or margarine
2 pounds powdered sugar, sifted
½ cup mashed bananas
1 teaspoon freshly squeezed lemon juice
1 cup toasted coconut
⅔ cup finely chopped nuts

Cream butter; add sugar and bananas, which have been sprinkled with lemon juice; blend well. Add coconut and nuts; mix well.

Note: To make icing more attractive, add few drops of yellow food coloring.

Lane Cake

8 egg whites
1 cup butter or margarine
2 cups sugar
3½ cups all-purpose flour
3 teaspoons baking powder
1 cup milk
1 teaspoon vanilla extract (optional)

Beat egg whites until they hold a peak, but are not dry. Set aside, then cream butter or margarine and sugar well. Sift flour and baking powder together and add to creamed mixture alternately with milk. Fold in beaten egg whites and vanilla. Bake in four layers at 350° until brown.

Filling

1 cup chopped nuts
1 cup flaked coconut
1 cup seedless raisins
½ cup butter or margarine
2 cups sugar
8 egg yolks
¾ cup grape juice

Grind nuts, coconut, and raisins. Put these in a saucepan with the butter or margarine, sugar, and egg yolks. Cook for 15 to 20 minutes. Stir in grape juice to thin filling. Spread between layers, and use a white frosting for top and sides of cake.

Lord Baltimore Cake

2¾   cups all-purpose flour
2¾   teaspoons baking powder
 ½   teaspoon salt
 ¾   cup butter
1¼   cups sugar
  8   egg yolks
 ¾   cup milk
 ½   teaspoon lemon extract

Combine flour, baking powder, and salt, and sift together three times. Cream butter thoroughly, add sugar gradually, and cream together until light and fluffy. Beat egg yolks very thoroughly until lemon colored. Add to creamed mixture and beat until very smooth. Add dry ingredients, alternately with milk, a small amount at a time, beating very thoroughly after each addition. When all flour is added, beat thoroughly again. Add lemon extract. Bake in three greased 9-inch layer pans at 375° for about 25 minutes, or until done. Spread Lord Baltimore Frosting between layers and on top of cake.

Lord Baltimore Frosting

1½   cups sugar
  1   tablespoon light corn syrup
 ½   cup water
  2   egg whites, stiffly beaten
 ¼   teaspoon orange juice
  2   teaspoons freshly squeezed
        lemon juice
 12   candied cherries, cut into quarters
 ½   cup macaroon crumbs
 ½   cup blanched almonds, chopped
 ¼   cup chopped pecans

Combine sugar, corn syrup, and water and cook until syrup forms a soft ball in cold water, or spins a long thread when dropped from tip of spoon (240°).

Pour syrup in fine stream over egg whites, beating constantly. Add orange and lemon juice to fruit, macaroon crumbs, and nuts and combine the two mixtures. Cool and spread between layers of cake. Yield: enough frosting to cover tops of 3 (9-inch) layers.

Lady Baltimore Cake

 ½   cup butter or margarine
  1   cup sugar
1¾   cups all-purpose flour
 ⅛   teaspoon salt
  2   teaspoons baking powder
 ½   cup milk
  1   teaspoon vanilla extract
  3   egg whites, stiffly beaten

Cream butter or margarine. Add sugar and cream again thoroughly. Sift dry ingredients and add alternately with milk. Add vanilla and fold in stiffly beaten egg whites. Bake in two layers at 350° for 25 minutes. Put layers together with Lady Baltimore Frosting. There are many variations. Some recipes call for covering cake with a thick syrup made of 1 cup sugar, 1½ cups water. This is put on as soon as cakes are removed from pan. Frosting is then put on top of syrup mixture.

Lady Baltimore Frosting

  2   cups sugar
 ⅔   cup water
  2   egg whites, stiffly beaten
  5   figs
 ⅔   cup raisins
 ⅔   cup nuts
        Candied cherries

Boil sugar and water to soft-ball stage (238°). Pour slowly over well beaten egg whites, beating constantly. Set aside to cool. Put figs, raisins, and nuts through chopper. Add to cooled frosting. Spread between layers and on top and sides of cake. Garnish with nuts and halved candied cherries.

Chocolate Pound Cake

½ pound margarine
½ cup vegetable shortening
3 cups sugar
5 eggs
3 cups all-purpose flour
2 teaspoons baking powder
½ cup cocoa
½ teaspoon salt
1¼ cups milk
1 tablespoon vanilla extract

Cream margarine and shortening, adding sugar gradually. Add eggs one at a time, beating well after each addition. Sift together three times the flour, baking powder, cocoa, and salt. Add to mixture alternately with the milk. Add vanilla. Pour batter into a tubepan that has been greased and dusted with flour. Batter will be very thin. Bake at 325° for 1¼ to 1½ hours.

Apple Dapple Cake

3 eggs
1½ cups salad oil
2 cups sugar
3 cups all-purpose flour
1 teaspoon salt
1 teaspoon soda
2 teaspoons vanilla extract
3 cups chopped apples
1½ cups chopped pecans

Mix eggs, salad oil, and sugar, and blend well. Add flour, salt, and soda mixed well. Add vanilla, chopped apples, and nuts. Put into greased 8- or 9-inch tubepan. Bake at 350° for one hour. While cake is still hot, pour hot Topping over it in the pan.

Topping

1 cup brown sugar
¼ cup milk
1 stick margarine

Combine all ingredients and cook for 2½ minutes. Pour hot Topping over hot cake in pan. Let set until cold; when completely cold, remove cake with Topping from pan.

Fresh Apple Cake No. 1

1¼ cups corn oil
2 cups sugar
3 cups all-purpose flour
1 teaspoon salt
1 teaspoon soda
3 eggs
2 teaspoons vanilla extract
2 cups chopped fresh apples
1 cup chopped nuts
1 (3½-ounce) can flaked coconut

Mix corn oil and sugar together with spoon until sugar is dissolved. Combine dry ingredients and add to sugar mixture alternately with eggs, beating after each addition.

Add vanilla, chopped apples, nuts, and coconut. Batter will be very thick. Put into greased and floured tubepan. Bake at 350° for 1 hour and 15 minutes. Cool in pan.

Fresh Apple Cake No. 2

2½ cups all-purpose flour
 1 teaspoon ground cinnamon
 1 teaspoon ground allspice
 1 teaspoon soda
 1 cup butter or margarine
 2 cups sugar
 4 eggs
½ cup water
 3 medium apples, chopped
 1 cup pecans, chopped fine
 1 teaspoon vanilla extract

Mix and sift flour, spices, and soda. Cream butter or margarine, using medium speed on mixer. Add sugar, and eggs, one at a time. Add dry ingredients and water alternately. Fold apples and nuts into mixture. Add vanilla. Pour into greased tubepan lined with waxed paper. Bake at 350° for 1½ hours; or bake in layer pans at 400° for 30 minutes.

Applesauce Cake

½ cup shortening
 1 cup sugar
 1 egg
1¾ cups all-purpose flour
 1 cup raisins
 1 cup finely chopped nuts
½ teaspoon salt
 1 teaspoon soda
½ teaspoon ground cinnamon
¼ teaspoon ground cloves
 1 cup applesauce

Cream shortening and sugar well; add egg and beat until light and fluffy. Sprinkle 2 tablespoons flour over the combined raisins and nuts. Combine remaining flour with salt, soda, cinna-mon, and cloves. Heat applesauce and add to creamed mixture alternately with the dry ingredients, mixing only until well blended. Stir in raisins and nuts. Pour into a greased and floured 9-inch tubepan. Bake at 350° for 40 minutes. Cool thoroughly.

Confederate Cake

½ cup butter
 1 cup sugar
½ cup milk
 3 eggs
1½ cups all-purpose flour
 2 teaspoons baking powder
    Ground nutmeg
    Chopped nuts

Cream butter and sugar; add milk and unbeaten eggs, and mix well. Sift flour and baking powder together and blend with the creamed mixture. Add a dash of nutmeg. Pour into greased loafpan and sprinkle the top with nutmeg, nuts, and sugar. Dot with butter and bake at 375° for about 20 minutes.

Orange Rum Cake

 1 cup margarine
 1 cup sugar
 2 eggs
    Grated rind of 2 large oranges
    Grated rind of 1 lemon
2½ cups all-purpose flour
 2 teaspoons baking powder
 1 teaspoon soda
½ teaspoon salt
 1 cup buttermilk
 1 cup chopped pecans
    Orange Glaze

Beat margarine until light and fluffy; add sugar and beat well. Add eggs and grated rind and beat until mixture is very light. Combine dry ingredients and add to creamed mixture alternately with buttermilk, beginning and ending with dry ingredients. Stir in chopped pecans. Spoon mixture into a well greased 10-inch tubepan. Bake at 350° for 1 hour, or until cake tests done. Leave in pan and pour glaze over top of cake. It is best if cake is covered and left in pan several days before serving.

Orange Glaze

Juice of 2 large oranges
Juice of 1 lemon
1 *cup sugar*
2 *tablespoons rum flavoring*

Mix all ingredients and bring to a boil. Pour over hot Orange Rum Cake. Yield: about ¾ cup.

Sweet Potato Cake

¼ *cup butter*
1½ *cups sugar*
2 *eggs*
½ *cup milk*
2 *cups all-purpose flour*
2 *teaspoons baking powder*
1 *teaspoon ground cloves*
2 *teaspoons ground cinnamon*
1 *cup nuts*
1 *(2-ounce) bottle maraschino cherries, drained*
1 *cup flaked coconut*
1 *cup cooked, mashed sweet potato*
1 *tablespoon peanut butter*

Cream butter and sugar; add eggs, milk, and dry ingredients and mix well. Add

other ingredients and mix well. This makes a very stiff dough. Put into a greased loafpan or tube cakepan. Bake at 350° for 1 hour and 45 minutes.

John Garner Cake

1 *pound raisins*
½ *cup shortening*
2 *cups sugar*
2 *teaspoons ground cinnamon*
½ *teaspoon ground cloves*
2 *cups boiling water*
½ *cup hot water*
2 *teaspoons soda*
3¾ *cups all-purpose flour*
⅛ *teaspoon salt*

Boil raisins, shortening, sugar, cinnamon, cloves and 2 cups boiling water for 10 minutes. When cool add ½ cup hot water with soda dissolved in it. Stir in flour and salt sifted together. Bake in a greased loafpan at 275° for 1½ hours.

Vanilla Wafer Cake

1 *cup margarine or butter*
2 *cups sugar*
6 *eggs*
1 *(12-ounce) box vanilla wafers, crushed*
½ *cup milk*
1 *(7-ounce) package flaked coconut*
1 *cup chopped pecans*

Cream margarine or butter, add sugar, and beat until smooth. Add eggs, one at a time, beating well after each addition. Add vanilla wafers alternately with milk. Add coconut and pecans. Pour batter into a greased and floured tubepan. Bake at 275° for 1½ hours.

Texas Date Cake

- 1 cup dates, chopped
- 1 teaspoon soda
- 1 cup boiling water
- ½ cup butter or margarine
- 2 cups sugar
- 1 egg
- 1 teaspoon vanilla extract
- 1⅓ cups all-purpose flour
- 1 cup pecans

Put chopped dates and soda into large bowl; add boiling water. Mash until as smooth as mush. (This is a most important step. It takes time, but is worth it.) Cream butter or margarine and 1 cup of the sugar. Add the other cup of sugar, the egg, and vanilla. Stir in the date mixture. Then add flour and pecans. Bake in a greased tubepan at 350° for about 1 hour.

Raisin Cake

- ⅓ cup shortening
- 1 cup brown sugar
- 2 cups raisins
- 1 teaspoon ground cinnamon
- ½ teaspoon ground cloves
- ¼ teaspoon ground nutmeg
- ¼ teaspoon salt
- 1 cup water
- 2 cups all-purpose flour
- 1 teaspoon soda
- ½ teaspoon baking powder

Combine shortening, sugar, raisins, spices, salt, and water in a saucepan, and boil for 3 minutes. Let cool and add the flour, soda, and baking powder. Beat until smooth. Pour into a greased or lined loafpan and bake at 350° for 1 hour.

Lightning Cake

- 1 cup all-purpose flour
- 2 teaspoons baking powder
- ¾ cup sugar
- ¼ teaspoon salt
- ¼ cup melted butter or margarine
- 2 eggs
  Milk
- 1 teaspoon vanilla extract or ground nutmeg

Sift dry ingredients into mixing bowl. Pour melted butter or margarine into 1-cup measuring cup; add eggs, and finish filling the cup with milk. Add to the dry ingredients, and beat thoroughly. Add flavoring. Bake in an oiled and floured 9-inch cakepan at 350° for 30 minutes.

Ginger Pound Cake

- 1 pound butter or margarine
- 1¼ cups brown sugar, firmly packed
- 6 eggs
- 5 cups all-purpose flour
- 2 teaspoons ground cinnamon
- 2 tablespoons ground ginger
- 1 teaspoon ground nutmeg
- ½ tablespoon soda
- 2 cups dark molasses
- ½ cup milk

Cream butter or margarine and sugar until fluffy, add eggs, and beat well. Sift dry ingredients together and add to creamed mixture alternately with molasses and milk. Pour batter into a tubepan which has been greased and floured on the sides, and the bottom lined with greased and floured brown paper. Bake at 300° for about 1 hour.

Half–Pound Cake

½ *pound butter or margarine*
2 *cups sugar*
6 *eggs*
2 *cups all-purpose flour*
¼ *teaspoon salt*
1 *teaspoon lemon extract*

Mix butter or margarine and sugar and beat thoroughly. Add eggs, one at a time, beating well after each addition. Add flour and salt; beat thoroughly. Bake in a loafpan at 325° for 1 hour.

Old-Fashioned Pound Cake

2 *cups all-purpose flour*
1 *cup butter (decreased by 1 tablespoon if other shortening used)*
1⅔ *cups sifted sugar*
5 *eggs*
1 *teaspoon vanilla extract*

Sift flour, measure, and sift again five times. Cream butter, add sugar, and beat until sugar is no longer grainy. Then add eggs, one at a time, beating well after each addition. Continue beating until batter is fluffy. Add flour, beat until blended, and add vanilla. Pour into greased, floured tubepan. Bake at 275° for 2 hours, or until done.

Lemon Pound Cake

2 *cups butter or margarine*
2 *cups sugar*
6 *eggs*
4 *cups all-purpose flour*
1 *pound white raisins (dredged in a little flour)*
1 *pound pecans, chopped*
1 *(2-ounce) bottle lemon extract*

Cream butter or margarine and sugar well. Add eggs one at a time, then flour, then raisins, then nuts and flavoring. Bake in paper-lined greased tubepan at 325° for 1½ hours.

Buttermilk Pound Cake

1 *cup shortening*
2 *cups sugar*
4 *eggs*
1 *teaspoon vanilla extract*
1 *teaspoon orange flavoring*
3 *cups all-purpose flour*
¾ *teaspoon salt*
½ *teaspoon soda*
½ *teaspoon baking powder*
1 *cup buttermilk*

Cream shortening and sugar until light and fluffy. Add eggs and beat well. Add vanilla and orange flavoring. Sift dry ingredients together three times. Add dry ingredients to creamed mixture alternately with buttermilk. Spoon into greased tubepan and bake at 300° for about 1 hour.

7-Up Pound Cake

    2 sticks margarine
  ½ cup vegetable shortening
    3 cups sugar
    5 eggs
    1 teaspoon lemon extract
    3 cups all-purpose flour
    1 (7-ounce) bottle 7-Up

Cream margarine and shortening with sugar; add eggs one at a time, beating well after each addition. Add lemon extract; add flour and 7-Up alternately, beating after each addition. Bake in a greased and floured tubepan at 300° for 1½ hours, or until cake tests done.

Silver Cake

    1 cup shortening
    2 cups sugar
3½ cups all-purpose flour
  ½ teaspoon soda
    2 teaspoons baking powder
  ¼ teaspoon salt
    1 cup buttermilk
    1 teaspoon vanilla extract
    6 egg whites, stiffly beaten

Cream shortening and sugar until light and fluffy. Sift together flour, soda, baking powder, and salt. Combine buttermilk and vanilla. Add dry mixture to creamed mixture alternately with buttermilk, beating constantly after each addition.

Spoon batter into three 8-inch greased layer pans or a greased Bundt pan. Bake at 350° for 25 to 30 minutes for the layers, or 50 minutes for the Bundt cake. Yield: 12 servings.

Modern Marble Cake

  ½ cup shortening
    1 cup sugar
    2 eggs, beaten
1¾ cups sifted cake flour
    2 teaspoons baking powder
  ½ teaspoon salt
  ½ cup milk
    1 teaspoon vanilla extract
    1 ounce (square) chocolate
    2 tablespoons milk

Cream shortening with sugar until fluffy. Add beaten eggs. Add sifted dry ingredients and milk alternately in small amounts, beating well after each addition. Add vanilla. Divide batter into halves. Melt chocolate and add with 2 tablespoons milk to one half; blend well. Drop batter by tablespoonfuls into greased 8- x 8-inch pan, alternating white and chocolate. Bake at 350° for 50 to 60 minutes.

Chocolate-Oatmeal Cake

    1 cup uncooked oatmeal
1½ cups boiling water
  ½ cup shortening
1½ cups sugar
    2 eggs
    1 cup all-purpose flour
    1 teaspoon soda
  ½ teaspoon salt
  ½ cup cocoa
    1 teaspoon vanilla extract
    1 cup chopped nuts (optional)

Mix oatmeal with boiling water and let cool. Cream shortening, sugar, and eggs until light and fluffy. Add oatmeal mixture along with mixture of dry ingredients. Stir in vanilla, and beat until smooth. Add nuts, if desired. Spoon mixture into greased 13- x 9- x 2-inch pan and bake at 350° for 35 to 40 minutes, or until cake pulls away from sides of pan. Yield: 12 servings.

Shortbread

6 cups sifted all-purpose flour
1 cup sugar
  Dash ground mace
1 pound softened butter
2 egg yolks
  Sugar

Sift flour and sugar and mace together; cut in butter until mixture resembles coarse cornmeal. Add egg yolks, one at a time, kneading dough between each addition. Pat dough into two fluted pans with removable bottoms (flan pans). Lightly mark wedges (pie fashion). Prick with fork and sprinkle generously with granulated sugar; chill for half an hour before baking.

Bake at 350° for 15 minutes. Reduce heat to 300° and bake 30 minutes longer. Watch very carefully the last 15 minutes of baking — the cake should not brown. As soon as it is removed from the oven, cut each section all the way through. Cool. Yield: 2 cakes.

Shortbread Cookies

Use recipe for Shortbread. After dough has chilled, roll ¼ inch thick and cut in desired shapes. Place on ungreased cookie sheets. Spread each cookie with jam or preserves, and top with half a blanched almond. Bake at 350° for 12 to 15 minutes. Yield: about 4 dozen.

Ginger Cake (Noel)

½ cup softened butter
1 cup sugar
3 eggs
1 teaspoon ground cinnamon
1 teaspoon ground ginger
2 teaspoons ground cloves
1¾ cups all-purpose flour
1 teaspoon soda
⅔ cup commercial sour cream
1½ cups applesauce
  Frosting or whipped cream

Cream butter and sugar until light and fluffy. Add eggs and spices and beat well. Sift flour and soda together; add to creamed mixture alternately with sour cream, and stir until well blended. Spoon batter into two greased 8-inch cakepans and bake at 325° for 15 minutes; reduce heat to 250° and bake 15 to 20 minutes longer, or until cakes test done. Cool. Put layers together with applesauce. Cover top with a frosting or whipped cream and decorate as desired.

Hot Water Gingerbread

⅓ cup shortening
⅔ cup boiling water
1 cup sorghum
1 egg
2¾ cups all-purpose flour
2 teaspoons soda
1 teaspoon salt
1 teaspoon ground cinnamon
1½ teaspoons ground ginger
¼ teaspoon ground cloves

Melt shortening in boiling water, add sorghum and well beaten egg, then the dry ingredients sifted together. Bake in greased 13- x 9- x 2-inch pan at 350° for about 30 minutes.

Prune Roll

> 1 (13¾-ounce) package hot roll mix
> 1½ cups chopped, pitted cooked prunes
> 3 tablespoons sugar
> ½ teaspoon grated lemon rind
> 3 tablespoons freshly squeezed lemon juice
> ½ cup powdered sugar
> 2 tablespoons water

Follow directions on package for preparing rolls; let rise. While dough is rising, prepare prune filling: Combine prunes, sugar, lemon rind and juice.

Punch down raised dough. Place on lightly floured surface and roll into a rectangle 14 x 12 inches. Place rectangle on a greased cookie sheet. Spread prune filling lengthwise over half the dough. Fold dough over. Brush edges with water and press lightly to seal. Cover and let rise in a warm place until almost double. Bake at 350° for 15 to 20 minutes. While it is still warm, frost with a powdered sugar frosting made by mixing powdered sugar with water.

Graham Cracker Cake

> 1 (16-ounce) box graham crackers
> 2 teaspoons baking powder
> 1 cup undiluted evaporated milk
> 2 sticks butter or margarine
> 2 cups sugar
> 4 eggs
> 1 teaspoon vanilla extract
> 1 cup chopped pecans
> 1 (3½-ounce) can coconut
> Pineapple Filling

Crumble crackers, add baking powder, mix well, and add milk. Set aside.

Cream margarine and sugar. Add eggs one at a time, beating well after each addition. Combine with cracker mixture. Stir in vanilla extract, pecans, and coconut. Bake in greased 13- x 9- x 2-inch pan at 350° for 50 minutes or until done. Spread with Pineapple Filling.

Pineapple Filling

> 1 cup sugar
> 4 teaspoons flour or cornstarch
> 1 (20-ounce) can crushed pineapple

Combine sugar and flour. Add pineapple and cook until thick (about 10 minutes). Spread over cake in the pan and cut into squares. Yield: 12 to 15 servings.

Roulage

> ½ cup all-purpose flour
> ½ cup cocoa
> 1 teaspoon baking powder
> ¼ teaspoon salt
> 3 eggs
> 1 cup sugar
> ¼ cup water
> 1 teaspoon vanilla extract
> Sweetened and flavored whipped cream
> Nuts or coconut (optional)

Sift flour, cocoa, baking powder, and salt together three times. Beat eggs in a large bowl until thick and lemon colored; gradually beat in the sugar. Add the water and vanilla, beating at slow speed. Add dry ingredients, beating only until smooth. Pour into greased, paper-lined 15- x 10- x 1-inch pan and bake at 400° for 15 to 20 minutes, or until cake springs back from a light touch of your finger. Turn out immediately onto a tea towel sprinkled with powdered sugar; carefully peel off the paper; trim any crusty edges away; then roll up, starting at narrow end of cake, towel and all, from the end. Cool on a rack. Unroll and spread with sweetened and flavored whipped cream and sprinkle with nuts or coconut, if desired. Reroll on the tea towel so that the towel may be gently wrapped about the roll to keep it in shape while it is stored in the refrigerator until serving time. Yield: 8 servings.

Pineapple-Cherry Upside-Down Cake

3 eggs, separated
5 tablespoons water
1 cup sugar
1 cup all-purpose flour
½ teaspoon salt
1 teaspoon vanilla extract
  Filling

Beat egg yolks until thick and lemon colored. Add the water, then the sugar gradually; beat until light and fluffy. Fold in egg whites, beaten stiff but not dry. Sift flour and salt together. Fold

gently into mixture, then add vanilla. Line cakepan with Filling and pour batter over Filling. Bake at 350° for about 50 minutes, or until brown.

Filling

¾ cup butter or margarine
1 cup firmly packed brown sugar
  Pineapple slices
  Maraschino cherries

Cream butter or margarine and sugar together. Spread in bottom of pan, and cover with pineapple slices and cherries.

Jellyroll

4 eggs
¾ cup sugar
¾ cup all-purpose flour
¾ teaspoon baking powder
¼ teaspoon salt
1 teaspoon vanilla extract
1 cup jelly or jam

Place eggs in a bowl and beat with rotary egg beater or mixer. Add sugar gradually, and beat until mixture is thick and lemon colored. Sift dry ingredients together. Fold with vanilla into egg mixture. Turn into shallow pan, 15 x 10 inches, lined with greased paper. Bake at 400° for about 13 minutes, or until done. Cut crisp edges off cake. Turn pan at once onto a clean cloth sprinkled with powdered sugar.

Remove paper from cake. Spread cake with softened jelly or jam to within ½ inch of edges. Then roll it up quickly, starting at the narrow side of the cake. Finish with open edge on the underside. Wrap in towel and cool on rack.

Strawberry Shortcake

    2 cups all-purpose flour
    3 teaspoons baking powder
    ½ teaspoon salt
    ½ cup butter or margarine
    1 cup milk
       Sweetened strawberries
       Melted butter or margarine
       Whipped cream (optional)

Mix flour, baking powder, and salt and sift into a bowl. Add butter or margarine, and chop in with a knife until mealy. Add cold milk. Stir to make a soft dough. Pat or roll out dough ¼ inch thick on lightly floured board. Cut with 2-inch, round cutter into 12 to 16 rounds. Place on ungreased cookie sheets; brush tops lightly with melted butter or margarine, and place in pairs one on top of other. Bake at 450° for 10 to 12 minutes. Separate, and fill with strawberries. Replace tops, and spoon additional strawberries over shortcake. Add whipped cream, if desired. Yield: 12 servings.

Susie's "Rush-Up" Cake

    ¾ cup shortening
    2 cups brown sugar
    2 eggs, separated
    1 teaspoon soda
  1¼ cups buttermilk
  2⅓ cups all-purpose flour
    1 teaspoon baking powder
    1 teaspoon ground cloves
    1 teaspoon ground cinnamon
    1 teaspoon vanilla extract
       Brown Sugar Meringue

Cream together shortening and sugar; add egg yolks, and beat well. Dissolve soda in buttermilk and add alternately with sifted dry ingredients. Add vanilla. Mix until smooth and pour into greased 8- x 12-inch pan. Cover with Brown Sugar Meringue and bake at 350° for 45 to 50 minutes.

Brown Sugar Meringue

    2 egg whites
    1 cup brown sugar
    ½ cup nuts

Beat egg whites until stiff. Slowly add sifted brown sugar, and beat until smooth. Add nuts. Spread on cake batter and bake.

Two-Minute Cake

    ½ cup butter or margarine
    2 eggs, unbeaten
       Milk
    1 cup sugar
    1 cup all-purpose flour
    2 teaspoons baking powder
    2 teaspoon vanilla extract
    ⅛ teaspoon salt

Combine butter or margarine and eggs in a 1-cup measuring cup; finish filling cup with milk. Sift dry ingredients together twice. Then combine all ingredients and beat for 2 minutes. Add vanilla and salt. Pour into a 9-inch layer pan and bake at 350° for 20 to 30 minutes.

Caramel Frosting

3 cups firmly packed brown sugar
1 cup water
1 tablespoon butter or margarine
1 teaspoon vanilla extract
   Cream or rich milk, to soften

Boil the sugar and water until the syrup reaches the soft-ball stage (238° to 240°). Add the butter or margarine and vanilla and remove from heat. Let cool, then beat until thick and creamy. Add cream until consistency to spread. Yield: enough frosting for 2 (9-inch) layers.

Cooked Chocolate Frosting

¼ pound butter or margarine
1½ squares unsweetened chocolate
½ cup milk
2 cups sugar
1 teaspoon vanilla extract

Put all ingredients except vanilla into saucepan. Stir over medium heat until sugar is dissolved. Then let come to a boil and boil for 2½ minutes. Remove from heat, add vanilla, cool, and beat. Yield: enough frosting for tops and sides of 2 (8-inch) layers.

Chocolate-Cream Cheese Frosting

5 squares unsweetened chocolate
2 (3-ounce) packages cream cheese
¼ cup milk
¼ teaspoon salt
1 teaspoon vanilla extract
4 cups powdered sugar

Melt and cool chocolate. Work cream cheese and milk together until smooth and soft. Remove and reserve 3 tablespoons of cheese mixture. To remaining part, add and blend in the salt, vanilla, and melted chocolate. Add sugar gradually, beating until smooth after each addition. Beat in the reserved cheese mixture, 1 tablespoonful at a time. Continue beating until smooth and creamy. Yield: enough frosting for tops and sides of 2 (8-inch) layers.

Cocoa Mocha Frosting

6 tablespoons coffee
1 teaspoon vanilla extract
1 pound powdered sugar
1 cup sifted cocoa
½ teaspoon salt
6 tablespoons butter or margarine

Combine medium-strength, cold coffee and vanilla in mixing bowl. Sift sugar. Then sift all dry ingredients together. Add to liquids in three parts, beating until smooth after each addition. Gradually beat in soft butter or margarine, 1 tablespoonful at a time. Beat until smooth and creamy. Yield: enough frosting for 2 (9-inch) layers.

All-Purpose Quick Mix Frosting

Beat powdered sugar into 2 egg whites until thick enough to spread. Add ¾ teaspoon vanilla extract or any other flavoring desired. For a chocolate flavor, add 2 squares melted chocolate. Yield: enough topping for 2 (8-inch) layers.

Quick Chocolate Frosting

2 squares unsweetened chocolate
1 can sweetened condensed milk
1 tablespoon water
  Dash salt
½ teaspoon vanilla extract

Melt the chocolate in the top of a double boiler. Add the condensed milk gradually, mixing well. Then add the water and salt and blend. Cook for 5 minutes over rapidly boiling water, stirring constantly. Remove from heat and add vanilla. Cool. Yield: enough frosting for tops of 2 (9-inch) layers.

Glossy Chocolate Frosting

1 cup sugar
½ cup cocoa
¼ cup butter or margarine
¼ cup milk
¾ teaspoon vanilla extract
¼ teaspoon ground cinnamon (optional)

Mix all ingredients except vanilla and cinnamon. Stir and cook slowly until mixture comes to the boiling point. Increase heat and boil rapidly for 1 minute. Let cool for a few minutes. Add vanilla and cinnamon and beat to spreading consistency. Yield: enough frosting for top of 1 (8-inch) cake.

Broiled Coconut Frosting

¼ cup butter or margarine
½ cup firmly packed brown sugar
3 tablespoons top milk
1 cup coconut

Soften the butter or margarine and blend in remaining ingredients. Spread over the top of warm or cooled cake. Place 3 inches from broiler unit. Broil until mixture bubbles and turns golden brown (about 3 to 5 minutes). Yield: enough frosting for 9-inch cake square.

Fudge Frosting

2 ounces unsweetened chocolate, finely cut
1½ cups sugar
7 tablespoons milk
2 tablespoons shortening
2 tablespoons butter or margarine
1 tablespoon corn syrup
¼ teaspoon salt
1 teaspoon vanilla extract

Put chocolate, sugar, milk, shortening, butter or margarine, corn syrup, and salt into a saucepan. Bring slowly to a full rolling boil, stirring constantly, and boil briskly for 1 minute (1½ minutes if the day is damp). Remove from heat and cool to lukewarm. Add vanilla and beat until thick enough to spread. Yield: enough frosting for tops of 2 (8-inch) layers, or top and sides of 1 (12- x 8- x 2-inch) cake.

Coconut-Marshmallow Frosting

1 cup sugar
⅓ cup boiling water
¼ teaspoon vinegar
2 egg whites, stiffly beaten
10 marshmallows, quartered
1 cup thin-flaked coconut

Place sugar, water, and vinegar in a saucepan and cook over low heat until sugar is dissolved. Cover, and cook for 2 minutes. Remove cover and cook until the soft-ball stage is reached (238° to 240°). Pour in a thin stream over stiffly beaten egg whites, beating constantly. Add marshmallows, and continue stirring until cool and thick enough to spread. Spread on cake and sprinkle with the coconut. Yield: enough frosting for 2 (8-inch) layers.

Skillet Chocolate Mocha Frosting

1 cup sugar
2 tablespoons evaporated milk
1 egg
2 ounces unsweetened chocolate, cut fine
2 teaspoons dry instant coffee

Combine sugar, milk, egg, and chocolate in a skillet. Place over medium heat and bring to a boil, stirring constantly. Remove from heat and add the instant coffee. Beat until frosting is creamy and thick. Yield: enough frosting for top of 1 (8- or 9-inch) cake.

Fresh Coconut Frosting

3 cups sugar
1 cup water
2 teaspoons vinegar
3 egg whites, beaten
½ teaspoon cream of tartar
1 teaspoon lemon extract
1 teaspoon vanilla extract
1½ cups freshly grated coconut

Stir together the sugar, water, and vinegar. Cook until it spins a fine hair-like thread. Beat egg whites with cream of tartar. Gradually add sugar mixture, beating constantly. Add lemon and vanilla extracts and mix well. Stir in coconut and spread on cooled cake layers. Yield: enough for 3 layers.

Browned Butter Frosting

½ cup butter
4 cups sifted powdered sugar
1½ teaspoons vanilla extract
4 tablespoons cream
3 to 4 tablespoons hot water

Melt the butter over low heat until golden brown, stirring constantly. Remove from heat and blend in the sugar, vanilla, and cream. Add hot water, and stir vigorously until cool and the right consistency to spread. If it gets too thick to spread, warm slightly over hot water. Yield: enough frosting for 2 (9-inch) layers.

Baked Frosting

3 egg whites
¼ teaspoon cream of tartar
¾ cup firmly packed brown sugar
½ cup chopped walnuts

Beat egg whites with cream of tartar until foamy. Add sugar gradually, beating until whites stand in peaks. Spread over cake batter and sprinkle walnuts over the frosting. Bake according to cake directions. Yield: enough frosting to cover 2 (8- or 9-inch) layers, a 9- x 14- x 2-inch loaf cake, or 18 cupcakes.

Mile High Frosting

2 egg whites
1 cup jelly or 1 cup corn syrup
1 teaspoon vanilla extract

Put all ingredients into large bowl of mixer. Turn on low, then increase to medium, then high speed. Beat until very stiff. It never gets hard. Yield: 1½ cups.

Pecan Broiled Frosting

6 tablespoons soft butter or margarine
¾ cup firmly packed brown sugar
4 tablespoons cream
½ cup pecans, chopped

Mix all ingredients together and spread on top of warm cake. Place about 3 inches under the broiler and broil until mixture browns. Yield: enough frosting for top of 13- x 9-inch cake.

Orange Frosting

3 tablespoons sugar
1 tablespoon cornstarch
½ cup evaporated milk
3 egg yolks
½ cup freshly squeezed orange juice
1 teaspoon grated orange rind

Mix together the sugar and cornstarch in the top of a double boiler. Add the milk, and mix until smooth. Cook over hot water until slightly thickened. Beat egg yolks. Add orange juice and rind to the yolks. Stir into milk mixture. Continue cooking, stirring constantly, until thick. Cool before spreading. Yield: enough frosting for 2 (8-inch) layers.

Moon Glow Frosting

Grated rind of 1 lemon
4 tablespoons freshly squeezed lemon juice
2 egg yolks, unbeaten
4½ cups powdered sugar
2 tablespoons melted butter or margarine

Add lemon rind and juice to the egg yolks. Stir in sugar until smooth and stiff enough to spread. Add melted butter or margarine last. Yield: enough frosting for 2 (8-inch) layers.

Jelly and Cream Cheese Frosting

1 cup blackberry jelly
1 (3-ounce) package cream cheese

Mix jelly and cream cheese. Beat until mixture is smooth and stands in peaks. Use on cakes, cupcakes, or filled cookies.

Ornamental Frosting

1 cup shortening
2 pounds sifted powdered sugar
1 unbeaten egg white
½ teaspoon salt
1 teaspoon vanilla extract
⅓ to ½ cup lukewarm cream

Cream the shortening and a part of the sugar gradually. Add the egg white, salt, and vanilla. Then alternately add the cream and the remaining sugar. Beat until fluffy and creamy. This frosting will keep in a tight container in the refrigerator. Yield: about 3 cups.

Peanut Butter Broiled Frosting

⅔ cup firmly packed brown sugar
 4 tablespoons soft butter or margarine
 4 tablespoons cream
 4 tablespoons peanut butter
 1 cup peanuts, chopped

Mix all ingredients together and spread on cold cake. Place about 3 inches under the broiler and broil until mixture browns. Yield: enough frosting for top of 13- x 9-inch cake.

Boiled Taffy Frosting

 2 cups sugar
½ cup water
¼ cup molasses
    Dash salt
 2 egg whites, beaten
 1 teaspoon flavoring

Thoroughly mix the sugar, water, molasses, and salt. Cook without stirring to the firm-ball stage (245°). Gradually add the hot syrup to the beaten egg whites, beating all the time. Continue beating until mixture stands in high peaks. Beat in flavoring. If frosting hardens before spreading, beat in a few drops of hot water. Yield: enough frosting for 2 (9-inch) layers.

Mocha Whipped Cream

 2 teaspoons instant coffee
 2 tablespoons sugar
 1 teaspoon cocoa
½ pint cream, whipped

Sift dry ingredients and fold into whipped cream. Serve as topping on cake or other dessert. Yield: 1 pint.

Peppermint Frosting

 5 tablespoons cold water
 1 tablespoon white corn syrup
1½ cups sugar
¼ teaspoon cream of tartar
 2 egg whites
 1 teaspoon vanilla extract
    Red coloring
½ cup crushed peppermint candy

Combine all ingredients except vanilla, red coloring, and candy, and mix well. Set over rapidly boiling water and beat constantly until mixture will hold a soft peak. Remove from heat and set over cold water. Add vanilla, and beat until mixture will hold a sharp peak. This frosting does not get hard or grainy. Add the cake coloring and the peppermint candy just before spreading. Yield: enough frosting for 2 (8-inch) layers.

Uncooked Butter Frosting

 4 tablespoons butter or margarine
 2 cups sifted powdered sugar
    Grated rind of 1 lemon
    Juice of 1 lemon

Melt butter or margarine and add sugar, grated rind, and lemon juice. Beat well. Add milk if needed to make frosting spreading consistency. Yield: enough frosting to cover 1 (8- or 9-inch) layer.

Seven-Minute Frosting

    5 tablespoons cold water
    1 tablespoon white corn syrup
1½ cups sugar
    ¼ teaspoon cream of tartar
    2 egg whites
    1 teaspoon vanilla extract

Combine all ingredients except the vanilla, and mix well. Set over rapidly boiling water, and beat constantly until the mixture will hold a soft peak (with rotary beater, about 6 to 7 minutes; with electric beater, about 3 to 4 minutes). Remove from heat and set over cold water. Add vanilla, and continue beating until mixture is cool and will hold a sharp peak. This usually takes about twice as long as the time of the beating over the boiling water. Yield: enough frosting for 3 (8-inch) layers.

Bittersweet Mocha Frosting

    1 cup sugar
    1 cup cocoa
    ¼ teaspoon salt
    ½ cup strong coffee
    ½ cup nuts, chopped
    ¼ teaspoon vanilla extract

Combine sugar, cocoa, and salt in a saucepan. Blend in the coffee. Cook over low heat until smooth and glossy, stirring often (about 15 minutes). Cool. Beat in nuts and vanilla. Chill until firm. Spread on cake with spatula dipped in hot water. Yield: enough frosting for 24 tiny cupcakes or top and sides of 1 (9-inch) layer.

Spanish Cream Filling

    1 cup milk
    1 stick cinnamon
       Piece of lemon rind
    ¾ cup sugar
    ¼ cup all-purpose flour
    ½ teaspoon salt
    1 tablespoon butter or margarine
    4 egg yolks
       Powdered sugar

Combine milk, cinnamon, lemon rind, and bring to a boil. Strain. Combine sugar, flour, and salt, and add slowly to the milk, cooking in a double boiler for 15 minutes. Then add butter or margarine and beaten egg yolks. Cook for about 3 more minutes. Spread on a flat cake and roll as for jellyroll. Dust with powdered sugar. Yield: enough filling to cover a 13- x 9- x 2-inch layer.

Persimmon Cake Filling

2½ cups sugar
    ¾ cup boiling water
    1 teaspoon baking powder
    2 egg whites
    1 teaspoon freshly squeezed
       lemon juice
  12 large persimmons

Boil sugar, water, and baking powder without stirring until syrup spins a thread. Beat whites of eggs until dry. Cool syrup and add to egg whites gradually, beating constantly until right consistency to spread. Add 1 teaspoon lemon juice and cool. To one-third of this mixture, add 12 persimmons, seeded and chopped fine. Spread quickly between layers. Cover top and sides of cake with remaining plain frosting. Yield: enough filling for 3 layers.

Caramel Filling

4 cups sugar, divided
1 cup milk
1 tablespoon butter or margarine

Put 3 cups of the sugar and the milk in a saucepan and bring to a boil. Put the other cup of sugar into a heavy skillet and cook until sugar is caramelized, stirring constantly. Add the hot syrup mixture to the caramelized sugar, stirring constantly. Add the butter or margarine, and cook until it reaches the soft-ball stage (238° to 240°). Remove from heat, and beat until creamy. Yield: enough filling for 2 (9-inch) layers.

Fig Filling

½ pound figs, finely chopped
⅓ cup sugar
⅓ cup boiling water
1 tablespoon freshly squeezed
   lemon juice

Mix ingredients in order given and cook in double boiler until thick enough to spread. Spread while hot. Yield: enough filling for 2 (8-inch) layers.

Lemon Butter

7 egg yolks
2 cups sugar
¼ cup all-purpose flour
¼ cup freshly squeezed lemon juice
   Grated rind of 2 lemons
1 cup butter

Beat egg yolks thoroughly. Mix sugar and flour and add to egg yolks. Add lemon juice, rind, and butter. Cook in top of double boiler, letting the water simmer but not boil. Stir constantly. Cook until mixture is thick enough to hold its shape in a spoon. Remove from heat. Beat until cool and a good consistency for spreading. May be used as a filling between layers of cake, for pies, tarts, or in éclairs. Yield: enough filling for 3 layers.

Date Filling

1½ cups chopped dates
¼ cup sugar
½ cup water
1 tablespoon freshly squeezed
   lemon or orange juice

Cook dates, sugar, and water together until thick. Cool and add lemon or orange juice. Yield: enough filling for 2 layers.

Zesty Lemon Filling

1 cup sugar
3 tablespoons cornstarch
½ teaspoon salt
1 cup boiling water
2 tablespoons grated lemon rind
½ cup freshly squeezed lemon juice
2 tablespoons butter or margarine

Combine all ingredients. Bring to a full rolling boil, stirring occasionally. Turn down the heat and boil for 1 minute, stirring all the time. Let cool at room temperature. Beat well before spreading on cake. Yield: enough filling for 2 (8- or 9-inch) layers.

Raisin Filling No. 1

1½ cups seedless raisins, chopped
¾ cup water
¼ cup molasses
2 tablespoons cornstarch
½ teaspoon ground cinnamon
¼ teaspoon ground cloves
1 tablespoon butter or margarine
½ teaspoon grated lemon rind

Grind the raisins in a food chopper twice, using the coarsest blade. Add water, molasses, cornstarch, and spices. Mix well. Cook until the mixture is thick and clear, stirring constantly. Stir in butter or margarine and lemon rind. Yield: enough filling for 2 (9-inch) layers.

Raisin Filling No. 2

1 cup sugar
¼ cup water
2 egg whites, beaten until stiff
1 cup chopped raisins

Cook sugar and water until it spins a thread. Pour slowly into egg whites. Beat until thick enough to spread. Fold in raisins. Yield: enough filling for 2 (8-inch) layers.

Orange Filling

2 tablespoons butter or margarine
¼ cup sugar
2 eggs, beaten
1 tablespoon grated orange rind
1 tablespoon freshly squeezed lemon juice
½ cup orange juice

Combine all ingredients and mix until well blended. Cook in top of double boiler until well thickened, for about 15 minutes. Chill before spreading on cake. Yield: enough filling for 2 layers.

Pineapple Filling

¼ cup sugar
1 tablespoon cornstarch
Dash salt
⅔ cup pineapple juice
2 slightly beaten egg yolks
1 tablespoon butter or margarine
1 cup drained crushed pineapple

Combine sugar, cornstarch, and salt in a saucepan. Add the pineapple juice to the slightly beaten egg yolks and blend. Then add gradually to the sugar mixture, mixing thoroughly. Place over medium heat and bring to a boil, stirring constantly. Remove from heat. Add butter or margarine and pineapple. Mix well. Cool before spreading on cake. Yield: enough frosting for tops and sides of 2 (8-inch) layers.

Prune Whip Cake Filling

2 teaspoons unflavored gelatin
½ cup liquid from cooked prunes
¼ cup sugar
2 cups cooked, pitted, mashed prunes
1 cup cream, whipped

Cut 2 (8-inch) layer cakes into four thin layers. Soften gelatin in prune liquid and dissolve over hot water. Stir gelatin and sugar into cooked prunes. Cool until slightly thickened, then combine with whipped cream. Yield: enough filling for 3 layers.

Candies & Confections

Candymaking is an art, using wooden spoons for brushes and pans for easels. The candymaker has one advantage over the artist, however. She can rely on a recipe rather than unpredictable talent, and the end result is likely to draw few critics.

Candies come before Christmas in more than one sense. The candies and confections we bake in the weeks preceding December 25 are the descendants of the fruits, sweet herbs, and honey first combined by primitive man.

Honey remained the sugar basis for candy until explorers reached the New World and took back not only sugar but cocoa and vanilla as well.

Understanding the basic chemistry involved in making candy makes it clear why more than in any other type of food preparation, careful attention to directions is vital.

Granulated sugar is the basis of candy. Different chemical reactions during cooking cause this sugar to have the various textures of fudges and fondants or taffies, caramels, and brittles. Moisture must be driven from the candy mixture. At the point when the proper amount has been removed, candy is done.

If the praise you receive from serving good candy isn't enough, remember that you are now not only cook, but also artist and chemist — and you can smile a satisfied smile.

Creamy Caramels

    2 cups sugar
    2 cups warm light cream
    1 cup white or dark corn syrup
    ½ teaspoon salt
    ⅓ cup margarine or butter
    1 teaspoon vanilla extract
    ½ cup chopped nuts

Combine sugar, 1 cup of cream, corn syrup, and salt in a large heavy saucepan. Cook over medium heat for about 10 minutes; stir constantly throughout all cooking periods. Pour in remaining cup of cream very slowly, so that mixture does not stop boiling at any time. Cook for about 5 minutes longer. Stir in margarine about a teaspoonful at a time.

Turn heat to low and cook slowly to 248° or until small amount of mixture forms a firm ball when tested in very cold water. Remove from heat; add vanilla and nuts and mix gently. Allow to stand for about 10 minutes, and then stir only enough to distribute the nuts. Pour into one corner of a lightly buttered 8- x 8- x 2-inch pan, letting mixture flow to its own level in the pan.

Do not scrape the cooking pan. Cool to room temperature. Turn the block of candy onto a cutting board; if candy sticks, heat bottom of pan slightly, and turn onto board. Cool before cutting. Mark off into ¾-inch squares and cut with a large, sharp knife. Wrap each caramel in waxed paper. If candy is to be eaten right away, it may be dusted with powdered sugar. Yield: about 2 pounds.

Variation
Creamy Chocolate Caramels — Follow recipe for Creamy Caramels, adding 3 or 4 squares of unsweetened chocolate to the sugar-corn syrup-cream mixture.

Nut Caramels

    1 cup evaporated milk
    ¼ cup butter or margarine
    1 cup sugar
    1 cup white corn syrup
    ¼ teaspoon salt
    1 teaspoon vanilla extract
    1 cup chopped nuts

Heat the milk and butter or margarine, and set aside in a warm place. In a heavy pan cook the sugar, corn syrup, and salt until it comes to a boil and sugar is dissolved. Boil until mixture reaches the firm-ball stage, stirring often. Stir in the hot milk mixture slowly so that the sugar mixture does not stop boiling. Cook and stir until candy again reaches the firm-ball stage. Remove from heat and stir in vanilla and nuts. Pour into buttered pans. When firm, turn out onto cutting board or waxed paper. Cut into squares. Yield: about 1 pound.

Patience (Caramel)

    3 cups sugar
       Pinch soda
    ½ cup boiling water
    1 cup milk
    1 cup nuts
    1 tablespoon vanilla extract
    1 tablespoon butter or margarine

Caramelize 1 cup sugar until light brown. Add pinch of soda and about ½ cup boiling water. When dissolved and smooth, add to boiling milk. Cook to cream stage. Set aside and cool. Add nuts, flavoring, and butter. Beat until glassy look disappears. Pour quickly onto buttered plate. Cool and cut into squares. Yield: about 1 pound.

Divinity

2 cups sugar
½ cup white corn syrup
½ cup boiling water
2 egg whites, beaten
1 teaspoon vanilla extract
Cherries (optional)
Nuts (optional)

Combine sugar, corn syrup, and water. Cook over moderate heat until mixture spins a thread when dropped from a spoon. Gradually add to the beaten egg whites, beating all the while. Add vanilla and beat until candy loses its gloss and stands in peaks. Drop by teaspoonfuls onto waxed paper. Top with cherries or nuts, if desired. Yield: 1½ pounds.

Butter Fondant

2 cups sugar
¾ cup milk
1 tablespoon white corn syrup
1 tablespoon butter
1 teaspoon vanilla extract

Cook the sugar, milk and corn syrup together to 238° or until a soft ball forms when a small amount is dropped into cold water. Stir the mixture occasionally to prevent sticking. When the syrup is removed from heat, add the butter and vanilla, and pour it at once onto a cold, wet platter. Cool the mixture to 110° (or until it is lukewarm), and then beat it with a wide spatula until it becomes white and creamy. Next, knead it until the mass is smooth and no lumps remain. Put the fondant in a covered crock or glass jar and allow it to "ripen" for 2 to 3 days. It may be used to stuff dates or to coat cherries; it may be shaped and coated with chocolate; or chopped nuts may be worked into it; or it may merely be shaped and decorated on top with a nut or a cherry.

Orange Fondant

3 cups sugar
½ cup evaporated milk
⅔ cup orange juice
¼ cup butter or margarine

Combine all ingredients and cook to the soft-ball stage. Pour onto a large buttered platter and let cool until mixture retains a dent made by the finger. Stir with a spatula or large spoon until fondant is smooth and creamy. Drop by teaspoonfuls onto waxed paper or shape into small balls. Yield: about 1 pound.

Variations

Orange Creams — Roll fondant into balls. Top each with a strip of candied orange peel.

Orange Nut Creams — Top fondant balls with pecan halves.

Orange Cream Dates — Stuff pitted dates with Orange Fondant.

Chocolate Orange Creams — Coat fondant balls by dipping into melted dipping chocolate.

Orange Coconut Creams — Knead coconut into fondant mixture. Shape into balls.

Speedy Cream Fondant

3 tablespoons butter or margarine
¼ teaspoon salt
3 cups powdered sugar
1 to 1½ tablespoons cream
1 teaspoon vanilla extract

Beat butter or margarine until soft. Blend in salt and 1½ cups of the sifted sugar until evenly crumbled. Add remaining sugar alternately with cream and vanilla (½ teaspoon at a time) until mixture is stiff enough to leave sides of bowl in a ball. Blend until smooth. Yield: about 1 pound.

Uncooked Orange Fondant

2 tablespoons butter
1 cup powdered sugar
1 egg yolk
  Grated rind of 1 orange
  Orange juice

Cream butter; stir in powdered sugar, egg yolk, and the grated rind of 1 orange. If the fondant is too stiff, add a little orange juice. This may be used for stuffing dates. Yield: ¼ pound.

Seafoam Candy

1 (1-pound) box brown sugar
1 cup water
1 teaspoon vinegar
⅛ teaspoon cream of tartar
1 egg white
1 teaspoon vanilla extract
  Nuts (optional)

Mix sugar, water, vinegar, and cream of tartar and cook until a firm ball forms when dropped into cold water. Pour slowly over stiffly beaten egg white. Add vanilla. When candy thickens, add nuts, and drop with a small spoon onto waxed paper. Yield: about 1 pound.

Buttermilk Fudge

2 cups sugar
¾ cup buttermilk
½ cup white corn syrup

Cook these three ingredients together until a few drops will form a soft ball when dropped into cold water. Remove from heat, cool. When candy is slightly warm, beat until it begins to get creamy, then pour onto buttered platter, or pour on damp cloth and shape into a roll. When firm, cut into small pieces. Yield: about 1 pound.

Never-Fail Fudge

2 cups sugar
¼ cup cocoa
¼ cup white corn syrup
1 cup milk
3 tablespoons butter
1 teaspoon vanilla extract

Mix sugar and cocoa. Add corn syrup and milk. Set over heat and stir until all sugar is dissolved. As mixture begins to boil, wipe sides of pan with wet cloth to remove any undissolved sugar. Let boil hard until it reaches a soft-ball stage (240°). Add butter, but do not stir. Let cool and add vanilla. Beat until candy is stiff, then pour onto greased platter. Yield: about 1 pound.

Double Fudge

Chocolate Mixture

2 cups sugar
1 square unsweetened chocolate, chipped
⅔ cup water
4 tablespoons butter or margarine
½ teaspoon vanilla extract

Combine sugar, chocolate, and water. Stir until the sugar is dissolved. Boil until the soft-ball stage is reached. Remove from heat and add butter or margarine and vanilla. Cool until lukewarm and beat until thick and creamy. Pour into a greased pan, spreading ⅓ to ½ inch thick. Cover with Panocha Mixture.

Panocha Mixture

2¼ cups brown sugar
½ cup water
3 tablespoons butter or margarine
½ teaspoon vanilla extract
1 cup chopped pecans

Combine brown sugar and water. Stir until sugar is dissolved. Boil until soft-ball stage is reached. Remove from heat and add butter or margarine, vanilla and pecans. Cool until lukewarm and beat until thick and creamy. Pour over the Chocolate Mixture. Let cool, and cut into squares. Yield: about 2 pounds.

Hawaiian Fudge

2½ cups sugar
1 cup rich milk or cream
1 (8-ounce) can crushed pineapple
1 cup pecans
Few drops green cake coloring

Combine sugar, milk or cream, and pineapple. Bring to a boil over medium heat and cook until mixture reaches the soft-ball stage. Remove from heat, and add pecans and coloring. Let cool slightly, and beat until creamy. Pour into greased pan. Cut into squares when cool. Yield: about 1 pound.

Million-Dollar Fudge

4¼ cups sugar
6 tablespoons butter or margarine
1 (14½-ounce) can evaporated milk
2 (6-ounce) packages chocolate pieces
1 (8-ounce) jar marshmallow cream
4 cups chopped nuts

Boil together the sugar, butter or margarine, and evaporated milk for about 7 minutes after first bubbles appear, or until the soft-ball stage is reached. Put chocolate pieces, marshmallow cream, and nuts into a large bowl. Pour syrup over and stir until chocolate is dissolved. Beat until cool and creamy. Drop on waxed paper or pour into greased pan, cool, and cut into serving pieces. Yield: about 2 pounds.

Peanut Butter Fudge

2 cups sugar
1 cup milk
¼ cup corn syrup
1 cup peanut butter
1 teaspoon vanilla extract
Dash salt

Mix all ingredients together, and continue stirring as it cooks. When it forms a soft ball in cold water, remove from heat and cool without stirring. Beat well, pour into well-greased pan, and cut into squares. Yield: about 2 pounds.

Walnut Fudge

2 cups sugar
2 squares unsweetened chocolate, chipped
⅔ cup cream, milk, or water
2 tablespoons white corn syrup
2 tablespoons butter
  Few grains salt
1 teaspoon vanilla extract
1 cup broken walnut kernels

Put sugar, chocolate, liquid, corn syrup, butter, and salt into a saucepan and heat slowly, stirring until the sugar is dissolved. Cover until boiling point is reached. Cook without stirring until the temperature of 240° is reached, or until a soft ball is formed when a few drops are placed in cold water. Add vanilla, then cool, without stirring, to lukewarm (110°). Add walnut kernels and beat until creamy and mixture loses its shine. Pour into a buttered square pan and mark into squares. Yield: about 1½ pounds.

Easy-Do Pralines

1 (3¾-ounce) package butterscotch
  pudding mix
1 cup sugar
½ cup brown sugar
½ cup evaporated milk
1 tablespoon butter or margarine
1½ cups chopped pecans

Combine all ingredients except pecans. Cook over low heat until dissolved. Add the pecans, and cook slowly until candy reaches the soft-ball stage. Remove from heat and let cool slightly. Beat until mixture thickens. Drop by spoonfuls onto waxed paper to cool. Yield: 3 dozen.

Pralines

3 cups sugar
½ cup cream
1½ cups cane syrup
½ teaspoon salt
1 cup milk
½ cup butter
1 tablespoon vanilla extract
2 cups nuts

Combine first six ingredients and cook until mixture forms a soft ball in cold water. Remove from heat, and add flavoring and nuts. Stir rapidly until it begins to thicken; and before it begins to sugar, pour or drop from spoon into cupcake liners or in medium-sized circles on a buttered platter. Yield: 3 dozen.

Oldtime Pralines

3 cups sugar
1 cup cream or rich milk
1 teaspoon grated orange rind
1 cup sugar
1 teaspoon vanilla extract
2 cups pecans or mixed nuts (pecans and
  black walnuts)
  Dash salt

Boil the 3 cups sugar with the cream and rind in a large, deep kettle, until it forms a soft ball (as for fudge) when dropped in cold water. While this syrup is cooking, melt the remaining cup of sugar in a heavy frying pan, stirring constantly until it reaches the pale golden brown caramel stage. When both syrups are ready, carefully add the caramelized sugar to the first syrup, stirring with a long spoon, and being careful not to get burned when it foams up. Test immediately for the soft-ball stage; if unsatisfactory, remove from heat and let cool almost to lukewarm. Then add the vanilla, nuts, and salt, and beat until stiff and creamy, as for fudge. Drop in fat cakes onto a buttered cookie sheet.

Allow to cool before removing from sheet. Yield: 3 dozen.

Texas Pralines

2 cups sugar
½ teaspoon salt
1 cup butter or margarine
1 cup toasted pecans, unsalted

Melt sugar to golden brown color. Add other ingredients. Drop onto greased slab by large spoonfuls. Cool. Yield: 2 dozen.

Yam Pralines

3 cups sugar
1 cup light cream
1¼ cups cooked, mashed sweet potatoes
Dash salt
1 cup firmly packed brown sugar
2 cups chopped pecans

Combine sugar, cream, sweet potatoes, and salt in a heavy saucepan. Mix well. Cook over medium heat until mixture reaches soft-ball stage (234°). Stir occasionally. Melt brown sugar in a heavy skillet over medium heat. Then quickly add melted sugar and pecans to candy mixture. Blend thoroughly. Remove from heat and drop by spoonfuls onto greased cookie sheet. Allow pralines to cool until crystallized. Yield: about 2 dozen.

Favorite Pralines

3 cups light brown sugar
¼ cup butter
1 cup cream
1½ cups chopped pecans
⅛ teaspoon ground cinnamon

Mix the sugar, butter, and cream, and cook until a small quantity dropped in cold water forms a soft ball. Add the chopped pecans and cinnamon. Beat until cool, then drop by spoonfuls onto waxed paper. Yield: 2 dozen.

Minted Nuts

1 cup sugar
½ cup water
⅛ teaspoon salt
1 tablespoon white corn syrup
6 marshmallows
½ teaspoon essence of peppermint
3 cups pecan halves

Cook together slowly the sugar, water, salt, and corn syrup until it reaches 230° on candy thermometer. Add marshmallows; stir until they are melted. Add peppermint and pecans; stir with circular motion until every nut is coated and mixture hardens. Drop onto unglazed paper. Cool. Yield: 2 dozen.

Butter Mints

¼ cup butter
1 (1-pound) box powdered sugar
  Coloring
  Flavoring

Cream butter until quite soft, but not melted. Add as much powdered sugar as it will take to make a soft, creamy mint that can be forced through a pastry tube. Add coloring and flavoring as desired. Yield: 1 pound.

Pulled Mints

2 cups sugar
1 cup water
¼ cup butter or margarine
  Few drops oil of peppermint
  Food coloring

Combine sugar and water. Cook slowly, stirring constantly until mixture boils. Add butter or margarine. Boil slowly without stirring to the hard-ball stage (258° to 261° on your candy thermometer). To test candy, if you do not have a thermometer, pour from a spoon into cup of cool water, circling spoon to form a coil. This coil should be brittle. Remove immediately from heat and pour out in a circle on a cold marble slab. Try to make thickness of circle the same around. When candy is brittle on surface and soft in center, loosen from slab. Fold candy and pull gently but firmly with tips of fingers. Smear a few drops of food coloring and oil of peppermint in center of candy. Continue folding and pulling until color is distributed. Stretch into a long rope, continually turning, and cut off pieces into desired lengths

with scissors. (Turning rope gives the "pillow" effect.) Place pieces on cloth to dry overnight. When hard and dry, put into airtight container and mints will become soft and creamy. Yield: about 3 dozen.

Apricot-Coconut Drops

¼ cup butter or margarine
2 tablespoons orange juice
1½ cups sifted powdered sugar
¾ cup nonfat dry milk solids
½ cup coconut
1 cup dried apricots, chopped

Melt the butter or margarine. Remove from heat and add the orange juice. Stir in the mixture of powdered sugar and dry milk, ½ cup at a time. Mix in the coconut and chopped apricots. If mixture is too dry, add a few drops of water. Drop by teaspoonfuls onto waxed paper. Chill. Yield: 15 servings.

Candied Grapefruit Peel

1 large grapefruit
1½ cups sugar
  Coloring (optional)

Cover grapefruit peel (cut into strips) with water and bring to a brisk boil. Drain well, and repeat five times to remove bitter flavor. After last draining, cover with sugar and do not add water. Stir over low heat until syrup forms. Add coloring, if desired. Cook until peel absorbs all the syrup. Remove to platter covered with granulated sugar and let peel take up as much sugar as it will hold. Store in airtight containers. Yield: 3 dozen.

Candied Orange and Lemon Rind

Rind from 3 oranges (or 4 lemons)
1 *cup sugar*
½ *cup water*

Choose clean-skinned fruit and remove rind in quarters. Cover with water to which 1 teaspoon salt has been added. Boil for 30 minutes; then drain. Cover with fresh water and boil again until rind is tender (about 30 minutes). Lemon rind may need to boil longer. Drain again. Bring sugar and water to a boil, add the rind, and boil gently until rind absorbs syrup. Drain and roll in sugar. Cut into strips with scissors. Yield: 3 dozen.

Flatten to a 5- x 12- x ¼-inch rectangle, using palms of hands or lightly greased rolling pin. Mix last three ingredients together, and with buttered fingers spread it thinly to ½ inch from edge, over surface of candy. Roll as for jelly-roll, starting from the side rather than from end. Stretch roll into a long rope ½ inch wide. Cut into 1-inch pieces. Wrap each piece in waxed paper. Yield: about 3 dozen.

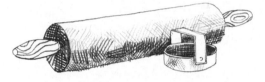

Fruited Molasses Taffy

1¼ *cups molasses*
1 *cup sugar*
1 *tablespoon butter or margarine*
⅔ *cup ground dates or raisins*
½ *cup chopped nuts or coconut*
1 *tablespoon molasses*

Cook first three ingredients together in saucepan until syrup separates into threads which are hard, but not brittle (270° or soft-crack stage). Stir constantly. Pour at once onto greased platter or cookie sheet. As edges cool, fold them toward center with spatula or they will harden before center is ready to pull. (Do not disturb that part of taffy which has not cooled, or candy will stick to pan.) When taffy is cool enough to pull, fold into a ball. Butter fingers lightly, and pull until candy is light in color.

Heavenly Delight

3 *cups sugar*
1 *cup white corn syrup*
1½ *cups cream or undiluted evaporated milk*
1½ *pounds candied cherries*
1½ *pounds candied pineapple*
½ *pound chopped walnuts*
½ *pound chopped pecans*
½ *pound chopped Brazil nuts*

Cook sugar, corn syrup, and cream or milk to the firm-ball stage. Beat until mixture starts to lose glossiness. Add fruit and nuts. Mold into a buttered or waxed paper-lined pan. Garnish the top with pineapple and nuts if desired. Let set in refrigerator until hard. Cut into slices after 24 hours. Store in refrigerator until ready to use. Yield: 5½ pounds.

Mary Butler's Fruit Balls

1 *pound figs*
1 *pound raisins*
1 *pound dates*
2 *to 3 pounds pecans*
1 *cup citrus juice*
   Powdered sugar

Combine and grind all ingredients. Soak for a week in 1 cup of fruit juice. Roll into balls; dip in powdered sugar. Yield: 3 dozen.

Chocolate-Rum Balls

1 *(6-ounce) package semisweet chocolate pieces*
1 *(7-ounce) jar marshmallow creme*
1 *tablespoon rum flavoring*
3 *cups crisp rice cereal*
½ *cup shredded coconut*
½ *cup chopped pecans*

Melt chocolate over hot, not boiling, water. Combine marshmallow creme and rum flavoring. Stir in chocolate; mix well. Add cereal, coconut, and nuts; form into balls. Roll in additional coconut or nuts if desired. Chill until firm. Yield: 4 dozen.

Creamy Pecan Candy

2½ *cups sugar*
1 *cup evaporated milk*
2 *tablespoons butter or margarine*
2 *tablespoons white corn syrup*
½ *cup sugar*
1 *tablespoon butter or margarine*
2 *cups pecans*

Bring the 2½ cups sugar, milk, 2 table-spoons butter or margarine, and corn syrup to a boil. Add the additional ½ cup sugar and 1 tablespoon butter or margarine. Pour in the pecans and cook to the soft-ball stage. Remove from heat and beat until creamy. Drop by spoon-fuls onto greased surface. Yield: about 18.

Orange-Coconut Creams

3 *cups sugar*
1¼ *cups cream or undiluted evaporated milk*
½ *teaspoon salt*
3 *tablespoons white corn syrup*
2 *tablespoons butter or margarine*
2 *tablespoons grated orange peel*
1½ *cups coconut*

Mix sugar, milk or cream, salt, and corn syrup together. Stir over low heat until sugar is dissolved. Heat to boiling. Boil for 3 minutes with cover on pan. Remove cover and cook to soft-ball stage. Remove from heat and add butter or margarine and grated orange peel. Cool to lukewarm without stirring. Add coconut and beat until creamy. Spread in a buttered pan and cut into squares when firm. Yield: about 2 pounds.

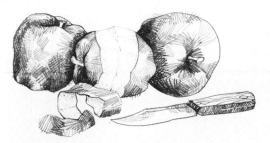

Date Roll

  3 cups sugar
1½ cups milk
  2 cups chopped dates
  1 cup pecans
  1 teaspoon vanilla extract
  1 tablespoon butter

Boil sugar and milk until it forms a soft ball in water (236°). Do not scrape sides of pan. Add dates and nuts and cook until it forms a firm ball in water (240°). Add vanilla, and remove from heat. Let stand until lukewarm. Beat as fudge. When it begins to thicken, pour onto damp cloth and roll. Let stand for 24 hours; then slice. Date Roll can be kept in a damp cloth in a cool place for several weeks. Yield: about 1 pound.

Foolproof Candy

  1 cup chopped nuts
  1 (6-ounce) package semisweet
    chocolate pieces
¼ pound butter or margarine
  1 teaspoon vanilla extract
  2 cups sugar
  1 (6-ounce) can evaporated milk
10 large marshmallows

Put the nuts, chocolate pieces, butter, and vanilla into a large bowl. Set aside. Mix sugar, evaporated milk, and marshmallows in a saucepan. Place on low heat and stir until sugar is dissolved. Cook over high heat until mixture comes to a boil. Reduce heat as much as possible and cook for 15 minutes. Pour over first mixture in bowl and stir until chocolate and butter are completely melted. Pour into a buttered dish; cut into squares when candy has cooled. Yield: 2 dozen.

Date-Nut Roll

  2 cups sugar
  1 cup milk
½ (8-ounce) package dates
½ cup chopped pecans
  1 teaspoon vanilla extract

Combine sugar and milk in heavy saucepan. Cook over moderate heat until mixture forms a firm ball when dropped into cold water. Remove from heat and add chopped dates. Beat until mixture becomes stiff, then add nuts and vanilla. Pour onto a damp cloth. Shape into a roll and allow to stand and cool. Slice. Yield: 1 pound.

Peanut Brittle

  2 cups sugar
  1 cup white corn syrup
½ cup water
  1 teaspoon salt
  2 tablespoons butter
  2 cups raw peanuts
  2 teaspoons vanilla extract
1½ teaspoons soda

Mix first four ingredients and bring to boil. Cover and boil for 3 minutes. Remove cover and boil to 250°, or to a hard-ball stage, then add butter and peanuts. Cook slowly to 300° or a hard-crack stage, then stir vanilla and soda into mixture quickly. Pour onto greased slab or platter. Let stand for 1 minute or so, then turn over like a pancake, and pull from edges to desired thinness. Yield: 2 pounds.

Note: Roasted peanuts may be used and added at the last. Never pour onto tin or enamelware.

Peanut Butter Crunchies

    4 cups sugar-coated cornflakes
    ½ cup sugar
    ⅛ teaspoon salt
    ⅛ teaspoon soda
    ¼ cup dark corn syrup
    ⅔ cup milk
    1 teaspoon vanilla extract
    ¼ cup butter or margarine
    ⅓ cup crunchy peanut butter

Place cereal in a large greased bowl. Combine sugar, salt, soda, corn syrup, and milk in saucepan. Bring to a boil over medium heat, stirring only until sugar is dissolved. Continue boiling, stirring occasionally, until a small amount of mixture forms a soft ball in cold water (or to a temperature of 236°). Remove from heat and cool for 1 minute.

Add vanilla, butter, and peanut butter; beat until thick. Pour over cereal and mix well. Press into greased 9- x 9-inch pan. When cold, cut into squares. Yield: about 3 dozen.

Peanut Butter Roll

    2 cups sugar
    1 cup brown sugar
    ½ cup white corn syrup
    1 cup light cream or undiluted
        evaporated milk
    1 teaspoon white vinegar
    ½ cup peanut butter
    1 cup sifted powdered sugar
    ½ cup chopped pecans

Combine sugars, corn syrup, cream or milk, and vinegar. Cook to the soft-ball stage, stirring until sugar is dissolved. Cool, without stirring, to lukewarm.

Beat until creamy, then stir in the peanut butter. Turn onto a surface dusted with powdered sugar. Knead in the sugar to make firm. Shape into a 2-inch roll, 12 inches long. Roll in chopped pecans, pressing the nuts firmly into the roll. Wrap in waxed paper and chill. Cut into slices. Yield: about 1½ pounds.

Pecan Nougat

    1 cup ground pecans
    ½ cup sugar
    1½ teaspoons vanilla extract
    ½ teaspoon salt
        Portion of unbeaten egg white

Mix ingredients. Add just enough of the unbeaten egg white to hold mixture together when pressed lightly with hand. A teaspoon of mixture will make a nice-sized nougat. The trick lies in the proper handling of mixture. Lightly mold into roundish pats, and bake on greased baking sheet at 250° until golden brown. Allow the nougats to get cold before removing them from baking sheets. Yield: about 1 dozen.

Mexican Pecan Candy

    2 cups sugar
    1 cup milk
    2 tablespoons butter
    2 tablespoons white corn syrup
    ½ teaspoon salt
    ½ teaspoon soda
    1 cup chopped pecans
    1 teaspoon vanilla extract

Mix all ingredients except pecans and vanilla in a large saucepan, and bring to a boil. When mixture comes to a boil, add pecans and cook until it reaches 234°, or until it forms a soft ball when dropped into cold water. Add vanilla and beat until creamy. Drop by spoonfuls onto waxed paper, or spread in buttered pan and cut into squares. Yield: about 2 dozen.

Pecan Roll

2 cups sugar
¼ cup corn syrup
1 cup milk
1 cup brown sugar
2 tablespoons butter
Pecans

Cook all ingredients together except butter and pecans until the mixture forms a soft ball when dropped into cold water. Remove from heat, add butter, and cool. Beat until creamy. Turn out onto pastry board or marble slab dusted with powdered sugar. Knead until firm. Shape into a roll about 2 inches thick. Dip into corn syrup and roll into chopped pecans. Keep in a cold place until firm enough to slice. Yield: about 1 pound.

Penuche

1 (1-pound) box brown sugar
¾ cup light cream or half-and-half
1 tablespoon white corn syrup
2 tablespoons butter
1 teaspoon vanilla extract
1 cup coarsely chopped walnuts or pecans

Measure all ingredients except vanilla and nuts into large saucepan. Heat to boiling, stirring constantly, and boil gently to 238° or until a few drops form a soft ball in cold water. (Don't worry if mixture curdles; beating will make it smooth.) Remove from heat and let stand without stirring until bottom of pan feels lukewarm. Stir in vanilla and nuts; then beat with spoon until thick and creamy and mixture begins to lose its gloss. Pour into buttered 8-inch square pan. Cut into squares while warm. Yield: about 1 pound.

To Make Good Candy

Candies are energy foods; with fruits and nuts added they offer additional nutrients. Candies are welcome gifts at any season of the year, and the boxes of homemade candy are always the first to be sold at bazaars.

Candymaking, to be successful, is more than a matter of luck. Just as in any other cooking process, there are some special rules. With careful attention to the rules that apply, there is no reason why you cannot make perfect candy every time. Here are some of the rules to follow:

Organize Your Work: Check to see that you have all the equipment and ingredients needed before starting candy.

Right Equipment: A large, heavy saucepan is best for candymaking. Select one that will allow the mixture to boil up without boiling over. Wooden spoons are preferable to metal ones since they are more comfortable to hold and will not scratch the pan. Remove the spoon while the candy is cooking.

Thermometer: A candy thermometer is very helpful because it is important to cook candy at exactly the right temperature and to the right stage. Some people can judge fairly well by dropping a small bit of the candy into cold water, but this is not entirely dependable and takes a great deal of experience.

Stirring: Occasional stirring of candies made with milk or cream is often necessary to keep the candy from sticking or scorching. If fruit or nuts are cooked in the candy, it is usually necessary to stir it.

Using Lid: A tight-fitting lid on the saucepan is necessary for the first few minutes of cooking. As soon as the syrup has begun to boil, the lid should be removed and the cooking completed. The steam that forms in the first few minutes helps to dissolve the sugar crystals which might form on the sides of the pan.

Heat Control: Candy in which milk or cream is used should be cooked at medium temperature to prevent scorching. Candy using water or fruit juice may be cooked at a higher temperature.

Weather: A clear day is better for making candy, since there is less moisture in the air. If candy is made on a cloudy or damp day, it should be cooked to a slightly firmer stage.

Beating Candy: Candy to be beaten should always be allowed to cool first. For a fine grained, creamy product, allow the candy to cool to 110° before beating.

Ingredients: All ingredients used in candies should be fresh and of good quality. When measuring brown sugar, remember to pack it firmly into the measuring cup. In recipes calling for coconut, you may use fresh coconut grated, or canned, packaged, or frozen. There are several types of coconut on the market . . . flaked, shredded, and grated. Any of these may be used. However, the flaked makes a smoother product for dropping or for cutting into squares.

Testing the Candy

In using a candy thermometer, the following degrees will show the degree of doneness of the candy.

Soft-ball stage	234° to 240°
Firm-ball stage	244° to 250°
Hard-ball stage	250° to 265°
Hard-crack stage	290° to 310°

If you have no candy thermometer, you may use the cold water test, although it is not as accurate. In making these tests, use fresh, cold water each time you test a sample. Drop a very little of the boiling syrup into a cup of cold water. Be sure to remove the syrup from the heat while testing is being done. When the syrup in the cold water can be gathered up between the fingers into a ball that holds its shape fairly well, it has reached the soft-ball stage.

The firm-ball stage has been reached when the ball will hold its shape.

When the ball reaches the stage that it holds its shape and is hard enough to be rolled on an oiled surface, the hard-ball stage has been reached.

The hard-crack stage is reached when the ball removed from the water is quite firm and cracks when knocked against the side of the cup.

Cookies

The delight of a small boy's heart, an essential at teas and receptions, a portable expression of love to a son or daughter away from home for the first time — all equal cookies.

As down to earth as a cut-out clown, as filled with holiday spirit as iced Santas, as old-fashioned as gingersnaps, cookies are one of the nicer parts of life for any age.

Cookies are the first experiment in kitchen magic for a child who will know the spells by heart when she is a grandmother making tea cakes without a recipe.

Many cookies include traditions among their ingredients handed down from the first settlers. Moravian Christmas Cookies, synonymous with the holiday in North Carolina, have found their way to other parts of the South where the people are of very different lineage.

The wooden cookie mold of yesterday has taken a back seat to lightweight plastic and aluminum cutters, but cookies in fanciful shapes are still recognized favorites.

Basic ingredients remain much the same, although we no longer use a feather and rose water for glazing. Spices, nuts, and fruits continue to add variety to conventional cookies.

It may be the simplest sweet, but the charm of a cookie is undisputed.

Ambrosia Cookies

  2 cups all-purpose flour
  ½ teaspoon baking powder
  ½ teaspoon salt
  1 teaspoon soda
  1 cup shortening
  1 cup white sugar
  1 cup firmly packed brown sugar
  2 eggs
  1 teaspoon vanilla extract
1½ cups uncooked oatmeal
  1 cup flaked coconut
  1 cup seedless raisins
  1 cup chopped dates
  1 cup chopped nuts

Combine first four ingredients. Cream shortening and sugar until light. Add eggs, one at a time, beating well after each addition. Add vanilla. Stir in dry ingredients.

Combine oatmeal, coconut, raisins, dates, and nuts; stir into creamed mixture. Shape into small balls and place on greased cookie sheets. Bake at 375° for about 12 to 14 minutes. Yield: about 5 dozen.

Brown Sugar-Pecan Cookies

1½ cups all-purpose flour
  ¼ teaspoon salt
  ½ cup shortening
  ½ cup sugar
  1 cup firmly packed brown sugar
  1 egg
  1 teaspoon vanilla extract
    Pecan halves

Sift together flour and salt. Cream the shortening. Add sugars gradually and cream until light and fluffy. Add the egg and vanilla. Blend in dry ingredients, gradually. Shape into small round balls and place on a greased cookie sheet. Flatten with fork or spatula to ⅛-inch thickness. Top each cookie with 2 or 3 pecan halves. Bake on ungreased cookie sheets at 375° for 10 to 12 minutes. Yield: 3 dozen.

Peanut Butter Cookies

  ¼ cup vegetable shortening
  ¼ cup butter or margarine
  ½ cup white sugar
  ½ cup firmly packed brown sugar
  1 egg
  ½ cup peanut butter
  ¼ teaspoon vanilla extract
1½ cups all-purpose flour
  1 teaspoon soda
  ¼ teaspoon salt

Cream shortening and butter or margarine together until light and fluffy. Add sugars, and cream until smooth. Add the egg, and beat well. Beat in peanut butter and vanilla. Combine flour, soda, and salt and add to creamed mixture. Roll dough into balls about 1 inch in diameter. Place on greased cookie sheets and flatten by pressing with tip of teaspoon. Bake at 400° for 10 to 12 minutes. Yield: 4 dozen.

Gingerbread Men

1½ cups heavy cream
2½ cups firmly packed brown sugar
1½ cups molasses, dark or light
  1 tablespoon ground ginger
  2 tablespoons soda
  9 cups all-purpose flour

Whip cream; add sugar, molasses, ginger, and soda. Stir and beat for 10 minutes. Add flour and work until smooth. Cover and put in a cool place overnight. Roll out portions on lightly floured board and cut in desired shapes. Brush flour from cookies-even a trace of flour on gingerbread spoils the looks. Lightly brush each cookie with water. Bake at 250° for 15 minutes. Scraps of dough may be cut in strips, baked, and decorated. Yield: about 3 dozen.

Soft Molasses Cookies

- 1 cup shortening
- 3 teaspoons ground ginger
- 1 teaspoon ground cinnamon
- ½ teaspoon ground nutmeg
- ½ teaspoon ground cloves
- 2 teaspoons salt
- 1 cup firmly packed brown sugar
- 1 cup molasses
- 2 eggs, unbeaten
- 4 cups all-purpose flour
- 2 teaspoons soda
- ½ cup sour milk

Combine shortening, spices, salt, brown sugar, molasses, and eggs and beat thoroughly. Sift flour with soda and add to the first mixture. Add sour milk and mix well. Chill dough overnight. Roll ¼ inch thick on floured board, and cut with large cookie cutter. Place on greased cookie sheets. Bake at 400° for 8 to 10 minutes. Yield: about 3½ dozen 3-inch cookies.

Note: Molasses cookies team up well with spices, particularly ginger. To handle deftly and cut neatly, keep dough chilled. Soft cookies should not be rolled too thin. To keep cookies soft, store in airtight container. Serve with hot tea, coffee, buttermilk or milk.

Molasses Cookies

- ½ cup melted shortening
- ½ cup melted butter or margarine
- 1 cup molasses
- 1 egg, beaten
- 2 teaspoons freshly squeezed lemon juice
- ½ teaspoon grated lemon rind
- 4½ cups all-purpose flour
- 1 teaspoon ground ginger
- ⅛ teaspoon ground cloves
- 1 teaspoon soda
- 1 teaspoon salt

Combine shortening, butter or margarine, and molasses; add egg, lemon juice, and lemon rind. Stir until mixture is blended. Sift flour, ginger, cloves, soda, and salt together and mix with other ingredients. Chill dough until firm. Roll, cut with cookie cutter and bake on greased cookie sheets at 375° for 12 to 15 minutes. Yield: 6 dozen.

Gingersnaps

- 1 cup molasses
- ½ cup shortening
- ¼ teaspoon salt
- 3 cups all-purpose flour
- 1 teaspoon soda
- 2 teaspoons ground ginger

Heat molasses and shortening. Mix and sift dry ingredients and add to first mixture (need not wait for it to cool). Thoroughly chill, toss on lightly floured board, roll very thin, and cut. Handle quickly and do not let get warm. Bake on greased cookie sheets at 375° for 8 to 10 minutes. Yield: 4 dozen.

Moravian Christmas Cookies

¾ cup butter and shortening, mixed
¾ cup firmly packed brown sugar
2 cups black molasses
7½ cups all-purpose flour
4 tablespoons ground cinnamon
4 tablespoons ground ginger
1 teaspoon salt
1 tablespoon soda
¼ cup hot water

Cream butter and shortening with sugar. Add molasses. Sift flour, cinnamon, ginger, and salt together. Add soda to boiling water. Add flour mixture and water alternately to creamed mixture. Work well with the hands. Cover, and store in refrigerator overnight. Roll as thin as paper. Bake on greased cookie sheets at 375° for a few minutes, or until they just begin to brown. When cool, store in a tightly covered container. Yield: 15 dozen.

Note: The best way to roll cookies extra thin is on a cloth or covered board with a rolling pin tightly covered with a child's new white sock. Do not add extra flour.

Surprise Cookies

1 cup butter or margarine
¾ cup firmly packed brown sugar
¾ cup white sugar
2 eggs, slightly beaten
1 teaspoon soda
2 teaspoons hot water
1 teaspoon vanilla extract
3 cups all-purpose flour
¼ teaspoon salt
2 (6-ounce) packages chocolate chips
1 cup chopped nuts
1 cup chopped candied cherries

Cream butter or margarine and sugars until light; add beaten eggs and soda dissolved in hot water. Mix well. Add vanilla. Beat in flour mixed with salt. Fold in remaining ingredients. Blend well. Chill and shape into balls 1 inch in diameter. Bake on greased cookie sheet at 375° for 10 to 12 minutes. Yield: 6 dozen.

Scotch Shortbread

1 cup soft butter or 2 sticks margarine
⅝ cup sugar
2½ cups all-purpose flour

Cream butter, add sugar gradually while creaming. Stir in flour, and mix thoroughly with hands. Add chopped nuts, if desired. Chill for ½ hour. Roll out to about ¼-inch thickness. Cut with cookie cutter, or cut in strips like fingers. Place on ungreased baking sheets and bake at 300° for 20 to 25 minutes. Yield: 3 dozen.

Heavenly Delight Cookies

½ cup butter
½ cup shortening
½ cup powdered sugar
½ cup nuts
2 cups all-purpose flour
½ teaspoon vanilla extract
⅓ teaspoon almond extract

Cream butter, shortening and sugar together. Add finely chopped nuts, flour and extracts. Chill for easier handling. Form into small balls. Bake on ungreased cookie sheets at 350° for about 20 minutes. Roll in powdered sugar while still warm. Yield: 4 dozen.

Nut and Raisin Cookies

  1 cup butter or margarine
1 ½ cups sugar
  3 eggs, well beaten
  1 teaspoon soda
1 ½ tablespoons hot water
3 ¼ cups all-purpose flour
  ½ teaspoon ground ginger
  ½ teaspoon ground mace
  ½ teaspoon lemon
1 ½ cups chopped nuts
  1 cup seedless raisins
  ½ teaspoon salt

Cream butter or margarine and sugar until light and fluffy. Then add the well beaten eggs and the soda which has been dissolved in hot water. To this mixture add flour and rest of ingredients. Mix well and chill. Roll out and cut with cookie cutter. Bake on ungreased cookie sheets at 350° for about 10 minutes. Yield: 10 dozen.

Confederate Jumbles

  ¾ cup butter
1 ½ cups sugar
  3 eggs
  1 teaspoon baking powder
  ¼ teaspoon salt
    About 2 cups all-purpose flour
  3 tablespoons milk

Cream butter and sugar. Add eggs, and beat well. Sift baking powder, salt, and flour together and add to the creamed mixture. Add the milk. This dough should be stiff enough to roll. Roll and sprinkle with sugar. Cut and bake on a greased cookie sheet at 350° for 8 to 10 minutes. Yield: about 4 dozen.

Peanut Butter-Marshmallow Cookies

  ½ cup shortening
  ½ cup sugar
  ½ cup firmly packed brown sugar
  ½ cup peanut butter
  1 egg, beaten
1 ¼ cups all-purpose flour
  ¾ teaspoon baking soda
  ¼ teaspoon salt
  ¼ teaspoon baking powder
  1 cup miniature marshmallows

Cream shortening, sugars, peanut butter, and beaten egg. Combine dry ingredients. Add to creamed mixture. Fold in marshmallows. Form into balls about 1 inch in diameter. Bake on greased cookie sheets at 350° for 8 to 10 minutes. Yield: 5 dozen.

Sand Tarts

  2 cups all-purpose flour
1 ½ teaspoons baking powder
  ½ cup butter or margarine
  1 cup sugar
  1 egg
    Egg white
    Sugar
    Cinnamon

Sift flour with baking powder. Cream butter or margarine thoroughly; add sugar, and cream until light and fluffy. Add egg and flour. Blend and chill until firm enough to roll ⅛ inch thick. Cut with doughnut cutter. Brush with egg white and sprinkle with mixture of sugar and cinnamon. Bake on ungreased cookie sheets at 375° for 10 minutes. Yield: 4 dozen.

Pfeffernuesse

>   3 cups all-purpose flour
>   ½ teaspoon ground cinnamon
>   ½ teaspoon ground cloves
>   ¼ teaspoon salt
>   ⅛ teaspoon ground white pepper
>   1 cup finely chopped blanched almonds
>   ¼ cup finely chopped candied citron
>   ¼ cup finely chopped candied
>   orange peel
>   3 eggs
>   1½ cups sugar

Combine flour, cinnamon, cloves, salt, and pepper. Stir in almonds, citron, and orange peel. Beat eggs until foamy. Add sugar gradually and continue beating until thick and light. Add flour mixture to eggs and mix thoroughly. Cover and chill for several hours or overnight. Dust hands lightly with flour and form dough into balls using about 1 tablespoonful of dough for each cookie. Place on greased baking sheets. Bake at 350° for 15 to 20 minutes or until lightly browned. Yield: 5½ dozen.

Praline Cookies

>   ¾ cup shortening
>   ¾ cup sugar
>   ½ cup unsulphured molasses
>   1 egg
>   2¼ cups all-purpose flour
>   1 teaspoon ground cinnamon
>   1½ teaspoons soda
>   ½ teaspoon salt
>   ½ teaspoon ground ginger
>   1 (6-ounce) package butterscotch-
>   flavored morsels
>   Sugar
>   Pecan halves

Cream together shortening and sugar until light and fluffy. Add molasses and egg; mix well. Combine dry ingredients and add to creamed mixture. Stir in butterscotch morsels. Chill in refrigerator for 2 hours. Form into 1-inch balls; roll in sugar. Place on greased baking sheets. Top each with a pecan half. Bake at 375° for 10 to 12 minutes. Yield: about 5 dozen.

Orange Cookies

>   ⅔ cup butter or margarine
>   1¼ cups sugar
>   2 eggs
>   3 cups all-purpose flour
>   1½ teaspoons salt
>   2 teaspoons baking powder
>   Juice of 1 orange
>   Grated rind of 1½ oranges

Cream butter or margarine and sugar. Beat in eggs. Sift flour, measure, then sift together with other dry ingredients. Add to creamed mixture. Then add orange juice and grated orange rind. Mix well. Chill. Roll thin, cut, bake on ungreased cookie sheets at 400° for about 8 minutes. Yield: 4 dozen.

Butter-Pecan Cookies

>   1 cup butter or margarine
>   ¾ cup firmly packed brown sugar
>   ¾ cup white sugar
>   2 eggs
>   1 teaspoon vanilla extract
>   2¼ cups all-purpose flour
>   1 teaspoon soda
>   ½ teaspoon salt
>   1 cup chopped pecans

Cream butter and sugars until light and fluffy. Beat in eggs and vanilla. Combine dry ingredients; add to creamed mixture and mix well. Stir in pecans. Drop by teaspoonfuls onto ungreased cookie sheets. Bake at 375° for about 10 minutes or until lightly browned. Yield: about 4 dozen.

Swedish Pecan Balls

1 cup ground pecans
2 tablespoons sugar
½ cup butter or margarine
1 cup all-purpose flour
1 teaspoon vanilla extract
⅛ teaspoon salt
  Powdered sugar

Combine all ingredients except powdered sugar and mix well. Shape dough into balls the size of walnuts. Place on ungreased cookie sheet and bake at 275° for about 30 minutes or until light brown. Roll in powdered sugar while hot and again after cookies have cooled. Yield: 2 dozen.

Crisp Peanut Butter Cookies

1 cup shortening
1 cup white sugar
1 cup firmly packed brown sugar
1 teaspoon vanilla extract
2 eggs, beaten
1 cup peanut butter
2 cups all-purpose flour
2 teaspoons soda
1 teaspoon salt

Cream shortening, sugars, and vanilla. Add beaten eggs, and beat thoroughly.

Stir in peanut butter. Combine dry ingredients; stir into creamed mixture. Drop by teaspoonfuls onto ungreased cookie sheets. Press with back of floured fork to make a criss-cross design. Bake at 350° for about 10 minutes, or until lightly browned. Yield: about 6 dozen.

Crisp Almond Cookies

1 cup butter
1 cup sugar
1 cup thick sour cream
⅛ teaspoon soda
2 egg yolks
1½ teaspoons grated lemon rind
1 teaspoon soda
½ teaspoon salt
3 to 3⅓ cups all-purpose flour
¾ cup almonds
2 tablespoons sugar

Combine butter, 1 cup sugar, cream, and ⅛ teaspoon soda in heavy saucepan. Place over heat. Stir until sugar is dissolved. Boil, stirring occasionally, until thick (10 to 15 minutes). Cool to lukewarm. Beat in egg yolks, lemon rind, 1 teaspoon soda, and salt. Add enough flour to make a medium-stiff dough. Roll dough, ½ teaspoon at a time, in palm of hands to form small balls. Place 3 inches apart on ungreased cookie sheet. Press flat with bottom of glass dipped in sugar. Sprinkle with mixture of almonds and 2 tablespoons sugar. Bake on ungreased cookie sheets 325° for 10 to 12 minutes or until edges are browned. Yield: 10 dozen.

Festive Fruit Cookies

½ cup shortening
½ cup firmly packed brown sugar
¾ cup white sugar
1 teaspoon vanilla extract
1 egg, slightly beaten
1 (6-ounce) can frozen orange juice concentrate
2½ cups all-purpose flour
1 teaspoon soda
½ teaspoon baking powder
¼ teaspoon salt
¾ cup flaked coconut
¾ cup chopped nuts
2 cups powdered sugar
½ cup soft butter

Cream shortening and sugars until light and fluffy. Add vanilla and egg. Add ½ cup orange juice, reserving remainder for frosting. Stir until well blended. Combine flour, soda, baking powder, and salt. Add to orange mixture, stirring until smooth. Add coconut and nuts. Drop by teaspoonfuls onto ungreased baking sheets. Bake at 350° for 9 to 11 minutes. Remove to cooling rack. Blend sugar with butter and reserved orange concentrate. Frost hot cookies. Yield: 5 dozen.

Butterscotch Drop Cookies

1 (6-ounce) package butterscotch morsels
½ cup butter or margarine
⅔ cup firmly packed light brown sugar
1 egg
1⅓ cups all-purpose flour
¾ teaspoon soda
⅓ cup chopped nuts
¾ teaspoon vanilla extract

Melt morsels and butter or margarine over hot (not boiling) water. Remove from heat. Beat in brown sugar and egg. Combine flour and soda and beat into mixture. Add chopped nuts and vanilla. Drop by half-teaspoonfuls onto greased cookie sheets. Bake at 375° for about 6 to 8 minutes. Cool slightly. Remove from cookie sheet. Yield: about 5 dozen.

Black Walnut Drop Cookies

½ cup shortening
⅓ cup butter or margarine
¼ cup powdered sugar
1 teaspoon vanilla extract
2 tablespoons thick cream
2 cups all-purpose flour
1 teaspoon soda
2 cups chopped black walnuts
Sifted powdered sugar

Cream shortening and butter or margarine together. Add sugar, and cream until light. Stir in vanilla and thick cream. Sift flour and soda together. Add nuts, and chop the nuts in the flour mixture. Stir into creamed mixture. Shape into small balls the size of hickory nuts. Place on cookie sheet and bake at 325° until a delicate brown, about 20 to 30 minutes. When cool, roll in sifted powdered sugar. Yield: 4 dozen.

Pecan Drop Cookies

3 egg whites
1 cup firmly packed brown sugar
½ cup white sugar
3 tablespoons all-purpose flour
4 cups pecans, chopped
½ teaspoon salt

Beat egg whites until stiff, beat in sugar and flour until well mixed. Add chopped pecans and salt and drop by teaspoonfuls onto greased cookie sheet. Bake at 350° until golden brown. Yield: 3 dozen.

Crunchy Brown Sugar Cookies

½ cup shortening
1 cup firmly packed brown sugar
2 eggs, well beaten
1½ cups all-purpose flour
1½ teaspoons baking powder
¼ teaspoon ground nutmeg
½ teaspoon ground cinnamon
½ teaspoon salt
½ cup toasted breadcrumbs
1 cup raisins

Cream shortening and sugar; add well beaten eggs, and mix well. Sift flour, baking powder, and spices together, and add crumbs and raisins to flour and mix well. Add dry mixture to creamed mixture; stir until all flour is dampened. Place in refrigerator to chill. Drop by spoonfuls onto greased baking sheet. Bake at 400° for 8 to 10 minutes. Yield: 3 dozen.

Williamsburg Cookies

1 egg white
¼ teaspoon salt
1 cup firmly packed brown sugar
1 cup chopped nuts
1 tablespoon all-purpose flour
½ teaspoon vanilla extract

Beat egg white until stiff; add salt. Add brown sugar gradually. Chop nuts and sprinkle with flour, then add to egg white mixture. Add vanilla and drop by teaspoonfuls onto greased cookie sheet. Bake at 275° for 15 minutes. Allow cookies to cool for 1 minute before removing from cookie sheet. Yield: 2 dozen.

Chocolate-Coconut Chews

½ cup chocolate chips
1½ cups corn flakes
1½ cups flaked coconut
1 cup sugar
2 eggs, beaten
1 teaspoon vanilla extract

Combine chocolate chips, corn flakes, coconut, and sugar in a large bowl. Add eggs and vanilla, and mix well. Let set for 5 minutes. Drop from teaspoon onto greased cookie sheet and bake at 350° for about 10 minutes. Yield: 3 dozen.

Peanut Butter Cookies

1 cup shortening
1 cup peanut butter
1 cup white sugar
1 cup firmly packed brown sugar
2 eggs, lightly beaten
2½ cups all-purpose flour
2 teaspoons soda

Cream shortening, peanut butter, and sugar until smooth. Add eggs, then flour sifted with soda. Roll into small balls, place on cookie sheet, and with a wet fork flatten in a crisscross design. Bake at 400° for about 10 minutes. Yield: 4 dozen.

Christmas Snowcaps

 3 egg whites
⅛ teaspoon cream tartar
½ teaspoon peppermint extract
    Dash salt
¾ cup sugar
⅔ cup diced, candied cherries

Beat egg whites, to which cream of tartar has been added, until stiff but not dry. Add peppermint extract and salt; add sugar gradually and beat until well blended and smooth. Save some of the candied cherries for topping the cookies, but add the rest, a few at a time, to egg mixture. Cover cookie sheet with plain brown paper. Drop cookie mixture by teaspoonfuls onto the paper. Bake at 325° for about 20 minutes. Let stand for a few minutes after removing from oven; then remove warm cookies with a spatula and place on a rack. Top with remaining cherries. Yield: about 2½ dozen.

Christmas Rocks

1½ cups all-purpose flour
 ½ tablespoon cocoa
 ½ teaspoon each of ground cinnamon, mace, and nutmeg
 ¼ teaspoon each of ground ginger and allspice
 ½ teaspoon soda
 ½ pound nuts
  1 pound mixed candied fruit
 ½ cup butter or margarine
 ¾ cup sugar
  2 eggs, well beaten
 ½ tablespoon strong coffee

Sift flour with cocoa, spices, and soda. Break nuts into pieces; cut fruits into slivers. Dredge both in a small quantity of flour mixture. Cream butter or margarine with sugar until light. Beat eggs until foamy. Mix them in. Add flour, mix thoroughly. Add coffee. Stir in nuts and fruits. Drop batter by teaspoonfuls onto greased baking sheet — not too close together. Bake at 325° for 12 to 15 minutes. They'll be crisp when done. Yield: 5 dozen.

Chocolate Fudge Cookies

2 squares unsweetened chocolate
1 (15-ounce) can sweetened condensed milk
1 cup nuts

Melt chocolate in top of double boiler. Add sweetened condensed milk and stir over rapidly boiling water for 5 minutes or until mixture thickens. Cool and add chopped nuts. Blend thoroughly. Drop by spoonfuls onto greased baking sheet. Bake at 350° for 15 minutes or until delicately browned. Remove from pan at once. Yield: about 2 dozen.

Mexican Wedding Cakes

½ cup butter or margarine
¼ cup powdered sugar
 1 cup all-purpose flour
 1 teaspoon vanilla extract
½ cup chopped nuts

Cream butter or margarine with sugar. Add flour gradually, beating well after each addition. Add vanilla and nuts and blend. Shape into crescents, place on ungreased cookie sheet, and bake at 325° for 15 to 18 minutes. Yield: about 4 dozen.

Maryland Black Pepper Cookies

2 eggs, separated
1 cup firmly packed brown sugar
1 cup all-purpose flour
1 teaspoon ground cinnamon
¼ teaspoon salt
½ teaspoon ground cloves
¼ teaspoon black pepper
¼ teaspoon soda
¼ teaspoon baking powder
1 cup seeded raisins and nuts

Beat egg whites and yolks separately, then together. Add sugar, and mix well. Sift dry ingredients together and add to eggs. Stir in raisins and nuts. Add more flour, if needed. The dough should be stiff. Drop by tablespoonfuls onto greased baking sheet. Bake at 375° for about 7 minutes. Yield: 5 dozen.

Coconut Cookies

1 cup firmly packed brown sugar
1 cup white sugar
1 cup shortening
2 eggs
2 cups coconut
2 cups uncooked quick-cooking oatmeal
2 cups all-purpose flour
1 teaspoon baking powder
½ teaspoon salt
1 teaspoon soda
1 teaspoon vanilla extract

Mix ingredients in the order listed, sifting flour, baking powder, salt, and soda together before adding. Drop on greased cookie sheet and bake at 375° for 10 to 15 minutes. Yield: 4 dozen.

Black Walnut Cookies

2⅓ cups all-purpose flour
2 teaspoons baking powder
1 teaspoon salt
1 cup shortening
¾ cup white or brown sugar
½ cup light or dark corn syrup
2 eggs
1 teaspoon vanilla extract
1 cup coarsely chopped black walnuts
¼ cup milk

Combine flour, baking powder, and salt. Cream shortening. Add sugar gradually and cream until light and fluffy. Add corn syrup and blend thoroughly. Add eggs, one at a time, beating well after each addition. Stir in vanilla and walnuts. Add dry ingredients alternately with milk. Drop by teaspoonfuls onto greased baking sheet. Bake at 375° for 12 to 15 minutes. Yield: 5 dozen.

Note: Walnuts or pecans may be substituted for the black walnuts.

Date-Nut Drops

¼ cup butter or margarine
2 tablespoons orange juice
1½ cups sifted powdered sugar
¾ cup nonfat dry milk solids
½ cup pecans, chopped fine
1 cup dates, chopped fine

Melt butter or margarine and add orange juice. Remove from heat. Stir in powdered sugar and nonfat dry milk solids, which have been sifted together. Mix in pecans and dates. Drop by spoonfuls onto waxed paper. These cookies do not need baking, but should be chilled. Yield: 3 dozen.

Molasses–Oatmeal Cookies

- ½ cup shortening
- 1 cup molasses
- 1 egg, well beaten
- 1½ cups all-purpose flour
- ½ teaspoon salt
- ½ teaspoon soda
- 1 teaspoon baking powder
- 1 teaspoon ground cinnamon
- ½ teaspoon ground nutmeg
- 1½ cups uncooked oatmeal
- ½ cup nuts
- ½ cup raisins
- ½ cup mixed candied fruits

Cream shortening; add molasses and egg. Sift flour and measure. Add salt, soda, baking powder, and spices; re-sift. Add with remaining ingredients to molasses mixture. Drop by teaspoonfuls onto a greased baking sheet. Bake at 375° to 400° for 12 to 15 minutes. Yield: 6 dozen.

Coconut-Gumdrop Cookies

- 1 cup shortening
- 1 cup firmly packed dark brown sugar
- 1 cup white sugar
- 2 eggs, well beaten
- 1 teaspoon vanilla extract
- 2 cups all-purpose flour
- ¼ teaspoon salt
- 1 teaspoon soda
- 1 teaspoon baking powder
- 1 cup flaked coconut
- 2 cups uncooked oatmeal
- 1 cup pecans, chopped
- 1 cup gumdrops, chopped

Cream shortening and sugar; add well beaten eggs and vanilla and mix well. Sift dry ingredients together and add to the creamed mixture. Stir in coconut, oatmeal, pecans, and gumdrops. Form cookies into balls and put on a greased baking sheet; press flat with a fork. Bake for 10 minutes at 375°. Yield: 5 dozen.

Holiday Fruit Cookies

- 2 eggs, beaten
- ¾ cup sugar
- ½ cup molasses
- 1½ teaspoons soda
- 1½ tablespoons water
- ½ teaspoon each of ground cinnamon, nutmeg, and cloves
- ¼ cup fruit juice (any flavor)
- 2 cups all-purpose flour
- 1 box seedless raisins
- 1 pound shelled nuts

Beat the eggs; add sugar and molasses, and mix well. Add soda dissolved in water. Add spices, fruit juice, and half the flour. Dredge raisins and nuts with other half of flour, and add to batter. Drop by teaspoonfuls onto a greased cookie sheet and bake at 350° for about 12 to 15 minutes. These cookies will remain fresh over a long period. Yield: 4 dozen.

Peanut Crunchies

- 1 cup butter or shortening
- ¾ cup sugar
- 1 cup firmly packed brown sugar
- 1 teaspoon vanilla extract
- 2 eggs
- 2 cups all-purpose flour
- 1 teaspoon soda
- 2 cups uncooked oatmeal
- 1 cup chopped salted peanuts

Cream butter or shortening. Add sugar and cream together. Stir in vanilla. Add eggs, one at a time, beating well. Sift flour and soda; add to creamed mixture, stirring until blended. Stir in oatmeal and peanuts. Drop batter by teaspoonfuls onto well greased cookie sheet. Bake at 400° for 10 to 15 minutes, or until lightly browned. Yield: 5 dozen.

Delaware Butter Balls

- 1 cup butter or margarine
- ½ cup powdered sugar
- 1 teaspoon vanilla extract
- 2½ cups all-purpose flour
- ½ teaspoon salt
- ¾ cup walnuts, chopped fine

Cream butter or margarine and add sugar gradually; add vanilla. Sift flour, measure, and add to creamed mixture. Add salt and nuts. Roll in ¾-inch balls. Bake in greased pan at 350° for 20 minutes. Roll in powdered sugar while still warm, and again when cool. Yield: 4 dozen.

Ladyfingers

- 3 egg whites
- Pinch salt
- ⅓ cup powdered sugar
- 2 egg yolks
- ¼ teaspoon vanilla extract
- ⅓ cup all-purpose flour

Beat egg whites until stiff; add salt. Fold in powdered sugar. Add beaten egg yolks. Add vanilla, then fold in flour. Form into finger shapes on slightly greased and floured pan. Bake at 350° for about 10 minutes. Yield: 2 dozen.

Drop Ginger Cookies

- ⅓ cup shortening
- ½ cup sugar
- 1 egg
- 1½ cups all-purpose flour
- 1 teaspoon soda
- ½ teaspoon salt
- ½ teaspoon ground cinnamon
- ½ teaspoon ground ginger
- ⅓ cup milk
- 1 teaspoon vinegar
- ¼ cup molasses

Cream together shortening and sugar. Add egg, beating vigorously. Sift together flour, soda, salt, and spices. Mix together milk and vinegar. Add molasses, and mix well. Add flour mixture alternately with milk mixture, beating until smooth after each addition. Begin and end with flour mixture.

Drop by level teaspoonfuls onto greased pan, leaving plenty of space between each cookie (about 2 inches apart). Bake at 350° to 375° for about 10 minutes. Yield: 4 dozen.

Macaroons

- 6 egg whites
- 3 cups sugar
- ½ cup water
- 1 cup pecans
- 1 teaspoon vanilla extract

Beat egg whites until stiff. Boil sugar and water until it spins a thread. Add to egg whites, and continue beating until cool. Fold in nuts and vanilla. Drop by spoonfuls on buttered cookie sheets. Bake at 275° for 45 minutes. Yield: about 8 dozen.

Oatmeal Macaroons

½ cup liquid shortening
¾ cup sugar
1½ teaspoons vanilla extract
1 egg, well beaten
½ cup all-purpose flour
¼ teaspoon baking powder
½ teaspoon salt
1 cup chopped pecans
1 cup uncooked oatmeal

Beat shortening and sugar together. Stir in vanilla and egg. Combine flour, baking powder, and salt. Add to shortening mixture. Stir in pecans and oatmeal. Drop by teaspoonfuls onto greased cookie sheets. Bake at 375° for 10 to 12 minutes. Cool for about 1 minute before removing from cookie sheets. Yield: 3½ dozen.

Lemon Drops

½ cup shortening
1 tablespoon grated lemon rind
1 cup sugar
1 egg, unbeaten
¼ cup freshly squeezed lemon juice
¼ cup cold water
2 cups all-purpose flour
3 teaspoons baking powder
¼ teaspoon salt

Blend shortening and rind together. Gradually add sugar, creaming well. Beat in the egg, lemon juice, and water. Sift flour, baking powder, and salt together, and blend thoroughly into the creamed mixture. Drop by level tablespoonfuls, 1 inch apart, onto greased cookie sheet. Bake at 400° for about 8 minutes. Cool before storing. Yield: 5 dozen.

Almond Macaroons

½ pound almond paste
3 egg whites, slightly beaten
½ cup all-purpose flour
½ cup sugar
½ cup powdered sugar

Work the almond paste with a wooden spoon until it is smooth. Add the slightly beaten egg whites and blend thoroughly. Add flour, sifted with the sugars. Cover cookie sheets with ungreased white paper. Drop cookie mixture from tip of a teaspoon or press through a cookie press. Bake at 300° for about 30 minutes. Remove macaroons from paper with a spatula while still warm. Yield: about 2½ dozen.

Gumdrop Bar Cookies

1 (1-pound) box dark brown sugar
4 eggs
2 cups all-purpose flour
1 cup gumdrops, cut into small pieces
½ cup chopped nuts

Beat the brown sugar with the eggs until well blended. Add other ingredients and mix well. Put into two greased 8-inch-square cakepans and bake at 325° for 30 minutes. Cut into bars while still warm. Yield: 2 dozen.

Bar Cookies No. 1

¼ cup shortening
1 cup firmly packed brown sugar
1 egg
1 cup all-purpose flour
1 teaspoon baking powder
1 cup nuts, chopped
1 teaspoon vanilla extract

Cream shortening and sugar. Add egg, and beat well. Stir in sifted dry ingredients, nuts, and vanilla. Bake in a greased 8- x 8- x 2-inch pan at 300° for 30 minutes. Cut into bars while still warm. Yield: 2 dozen.

Bar Cookies No. 2

½ cup butter or margarine
1 cup firmly packed light brown sugar
1 cup firmly packed dark brown sugar
2 eggs
1½ cups all-purpose flour
1½ teaspoons baking powder
1 teaspoon vanilla extract
1 cup chopped pecans

Blend margarine or butter and sugar. If a chewy cookie is desired, do not mix too much. Add eggs and beat well. Stir in flour sifted with baking powder, then vanilla and nuts. Spread in two 8- x 8- x 2-inch greased pans. Bake at 300° for 30 minutes. Cut into bars while warm, but leave in pan until cool. Yield: 4 dozen.

Oatmeal Lace Cookies

2 tablespoons melted shortening
1 cup sugar
2 eggs
½ teaspoon vanilla extract
½ teaspoon almond extract
¾ teaspoon salt
2 teaspoons baking powder
2 cups uncooked oatmeal

Combine shortening and sugar. Add eggs, and beat until light and fluffy. Add vanilla and almond extracts. Mix salt and baking powder with oatmeal and add to first mixture. Drop by teaspoonfuls onto greased cookie sheet, 2 inches apart. Bake for 12 to 15 minutes at 350°. Remove from cookie sheet immediately after baking. Yield: 3 dozen.

Sugar Cookies

½ cup butter, softened
1 cup sugar
1 egg
2 tablespoons milk or cream
½ teaspoon vanilla extract
2 cups all-purpose flour
½ teaspoon salt
2 teaspoons baking powder
Raisins
Granulated sugar

Combine butter, sugar, egg, milk or cream, and vanilla and beat until light and fluffy. Combine flour, salt, and baking powder and stir in, mixing well. Chill dough thoroughly. Roll small portions of the dough at a time on lightly floured board. (Dough may be rolled thick or thin.) Cut with a 3-inch cookie cutter, press a raisin in center of each cookie, and sprinkle generously with granulated sugar. Place on lightly greased cookie sheets and bake at 375° about 8 minutes. Cool and store in tightly covered containers. Yield: about 4 dozen.

Note: You can successfully double this recipe and keep a part of the dough refrigerated for several weeks.

Mushroom Cookies

        5 cups all-purpose flour
  1 ½ teaspoons soda
      ½ teaspoon salt
        1 tablespoon ground cinnamon
        1 tablespoon ground cloves
        1 tablespoon ground nutmeg
        1 tablespoon ground cardamom
        1 cup honey
        6 tablespoons granulated sugar
      ½ cup granulated sugar
      ¼ cup butter
        1 tablespoon grated lemon peel
        1 tablespoon grated orange peel
      ¼ cup commercial sour cream
        2 eggs, slightly beaten
           Decorating Frosting
           Poppy seed
           Cocoa

Sift flour, soda, salt, and spices together and set aside. Put honey in a large saucepan over moderate heat. Place the 6 tablespoons sugar in a small heavy skillet over moderate heat; stir until sugar melts and caramelizes. Pour into hot honey; continue cooking and stirring until caramelized sugar is dissolved. Remove from heat; add ½ cup sugar and the butter, and stir until butter is melted. Stir in lemon and orange peel. Add sour cream and eggs alternately with dry ingredients, mixing until well blended. Cover and chill several hours in the refrigerator.

To make mushroom caps: Break off small pieces of dough and shape in palm of hand which has been coated with flour. Make caps about 1 to 2 inches in diameter and ¼ inch thick. Shape caps so that they are rounded on one side and have a slight indentation on the other. Place rounded side down on well greased cookie sheets and bake at 350° for 7 to 10 minutes. Place caps on cake racks and let cool.

To make stems: Roll dough into ropes about 12 inches long; place on brown paper and cut into desired lengths (you will need about 7 dozen). Carefully roll brown paper around ropes, leaving ends open and securing roll with cellophane tape. Place on cookie sheets and bake at 350° about 7 to 10 minutes. Remove paper immediately. Place on racks and let cool.

To assemble mushroom cookies: Turn mushroom caps over and enlarge indentation on flat side with tip of a knife to make a place for stems to fit. Prepare Decorating Frosting; keep frosting covered with a damp towel as you work. Dip one end of stem in frosting and place in indentation. Set aside. After frosting has had a chance to set, frost stems and flat side of caps and sprinkle poppy seed around bottom of stems. Let stand for frosting to harden. Cover caps with frosting to which cocoa has been added; sprinkle with poppy seed and set aside for frosting to harden. Yield: 7 dozen.

Decorating Frosting

        3 egg whites
      ½ teaspoon cream of tartar
        5 cups sifted powdered sugar

Put egg whites in a perfectly clean mixer bowl; add cream of tartar and beat until stiff peaks form. Gradually add sugar and beat until stiff. Remove small amounts at a time, and keep bowl covered with a damp cloth.

Lemon Crumb Squares

1 (15-ounce) can sweetened
condensed milk
½ cup freshly squeezed lemon juice
1 teaspoon grated lemon rind
1½ cups all-purpose flour
1 teaspoon baking powder
½ teaspoon salt
⅔ cup butter
1 cup firmly packed dark brown sugar
1 cup uncooked oatmeal

Blend together milk, juice, and rind of
lemon and set aside. Combine flour, baking powder, and salt. Cream butter and
blend in sugar. Add flour mixture and
oatmeal; mix until crumbly. Spread
half the mixture in a buttered 13- x 9-
x 2-inch pan. Pat mixture down and
spread sweetened condensed milk mixture over it. Cover top with remaining
crumb mixture. Bake at 350° until
brown around edges (about 25 minutes).
Cool in pan at room temperature for 15
minutes; cut into 1¾-inch squares and
chill in pan until firm. Yield: 2 dozen.

Coconut Dream Bars

½ cup butter or margarine
½ cup firmly packed brown sugar
1 cup all-purpose flour
2 eggs
1 cup brown sugar
½ teaspoon baking powder
2 tablespoons all-purpose flour
¼ teaspoon salt
1½ cups coconut
½ cup chopped nuts
1 teaspoon vanilla extract

Cream the ½ cup butter or margarine
and ½ cup brown sugar. Add 1 cup flour,
and mix. Spread in well greased 8-inch
square cakepan. Bake at 350° for
10 minutes.

Beat the eggs and add 1 cup brown
sugar, baking powder, 2 teaspoons flour,
and salt. Add coconut, nuts, and vanilla.
Pour over top of baked layer and continue baking at 350° until set (about 10
to 15 minutes). Cut into bars when
slightly cool. Remove from pan with
wide spatula and cool on wire rack.
Yield: 2 dozen.

Coconut Vanities

2 cups all-purpose flour
2 teaspoons baking powder
¼ cup margarine or butter
1 cup sugar
1 egg
Grated rind of 1 orange
¼ cup milk
½ cup orange juice
½ cup shredded coconut
1 egg white
3 tablespoons sugar

Sift flour and baking powder. Cream
butter and sugar. Add egg and beat well.
Combine grated rind, milk, and orange
juice. Add flour mixture alternately with
liquid, mixing after each addition. Add
coconut. Pour into shallow, greased,
paper-lined pan. Beat egg white until
frothy, add 3 tablespoons sugar gradually, and continue beating until mixture
is stiff. Spread on batter. Bake at 300°
for 30 minutes. Yield: 3 dozen.

Brown Sugar Brownies

1¾ sticks margarine
2 cups firmly packed light brown sugar
2 eggs
1 cup all-purpose flour
1 cup chopped nuts
½ teaspoon vanilla extract

Beat margarine until creamy; add sugar and continue beating until mixture is smooth. Add eggs and mix well. Stir in flour, nuts, and vanilla. Bake in a greased 9- x 9- x 2-inch pan at 375° for 25 to 30 minutes. Cut into squares as soon as taken from the oven. Yield: 3 dozen.

Black Walnut Bar Cookies

½ cup brown sugar
1 cup all-purpose flour
½ cup butter or margarine
1 cup firmly packed brown sugar
2 eggs, beaten
¼ teaspoon salt
1 teaspoon all-purpose flour
1 teaspoon vanilla extract
1½ cups flaked coconut
1 cup black walnuts, chopped

Sift the ½ cup brown sugar with the 1 cup flour. Cut in the butter or margarine. Press into a 10- x 10-inch pan and bake at 375° for 10 minutes. Remove pan from oven and let cool. Mix 1 cup brown sugar with beaten eggs, salt, 1 teaspoon flour, vanilla, coconut, and black walnuts. Pour over baked layer and return to oven. Bake at 375° for 20 minutes. Remove and cool before cutting into bars or squares. Yield: 3 dozen.

Date-Nut Bars

1 cup sugar
3 egg yolks, beaten
1 teaspoon vanilla extract
¼ cup melted butter or margarine
3 egg whites, stiffly beaten
1 cup all-purpose flour
1 teaspoon baking powder
Pinch salt
1 cup dates, chopped
¾ cup pecans, chopped

Gradually beat sugar into egg yolks, add vanilla and melted butter or margarine, blending well. Fold in stiffly beaten egg whites. Combine flour with baking powder and salt; add to creamed mixture and blend well. Stir in dates and pecans. Pour into two greased 8- x 8- x 2-inch pans. Bake at 350° for about 20 minutes. Yield: 4 dozen.

Cereal-Chocolate Squares

¾ cup sugar
1 egg
¼ teaspoon salt
1 cup crushed corn flakes, divided
1 tablespoon milk
½ teaspoon vanilla extract
2 squares unsweetened chocolate
2 tablespoons butter or margarine

Beat sugar gradually into egg. Add salt, ½ cup corn flakes, milk, and vanilla. Combine melted chocolate and butter or margarine; add to egg mixture and blend. Sprinkle greased 8- x 8- x 2-inch pan with ¼ cup corn flakes, pour in chocolate mixture, and sprinkle remaining corn flakes on top. Bake at 325° for 40 minutes. Cut into squares before removing from pan. Yield: 2 dozen.

Easy Fudge Squares

1 cup sugar
¾ cup cocoa
½ cup all-purpose flour
2 eggs, beaten
¼ cup milk
1 cup chopped nuts
⅓ cup melted butter or margarine
   Powdered sugar

Combine sugar, cocoa, and flour. Add beaten eggs and milk and stir until smooth. Add nuts, and melted butter or margarine. Bake in a greased 8-inch square pan at 350° for about 40 minutes. When cool, cut into squares and roll in powdered sugar. Yield: 2 dozen.

Almond-Jam Bars

1½ cups all-purpose flour
½ cup sugar
½ teaspoon baking powder
½ teaspoon ground cinnamon
¼ teaspoon ground cloves
½ cup shortening
½ teaspoon almond extract
1 egg, beaten
¼ cup milk
¾ cup jam (any flavor)

Sift together flour, sugar, baking powder, cinnamon, and cloves. Cream together shortening and extract. Cut or rub shortening into flour mixture. Add beaten egg and milk and mix until well blended. Spread half of mixture into greased 7- x 11-inch pan. Cover evenly with jam. Spread with remainder of mixture over jam. Bake at 400° for 25 to 30 minutes. When cool, cut into bars. Yield: about 28 (1- x 2½-inch) bars.

Seven-Layer Cookies

½ stick butter
1 cup graham cracker crumbs
1 cup flaked coconut
1 (6-ounce) package chocolate chips
1 (6-ounce) package butterscotch morsels
1 (15-ounce) can sweetened
   condensed milk
1 cup chopped pecans

Melt butter in a 13- x 9- x 2-inch pan. Add ingredients by layers, in order listed. Bake at 325° for about 30 minutes. Let cool in pan, then cut into small squares. Yield: 4 dozen.

Brownies

⅓ cup butter or margarine
1½ squares unsweetened chocolate
2 eggs
1 cup white or brown sugar
⅔ cup all-purpose flour
½ teaspoon baking powder
¼ teaspoon salt
¾ cup broken nuts
1 teaspoon vanilla extract

Melt butter or margarine and chocolate together over hot water. Beat eggs until lemon colored, and gradually add sugar, beating well. Blend in chocolate mixture. Sift flour, baking powder, and salt together, and stir into batter until smooth. Add nuts and vanilla. Turn into greased 8- x 8- x 2-inch pan. Bake at 350° for 25 minutes. Cut into squares. Yield: 2 dozen.

Oatmeal Crispies

   1 cup shortening
   1 cup brown sugar
   1 cup white sugar
   2 eggs
   1 teaspoon vanilla extract
1 ½ cups all-purpose flour
   1 teaspoon salt
   1 teaspoon soda
   3 cups uncooked quick-cooking oatmeal
   ½ cup nuts

Cream shortening and sugar. Add eggs and vanilla and beat well. Combine flour, salt, and soda. Add to creamed mixture. Stir in oatmeal and nuts and mix well. Form into rolls, wrap in waxed paper, chill thoroughly and slice. Place on greased cookie sheets and bake at 350° for about 10 minutes. Yield: 4 dozen.

Coconut-Oatmeal Cookies

   1 cup butter or margarine
   2 cups brown sugar
   2 eggs, well beaten
1 ½ teaspoons vanilla extract
   1 teaspoon soda
   4 cups quick-cooking oatmeal
   2 cups all-purpose flour
   1 cup flaked coconut

Mix butter or margarine and brown sugar together. Add well beaten eggs and vanilla. Mix soda, oatmeal, flour, and coconut together and add to the first mixture. Form into two 2-inch rolls, wrap in waxed paper, and let chill in refrigerator for 4 to 5 hours. Slice very thin and bake on greased cookie sheets at 350° for about 10 to 12 minutes. Yield: 10 dozen.

Lemon Refrigerator Cookies

   1 cup butter or margarine
   ½ cup dark brown sugar
   2 eggs
     Grated rind of 1 lemon
   2 tablespoons freshly squeezed lemon juice
   1 teaspoon vanilla extract
2 ¾ cups all-purpose flour
   ¼ teaspoon soda
   ¼ teaspoon salt
   ½ cup pecans, finely chopped
   1 cup semi-sweet chocolate drops

Cream butter or margarine and brown sugar until smooth. Then add eggs one at a time and beat well after each addition. Stir in grated lemon rind, lemon juice, and vanilla. Add sifted dry ingredients, nuts, and chocolate. Form into two 12-inch rolls 1 ½ inches in diameter. Chill in waxed paper. When chilled, slice thin and place on ungreased cookie sheets. Bake at 375° for 8 minutes. Yield: 12 dozen.

Sumrall Cookies

   1 (1-pound) box brown sugar
   4 eggs
   2 cups all-purpose flour
   1 teaspoon baking powder
   ½ teaspoon soda
   2 cups pecans
   1 teaspoon vanilla extract

Combine brown sugar and eggs and beat well. Add flour which has been combined with baking powder and soda. Stir in pecans and vanilla. Mix well with hands. Spread batter on a greased 15- x 10- x 1-inch cookie sheet. Bake at 350° for about 25 minutes. Cut into bars while hot. Yield: about 4 dozen.

Oatmeal Drop Cookies

½ cup butter or margarine
½ cup firmly packed brown sugar
½ cup corn syrup
1 egg
1 cup all-purpose flour
½ cup cocoa
¼ teaspoon soda
½ teaspoon salt
1¼ cups uncooked quick-cooking oatmeal
½ cup chopped nuts
½ cup milk

Cream butter or margarine. Add sugar gradually and cream until light and fluffy. Add corn syrup and egg and mix well. Combine dry ingredients; stir in oatmeal. Add nuts. Add creamed mixture and milk to dry ingredients. Drop by teaspoonfuls onto lightly greased cookie sheets. Bake at 350° for 15 minutes, or until done. Yield: about 3 dozen.

Refrigerator Cookies

1 cup shortening
½ cup brown sugar
½ cup white sugar
1 egg, beaten
2 tablespoons orange juice
2 tablespoons grated orange rind
2 cups all-purpose flour
¼ teaspoon soda
½ cup pecans, chopped fine

Cream shortening and sugar. Add the beaten egg, orange juice, and grated rind, beating until smooth. Sift flour and soda together, and add to creamed mixture. Stir in chopped pecans. Shape into a roll and chill overnight in refrigerator. Slice thin and bake on ungreased cookie sheets at 375° for 10 to 12 minutes. Yield: 5 dozen.

Honey Refrigerator Cookies

¾ cup honey
½ cup butter or margarine
1 egg
2½ cups all-purpose flour
1½ teaspoons baking powder
¼ teaspoon soda
½ teaspoon salt
½ cup nuts

Cream honey, butter or margarine, and egg. Mix and sift dry ingredients and add to creamed mixture. Then mix in nuts. Shape into long, round rolls the size desired for cookies, wrap in waxed paper, and place in refrigerator for 2 to 3 days. Slice thin and bake on greased cookie sheets at 400° to 425° for about 10 to 12 minutes. Yield: 4 dozen.

Butterscotch Cookies No. 1

½ cup butter or margarine
2 cups firmly packed brown sugar
2 eggs
3½ cups all-purpose flour
3 teaspoons baking powder
  Pinch salt
1 teaspoon vanilla extract

Cream butter or margarine and sugar until light and fluffy. Add eggs and beat well. Work in sifted dry ingredients and add vanilla. Make into two rolls and store in refrigerator for several hours or overnight. Slice fairly thin and bake on ungreased cookie sheets at 400° until lightly browned. Remove immediately to wire rack to cool. Yield: 5 dozen.

Butterscotch Cookies No. 2

    2 cups firmly packed brown sugar
    3 cups all-purpose flour
  1½ teaspoons soda
  1⅓ teaspoons cream of tartar
   ½ cup melted butter or margarine
    2 eggs, beaten

Combine sugar, flour, soda, and cream
of tartar. Add melted butter or margarine and beaten eggs. Turn onto a lightly
floured board and knead. Shape into
small rolls and wrap in waxed paper.
Refrigerate overnight. Slice and bake on
greased cookie sheets at 350° for 12
minutes. Yield: about 7 dozen.

Old-Fashioned Sugar Cookies

    1 cup shortening (part butter)
  1½ cups sugar
    2 eggs
  2¾ cups all-purpose flour
    2 teaspoons soda
    2 teaspoons cream of tartar
   ½ teaspoon salt
    2 tablespoons sugar
    2 teaspoons ground cinnamon

Cream together shortening and 1½ cups
sugar. Add eggs, and beat until light
and fluffy. Combine flour, soda, cream of
tartar, and salt and add to creamed mixture. Chill for at least 1 hour in refrigerator. Roll in a mixture of 2 tablespoons sugar and 2 teaspoons ground
cinnamon. Cut into desired shapes. Bake
on ungreased cookie sheets at 350° for
about 10 to 12 minutes. Yield: 4 to
5 dozen.

Sugarplum Cookies

  2¼ cups all-purpose flour
  1½ teaspoons baking powder
   ¾ teaspoon salt
   ⅔ cup butter or margarine
   ½ cup sugar
    1 egg, unbeaten
  1½ teaspoons grated lemon rind
   18 seeded raisins

Sift dry ingredients together. Cream
butter or margarine with sugar until
very light. Add unbeaten egg and mix in
well. Add lemon rind. Mix flour into
this mixture and work it well with your
hands. Now, pack the cookie dough into
a round pint-sized ice cream container.
Chill for 3 hours. Strip off the carton
and slice thin. Place large, seeded raisin
in center of each cookie; put on greased
baking sheets; bake at 400° for 10 to 12
minutes. Yield: about 1½ dozen.

Nut Refrigerator Cookies

  1½ cups butter or margarine
    2 cups brown sugar
    2 eggs, well beaten
    3 cups all-purpose flour
    2 teaspoons baking powder
   ½ cup nuts

Cream butter, add sugar and well beaten
eggs. Mix well; add flour and baking
powder sifted together. Mix to a dough
and add nuts. Shape into rolls. Wrap in
waxed paper. (May need to spoon dough
onto waxed paper as dough may be
soft.) Chill, slice, and bake on ungreased
cookie sheets at 375° for about 15 minutes. Yield: 6 dozen.

Desserts

Dessert is an expression of love in a meal, and in the South where so much care goes into the preparation of fine foods, a meal without dessert is a contradiction in terms. It doesn't have to be elegant or rich, but it must be *there*.

Many of the desserts on which Southerners for generations have cut their sweet tooth are as simple in preparation and form as boiled custards and puddings, with ingredients ranging from rice to fruits.

Some of the desserts we cherish have seasonal connotations. Ambrosia is as much a part of Christmas as the traditional tree. It was once considered the food by which the Greek gods preserved their immortality, and more than a few Southern mothers and grandmothers attained their own share of the same with family and friends as they went through the annual ritual of mixing coconut and oranges.

Summer is the South's season, and ice cream the dessert it claims for its own. One authority of previous years wrote that "after having tried many new and patent freezers, some of the best housekeepers have come to the conclusion that the old-fashioned freezer is the best. It is well, however, to keep a patent freezer on hand, in case of your wanting ice cream on short notice; but for common use an old-fashioned one is the best."

Today, electric freezers make the process fairly simple. But the recipes for custard and an almost universal preference for fresh peaches remain virtually unchallenged.

The word dessert comes from an old French verb meaning "to clear the table." And with our rich store of desserts, plain and fancy, finishing a meal without dessert would be almost like clearing the table before anyone sat down to dinner.

Buttermilk Ice Cream

Juice of 1 lemon
1 cup sugar
2 (14½-ounce) cans evaporated milk
4 cups buttermilk
4 egg whites, beaten

Mix lemon juice and sugar, then slowly add evaporated milk, next buttermilk, and then the beaten egg whites. Freeze. Yield: ½ gallon.

Custard Ice Cream

1 cup sugar
1 tablespoon cornstarch
4 eggs, beaten
8 cups milk
1 (14½-ounce) can evaporated milk
½ cup sweetened condensed milk
1½ tablespoons vanilla extract

Cook sugar, cornstarch, beaten eggs, and 2 cups of the milk together in top of double boiler until mixture coats spoon. Remove from heat. Add remaining ingredients. Let cool, then freeze. Yield: 1 gallon.

Peppermint Ice Cream

1 cup milk
½ cup sugar
⅛ teaspoon salt
1 teaspoon all-purpose flour
1 egg, well beaten
½ teaspoon unflavored gelatin
1 tablespoon cold water
¼ pound peppermint sticks
1 cup cream, whipped
    Pink coloring (optional)

Scald milk in top of a double boiler.

Add sugar, salt, and flour which has been mixed and moistened with a little of the scalded milk. Add egg, and cook until mixture coats spoon. Remove from heat, and add gelatin which has been dissolved in cold water. Cool. Add crushed peppermint sticks, whipped cream, and coloring. Freeze, stirring when half-frozen. Yield: 6 servings.

Chocolate Ice Cream

1½ squares unsweetened chocolate
     or ¼ cup cocoa
1 cup sugar
⅓ cup hot water
    Dash salt
1 tablespoon vanilla extract
1 quart thin cream

Melt chocolate. Combine melted chocolate (or cocoa), sugar, and water; cook until smooth and sugar is dissolved. Add salt and vanilla and cool. Add to cream and freeze. Yield: 8 servings.

Strawberry Ice Cream

12 eggs, well beaten
3 cups sugar
1 tablespoon all-purpose flour
½ teaspoon salt
3 teaspoons vanilla extract
2 cups half-and-half (cream and milk)
1 cup whipping cream
4 to 6 cups fresh strawberries, crushed
    Whole milk

Beat eggs. Combine sugar, flour, and salt and gradually add to beaten eggs; mix well. Add vanilla extract, half-and-half, cream, and crushed strawberries. Mix well and put into bucket of 1½- or

2-gallon freezer. Add milk to within one-third of top of bucket. Freeze until firm. Yield: 1½ gallons.

Fresh Peach Ice Cream

      6 cups light cream
      4 cups milk
 1 ½ cups sugar
    ¼ teaspoon salt
      2 teaspoons vanilla extract
    ½ teaspoon almond extract
      4 eggs
      4 cups peaches
 1 ½ cups sugar

Combine cream and milk. Stir in 1½ cups sugar, salt, flavoring, and beaten eggs. Add peaches which have been mashed and combined with 1½ cups sugar. Place in crank-type freezer, or refrigerator trays, and freeze. Yield: 1 gallon.

French Vanilla Ice Cream

 ½ cup sugar
 ¼ teaspoon salt
   1 cup milk
   3 egg yolks, beaten
   1 tablespoon vanilla extract
   1 cup whipping cream

Set refrigerator control for fast freezing. Blend sugar, salt, milk, and egg yolks in saucepan. Cook over medium heat, stirring constantly, just until mixture comes to a boil. Cool. Add vanilla. Pour into refrigerator tray and freeze until mixture is mushy and partly frozen. Whip cream until barely stiff. Empty partially frozen mixture into chilled bowl and beat until smooth. Fold

in whipped cream. Pour into two freezer trays and freeze until firm, stirring frequently and thoroughly during first hour of freezing. It will take about 3 to 4 hours to freeze thoroughly. Yield: 1 quart.

Rich Vanilla Ice Cream

   6 cups milk
   8 teaspoons cornstarch
   2 cups sugar
 ½ teaspoon salt
   4 eggs
   2 cups milk
   1 quart cream
   2 tablespoons vanilla extract

Scald 6 cups milk over hot water. Mix cornstarch, sugar, and salt; add scalded milk, stirring until sugar is dissolved. Cook in top of double boiler over boiling water for 20 minutes, stirring constantly, until slightly thickened. Beat eggs, and beat in remaining 2 cups milk; gradually stir hot mixture into egg mixture. Return mixture to top of double boiler and cook over boiling water for 10 minutes, stirring constantly. Cool and add cream and vanilla extract. Chill. Pour into a chilled 1-gallon ice cream freezer can. Freeze. Yield: 1 gallon.

Peanut Brittle Ice Cream

1 pound peanut brittle
1 pound marshmallows, quartered
2 cups cream, whipped

Run peanut brittle through food chopper, or chop very fine. Place in a mixing bowl. Add marshmallows and whipped cream and mix well. Pack in freezer for 3 hours, but do not turn crank. Or, freeze in refrigerator tray without stirring. Yield: 4 to 6 servings.

Buttermilk Sherbet

2 cups buttermilk
⅔ cup sugar
  Pinch salt
1 cup crushed pineapple and juice
1 teaspoon vanilla extract
1 egg white, beaten

Combine buttermilk, sugar, salt, pineapple, and vanilla. Pour into freezing tray and freeze to a soft consistency. Beat egg white until stiff. Transfer frozen mixture to a mixing bowl and beat until fluffy, then fold in egg white. Return to freezing tray and freeze. Yield: 3 cups.

Grape Sherbet

2 cups grape juice
2 tablespoons freshly squeezed lemon juice
  Dash salt
½ cup sugar
¼ cup water
2 egg whites, beaten

Combine grape juice, lemon juice, and salt, and freeze until firm in refrigerator tray. Boil sugar and water together for 3 minutes and pour slowly into beaten egg whites, beating constantly. Cool to lukewarm. Remove grape mixture from tray and fold into egg white mixture. Return to tray and freeze. Yield: 6 servings.

Lemon Sherbet

¾ cup sugar
1 cup water
  Dash salt
½ cup milk
½ cup freshly squeezed lemon juice
2 egg whites, beaten
¼ cup sugar

Combine ¾ cup sugar and water; cook for 5 minutes. Cool. Add salt, milk, and lemon juice. Freeze until firm in refrigerator tray. Turn into chilled bowl; beat thoroughly. Beat egg whites; gradually add remaining sugar, beating until sugar is dissolved and egg whites are stiff. Fold into frozen mixture. Return to tray and freeze firm. Yield: 6 servings.

Orange Sherbet

1 (3-ounce) package orange-flavored gelatin
2 cups boiling water
  Juice of 8 oranges
  Juice of 2 lemons
2 cups pineapple juice
¼ teaspoon salt
2 cups sugar
4 cups cream, lightly whipped

Dissolve gelatin in water. Add juices, salt, and sugar. Cool. Slowly add these ingredients to lightly whipped cream. Mix until well blended. Freeze in 1-gallon freezer. Yield: 1 gallon.

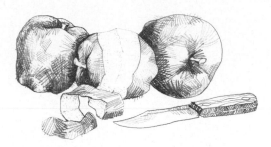

Pineapple Sherbet

    40 marshmallows
     2 cups pineapple juice
     1 cup water
     4 tablespoons freshly squeezed
        lemon juice
     4 teaspoons sugar
    ⅛   teaspoon salt
     5 egg whites, beaten

Combine marshmallows, pineapple juice, and water in top of double boiler and heat until marshmallows are melted. Cool. Add lemon juice and 2 teaspoons sugar. Freeze to a mush. Combine remaining sugar, salt, and beaten egg whites. Stir into sherbet, and complete freezing. Serve in chilled sherbet dishes. Yield: 4 to 6 servings.

Grandma's Boiled Custard

     4 cups milk
     6 egg yolks
    ½   cup sugar
        Pinch salt
     1 teaspoon vanilla extract

Scald milk. Beat egg yolks lightly, and add sugar and salt. Pour scalded milk over beaten egg mixture, a little at a time. Strain into top of a double boiler. Cook over simmering water only until mixture coats a spoon lightly, about 5 minutes. Remove from heat and cool; add vanilla. Yield: 6 servings.

Baked Custard

     3 cups milk
     6 tablespoons sugar
    ¼   teaspoon salt
     3 eggs, slightly beaten
     1 teaspoon vanilla extract
     1 tablespoon butter or margarine
        Ground nutmeg or cinnamon

Scald milk with sugar and salt. Stir slowly into beaten eggs, and add vanilla. Strain into custard cups or large baking dish, dot with butter or margarine, and add a dash or two of nutmeg or cinnamon. Set cups or baking dish in a shallow pan of hot water to come almost to top. Set on center rack of oven and bake at 325° until done, about 30 minutes. To test for doneness, insert knife in center of custard. When knife comes out clean, custard is done. Be careful not to overbake, as baking too long or at too high temperature will result in wheying or "weeping" of the cooled custard. Serve directly from custard cups, or spoon out into individual serving dishes and serve with any desired dessert sauce on top: chocolate, ground peppermint candy, or melted marshmallows. Yield: 6 servings.

Orange Pudding

    1 orange
1½ cups sugar, divided
    1 cup seedless raisins, ground
    ½ cup butter or margarine
    1 egg
    ⅔ cup buttermilk
    2 cups all-purpose flour
    1 teaspoon soda
    ½ teaspoon salt
       Whipped cream

Wash orange and squeeze out juice. Combine juice and ½ cup sugar; set aside, and stir occasionally. Grind peel of orange twice and add to ground raisins. Cream together remaining sugar and butter or margarine; add egg. Add buttermilk; combine dry ingredients and add raisin mixture. Spoon into a greased 1½-quart baking dish and bake at 350° for 30 minutes. While hot, pour orange juice over pudding and serve with whipped cream. Yield: 6 servings.

Snow Pudding

    1 package unflavored gelatin
    1 cup cold water
    2 cups boiling water
    2 cups sugar
       Vanilla extract to taste
    6 egg whites
    ½ to 1 cup flaked coconut
    1 (3-ounce) bottle maraschino cherries

Soak gelatin in 1 cup cold water to soften. Add 2 cups boiling water and stir until gelatin is dissolved. Then stir in sugar and vanilla. Chill thoroughly. When mixture is partially congealed, fold in stiffly beaten egg whites. Chill.

Serve with coconut sprinkled over the top. Garnish with cherries. Yield: 6 servings.

Ozark Pudding

    2 eggs
1¼ cups sugar
    2 teaspoons vanilla extract
    2 cups diced apples
    ½ cup chopped pecans
    ⅔ cup all-purpose flour
    3 teaspoons baking powder
    ½ teaspoon salt

Beat eggs; add sugar and vanilla, and mix well. Add apples and pecans, and mix well. Combine flour, baking powder, and salt; add to apple mixture. Pour into greased 12- x 8- x 1-inch pan, and bake at 350° for 20 to 30 minutes, or until a rich golden brown. Yield: 10 to 12 servings.

Plum Pudding

    1 cup seedless raisins
1½ cups mixed diced candied fruits
    ½ cup chopped walnuts
    1 cup all-purpose flour
    2 eggs, beaten
    ¾ cup molasses
    ¾ cup buttermilk
    ½ cup finely chopped suet
    ¼ cup cold, strong coffee
    1 cup fine, dry breadcrumbs
    ¾ teaspoon soda
    ¼ teaspoon ground cloves
    ¼ teaspoon ground allspice
    ¼ teaspoon ground cinnamon
    ¼ teaspoon ground nutmeg
    ¾ teaspoon salt

Combine fruits, walnuts, and ½ cup flour. Mix together eggs, molasses, buttermilk, suet, and coffee. Combine remaining flour, crumbs, soda, spices, salt, and add to egg mixture. Add to fruit, and mix well. Pour into well greased 1½-quart mold. Set on rack in deep pan; add boiling water to about 1 inch below cover of mold. Cover. Steam for 1½ to 2 hours. Yield: 10 to 12 servings.

Rice Pudding

- 2 eggs
- 2 cups milk
- 1¼ cups cold, cooked rice
- 1 cup seedless raisins
- ½ cup sugar
- ¼ teaspoon salt
- 1 teaspoon vanilla extract
  Dash ground cinnamon and nutmeg

Beat eggs until light and thick, and add to the milk. Lightly mix in the other ingredients. Place in a buttered 1½-quart casserole. Bake in a shallow pan of water at 350° for 1 hour, or until mixture is firm. Yield: 6 servings.

Creamy Rice Pudding

- ½ cup uncooked long-grain regular rice
- 2½ cups scalded milk
- ½ teaspoon salt
- ⅓ cup sugar
- ½ cup milk
- 1 teaspoon vanilla extract
- 1 (8½-ounce) can crushed pineapple, well drained
- 1 cup heavy cream, whipped
  Maraschino cherries

Combine rice, 2½ cups scalded milk, salt, and sugar in top of double boiler. Cook, stirring occasionally, over boiling water until rice is tender (about 1¼ hours). Add more water to bottom of double boiler if needed.

Remove from heat; stir in ½ cup milk and vanilla. Refrigerate until well chilled. Fold in drained pineapple and half of whipped cream. Top with remaining whipped cream and garnish with cherries. Yield: 8 to 10 servings.

Southern Sweet Potato Pudding

- 2 cups grated raw sweet potatoes
- ¼ cup melted butter or margarine
- 1 teaspoon grated lemon peel
- ¼ teaspoon ground ginger
- ½ teaspoon ground cinnamon
- ¼ teaspoon ground cloves
- 1 cup brown sugar, firmly packed
- 2 eggs, well beaten
- ½ cup chopped nuts
  Whipped cream (optional)

Grate peeled potatoes with fine grater. Measure and combine with next six ingredients. Add to well beaten eggs and blend. Pour into greased 1-quart casserole. Top with nuts. Bake at 325° for 1 hour. Serve warm — plain or with whipped cream. Yield: 6 to 8 servings.

Burnt Sugar Custard

 2 cups milk
 2 eggs
 3 tablespoons sugar
 1 teaspoon vanilla extract
 1/3 cup sugar
 2 tablespoons water

Mix milk, eggs, 3 tablespoons sugar, and vanilla. Cook 1/3 cup sugar and water until it is browned, stirring constantly. Pour browned sugar into four individual baking dishes. Let cool. Then pour the milk mixture on top of browned sugar. Set in a baking pan with 1/2-inch water in bottom of pan. Bake at 350° about 1 hour. Chill overnight, then turn upside down and serve. Yield: 4 servings.

Old-Fashioned Bread Pudding

 2 cups scalded milk
 1/4 cup butter or margarine
 2 eggs, slightly beaten
 1/2 cup sugar
 1/4 teaspoon salt
 1 teaspoon ground cinnamon
 3 cups soft bread cubes (about 5 slices)
 1/2 cup seedless raisins

Combine milk and butter or margarine. Stir milk mixture gradually into beaten eggs; add sugar, salt, and cinnamon. Put bread cubes and raisins in 1 1/2-quart baking dish; pour milk mixture over; stir gently to moisten bread. Place in a pan of hot water. Bake at 350° for 40 to 45 minutes or until knife inserted 1 inch from edge comes out clean. Remove from hot water. Serve warm or cold. Yield: 6 servings.

Banana Pudding

 3/4 cup sugar, divided
 1/3 cup all-purpose flour
 1/4 teaspoon salt
 2 cups scalded milk
 2 eggs, separated
 1 teaspoon vanilla extract
 25 vanilla wafers
 4 bananas, sliced

Blend 1/2 cup sugar, flour, and salt in top of double boiler. Add milk and cook until thick, stirring constantly. Cover and cook for 15 minutes. Beat egg yolks, combine with custard, and cook 2 minutes longer. Add vanilla. Line flat baking dish with vanilla wafers. Add sliced bananas. Top with custard. Repeat layers, if necessary. Beat egg whites until stiff, add remaining 1/4 cup sugar and spread over custard. Bake at 350° about 12 to 15 minutes. Yield: 6 servings.

Chocolate-Bread Pudding

 2 squares unsweetened chocolate
 4 cups scalded milk
 2 cups bread cubes
 1/4 cup melted butter or margarine
 1/2 teaspoon salt
 1 teaspoon ground cinnamon
 1/2 cup sugar
 2 eggs, slightly beaten
 1/2 teaspoon vanilla extract

Put chocolate in scalded milk and heat until chocolate is dissolved. Beat thoroughly. Soak bread in milk, and set aside to cool. Add other ingredients. Bake in a buttered 2-quart baking dish at 325° for 1 hour. Yield: 6 servings.
Note: If a firmer pudding is desired, reduce milk to 2 cups.

This meringue-topped Banana Pudding combines egg custard made from "scratch," sliced bananas, and vanilla wafers.

Woodford Pudding

> 1 cup sugar
> ½ cup butter or margarine
> 3 eggs, beaten
> 1 cup jam (any flavor)
> 1 teaspoon grated orange rind
> ½ cup all-purpose flour
> 1 teaspoon ground cinnamon
> 1 teaspoon ground nutmeg
> 1 teaspoon soda
> 3 teaspoons buttermilk

Cream sugar and butter or margarine. Stir in beaten eggs, jam, and grated orange rind. Add the dry ingredients and milk. Pour into a greased 8-inch baking pan. Bake at 300° about 30 to 40 minutes, or until firm. Yield: 6 servings.

Queen of Puddings

> 4 cups milk
> 2 cups broken or coarse breadcrumbs
> ½ stick butter or margarine
>   Salt to taste
> 6 egg yolks
> ½ cup sugar
> 1 teaspoon vanilla extract
>   Jelly or preserves
> 6 egg whites, stiffly beaten
> ⅔ cup sugar
>   Almond extract
>   Whipped cream

Scald milk. Add breadcrumbs, butter or margarine, and salt. Beat egg yolks with the ½ cup sugar and vanilla. Pour milk mixture slowly over the yolk mixture, stirring constantly. Pour into 6-cup casserole or pan, filling to about two-thirds full. Place in pan of hot water and cook at 350° until custard is the consistency of heavy cream in center when tested with a spoon. Remove from oven. Cover with favorite jelly or preserves (cherry or strawberry is good). Make a meringue of egg whites with ⅔ cup sugar; flavor with a few drops almond extract or other flavoring. Spread over custard. Return to oven to cook until meringue browns. Cool. Serve with unsweetened whipped cream. Yield: 6 servings.

Note: The custard part may be made a day ahead, and the meringue added the day of serving.

Georgia Kiss Pudding

> 4 cups milk
> 2 tablespoons butter or margarine
> 4 egg yolks
> 1½ cups sugar
> 3 tablespoons cornstarch
> 4 egg whites
> 4 tablespoons sugar

Bring milk to a boil, adding butter or margarine, egg yolks, and sugar as it boils. Dissolve cornstarch in a little milk and add to mixture, stirring well until it thickens. Remove from heat, and pour into greased 5-cup baking dish. Beat egg whites until stiff but not dry. Gradually add sugar; spread on pudding in baking dish. Bake at 350° about 30 minutes, or until brown. Yield: 4 servings.

Persimmon Pudding

> 2 eggs
> ¼ cup sugar
> 1½ cups hot milk
> ¼ teaspoon salt
> 1½ cups persimmon pulp

Beat together the eggs and sugar; add hot milk and salt. Pour slowly over persimmon pulp in a 5-cup baking dish, and stir together. Set dish in a pan of warm water, and bake at 250° until pudding is set. Yield: 6 to 8 servings.

Lemon Fluff Pudding

 3 egg whites
¾ cup sugar
 3 tablespoons all-purpose flour
¼ teaspoon salt
 2 tablespoons melted shortening
¼ cup freshly squeezed lemon juice
    Grated rind of 1 lemon
 3 egg yolks
 1 cup milk

Beat egg whites in small bowl of mixer at high speed for 2 minutes, or until peaks form. Combine other ingredients in large bowl of mixer and beat at lowest speed for 3 minutes. Add beaten whites and beat at low speed for 1 minute. Pour into a 3-cup baking dish. Place dish in a pan of hot water and bake at 350° for 40 to 45 minutes. Yield: 4 to 6 servings.

Lemon Pudding

 1 tablespoon unflavored gelatin
¼ cup cold water
 1 cup milk
 3 egg yolks
⅔ cup sugar
¼ teaspoon salt
½ cup freshly squeezed lemon juice
½ teaspoon grated lemon rind
 3 egg whites, beaten

Soak gelatin in cold water. Scald milk in top of a double boiler. Beat egg yolks and gradually add sugar and salt. Add hot milk to the egg mixture. Return to double boiler, and stir until slightly thickened. Remove from heat, add lemon juice, rind, and softened gelatin. Stir until gelatin is dissolved. Pour into a bowl and chill. Mix thoroughly and add the egg whites, beaten until stiff but not dry. Pour into container and set in refrigerator to chill. Yield: 6 to 8 servings.

Date Pudding

 1 cup chopped dates
 1 cup dark corn syrup
    Pinch salt
 1 cup water
 2 tablespoons freshly squeezed
    lemon juice
½ to 1 cup chopped nuts
 1 cup all-purpose flour
½ teaspoon baking powder
 1 teaspoon salt
 1 cup sugar
 1 cup milk
 1 teaspoon orange or lemon extract

Combine dates, corn syrup, salt, water, and lemon juice in saucepan. Cook until dates are partially softened. Pour mixture in a greased 13- x 9- x 2-inch baking pan. Sprinkle with chopped nuts.

Combine other ingredients in large mixing bowl. Beat until well mixed. Pour over date mixture. Bake at 350° for 30 minutes. Use the day it is baked, as this dessert does not keep well. Yield: 6 servings.

Brownie Pudding

    1   cup all-purpose flour
    2   teaspoons baking powder
    ½   teaspoon salt
    ¾   cup sugar
    2   tablespoons cocoa
    ½   cup evaporated milk
    1   teaspoon vanilla extract
    2   tablespoons melted butter or
        margarine
    1   cup chopped pecans
    ¾   cup brown sugar
    ¼   cup cocoa
    1¾ cups hot water

Combine flour, baking powder, salt,
sugar, and 2 tablespoons cocoa. Add
milk, vanilla, and melted butter or margarine. Mix until smooth. Add pecans.
Pour into greased 8-inch square cakepan. Mix brown sugar and ¼ cup cocoa,
and sprinkle over batter. Pour hot
water over entire batter. Bake at 350°
for 40 to 45 minutes. Yield: 6 to 8
servings.

Indian Pudding

    4   cups milk
    ½   cup plain cornmeal
    2   tablespoons butter or margarine
    ½   cup molasses
    1   teaspoon salt
    1   teaspoon ground cinnamon
    ¼   teaspoon ground ginger
    2   eggs

Scald the milk. Put cornmeal in top of
double boiler, and pour in the scalded
milk gradually, stirring constantly.
Cook over hot water for 20 minutes.
Mix together the other ingredients, and
add to the cornmeal mixture. Turn into
a buttered 1½-quart baking dish and
set in a pan of hot water. Bake at 350°
for 1 hour. Yield: 6 servings.

Andrew Jackson's Floating Island

    Enough sponge cake to cover bottom
    of a large bowl
    1   cup chopped blanched almonds
    1   tablespoon sherry flavoring
    4   cups plain boiled custard (flavored
        with vanilla or almond extract)

Cover bottom of large bowl with cake,
whole or broken into pieces. Sprinkle
almonds and then sherry flavoring over
the cake. Then pour the boiled custard
over all. If desired, top generously with
whipped cream, and dab bits of currant
jelly over it. Serve from the bowl.
Yield: 8 to 10 servings.

Chocolate Pudding

    4   cups milk
    1½ cups sugar
    4   tablespoons cocoa
    4   tablespoons cornstarch
    4   eggs, beaten
    1   teaspoon vanilla extract

Heat milk, keeping out enough to moist-
en cocoa and cornstarch. Add sugar.
When milk is hot, stir in cocoa and
cornstarch, then the beaten eggs. Bring
to a boil, remove from heat, and add
vanilla. Yield: 6 servings.

*Jelly jars that sparkle color, plump strawberry preserves, golden marmalades —
It's fun to say, "Yes, I made them myself." See recipes beginning on Page 369.*

Molasses Pudding

    4 cups milk
    2 cups soft breadcrumbs
    2 eggs
    ½ cup molasses
    ½ teaspoon salt
    ½ teaspoon ground nutmeg
    1 teaspoon ground cinnamon
       Grated rind of 1 lemon
    2 tablespoons butter or margarine

Scald milk. Put breadcrumbs in a well greased 1½-quart baking dish. Beat eggs, and add molasses, salt, spices, and lemon rind. Add milk to the egg mixture. Add butter or margarine, and pour over the breadcrumbs. Set baking dish in a pan of water and bake at 325° about 40 minutes or until pudding is firm in the center. Serve hot or cold. Yield: 6 to 8 servings.

Chocolate Mint Sauce

    2 squares unsweetened chocolate
    6 tablespoons water
    ½ cup sugar
       Dash salt
    3 tablespoons butter
    ¼ teaspoon vanilla extract
    ½ teaspoon peppermint extract

Combine chocolate and water in saucepan and place over low heat, stirring until blended. Add sugar and salt. Cook until sugar is dissolved and mixture very slightly thickened, stirring constantly. Add butter, vanilla, and peppermint extract; blend. Yield: 1 cup.

Lemon Sauce

    1½ tablespoons all-purpose flour
    ¼   cup sugar
    ¼   teaspoon salt
    1   cup boiling water
    ½   tablespoon butter or margarine
    4   tablespoons freshly squeezed
        lemon juice

Combine flour, sugar, and salt in top of double boiler, and mix until smooth. Add boiling water, stirring rapidly to prevent lumping. Cook until thickened, about 10 minutes. Add butter or margarine at end of cooking period. Let cool, then add lemon juice. Yield: about 1¼ cups.

Molasses-Pecan Praline Sauce

    1 tablespoon butter or margarine
    ½ cup pecan halves
    ¼ cup water
    1 cup unsulphured molasses

Melt butter or margarine in saucepan over medium heat. Brown pecans lightly in butter. Stir in water and molasses. Cook for 10 minutes. Serve hot or cold over ice cream. Yield: about 1⅓ cups.

Molasses-Butterscotch Sauce

1 tablespoon butter
¼ cup water
1 cup unsulphured molasses
½ cup evaporated milk

Melt butter in saucepan over medium heat. Stir in cold water and molasses. Cook for 10 minutes. Stir in the evaporated milk upon removing from heat. Chill. Serve on ice cream, puddings, or fruit desserts. Yield: 1½ cups.

Rum Sauce

2 tablespoons butter
¾ cup powdered sugar
1 egg yolk
2 tablespoons rum extract
1 egg white

Cream butter and sugar, add well beaten egg yolk. Cook over hot water until thickened. Add rum extract gradually, stirring constantly. Remove from heat and pour onto stiffly beaten egg white. Mix well. Serve warm. Yield: ¾ cup.

Corn Syrup Sauce

1 cup granulated sugar
1 cup dark corn syrup
1 cup heavy cream
⅛ teaspoon salt
½ teaspoon vanilla extract

Mix all ingredients (except vanilla), bring to a boil, stirring constantly, and cook for 3 minutes. Add vanilla and stir. Serve on biscuits, waffles, puddings, or ice cream. Yield: 3 cups.

Mocha Sauce

2 squares unsweetened chocolate
6 tablespoons strong coffee
½ cup sugar
   Few grains salt
4 tablespoons butter
½ teaspoon vanilla extract

Break chocolate into small pieces; add coffee and melt over low heat, stirring constantly. Add sugar and salt; cook, stirring until sugar is dissolved and mixture slightly thickened. Add butter and vanilla. Yield: 1 cup.

Pineapple Sauce

2 teaspoons cornstarch
½ cup cold water
½ cup drained, crushed pineapple
2 tablespoons brown sugar
1 tablespoon butter

Mix cornstarch and cold water to form a paste. Add drained crushed pineapple to paste. Add sugar and butter, and cook until thickened, stirring frequently. Yield: ¾ cup.

Glazed Baked Apples

1½ cups sugar
 ½ teaspoon ground cinnamon
1½ cups water
 1 tablespoon freshly squeezed
     lemon juice
 2 tablespoons freshly squeezed
     orange juice
 6 to 8 baking apples
 ¼ teaspoon red vegetable coloring

Combine 1 cup of the sugar with cinnamon in saucepan. Add water and strained fruit juices. Bring to a boil, and boil for 5 minutes. Wash medium-sized apples and remove about three-fourths of the core of each apple, cutting from stem end and leaving a solid base. Peel, leaving about ¼ inch of peel at base. Place in a shallow baking pan and pour boiling syrup over apples. Bake at 375° for about 30 minutes or until apples are tender. Baste frequently. Remove from oven when done.

To remaining ½ cup sugar, add the red vegetable coloring and stir with a fork until all sugar is thoroughly colored. Sprinkle tops of each apple with a little of the colored sugar. Put under broiler about 4 inches from heat. Baste with syrup in pan and continue sprinkling on more sugar until apples are glazed, about 15 minutes.

Remove from broiler and place apples on serving platter. If syrup is still somewhat thin, cook down until quite thick. Pour over apples, filling centers well. Cool until syrup is set, or chill in refrigerator if to be used for a meat accompaniment. Yield: 6 to 8 servings.

Cream Puffs

 1 cup water
 ½ cup butter
 1 cup all-purpose flour
 4 eggs

Place the water and butter in a saucepan and heat to boiling. Add all the flour at one time, stirring vigorously until mixture forms a ball and leaves the sides of the pan. Remove from heat and add unbeaten eggs, one at a time, beating thoroughly after each addition. Drop batter by rounded tablespoonfuls onto greased baking sheet. Bake at 400° for 30 to 40 minutes or until golden brown. Do not open oven door during early part of baking. Remove shells from baking sheet and put them on wire racks to cool. To serve, make a slit in cream puffs and fill with custard or ice cream. Yield: 12 cream puff shells.

Tutti-Frutti Marlow

20 large marshmallows
 1 cup milk
 1 cup whipping cream
 1 teaspoon vanilla extract
 ¼ cup chopped cherries
 3 slices pineapple, diced
 ½ cup chopped nuts

Dissolve marshmallows in hot milk. Cool thoroughly, then add cream which has been whipped until stiff. Add vanilla, cherries, pineapple, and nuts. Spoon into freezer tray of refrigerator. Allow to freeze for 30 minutes. Stir mixture, and return to refrigerator until frozen. Yield: 4 to 6 servings.

Strawberry Tart that's quick and easy to prepare and guaranteed to be delicious. See recipe on Page 330.

Charlotte Russe

4   envelopes unflavored gelatin
7   cups milk, divided
8   egg yolks
1   cup sugar
1   tablespoon vanilla extract
8   egg whites, beaten very stiff
8   tablespoons sugar
1   cup thick cream
6   teaspoons sugar

Dissolve the gelatin in 1 cup of milk.
Make a custard, using egg yolks,
remaining 6 cups of milk, sugar, and
vanilla. Add gelatin to the custard and
remove from heat when custard just
comes to a boil. (It will curdle if
allowed to boil.)

Let cool, then place in refrigerator
until it begins to congeal. Beat egg
whites until very stiff, and add 8 tablespoons sugar. Beat until sugar is dissolved. Whip cream and add 6 teaspoons sugar. Remove mixture from
refrigerator, and stir or beat until no
lumps are left. Fold in egg whites, then
cream mixture. Return to refrigerator
for several hours. Yield: 8 to 10
servings.

Molded Fruit Dessert

1   envelope unflavored gelatin
⅓   cup cold water
¾   cup syrup from canned fruit cocktail
¼   cup granulated sugar
¼   teaspoon salt
1   teaspoon grated lemon rind
2   tablespoons freshly squeezed
    lemon juice
⅔   cup whipping cream
1½ cups drained canned fruit cocktail

Soften gelatin in cold water. Heat syrup
with sugar and salt and dissolve gelatin
in it. Stir in lemon rind and juice. Cool
to consistency of unbeaten egg white.
Fold in whipped cream and fruit cocktail. Turn into molds and chill. Yield:
6 servings.

Fruit Whip

3   egg whites
½   cup sugar
3   tablespoons fruit juice
2   tablespoons freshly squeezed
    lemon juice
1   teaspoon grated lemon rind
⅛   teaspoon salt
½   cup chopped, cooked prunes, apricots,
    or other fruit

Combine egg whites, sugar, fruit juice,
lemon juice, lemon rind, and salt.
Cook slowly in top of a double boiler,
beating constantly with beater until
mixture forms peaks, about 7 minutes.
Fold in chopped fruit, and chill.
Serve with whipped cream or custard
sauce. Yield: 4 servings.

Jellyroll

4   eggs
¾   cup sugar
¾   cup all-purpose flour
¾   teaspoon baking powder
¼   teaspoon salt
1   teaspoon vanilla extract
1   cup jelly or jam
    Powdered sugar

Place eggs in a bowl and beat. Add sugar
gradually, and continue beating until
mixture is thick and lemon colored.

Combine dry ingredients and fold into egg mixture. Add vanilla and blend. Turn batter into a 15- x 10- x 1-inch jellyroll pan, lined with greased waxed paper; spread evenly toward corners. Bake at 400° about 13 minutes, or until done. Trim off crisp edges and immediately turn from pan onto a clean cloth sprinkled with powdered sugar. Remove waxed paper. Roll cake in cloth gently, evenly, and firmly. The cake should be completely covered by the cloth. Place on a cooling rack with loose edge of cloth underneath. When the cake is thoroughly cooled, unroll carefully. Spread with jelly or jam, and roll again. Sprinkle with powdered sugar. Slice to serve. Yield: 8 to 10 servings .

separate pans. Refrigerate until firm. Then cut in small cubes and return to refrigerator. Put crushed vanilla wafers in large bowl and combine with ½ cup sugar and melted margarine; spread half of this mixture over bottom of a 12- x 8- x 1-inch pan. Dissolve unflavored gelatin in 2 tablespoons cold water. Let stand 5 minutes, then add ½ cup hot pineapple juice. When gelatin cools, beat 2 envelopes of whipped topping with 1 cup milk, ½ cup sugar, and 1 teaspoon vanilla until stiff; then fold in the cooled unflavored gelatin. Gently fold in the gelatin cubes. Sprinkle other half of crumb mixture over top and refrigerate. This can be made a day or two before serving if kept refrigerated. Yield: 10 to 12 servings.

Jewel Dessert

    1 (3-ounce) package cherry-
      flavored gelatin
    1 (3-ounce) package lime-
      flavored gelatin
    1 (3-ounce) package orange-
      flavored gelatin
4½ cups hot water
1¾ cups crushed vanilla wafers
  ½ cup sugar
    1 stick margarine
    1 envelope unflavored gelatin
    2 tablespoons cold water
  ½ cup hot pineapple juice
    2 (4¼-ounce) envelopes
      whipped topping
    1 cup milk
  ½ cup sugar
    1 teaspoon vanilla extract

Dissolve each package of flavored gelatin in 1½ cups water and pour into

Fresh Peach Crumble

  ½ cup all-purpose flour
  ¾ cup nonfat dry milk solids
    3 tablespoons sugar
  ¼ teaspoon ground nutmeg
  ¼ teaspoon salt
    1 teaspoon ground cinnamon
  ⅓ cup butter or margarine
    3 cups sliced fresh peaches

Mix flour, nonfat dry milk solids, sugar, nutmeg, salt, and cinnamon. Cut butter or margarine in with pastry blender or two knifes until mixture is crumbly. Arrange fresh peach slices in shallow, well greased baking dish. Sprinkle with flour mixture. Bake covered at 350° about 25 minutes, or until peaches are tender. Remove cover, and bake for 10 minutes longer, or until crumbs are brown. Yield: 4 servings.

Ambrosia Dessert

13 to 14 vanilla wafers
¼ cup melted butter or margarine
1 tablespoon sugar
1 cup flaked coconut
1½ quarts vanilla ice cream
1 (6-ounce) can concentrated frozen orange juice
1 cup heavy cream, whipped

Roll vanilla wafers between waxed paper until crushed fine. Place in a bowl; add melted butter or margarine and sugar; blend well with fingers or pastry blender. Press evenly in bottom and on sides of a 10-inch pieplate. Chill for a few minutes. Sprinkle a handful of coconut over bottom. Spoon in ice cream, which has softened at room temperature. Spoon on one-half of the partially thawed orange juice. Add the last of the ice cream, then orange juice, then coconut. Cover entirely with whipped cream. Freeze. Yield: 6 servings.

Ambrosia

4 medium oranges
2 tablespoons sugar
½ cup flaked coconut
  Whipped cream (optional)

Peel and section oranges, remove seed, and sprinkle sugar over orange sections. Stir to mix. Place half of sections in bowl and sprinkle coconut over them. Add the rest of the sections and then the rest of the coconut. Cover dish and set in refrigerator until time to serve. Whipped cream may be added if desired. Yield: 6 servings.

Apple Crumble

½ cup all-purpose flour
¾ cup nonfat dry milk solids
¼ to ½ cup sugar
¼ teaspoon ground nutmeg
¼ teaspoon salt
1 teaspoon ground cinnamon
¼ cup butter or margarine
3 cups sliced apples

Mix flour, nonfat dry milk solids, sugar, nutmeg, salt, and cinnamon. Cut in butter or margarine with pastry blender until mixture is crumbly. Arrange apples in a shallow, well greased baking dish. Sprinkle apples with dry mixture, and cover baking dish. Bake at 350° about 30 minutes or until apples are tender. Remove cover, and bake for a few minutes until crumbs are brown. Yield: 6 servings.

Peach Snow

2 envelopes unflavored gelatin
½ cup cold water
1 cup boiling water
½ cup sugar
1 cup chopped cooked peaches
⅓ cup freshly squeezed lemon juice
2 egg whites, beaten
¼ cup sugar

Sprinkle gelatin in cold water; dissolve in boiling water. Add the ½ cup sugar; stir until dissolved. Add peaches and lemon juice. Mix together thoroughly. Beat egg whites until foamy, then add the ¼ cup sugar. Beat until mixture stands in peaks. Fold into thickened gelatin. Chill until set. Break up lightly with fork. Serve with boiled custard or chilled fruit. Yield: 6 servings.

Tacos are made by putting meat filling, shredded lettuce, and chopped tomatoes into a crisp fried, folded tortilla. See recipes for Tacos and Hot Chile Sauce on Page 340.

Apple Crisp

5 tart apples
¾ cup sugar
1 teaspoon ground cinnamon
½ cup all-purpose flour
½ cup butter or margarine
¼ cup water

Peel, core, and thinly slice the apples and arrange in a flat baking dish. Mix sugar, cinnamon, flour, and butter or margarine and set aside. Pour water over apples, and sprinkle sugar mixture over all. Bake at 325° for 30 to 40 minutes. Serve warm with whipped cream. Yield: 6 servings.

Virginia Fried Apples

Cook bacon at moderate temperature until crisp. Drain, and keep hot. Leave about 4 tablespoons drippings in the skillet. Fill with sliced, unpeeled apples and brown lightly. Sprinkle with sugar (½ cup per quart), cover, and cook slowly until tender. Remove cover and let apples brown and to cook off excess juice. Serve on a hot platter with bacon.

Blueberry Torte

2 cups graham cracker crumbs
1 teaspoon ground cinnamon
2 cups sugar, divided
½ cup soft butter or margarine
3 eggs, beaten
1½ cups cream cheese, softened
1 pint whipped cream
2 (1-pound) cans blueberries, drained
¼ cup cornstarch
2 teaspoons freshly squeezed lemon juice

Mix the graham cracker crumbs, cinnamon, ½ cup of the sugar, and the butter or margarine. Press mixture into a 13- x 9- x 2-inch baking pan. Set aside.

Cream the eggs, cream cheese, and ½ cup sugar together until smooth. Pour this mixture over the crumb crust. Bake at 375° for 20 minutes. Cool in refrigerator.

Drain the berries. Combine cornstarch, lemon juice, blueberry juice and 1 cup sugar and cook until thickened and clear. Stir in the berries, cool, and spread over cream cheese layer. Cool and cover with whipped cream. Serve cold. Yield: 10 to 12 servings.

Lemon Meringue

4 eggs, separated
1 cup hot milk
2 tablespoons butter or margarine
¼ cup all-purpose flour
¾ cup sugar
  Juice and grated rind of 2 lemons

Beat egg yolks until lemon colored. Add hot milk and butter or margarine and stir. Combine flour and sugar and stir into yolk mixture. Add lemon juice and rind. Fold in beaten egg whites.

Pour into custard cups. Set in a pan of warm water and bake at 325° about 30 minutes. Yield: 6 large or 8 small servings.

Pies & Pastries

Historians were absent the day the first pie was cut, and even the exact etymology of the term is a matter of speculation.

Terms and even spelling have changed, but the acceptance of the first bite of that first pie convinced homemakers that the dish was here to stay.

The result was an inexhaustible variety of chess, pecan, apple, and berry pies topped by meringue, whipped cream, and double crust. Even the language grew as such phrases as "pie and coffee" and "a sandwich and a piece of pie" became standard.

Mincement, sweet potato, and pumpkin are synonymous with Christmas, February, and Thanksgiving, but thanks to canned ingredients, are not seasonally limited.

Finding no way to avoid mention of the old cliché, if nothing is more American than apple pie, surely we can adapt it and say nothing is more Southern than pecan (or chess) pie.

Of course, no pie is any better than its pastry, whether it's made with shortening or lard, graham crackers, or cream cheese. One wonders if perhaps Eve had a flaky crust too good to waste when she picked that proverbial apple.

Amber Pie

1 cup sugar
1 tablespoon all-purpose flour
1 tablespoon butter or margarine
4 eggs, separated
1 teaspoon ground cinnamon
¼ teaspoon ground nutmeg
¼ teaspoon ground cloves
1 tablespoon vinegar
1 cup buttermilk
1 cup seedless raisins
1 baked 9-inch pie shell
½ cup sugar for meringue

Cream together sugar, flour, and butter or margarine. Add well beaten egg yolks and other ingredients in the order given. Cook slowly until thick. Pour into baked pie shell. Cover with meringue made from the 4 egg whites, and ½ cup sugar, and brown at 350°. Yield 1 (9-inch) pie.

Deep-Fried Apple Pies

3 cups sliced, peeled tart apples
½ cup water
1 teaspoon freshly squeezed lemon juice
¼ cup sugar
½ teaspoon ground cinnamon
⅛ teaspoon ground nutmeg
   Pastry for double crust
   Vegetable shortening or cooking oil for deep frying
   Butter or margarine
   Powdered sugar

Put apples into a saucepan; add water and lemon juice. Cover tightly and cook over low heat for 15 minutes, or until tender. Remove apples and drain. Blend in sugar, cinnamon, and nutmeg.

Shape pastry into two balls. Using one ball at a time, flatten on a lightly floured surface and roll out ⅛ inch thick. Cut out rounds, using a 3½-inch cutter. Heat shortening or oil to 375°.

Place 2 tablespoons apple mixture on each pastry round; dot with butter or margarine. Moisten half of the edge of each round with water. Fold the other half of round over filling. Press edges together with a fork to seal tightly.

Lower pies into hot shortening or oil. Deep-fry for about 3 minutes or until golden brown. Turn pies as they rise to surface and several times during cooking. Do not pierce.

Remove pies from shortening and drain over frying pan for a few seconds before removing onto absorbent paper. Sprinkle with powdered sugar; serve warm. Yield: 15 fried pies.

Old World Apple Pie

2 cups finely chopped tart apples
¾ cup sugar
2 tablespoons all-purpose flour
⅓ teaspoon salt
1 egg, beaten
½ teaspoon vanilla extract
1 cup commercial sour cream
1 unbaked 9-inch pie shell

Peel and chop apples and set aside. Combine sugar, flour and salt; add egg, vanilla, and sour cream. Beat until smooth. Add apples, mix well, and pour into pastry-lined piepan. Bake at 375° for 15 minutes; reduce heat to 325° and bake 30 minutes longer. Remove from oven and sprinkle with Topping.

Topping

⅓ cup all-purpose flour
¼ cup butter
⅓ cup brown sugar

Combine ingredients and blend well.
Sprinkle over baked pie. Return pie to
oven and bake at 325° for 20 minutes or
until topping is brown. Yield:
1 (9-inch) pie.

Tart Apple Pie

4 large tart apples
½ cup orange juice
½ cup sugar
Pinch salt
1 unbaked 9-inch double crust
1 egg white, beaten
3 tablespoons sugar, divided
⅓ cup sugar
1 stick margarine

Peel and slice apples. Cook with orange
juice, ½ cup sugar, and salt, until
tender. Cool. Line piepan with pastry.
Brush unbaked pie shell with some of
the beaten egg white; then sprinkle
generously with 1½ tablespoons sugar.
Add ⅓ cup more sugar to the cooled
apple mixture and put into pastry shell.
Cut margarine into small pieces and dot
over top of apples. Cut very narrow
strips from rolled-out pastry and twist
to make latticed top on pie. Brush with
remainder of egg white and sprinkle
with remaining 1½ tablespoons sugar.
Bake at 325° for 30 minutes on bottom
rack of oven. Move to center of oven
and bake 30 minutes longer. Yield:
1 (9-inch) pie.

Banana Meringue

5 egg whites
Dash salt
1 cup sugar
1 9-inch graham cracker crust
1 cup whipping cream
1 cup flaked coconut
2 large bananas, sliced

Combine egg whites and salt; beat to a
stiff foam. Add sugar slowly, beating
until sugar is dissolved and meringue
mixture is stiff. Pour into crust. Bake at
200° for 1 hour. Cool. Whip cream, add
coconut, and sweeten to taste. Place
alternate layers of bananas and whipped
cream on top of baked meringue. Chill.
Yield: 1 (9-inch) pie.

Blackberry Pie

2½ cups canned blackberries, drained
1 cup blackberry juice
3 tablespoons tapioca
Sugar to sweeten
Pastry for 9-inch pie

Combine drained blackberries, juice,
tapioca, and sugar. Let stand for 15
minutes, or while pastry is being made.
Line pan with pastry; add blackberries
and cover with strips of pastry. Bake
until pastry is browned. Yield:
1 (9-inch) pie.

Blackberry or Dewberry Cobbler

1   unbaked 10-inch double crust
4   to 6 cups very ripe blackberries
      or dewberries
1   cup sugar
¼   cup water
2   tablespoons all-purpose flour
¼   cup sugar
3   tablespoons butter

Make pastry; roll half very thin and use it to line a 2-inch-deep baking pan. Roll other half thin and cut into 2-inch strips. Bake half the strips in a preheated 375° oven until lightly browned.

Put berries, 1 cup sugar, and water into a saucepan. Cook until berries are soft. Mix flour and ¼ cup sugar and add to berries. Cook, stirring constantly until mixture has thickened slightly. Spoon berries into pastry-lined pan with cooked pastry strips stirred throughout filling. Dot with butter. Cover with remainder of pastry strips (uncooked). Bake at 425° until pastry is brown. Yield: 1 (10-inch) pie.

Blackberry Chiffon Pie

1   tablespoon unflavored gelatin
¼   cup cold water
4   eggs, separated
1   cup sugar, divided
½   cup freshly extracted blackberry juice
1   to 2 tablespoons freshly squeezed
      lemon juice
      Pinch salt
½   tablespoon grated lemon rind
      Drop of red vegetable
      coloring (optional)
1   9-inch graham cracker shell

Soften gelatin in cold water and set aside. Beat egg yolks; add ½ cup sugar, berry juice, lemon juice and salt. Cook to custard consistency over boiling water. Add lemon rind and softened gelatin; stir until the gelatin has dissolved. Cool mixture until it begins to set. Beat egg whites until stiff, and continue beating as you add ½ cup sugar until mixture is as stiff as meringue. Fold in the stiffly beaten egg whites and sugar. Blend in coloring. Pour into graham cracker shell and chill. Yield: 1 (9-inch) pie.

Variations

1.   Spread a layer of vanilla ice cream evenly in the graham cracker shell. Pour the berry mixture on top of the ice cream; spread it to cover completely. Put into freezer.
2.   Pile berry mixture in sherbet glasses and chill.

Butterscotch Pie

1   cup dark brown sugar
3   tablespoons all-purpose flour
      Pinch salt
1   cup milk
2   egg yolks
2   tablespoons butter
1   baked 8-inch pie shell
4   egg whites
¼   teaspoon cream of tartar
4   tablespoons sugar

Combine brown sugar, flour, and salt in top of double boiler. Heat milk and slowly stir into flour and sugar. Cook over boiling water until mixture begins to thicken. Beat egg yolks in small bowl and stir about 1 cup of hot liquid into egg yolks; combine the two mixtures in top of double boiler. Add butter and cook until thick and pour into pie shell. Make meringue by beating egg whites, and cream of tartar until stiff. Gradually add 4 tablespoons sugar to whites and continue beating until it holds a peak. Cover pie with meringue and bake at 400° until brown. Yield: 1 (8-inch) pie.

Lattice Cherry Pie

 1 cup sugar
 3 tablespoons cornstarch
 ¼ teaspoon salt
 1 cup cherry juice
 ¼ teaspoon red food coloring (optional)
 3 cups canned, water-packed red tart pitted cherries, drained
 2 tablespoons butter or margarine
 Pastry for 1 unbaked 9-inch pie shell and lattice top

Mix sugar, cornstarch and salt in saucepan. Add juice and coloring; stir until smooth. Cook until thickened and clear, stirring. Remove from heat; add cherries and butter or margarine. Pour into an unbaked 9-inch pie shell. Cover with lattice top crust. Bake at 425° for about 40 minutes. Yield: 1 (9-inch) pie.

Cracker Pie

 3 egg whites
 1 cup sugar
 1 teaspoon baking powder
 Dash salt
 20 round buttery crackers, rolled fine
 ¾ cup chopped walnuts

Beat egg whites until stiff. Fold in sugar, baking powder, and salt. Combine cracker crumbs and chopped walnuts. Fold very lightly into egg white mixture. Pour into buttered 8-inch pieplate and bake at 350° for 25 to 30 minutes. Cool, and top with whipped cream, cultured sour cream or ice cream. Yield: 1 (8-inch) pie.

Buttermilk Pie

 3 eggs
 1 cup sugar
 2 tablespoons all-purpose flour
 ½ cup melted butter or margarine
 1 cup buttermilk
 1 teaspoon vanilla or lemon extract
 1 unbaked 9-inch pie shell

Beat eggs slightly and add sugar and flour. Then add melted butter or margarine and mix well. Add buttermilk and flavoring and pour into unbaked pie shell. Bake at 325° until custard is set. Yield: 1 (9-inch) pie.

Sour Cream Pie

 2 eggs
 1 cup sugar
 1½ cups commercial sour cream
 ½ cup seedless raisins
 2 tablespoons all-purpose flour
 1 teaspoon vanilla extract
 ½ cup Brazil nuts or pecans
 1 unbaked 9-inch pie shell

Beat eggs slightly; add sugar, and blend well. Add sour cream, and mix well. Dredge raisins in flour and add to mixture. Add vanilla and nuts and turn into an unbaked pie shell. Bake at 400° for 10 minutes, reduce heat to 350° for 30 minutes longer. Yield: 1 (9-inch) pie.

Super Fudge Pie

½ cup butter or margarine
1 cup sugar, sifted
2 eggs, separated
2 ounces chocolate
⅓ cup all-purpose flour
1 teaspoon vanilla extract
Pinch salt
Whipped cream or vanilla ice cream

Cream butter or margarine until soft. Add sifted sugar gradually. Blend these ingredients until they are creamy. Beat in 2 egg yolks. Melt chocolate over hot water, cool slightly, and beat in. Sift flour before measuring. Beat the flour into the butter mixture. Add vanilla. Beat egg whites and ⅛ teaspoon salt until stiff. Fold into the batter. Bake in a well greased 8-inch piepan at 325° for about 30 minutes. Serve the pie topped with whipped cream or ice cream. Yield: 1 (8-inch) pie.

Chocolate Cream Pie

6 tablespoons cocoa
1 cup sugar
2½ cups cold milk
4 egg yolks, slightly beaten
4 tablespoons all-purpose flour
½ teaspoon salt
2 tablespoons butter or margarine
2 teaspoons vanilla extract
1 baked 9-inch pie shell
4 egg whites, stiffly beaten
8 tablespoons sugar

Add cocoa to sugar and mix well. Stir in 2 cups milk to make a smooth mixture, and heat in top of double boiler. Beat egg yolks; add flour blended with remaining ½ cup milk. Add salt, and stir into milk mixture. Cook until thick, stirring constantly. Add butter or margarine and vanilla. Cool and pour into baked pastry shell. Top with meringue made of the egg whites and 8 tablespoons sugar. Bake at 350° until meringue is lightly browned. Yield: 1 (9-inch) pie.

Chocolate Pie Topping

6 tablespoons butter or margarine
6 tablespoons powdered sugar
1½ squares unsweetened chocolate, melted
1 egg yolk

Cream butter or margarine and sugar; add melted chocolate and egg yolk. Mix well and spread on chilled pie. Yield: enough topping to cover a 9-inch pie.

Coconut Pie

½ cup sugar
⅓ cup all-purpose flour
3 egg yolks
2 cups milk, divided
¾ cup coconut
1 baked 9-inch pie shell
¼ teaspoon cream of tartar
3 egg whites
6 tablespoons sugar

Combine ½ cup sugar and flour in top of double boiler. Beat egg yolks in small bowl and add ¼ cup of milk. Heat remaining 1¾ cups milk and add to sugar and flour mixture; cook in top of double boiler, stirring until it thickens. Slowly add eggs and milk to mixture, stirring constantly. Cook until it thickens, stirring constantly. Add coconut and pour into a pie shell. Make meringue by beating egg whites and cream of tartar until stiff; add sugar gradually and continue beating until it holds a peak. Spread on pie and bake at 400° until brown. Yield: 1 (9-inch) pie.

French Coconut Pie

    3 eggs, separated
    1 unbaked 8-inch pie shell
1½ cups sugar
    1 teaspoon vanilla extract
  ½ cup melted butter or margarine
    1 cup flaked coconut

Brush a little egg white on unbaked pie shell and bake at 400° for about 1 minute. This prevents a soggy crust.

Beat eggs slightly; add other ingredients. Pour into pie shell. Bake for 10 minutes at 400°; 15 minutes at 375°; 15 to 20 minutes at 350°. Yield: 1 (8-inch) pie.

Jelly Cream Pie

    1 cup rich milk
    2 cups blackberry or grape jelly
    1 tablespoon butter or margarine
    3 tablespoons cornstarch
       Dash salt
    4 eggs, separated
    2 baked 8-inch pie shells
  ½ cup sugar

Heat milk and jelly together over low heat until jelly is melted. Melt butter or margarine in top of double boiler; stir in cornstarch and a dash of salt. Add milk and jelly, and cook over the boiling water until thick, stirring constantly.

Add a little of this hot mixture gradually to the beaten egg yolks, mixing well; return the egg-yolk mixture to top of double boiler. Continue cooking for 5 minutes longer, stirring constantly. Cool and pour into two cooled, baked pie shells.

Beat egg whites until stiff, and continue beating as you add ½ cup sugar and until mixture becomes a stiff meringue. Top cooled pies with meringue. Bake at 350° for about 18 minutes or until brown. Yield: 2 (8-inch) pies.

Gooseberry Pie

2½ cups gooseberries
1¼ cups sugar, divided
  ½ cup water
    1 tablespoon cornstarch
  ⅛ teaspoon salt
  ½ teaspoon ground cinnamon
  ¼ teaspoon ground nutmeg
    1 unbaked 9-inch pie shell
    1 egg white, unbeaten
    1 tablespoon butter or margarine

Cook gooseberries, ¾ cup sugar, and water until berries are soft. Combine remaining ½ cup sugar, with cornstarch, salt, and spices. Add to gooseberries and allow to cool.

Brush pie shell with unbeaten egg white. Fill with fruit mixture. Dot with butter or margarine. Top with pastry which has been gashed. Seal edges. Brush top with unbeaten egg white. Bake at 450° for 10 minutes. Reduce heat to 350° and continue baking for 25 minutes or until done. Yield: 1 (9-inch) pie.

Grape Juice Pie

    2 egg yolks
    1 cup grape juice
    ½ cup sugar
    1 tablespoon butter
    2 tablespoons all-purpose flour
    ¼ cup grape juice
    1 baked 8-inch pie shell
    2 egg whites, beaten
    2 tablespoons powdered sugar

Beat egg yolks; add 1 cup grape juice, sugar, and butter. Stir flour into ¼ cup grape juice and add to first mixture. Cook over low heat until mixture thickens, stirring constantly. Spoon mixture into baked pie shell. Top with meringue made with egg whites and powdered sugar. Bake at 350° for about 12 minutes, or until meringue is brown. Yield: 1 (8-inch) pie.

Jeff Davis Pie

Jeff Davis Pie was discovered and named by Aunt Jule Ann, a slave in the family of George B. Warren of Dover, Lafayette County, Missouri. Shortly before the war, Mr. Warren moved from the South to Dover, taking his slaves with him. Among them was Aunt Jule Ann, who was queen and tyrant in the kitchen in the Warren home. One Sunday when there were distinguished guests at the Warrens, Aunt Jule Ann served a new kind of pie, so delicious that there was a general desire to know how it was made.

Now Aunt Jule Ann, who admired Jefferson Davis, declared, "That's Jeff Davis Pie." Gradually the fame of the new pie spread across the South.

    2 cups sugar
    1 tablespoon all-purpose flour
    1 cup sweet cream
    1 cup butter
    6 eggs, beaten
    1 unbaked 9-inch pie shell

Combine sugar, flour, and cream with the butter and beat until light and frothy. Add beaten eggs. Pour into an unbaked pastry-lined pan. Bake as for custard pie about 40 minutes, starting with a hot oven to set the pastry, then reduce the temperature for the remainder of the baking. For the meringue, use 3 egg whites and "3 tablespoons sugar" (which in parlance of modern cooking means 6 to 9 level tablespoons). Yield: 1 (9-inch) pie.

Variations

1. Whip whites of eggs separately and fold into the pie.
2. Cook the pie in the top of a double boiler until it thickens, cool, put into baked shell, and top with meringue.

Lemon Pie

    ⅓ cup freshly squeezed lemon juice
    1 envelope unflavored gelatin
    4 eggs, beaten
    1½ cups sugar
    ⅛ teaspoon salt
    3 tablespoons butter or margarine
    ¾ teaspoon grated lemon rind
    ¾ teaspoon vanilla extract
    1½ cups heavy cream, whipped
    1 baked 9- or 10-inch pie shell

Put lemon juice in top of double boiler; add gelatin and stir until dissolved. Add beaten eggs, sugar, salt, and butter. Mix well. Stir and cook over boiling water until mixture thickens. Remove from heat and chill until mixture mounds slightly when dropped from spoon. Fold in lemon rind, vanilla, and whipped cream. Turn into baked pie shell and chill until firm and ready to serve. Yield: 1 (9- or 10-inch) pie.

Lemon Meringue Pie

   1 cup sugar
  ⅓ cup cornstarch
1 ½ cups hot water
   3 slightly beaten egg yolks
   3 tablespoons butter
   4 tablespoons freshly squeezed
      lemon juice
1 ⅓ tablespoons grated lemon rind
   1 baked 9-inch pastry shell
      Meringue

Mix sugar and cornstarch thoroughly. Gradually stir in hot water. Cook over moderate heat, stirring constantly until mixture boils. Boil for 1 minute or until mixture thickens. Slowly stir half the hot mixture into slightly beaten egg yolks and then beat into hot mixture in saucepan. Boil for 1 minute longer, stirring constantly. Remove from heat and continue stirring until smooth. Blend in butter, lemon juice, and lemon rind. Return mixture to heat for 1 or 2 minutes, stirring constantly, until firm. Pour into baked pie shell and cover with Meringue.

Meringue

  3 egg whites
 ¼ teaspoon cream of tartar
  6 tablespoons sugar

Beat egg whites with cream of tartar until frothy. Gradually beat in sugar. Continue beating until stiff and glossy. Pile meringue onto pie filling. Seal to edge of crust to prevent shrinking. Bake at 400° until brown. Yield: 1 (9-inch) pie.

Lemon Chiffon Pie

  1 envelope unflavored gelatin
 ¼ cup water
  1 cup sugar, divided
 ½ cup freshly squeezed lemon juice
 ½ teaspoon salt
  4 eggs, separated
     Grated rind of 1 lemon
  1 baked 9-inch pie shell

Sprinkle gelatin over water to soften. Mix ½ cup sugar, lemon juice, salt, and well beaten egg yolks in top of double boiler. Cook over hot water, stirring constantly, until mixture coats the spoon. Remove from hot water, stir in the softened gelatin and grated lemon rind, and stir until gelatin is completely dissolved. Pour into a bowl, cover tightly, and chill in refrigerator for about 1 hour. Beat egg whites until they are stiff but not dry. Add the remaining ½ cup sugar gradually, and continue beating until egg whites stand in peaks. Beat the chilled lemon mixture until fluffy. Fold into egg whites. Pour into baked, cooled pie shell, and chill in refrigerator until firm. Yield: 1 (9-inch) pie.

Lemon Chess Pie

2 cups sugar
½ cup butter or margarine
5 eggs
1 cup milk
1 tablespoon all-purpose flour
1 tablespoon cornmeal
¼ cup freshly squeezed lemon juice
  Grated rind of 3 large lemons
1 unbaked 9-inch pie shell

Cream sugar and butter or margarine; add eggs and milk, beat well. Then add flour, cornmeal, lemon juice, and grated lemon rind. Pour mixture in the pan, baking at 350° until done. Yield: 1 (9-inch) pie.

Key Lime Pie

1 (14-ounce) can sweetened condensed milk
3 egg yolks
½ cup lime juice
1 baked 9-inch pie shell
  Meringue or whipped cream

Beat the first three ingredients together until the lime juice has thickened the egg yolks. Pour the mixture in baked pie shell and top with Meringue or whipped cream as desired. Yield: 1 (9-inch) pie.

Meringue

3 egg whites
6 tablespoons sugar

Beat egg whites until stiff, continue beating as you add sugar and until mixture becomes smooth and quite stiff. Spread over top of pie and bake at 350° for about 15 minutes or until brown.

Never-Fail Chess Pie

4 eggs, beaten
1½ cups sugar
2 teaspoons cornmeal
  Pinch salt
¼ cup melted butter
4 tablespoons cream
1 teaspoon vanilla extract
1 unbaked 10-inch pie shell

Combine eggs, sugar, cornmeal, salt, butter, cream, and vanilla extract. Blend well before pouring into unbaked pie shell. Bake at 350° for 30 minutes. Yield: 1 (10-inch) pie.

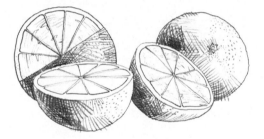

Molasses–Pecan Pie

3 eggs, beaten
¾ cup unsulphured molasses
¾ cup light corn syrup
2 tablespoons margarine or butter, melted
⅛ teaspoon salt
1 teaspoon vanilla extract
1 tablespoon all-purpose flour
1 cup pecans
1 unbaked 8-inch pie shell

Combine first six ingredients. Make a paste of small amount of mixture and flour; stir into remaining mixture. Add pecans. Turn into unbaked shell. Bake at 325° for 1 hour, or until firm. Yield: 1 (8-inch) pie.

Molasses Pie

½ cup all-purpose flour
½ cup brown sugar
½ teaspoon ground allspice
½ teaspoon ground cinnamon
½ teaspoon salt
1 teaspoon soda
1 cup buttermilk
¾ cup molasses
2 eggs
2 tablespoons melted butter or margarine
1 unbaked 9-inch pie shell

Sift all dry ingredients together except soda. Dissolve soda in buttermilk; mix in the molasses and add to dry ingredients. Add beaten eggs, then melted butter or margarine, and beat until smooth. Pour filling into unbaked pie shell and bake at 375° until pie begins to brown. Reduce heat to 350° and bake until the crust is brown and the filling firm. Yield: 1 (9-inch) pie.

Old-Fashioned Molasses Pie

1¼ cups molasses
1 tablespoon butter or margarine
3 eggs
1 tablespoon all-purpose flour
⅔ cup sugar
1 unbaked 8-inch pie shell

Place molasses and butter or margarine in saucepan and let come to a boil. Beat eggs until light and fluffy. Mix flour and sugar and add to eggs; add this mixture to molasses mixture. Pour in unbaked pie shell and bake at 325° for 30 minutes, or until set. Yield: 1 (8-inch) pie.

Mock Macaroon Pie

3 egg whites, beaten stiff
1 cup sifted sugar
½ teaspoon baking powder
⅛ teaspoon salt
10 salted crackers rolled fine
⅔ cup finely chopped pecans
1 cup whipped cream

Beat eggs until stiff but not dry. Sift together sugar, baking powder, and salt, and add to beaten eggs. Fold in crackers and pecans. Bake in a greased pan at 350° for 30 minutes. Open oven door and let pie cool in oven. Chill, and top with whipped cream 1 hour before serving. Yield: 6 servings.

Maids of Honor Tarts

1 cup sour milk
1 cup sweet milk
1 tablespoon melted butter or margarine
1 cup sugar
4 egg yolks
1 lemon, juice and rind
   Puff Pastry

Mix the two kinds of milk together in top of a double boiler and let become sufficiently heated to set the curd. Strain off the milk, rub the curd through a strainer, and add the butter or margarine to the curd, then the sugar, well beaten egg yolks, and lemon. Line tart pans with the richest of Puff Pastry (see index) and fill with the mixture. Bake at 400° for 15 to 20 minutes. Yield: 6 to 8 tarts.

Egg Custard Pie

  3 *cups milk*
  6 *eggs, slightly beaten*
½ *cup sugar*
  1 *teaspoon vanilla extract*
     Pinch salt
  1 *unbaked 9-inch pie shell*

Scald the milk. Mix together slightly beaten eggs, sugar, vanilla, and salt. Stir scalded milk gradually into egg mixture. Strain into pie shell. Bake at 450° for 10 minutes. Reduce heat to 325° and bake until a knife inserted in center of pie comes out clean. Cool. Yield: 1 (9-inch) pie.

Deep Dish Peach Pie

3 *cups all-purpose flour*
1 *teaspoon salt*
1 *teaspoon baking powder*
1 *cup shortening, chilled*
   About ½ cup ice water

Sift dry ingredients together and work in chilled shortening lightly. Add ice water slowly to form dough, and knead.

Filling

  4 *cups fresh, cooked peaches*
  1 *cup sugar*
     Pinch salt
  5 *or 6 kernels from peach seeds*
1¼ *cups sweet cream*

Drain peaches and pour juice into a saucepan; dice peaches and return to juice. Add ½ cup sugar and pinch of salt. Bring to a boil, add 5 or 6 kernels from peach seeds and boil until all sugar is dissolved. Then remove from heat, lift out peach seeds, and add 1 cup of cream.

Pour into a deep pan or casserole dish, filling up to within 1 inch of top. Roll out piecrust about ½ inch thick, and cover. Prick holes in crust to let steam escape. Bake at 425° to 450° until crust is brown. Then cover with a topping made with ½ cup sugar and ¼ cup cream blended well. Glaze top of pie and cook until topping is caramelized. Yield: 8 to 10 servings.

Osgood Pie

½ *cup butter or margarine*
  2 *cups sugar*
  4 *egg yolks, beaten*
  1 *cup raisins*
  1 *cup chopped pecans*
½ *teaspoon ground cinnamon*
½ *teaspoon ground cloves*
  4 *egg whites*
  1 *unbaked 9-inch pie shell*

Cream butter or margarine and sugar together until fluffy. Add beaten egg yolks, raisins, pecans, and spices. Fold in stiffly beaten egg whites. Bake at 325° for 50 minutes. Yield: 1 (9-inch) pie.

Peach Cobbler

3½ *cups cooked sliced peaches*
 ½ *cup sugar*
1½ *tablespoons cornstarch*
 ½ *teaspoon salt*
  1 *tablespoon butter or margarine*
 ¼ *teaspoon almond extract*
    Pastry for single crust

Drain syrup from peaches, and place peaches in a 9-inch pieplate or 1-quart baking dish. Measure 1 cup of the syrup and heat. Blend sugar, cornstarch, and salt; stir into hot syrup. Cook and stir until mixture boils. Stir in butter or margarine and almond extract. Pour over peaches. Roll pastry thin and cut in ½-inch strips. Arrange lattice fashion over top of baking dish. Bake at 400° for about 35 minutes, or until pastry is well browned. Serve warm. Yield: 1 (9-inch) pie.

Southern Peach Custard Pie

1 cup sliced fresh peaches
½ cup sugar
¾ cup milk
2 tablespoons cornstarch
2 egg yolks, beaten
¼ teaspoon ground cinnamon
1 unbaked 9-inch pie shell

Crush the fresh peaches and measure. Combine with the sugar. In a saucepan combine the milk and cornstarch and bring to a boil. Cook for 2 minutes and pour slowly over peaches, beating hard to blend. Add egg yolks and cinnamon. Beat again, and pour into unbaked pie shell. Bake at 350° until filling is firm. A meringue may be added if desired. Yield: 1 (9-inch) pie.

Note: Raspberries or plums may be used in place of the peaches, if desired.

Peanut Pie

½ cup sugar
1½ cups dark corn syrup
¼ cup shortening
¼ teaspoon salt
3 eggs, beaten
½ teaspoon vanilla extract
1½ cups roasted peanuts
1 unbaked 9-inch pie shell

Place sugar, corn syrup, shortening, and salt in saucepan and bring to a boil over low heat. Pour this hot mixture slowly over beaten eggs, stirring constantly. Cool. Add vanilla and peanuts. Pour into unbaked pie shell. Bake at 400° for 10 minutes. Reduce temperature to 375° and bake 35 to 40 minutes longer. Yield: 1 (9-inch) pie.

Favorite Pecan Pie

3 eggs
1 cup white sugar
1 cup dark corn syrup
1 cup whole pecans
⅛ teaspoon salt
1 teaspoon vanilla extract
1 unbaked 9-inch pie shell
   Whipped cream (optional)

Beat eggs, sugar, and corn syrup together. Add pecans, salt, and vanilla. Pour into unbaked pie shell. Bake at 425° for 10 minutes, then reduce heat to 350° and complete baking in 25 to 30 minutes. Brush melted butter or margarine over pecans while the pie is hot. Serve pie slightly warm or cold, with or without whipped cream. Yield: 1 (9-inch) pie.

Pecan Pie

¼ pound butter
3 tablespoons all-purpose flour
1 (1-pound) box light brown sugar
6 tablespoons milk
3 eggs
2 teaspoons vinegar
1½ teaspoons vanilla extract
1 cup chopped pecans
1 unbaked 9-inch pie shell

Melt butter; set aside to cool. Mix flour and sugar together. Add milk and eggs; beat well. Stir in vinegar and vanilla. Add melted butter and nuts; pour into unbaked pie shell. Bake at 300° for about 1 hour. Yield: 1 (9-inch) pie.

Special Pecan Pie

3 eggs, beaten
1 cup sugar
1 cup white corn syrup
⅔ cup pecans
1 teaspoon vanilla extract
Pinch salt
1 unbaked 9-inch pie shell

Combine all ingredients and mix well. Put into unbaked pastry shell and bake at 450° for 10 minutes, then reduce temperature and bake at 350° for 25 to 30 minutes. Yield: 1 (9-inch) pie.

Note: Bake 2½-inch tarts at 325° for 12 to 15 minutes.

Hawaiian Pineapple Pie

3 eggs, well beaten
1 cup light corn syrup
1 cup crushed pineapple, with juice
1 cup flaked or grated coconut
1 cup sugar
2 teaspoons all-purpose flour
½ stick margarine, melted
1 unbaked 10-inch pie shell

Combine eggs and corn syrup; beat until well blended. Stir in remaining ingredients and mix well. Spoon into pie shell and bake at 350° for about 30 minutes, or until pastry is brown and filling is firm. Yield: 1 (10-inch) pie.

Christmas Plum Pudding Pie

2 eggs, slightly beaten
1 cup orange marmalade
1 cup dates, chopped
1 cup flaked coconut
1 cup crystallized fruit, chopped
1 cup nuts, chopped
¼ cup slivers of ginger-preserved watermelon rind
2 tablespoons milk
1 tablespoon butter or margarine
1 unbaked 9-inch pie shell

Preheat oven to 425°. Beat eggs slightly; add all ingredients in order given, except the butter or margarine. Mix well and pour into unbaked pie shell. Dot the top with butter or margarine. Do not let set after putting filling into pastry. Bake at 425° for 25 minutes, or until crust is brown.

If the pie seems dry during baking period, add 1 tablespoon orange or pineapple juice and stir gently with a fork. Yield: 1 (9-inch) pie.

Pumpkin Pie No. 1

    3 eggs, slightly beaten
    1 cup granulated sugar
    ½ cup firmly packed brown sugar
    1 teaspoon all-purpose flour
    1 teaspoon ground cinnamon
    ½ teaspoon salt
    ¼ teaspoon ground nutmeg
    ¼ teaspoon ground allspice
  2½ cups cooked or canned pumpkin
    1 (13-ounce) can evaporated milk
    1 unbaked 9-inch pie shell

Combine eggs, sugars, flour, cinnamon, salt, nutmeg, and allspice. Blend in pumpkin gradually; add milk, and mix well. Pour into 9-inch unbaked pie shell. Bake at 450° for 10 minutes, then at 350° for 40 minutes or until a knife, inserted about halfway between center and outside edge of pie, comes out clean. Cool. Yield: 1 (9-inch) pie.

Pumpkin Pie No. 2

    2 cups cooked or 1 (16-ounce)
       can pumpkin
    1 cup firmly packed dark brown sugar
    1 tablespoon all-purpose flour
    ½ teaspoon salt
  1⅔ cups evaporated milk
  1¼ teaspoons ground cinnamon
    ½ teaspoon ground nutmeg
    ½ teaspoon ground ginger
    ½ teaspoon ground allspice
    ¼ teaspoon ground cloves
    2 eggs
    1 unbaked 9-inch pie shell

Combine pumpkin, brown sugar, flour, salt, milk, spices, and eggs. Beat with rotary beater. Pour mixture into unbaked pastry shell. Bake at 425° for 45 to 55 minutes, or until a knife inserted 1 inch from the edge of crust comes out clean. Serve warm. Yield: 1 (9-inch) pie.

Note: Center may still look soft, but will set later. Cooking pumpkin pie too long makes it watery.

Brown Sugar Pie

    ¼ pound butter or margarine
    1 (1-pound) box brown sugar
    4 eggs, beaten
    4 tablespoons milk
    2 teaspoons light corn syrup
    1 teaspoon vanilla extract
    2 unbaked 9-inch pie shells

Cream butter and sugar together. Add beaten eggs and other ingredients. Mix together, but do not beat at high speed if electric mixer is used. Pour into unbaked pie shells and bake at 375° until brown. Yield: 2 (9-inch) pies.

Sweet Potato Pie

    2 eggs
    1 cup sugar
    1 teaspoon salt
    ⅛ teaspoon ground nutmeg
    1 teaspoon ground cinnamon
    1 cup milk
    2 tablespoons butter or margarine
  1½ cups cooked mashed sweet potatoes
    1 unbaked 8-inch pie shell

Beat the eggs slightly; add sugar, salt, spices, and milk. Add butter or margarine to mashed sweet potatoes and blend with milk and egg mixture. Pour into unbaked pie shell and bake at 450° for 10 minutes. Reduce heat to 350° and bake for 30 to 40 minutes or until filling is firm. Yield: 1 (8-inch) pie.

Raisin Pie

2½ cups seedless raisins
1½ cups water
 ¾ cup white corn syrup
  2 tablespoons all-purpose flour
  2 tablespoons sugar
     Juice and grated rind of 1 lemon
 ½ cup chopped nuts
  1 unbaked 9-inch double crust

Combine raisins and water and boil for about 10 minutes. Combine white corn syrup, flour, sugar, lemon rind, and juice. Add to raisins, stir well, and let cook for 2 to 3 minutes. Add chopped nuts and let cool.

Pour cooled filling into unbaked pie shell. Cover with lattice strips of pastry, if desired. Bake at 400° for 10 minutes, reduce heat to 350° and bake for 20 to 30 minutes longer. Yield: 1 (9-inch) pie.

Three Story Pie

1 unbaked 9-inch pie shell
1 cup or more cooked dried fruit (peaches or apricots)
2 tablespoons all-purpose flour
1 cup sugar
1 cup milk
3 egg yolks, beaten
1 teaspoon vanilla extract
2 tablespoons butter or margarine
3 egg whites, beaten
   Pinch cream of tartar
6 tablespoons sugar

Line piepan with pastry. Mash cooked fruit until smooth and add sugar, if desired. Spread fruit into pie shell.

Mix flour and sugar. Heat the milk in top of double boiler. Gradually add small amount of hot milk to yolks; mix well, then add yolks to remaining hot milk in double boiler. Stir in sugar and flour mixture; cook over low heat, stirring constantly until mixture coats a spoon. Add vanilla and butter. Pour mixture over fruit. Bake at 350° for about 25 minutes.

Beat egg whites and cream of tartar until foamy. Add sugar, a small amount at a time, and continue beating until egg whites are stiff. Spread on pie and bake at 350° until brown. Yield: 1 (9-inch) pie.

Transparent Pie

 1 cup butter or margarine
 2 cups sugar
 4 egg yolks
 1 cup jelly (any flavor)
 1 teaspoon vanilla extract
 4 egg whites
½ cup sugar
 1 unbaked 10-inch pie shell

Cream butter or margarine and sugar together until well blended. Add egg yolks and jelly and mix well. Add vanilla. Pour into unbaked pie shell and bake at 325° for about 25 to 30 minutes, or until firm. Top with meringue made of 4 egg whites and ½ cup sugar. Return to oven until brown. Yield: 1 (10-inch) pie.

Tyler Pudding-Pie

John Tyler, Virginian, tenth President of the United States, was the first Vice President to become President on the death of a President. Of all our Presidents, Tyler had the most children — 14. The large family may explain this generous dessert, a modified transparent pudding in a piecrust.

½ cup butter
6 cups sugar
6 eggs
1 cup heavy cream
1 fresh coconut, grated
   Unbaked Puff Pastry

Cream butter and sugar, add well beaten eggs, cream, and coconut. Pour into four 8-inch piepans lined with uncooked Puff Pastry (see Index). Bake at 450° for 10 minutes to set pastry. Reduce heat to 350° and cook for 30 to 35 minutes until pies are firm. Yield: 4 (8-inch) pies.

Washington Pie

2 cups sifted cake flour
2 teaspoons baking powder
¼ teaspoon salt
1 cup sugar
2 eggs, well beaten
1 tablespoon melted butter or shortening
¾ cup hot milk
1 teaspoon vanilla extract
   Raspberry jelly or jam

Sift flour once, measure, add baking powder and salt, and sift together three times. Beat sugar gradually into eggs. Add butter; then flour, alternately with milk, a small amount at a time. Beat after each addition until smooth. Add vanilla. Bake in two greased 9-inch layer pans at 350° for 25 minutes. Spread raspberry jelly or jam between layers. Sift powdered sugar over top. To make Washington Cream Pie, spread Cream Filling between layers.

Cream Filling

¼ cup sugar
3 tablespoons all-purpose flour
1 cup scalded milk
1 egg, slightly beaten
1 tablespoon butter
½ teaspoon vanilla extract
⅓ cup pitted red tart cherries, drained

Combine sugar and flour. Add scalded milk and slightly beaten egg. Cook in top of a double boiler for about 15 minutes, or until of a creamy consistency. Add butter, vanilla, and well drained cherries. Cool and spread between layers of pie.

Party Rice-Pineapple Pie

1 (14-ounce) can sweetened condensed milk
½ cup freshly squeezed lemon juice
   Grated rind of 1 lemon
2 egg yolks
1 cup cooked rice
½ cup crushed pineapple
1 9-inch graham cracker crust or baked pie shell
2 egg whites, beaten
2 tablespoons sugar

Blend milk, juice, rind, and egg yolks. Fold in rice and pineapple. Pour into graham cracker crust or pastry pie shell. Cover with meringue made by beating egg whites until foamy, then adding sugar gradually. Beat until stiff but not dry. Bake at 350° for 10 minutes or until brown. Chill. Yield: 1 (9-inch) pie.

Note: This pie is also good topped with whipped cream.

Strawberry Tarts

1 (3¾-ounce) box French vanilla
   pudding and pie filling mix (not
   instant)
1½ cups milk
6 (3-inch) tart shells, baked
   Whipped cream
6 large fresh strawberries

Prepare pudding mix according to package directions, using 1½ cups milk. Pour into baked tart shells and refrigerate until set .Top with whipped cream and a large fresh strawberry. Yield: 6 tarts.

Vinegar Pie

2 tablespoons butter or margarine
½ cup sugar
3 tablespoons all-purpose flour
2 teaspoons ground cinnamon
½ teaspoon ground cloves
½ teaspoon ground allspice
1 egg
2 tablespoons vinegar
1 cup water
1 baked 8-inch pie shell

Cream the butter or margarine and sugar. Measure and sift flour, cinnamon, cloves, and allspice; add to creamed mixture. Then add egg, vinegar, and water. Cook in top of double boiler until thick. Pour into pastry shell that has been baked 2 or 3 minutes. Bake at 350° until done. Yield: 1 (8-inch) pie.

Almond Pastry

1½ cups all-purpose flour
¼ cup ground almonds
¼ cup sugar
¼ teaspoon salt
½ cup shortening
1 egg, beaten
   Cold water

Mix the first four ingredients and cut in the shortening. Add beaten egg and enough cold water to make a stiff dough. Chill thoroughly and line a 9-inch pie-plate. Yield: pastry for 1 (9-inch) crust.

Never-Fail Pastry

3 cups all-purpose flour
   Pinch salt
1 cup vegetable shortening
½ cup cold water

Put flour and salt into large bowl. Cut in ½ cup shortening with two knives until mixture resembles cornmeal. Cut in the remaining shortening until the particles are about the size of navy beans. Sprinkle the water a little at a time over the surface. Blend by tossing with a fork until mixture leaves sides of bowl and forms a ball. Avoid stirring. Wrap in waxed paper and chill for about 30 minutes before rolling. Yield: 3 (8- or 9-inch) single crusts.

Egg Pastry

    3 cups all-purpose flour
1 ½ teaspoons salt
    1 cup shortening
    1 egg, beaten
    1 teaspoon vinegar
    ½ cup ice water

Combine flour and salt; cut in shortening with two knives or a pastry blender
until mixture resembles coarse meal.
Combine egg, vinegar, and ice water.
Gradually add to dry ingredients; mix
until dough holds its shape. Yield:
pastry for 3 (9-inch) crusts.

Flaky Pastry

    2 cups all-purpose flour
    1 teaspoon salt
⅔ cup shortening
    4 tablespoons cold water

Measure flour and sift with salt. Add
shortening (at room temperature) and
blend with pastry blender or two knives.
Add water. Roll ⅛ inch thick and line
piepans. Prick pastry, and bake at 425°
for 12 to 15 minutes. Yield: pastry for
2 (8-inch) pie crusts.

Cheese Pastry

2 ¼ cups all-purpose flour
    1 teaspoon salt
¾ cup plus 2 tablespoons
        vegetable shortening
½ to 1 cup shredded American cheese
⅓ cup cold water

Mix flour and salt together in bowl.
With pastry blender or two knives, cut

two-thirds of shortening into flour until
mixture resembles coarse meal. Cut in
remaining shortening until it is the size
of large peas. Add cheese, and mix well.
Sprinkle water, 1 tablespoon at a time,
over the mixture, tossing quickly with
fork. Lightly form dough into a smooth
ball. Divide into two balls and roll out.
Yield: pastry for 1 (8- or 9-inch)
double crust.

Hot Water Pastry

    1 cup shortening
½ cup boiling water
    3 cups all-purpose flour
    1 teaspoon salt

Put half the boiling water in shortening.
Work until creamy. Then add the flour,
salt, and the rest of the water until mixture leaves sides of bowl. Divide into
four parts and roll. Yield: pastry for 2
(8-inch) double crusts.

Puff Pastry

    Pinch salt
1½ cups flour
¼   cup shortening
½   cup cold water
1½ teaspoons freshly squeezed
    lemon juice
¾   cup butter or margarine

Add salt to flour, cut in shortening, and mix into a dough with ½ cup cold water and lemon juice. Roll on floured board. Cream butter or margarine in a bowl until smooth but not soft. Divide it into three parts, spread ⅓ of butter or margarine in center of pastry. Fold pastry as an envelope. Leave in a cool place for 15 minutes and roll with short forward movements until very thin. Use another ⅓ of the butter or margarine, repeat process, and leave in cool place for 15 minutes; repeat with last ⅓ of butter or margarine. When finished, fold as an envelope; wrap in waxed paper, and leave in cool place overnight. Roll out and use as you would use any short pastry. Yield: pastry for 1 (9-inch) pie.

Tart Shells

1   cup all-purpose flour
½   teaspoon salt
⅓   cup shortening
3 to 4 tablespoons cold water

Sift together flour and salt. Cut in shortening with pastry blender until particles are size of navy beans. Pour in water carefully, mixing until dough sticks together. Lightly roll dough on floured pastry cloth to ⅛-inch thickness. Divide into six parts and press loosely into six 3½-inch fluted tart tins, smoothing out any air pockets underneath. Trim dough at edge. Pour filling into tart shells and bake at 400° for 30 minutes. Yield: pastry for 12 (2-inch) tart shells.

Short Pastry

1   cup all-purpose flour
½   teaspoon salt
⅓   cup shortening
3 or 4 tablespoons ice water
¼   cup butter
¼   cup sugar
¼   cup all-purpose flour

Combine 1 cup flour and salt. Cut in shortening with pastry blender. Add enough ice water to moisten flour. Chill pastry for about 1 hour.

Roll and fit into a 9-inch piepan. Soften butter and spread over bottom of pastry. Sprinkle sugar and ¼ cup flour over butter. Bake at 400° until pastry is brown. Yield: pastry for 1 (9-inch) pie shell.

Stir 'n' Roll Pastry

2   cups all-purpose flour
1½ teaspoons salt
½   cup salad oil
¼   cup cold milk

Mix flour and salt together. Put salad oil and cold milk into a measuring cup, but do not stir together. Then pour into flour. Stir lightly until mixed. Round up dough and divide into halves. Yield: pastry for 1 (8-inch) double crust.

Cottage Cheese Pastry

½ cup shortening
6 tablespoons sugar
½ teaspoon ground nutmeg
1 teaspoon ground ginger
1 cup cottage cheese
2 cups all-purpose flour

Work shortening with spoon until creamy. Add sugar gradually, beating until well blended. Then stir in nutmeg, ginger, and cottage cheese. Stir in flour, enough to make a dough that is easily handled. Chill several hours, or overnight. When ready to use, turn dough out on lightly floured board and roll about ¼ inch thick. Place on top of 9-inch pie or cobbler and bake at 425° until browned. Yield: pastry for 1 (9-inch) crust.

Cream Cheese Pastry

½ cup soft butter or margarine
1 (3-ounce) package cream cheese
1 cup all-purpose flour

Blend butter or margarine and cream cheese. Add flour gradually, mixing thoroughly. Work into a smooth dough by hand. Chill. Roll onto a sheet and cut, or roll into small balls and press into muffin tins. Bake at 350° for about 10 to 15 minutes. Yield: pastry for 1 (9-inch) crust.

Graham Cracker Crust

1½ cups finely rolled graham cracker crumbs
½ cup sugar
½ cup melted butter

Combine ingredients and line pieplate with the mixture. Pat firmly into place. Chill before adding filling. Yield: pastry for 2 (8-inch) crusts.

Oatmeal Pastry

1 cup all-purpose flour
1 teaspoon salt
⅓ cup shortening
½ cup uncooked oatmeal, regular or quick cooking
3 to 4 tablespoons cold water

Sift together flour and salt. Cut in shortening until mixture resembles coarse meal; add oatmeal; mix lightly. Add water, 1 tablespoon at a time, stirring until pastry can be formed into ball. Turn out onto lightly floured board. Roll dough to form 12-inch circle; fit loosely into 9-inch pieplate. Fold edges under; flute. Pierce bottom and sides. Bake in preheated 425° oven for 12 to 15 minutes. Yield: pastry for 1 (9-inch) crust.

Sweet Potato Crust

1 cup sifted all-purpose flour
1 teaspoon baking powder
½ teaspoon salt
1 cup mashed cooked sweet potatoes
⅓ cup melted butter
1 egg, well beaten

Sift flour, measure, add baking powder and salt, and sift again. Work in mashed sweet potatoes, melted butter, and egg. Roll ¼ inch thick and use as cover for chicken or meat deep dish pie. Yield: pastry for 1 (9-inch) crust.

Pastry Variations

1. Substitute ¼ cup finely chopped nuts for ¼ cup flour in the pastry.
2. Substitute ice-cold fresh orange juice for water in the pastry; add grated rind of 1 orange.
3. For grape pies or cobblers, use full-strength grape juice instead of water in pastry.

Hints for Making Pastry

1. All materials should be as cold as possible. Water used in making pastry should be ice cold.
2. Too much flour makes piecrust tough.
3. Too much shortening makes piecrust dry and crumbly.
4. Too much liquid makes piecrust heavy and soggy.
5. Measure all ingredients, and follow directions carefully.
6. Mix flour and salt and cut in the shortening with two knives or a pastry blender. Cutting in the shortening very thoroughly gives a tender crust; cutting it in coarsely gives a flaky crust.

7. Sprinkle cold water over the flour-shortening mixture very slowly, tossing the mixture with a fork until all particles are moistened. Do not mix with the hands.
8. Gather dough together in a ball and press together. Pie dough should be handled as little as possible.
9. Place ball of dough on lightly floured canvas or board. Roll with short strokes toward the edges. Lift rolling pin at edge and do not roll over the edge. Never turn dough while rolling.
10. The under crust should be rolled ⅛ inch thick and about 2½ inches larger than the top crust. The top crust should be rolled thinner than ⅛ inch and slightly larger than the pie it is to cover.
11. When the dough has been rolled to the shape and size to fit the pan, fold in half and lift it carefully into the pan with the fold in center of pan. Unfold dough and fit it loosely in the pan. Be sure that dough is not stretched as it is placed in the pan. Pat the entire surface with a little ball of dough to be sure there are no air pockets under the crust. Cut edges. If there are splits in edge, moisten and "patch" with a piece of rolled dough.
12. If pastry is to be baked before adding filling, prick crust with a fork to allow the escape of any air between crust and pan. Another way to prevent bulging is to place a second pan the same size inside the pastry-lined pan. Remove before crust is fully baked.

Foods with a Southwestern Flavor

The foods of the Southwest are a synthesis of Indian, Spanish, Mexican, and American tradition.

Corn, herbs, beef, rice, and beans are the staples for the richly colored and condimented Southwestern dishes.

Avocados are often used as vegetables, and chocolate serves not only as flavoring for meat and vegetables but also as a beverage.

Traditional cooking in the Southwest can almost be reduced to the spicing of staple beef, corn, and beans to produce a variety of dishes. Contrary to prevalent opinion, adding herbs and spices does not necessarily make Southwestern foods "hot."

The indispensable seasoning is chili powder. More than 90 kinds of chiles exist, but the basic powdered form is always a combination of chili peppers, cumin seeds, oregano, garlic, and table salt. The addition of bay leaf, ground cloves, ground allspice, and powdered onions results in flavor variations.

The chili con carne indigenous to the area is actually Texan rather than Mexican, although the combination of ground beef, onion, garlic, tomato paste, chili, and seasoned cooked beans has been traditionally considered an adopted specialty.

Connoisseurs of Southwestern food boast of the good health it brings. The Mexicans have long sought the oils of the powdered red chili peppers as aids to digestion and garlic for its medicinal qualities.

Many of the native dishes start from a simple cornmeal pancake called a tortilla. When not served alone with butter as bread or dessert, these tortillas take on seasoned meat or beans to become enchiladas and tacos.

The American side of Southwestern cookery finds its summation in barbecue. The beef roasted in deep pits and served in thin slices does, however, have a touch of Mexico in its accompanying sauce.

Obviously, a Spanish proverb has become a part of the Southwestern life-style: a full stomach makes a happy man.

Homemade Chili

3 pounds chuck or round steak
2 tablespoons cooking oil
2 large onions, chopped
2 or 3 cloves garlic, minced
3 cups hot water
2 to 4 tablespoons chili powder
1 teaspoon ground oregano
2 teaspoons ground cumin
2 tablespoons salt
2 jalapeño peppers, finely chopped

Cut meat into small pieces and cook in hot cooking oil until meat turns white. Add onion, garlic, and hot water; cover and simmer for 1 hour or until meat is tender.

Add chili powder, oregano, cumin, salt, and jalapeños; cook slowly for another hour, stirring occasionally. Add additional hot water if needed. Taste and add more seasoning if needed. Serve hot, with or without cooked pinto beans. Yield: 8 to 10 servings.

Texas Chili

 9 pounds chuck roast
¼ cup cooking oil
15 cloves garlic, minced
 5 large onions, finely chopped
10 cups hot water
¾ cup chili powder
 1 tablespoon oregano
 2 tablespoons ground cumin
 6 tablespoons salt
 6 jalapeño peppers, finely chopped
 2 tablespoons masa harina (cornflour)
½ cup cold water

Cut meat into small pieces and cook in hot cooking oil until meat turns white. Add garlic, onion, and hot water; cover and simmer for 1 hour or until meat is tender.

Add chili powder, oregano, cumin, and salt; cook slowly for another hour, stirring occasionally. Add additional water if needed. Taste and add more seasoning if needed. Add peppers. Sir masa harina (cornmeal can be substituted) into cold water; add to chili and cook and stir until mixture thickens. Serve hot. Yield: 12 to 16 servings.

Pinto Chili Beans

 1 pound dried pinto beans
 6 cups water
5¾ cups tomato juice
 3 cloves garlic, mashed or minced
¼ cup bacon drippings or melted shortening
 2 medium onions, chopped
 2 pounds ground beef
 1 green pepper, chopped
 4 large stalks celery, sliced
 2 (6-ounce) cans tomato paste
 1 to 2 tablespoons chili powder
 2 tablespoons salt
 1 teaspoon ground cumin

Wash beans and place in a heavy kettle. Cover with water, and bring to a boil. Boil for 3 minutes. Remove from heat and soak for about 1 hour. Add tomato juice and cook over low heat while preparing the meat mixture.

Sauté garlic in large frying pan with the bacon drippings; add onions, meat, green pepper, and celery. Cook until meat is brown, stirring constantly. Add tomato paste, chili powder, salt, and cumin. Mix well and add to beans. Cover and simmer about 2½ to 3 hours, or until beans are tender. Yield: 10 to 12 servings.

Quick Chili

    1   tablespoon shortening
    ½   cup chopped onion
    1   pound ground beef
    1   green pepper, chopped
    1   (10½-ounce) can condensed
        tomato soup
    1   teaspoon salt
    4   teaspoons (or more) chili powder
    ⅛   teaspoon black pepper
  1/16 teaspoon ground red pepper
    1   (1-pound) can red kidney beans

Melt shortening in heavy skillet. Add onion and cook until brown, then add ground beef and brown. Stir frequently so there will be no lumps of meat. Add green pepper, tomato soup, salt, chili powder, black and red pepper, and kidney beans. Heat mixture thoroughly and serve piping hot. Yield: 6 servings.

Chili Without Beans

  1½ cups ground baby beef suet
    3 pounds ground beef
    2 cloves garlic, minced
  1½ teaspoons paprika
    3 tablespoons chili powder
    1 tablespoon salt
    1 large onion, chopped fine
    1 teaspoon white pepper
    1 tablespoon cumin seed
  1½ tablespoons sugar or corn syrup
  1½ tablespoons finely ground dried
       chile peppers
    ½ (3-ounce) can tomato paste (optional)
    3 cups water

Melt the suet, add the beef, and sear thoroughly on all sides, using a very heavy pan. Add all the seasoning. Stir to prevent sticking. Add water, and cook slowly for 3 to 4 hours. More water may be needed. The flavor will improve if chili is allowed to stand for several hours or overnight before serving. Yield: 6 to 8 servings.

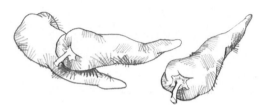

Soybean Chili

    1 cup soybeans
    1 onion, finely sliced
    4 tablespoons butter or
       margarine, divided
    2 cups tomatoes, drained
    1 teaspoon salt
    ½ teaspoon black pepper
    1 tablespoon chili powder
    ½ to 1 pound finely chopped lean beef
       (or lean pork or chicken)

Soak the beans overnight. Boil until tender the next morning and set aside. Brown onion in 2 tablespoons butter or margarine in kettle. Add drained tomatoes, which have been seasoned to taste with salt, pepper, and chili powder.

Brown the beef (or pork or chicken) in remaining 2 tablespoons butter or margarine in skillet; season with salt to taste, and add to the tomato sauce. Add the cooked beans, and simmer the mixture slowly for a few minutes before serving. Yield: 4 servings.

Hasty Chili

1 pound ground beef
3 tablespoons chopped suet
1 large onion, chopped
2 stalks celery, chopped
3 tablespoons shortening
2 cups canned tomatoes
1 (10½-ounce) can black bean soup
1 soup can water
1 teaspoon salt
½ teaspoon oregano
4 teaspoons chili powder

Brown the beef, suet, onion, and celery in shortening. Add tomatoes, soup, water, salt, oregano, and chili powder. Heat the mixture thoroughly and serve hot. Yield: 6 servings.

Enchiladas No. 1

2 pounds ground beef
1 tablespoon shortening
4 tablespoons chili blend
2 tablespoons chili powder
  Salt to taste
2 (11-ounce) cans tortillas
⅝ cup finely chopped onion
1 cup shredded cheese
  Sauce

Cook meat with shortening in skillet until well done, stirring occasionally so it will cook evenly. Add chili blend, chili powder, and salt; cook for about 2 minutes more. Spread 2 tablespoons meat mixture, 1 teaspoon finely chopped onion, and 1 teaspoon shredded cheese on each tortilla. Roll up and place in baking dish. Pour Sauce over tortillas; sprinkle shredded cheese on top, and bake at 350° for 20 minutes. Yield: 8 to 10 servings.

Sauce

1 (10½-ounce) can tomato soup
1 can water
2 tablespoons chili blend
  Juice of ½ lemon

Mix all ingredients and pour over enchiladas.

Note: If you plan to freeze the enchiladas, do so before you bake them. Place eight or nine enchiladas in a rectangular baking dish of oven-proof glass. Cover with aluminum foil and freeze.

Enchiladas No. 2

1½ pounds ground beef
2 tablespoons shortening
1 teaspoon salt
½ teaspoon pepper
1 teaspoon oregano
1 to 2 tablespoons chili powder
¼ teaspoon Tabasco sauce
1 clove garlic, minced
½ cup finely chopped onion
2 cups cooked tomatoes
2 (8-ounce) cans tomato sauce
  Enchilada Sauce
1 (11-ounce) can tortillas
1 pound cheese, shredded
½ cup chopped onion

Brown ground beef in shortening. Pour off excess shortening. Add salt, pepper, oregano, chili powder, Tabasco, garlic, onion, tomatoes, and tomato sauce. Cover and simmer for 30 minutes. Make Enchilada Sauce. Place each tortilla in Enchilada Sauce to soften. Fill each tortilla with 2 tablespoons meat mixture, 1 tablespoon shredded cheese, and 1 tablespoon chopped onion. Roll firmly, and place in a 13- x 9- x 2-inch baking dish. Top with remaining meat mixture and sauce. Sprinkle with remaining shredded cheese. Bake uncovered at 350° for 30 minutes. Serve hot. Yield: 4 to 6 servings.

Enchilada Sauce

3 tablespoons butter or margarine
1½ tablespoons all-purpose flour
1½ tablespoons chili powder
1½ cups water

Melt butter or margarine; add flour and chili powder, and blend until smooth. Add water and cook, stirring constantly, until thickened. Remove from heat.

Enchiladas No. 3

2 (11-ounce) cans tortillas
1 cup shortening
1 quart Enchilada Sauce or gravy
2 to 3 cups finely chopped onions
1 pound Cheddar cheese, shredded
   About 3 to 4 cups Enchilada Sauce or homemade chili
   Grated cheese

Use tongs to dip tortillas, one at a time, in medium hot shortening. Leave long enough to soften tortilla, but do not cook until crisp. Dip tortilla immediately into Enchilada Sauce or gravy and leave until soft. (This step may be reversed, if you like.)

Place softened tortilla on a flat surface. Sprinkle with chopped onion and shredded cheese and roll as you would a jelly-roll. Place in large flat pan with the flap of tortilla on bottom. When pan has been filled, cover with Enchilada Sauce or chili; sprinkle with grated cheese and place in oven preheated to 350°. Bake until cheese has melted and mixture is bubbly. Yield: 12 servings.

Enchilada Sauce

1 tablespoon salad oil
1 medium onion, chopped
3 cups tomato sauce or tomato puree
2 teaspoons chili powder
   Salt to taste
1 to 3 jalapeño peppers or green chiles, finely chopped

Heat salad oil in skillet. Cook onion in oil until wilted. Add tomato sauce and chili powder and cook for about 10 minutes. Add salt to taste, peppers or chiles, and keep mixture warm.

Note: You may want to substitute liquid from cooked pintos and some chili; then put in blender with cooked onion and peppers to make a smooth mixture. Adjust the seasoning; you might find you will need less chili powder and chiles if chili is used.

Caracas

2 tablespoons butter or margarine
1½ cups chopped dried beef
1 teaspoon chili powder
1 cup tomato pulp
1 cup shredded cheese
3 eggs, slightly beaten

Melt the butter or margarine in an iron pan; add the chopped beef, chili powder, and hot tomato pulp. Cook slowly until the beef is tender. Stir in the cheese, then the slightly beaten eggs. Stir and cook until the mixture becomes a soft mass like scrambled eggs. Serve at once on thin squares of toast. Yield: 6 servings.

Tacos

    1 (11-ounce) can tortillas
      Hot shortening
1½ cups shredded lettuce
    1 pound ground beef
   ½ teaspoon garlic salt
    3 tablespoons grated onion
   ¼ teaspoon oregano
   ¼ cup tomato sauce
      Hot Chile Sauce

With tongs dip each tortilla into hot shortening in skillet, folding it in half as it fries. Drain on paper towels. Cook meat until it turns white. Add seasonings and tomato sauce. Place a small amount of lettuce in each taco shell and top with cooked beef. Serve with Hot Chile Sauce. Yield: 6 to 12 servings.

Hot Chili Sauce

The sauce is made by combining ground hot peppers with tomato sauce or finely chopped fresh tomatoes. Jalapeños are very hot peppers, available in cans in most areas. If they are not sold in your area, canned green chiles or ground cayenne can be substituted.

This sauce may also be made by grinding the dried Mexican peppers, the canned green chiles, or jalapeños. These are often stewed with tomato sauce and seasoned to suit the cook, who usually adds a dash of oregano or cumin, or maybe both.

It's always safest to add just a small amount of this sauce to any Mexican food at first, then taste it and add as much as you think your tastebuds can stand.

Bunuelos (Mexican Fried Puffs)

    2 cups all-purpose flour
    1 tablespoon sugar
   ⅓ teaspoon salt
    1 tablespoon shortening
    1 egg, beaten
    6 tablespoons water
    2 teaspoons vanilla extract
      Powdered sugar

Combine flour, sugar, and salt; cut in shortening with pastry blender or two knives. Beat egg and mix with water and vanilla. Stir into dry ingredients to make a stiff dough. Roll very thin and cut in small rounds, then stretch these still thinner with the hands. They should be almost transparent. Fry in deep, hot shortening, and drain as soon as removed from shortening. Sprinkle with powdered sugar, and serve at once. Yield: 36 cakes.

Beef Tacos

    1 pound ground beef
    4 tablespoons bacon drippings
   ¼ teaspoon garlic salt
    1 teaspoon chili powder
      Salt to taste
    1 (11-ounce) can tortillas
      Shredded lettuce
      Chopped onion
      Chopped tomatoes

Cook ground beef in hot bacon drippings until meat turns white. Add garlic salt, chili powder, and salt; cook until meat is done.

Use taco shells or prepare your own from tortillas. Fold tortillas in half and fry until crisp in hot fat.

Place a layer of ground beef in bottom of each taco shell and finish filling with shredded lettuce, chopped onion, and chopped tomatoes. Yield: 6 servings.

Tamale Pie

- 1 onion, chopped
- 1 clove garlic, minced
- 1 sweet green pepper, chopped
- ½ cup shortening
- 1½ pounds ground beef
- 1½ cups cooked tomatoes
- ½ cup pitted ripe olives (optional)
- 2 chile peppers, cut fine
- 1 teaspoon salt
- ½ teaspoon pepper
- ½ cup shredded American cheese
- 2 tablespoons cornmeal
- 1 tablespoon chili powder
- 1 cup cornmeal
- 3 cups boiling water
- 1 teaspoon salt

Cook onion, garlic, and green pepper in hot shortening until tender; add ground beef and brown. Add tomatoes, ripe olives, chile peppers, 1 teaspoon salt, and pepper; simmer for 1 hour. Stir in shredded cheese, 2 tablespoons cornmeal, chili powder, and cook for 5 minutes. Gradually add 1 cup cornmeal to

3 cups boiling water to which salt has been added. Stir constantly until mixture thickens. Pour cornmeal mush over meat mixture in baking dish. Bake at 400° for 30 minutes. Yield: 6 to 8 servings.

West Texas Beef Soup

- 1 (4-pound) chine of beef (⅔ meat and ⅓ bone)
- 12 cups cold water
- 1 green pepper, chopped
- 1 cup minced onion
- 1 cup diced celery
- 1 cup sliced carrots
- 2 cups diced potatoes
- ½ cup diced turnips (optional)
- 2 cups cooked tomatoes
- 2 cups cooked corn
- 1 cup regular rice or macaroni
  Salt and pepper
- 1½ teaspoons chili powder
- ¼ teaspoon cumin seed, mashed

Have beef and bone sawed through in two or three places to extract all the flavor possible. Put into cold water and cook slowly until meat is tender. Remove meat from broth and strain to remove pieces of bone and undesirable fat. Set meat aside to cool, and return broth to kettle. Skim off excess fat. Add water, if necessary, to broth to make 3 cups liquid. Add the green pepper, onion, celery, carrots, potatoes, and turnips to the broth. Cook until vegetables are tender. Add tomatoes, corn, rice or macaroni, all seasonings, and the cooled cubed lean beef. Simmer for 30 minutes longer. Serve hot. Yield: 12 to 15 servings.

Cowboy Ranch Stew

1 tablespoon shortening
1 pound ground beef
1 medium onion, chopped
1 green pepper, diced
2 cups whole-kernel corn
2 cups canned kidney beans
2 cups canned tomatoes
1 teaspoon chili powder (optional)
¾ teaspoon salt

Put shortening in heavy kettle. Add beef, onion, and green pepper; cook, stirring occasionally, until meat is browned and onion and green pepper are tender. Drain corn, beans, and tomatoes; add liquids to meat, and cook until liquid is reduced to about one-half. Add corn, beans, tomatoes, chili powder, and salt; mix together and heat to serving temperature. Stir occasionally to prevent sticking. Serve at once. Yield: 6 servings.

Mexican Beef Pie

1½ pounds beef stew meat
1 teaspoon salt
½ teaspoon pepper
3 tablespoons all-purpose flour
3 tablespoons shortening
½ cup chopped onions
1 clove garlic, minced
2 teaspoons chili powder
1 (8-ounce) can tomato sauce
2 cups water
1 (16-ounce) can kidney beans
Cornmeal Mush

Cut meat into ½-inch cubes. Sprinkle with salt and pepper and roll in flour. Brown well in hot shortening. Add onions, minced garlic, chili powder, tomato sauce, and water. Cover, and cook slowly until meat is tender, for about 2 hours. Stir occasionally. Add kidney beans, and heat thoroughly.

Line bottom and sides of greased 2-quart casserole with Cornmeal Mush. Fill with meat mixture. Bake at 375° for 25 minutes. Yield: 5 servings.

Cornmeal Mush

½ cup cornmeal
¼ teaspoon salt
2 cups water

Stir cornmeal and salt into water and cook until thick.

South-of-the-Border-Style Chicken

1 (5-pound) hen
½ cup diced celery
½ cup diced carrots
2 tablespoons green pepper
1 onion, sliced thin
1 teaspoon salt
½ cup raisins, chopped
1 cup blanched, toasted almonds, chopped
½ cup dry breadcrumbs, browned
½ cup shortening
4 fresh tomatoes, peeled and chopped
½ teaspoon ground cinnamon
6 whole cloves
2½ cups strained chicken broth
2 tablespoons vinegar
¼ cup chopped ripe olives
2 tablespoons chopped pimiento

Clean and disjoint chicken; place in kettle, and cover with water. Add celery, carrots, green pepper, onion, and salt; cook until tender. Remove meat from bones and cut meat into bite-size pieces. Strain broth and save. Place raisins, almonds, and breadcrumbs in hot shortening; add tomatoes and spices. Pour in chicken broth and add cut up chicken meat. Simmer slowly for 30 minutes, until sauce begins to thicken. Add vinegar, ripe olives, and pimiento. Cook 10 to 15 minutes longer. Serve with hot buttered rice and a tossed green salad. Yield: 6 to 8 servings.

Hot Chicken Tacos

- 1 (3-ounce) can tomato paste
- 1 (6-ounce) can tomato sauce
- 1 medium onion, minced
- 1 teaspoon oregano
- 1 tablespoon vinegar
- 2 tablespoons salad oil
- 1½ teaspoons salt
- 2 canned green chile peppers, chopped
- 3 cups diced, cooked chicken or turkey
- 6 tablespoons chili sauce
- ½ teaspoon salt
- ¼ teaspoon pepper
- 1 (11-ounce) can tortillas
  Shredded cheese

Make a sauce by combining tomato paste, tomato sauce, minced onion, oregano, vinegar, salad oil, 1½ teaspoons salt, and chopped green chile peppers. Bring to a boil and simmer for 10 to 15 minutes and set aside. Moisten the chicken or turkey with chili sauce, and add salt and pepper to taste. Place about ¼ cup chicken mixture on each tortilla. Sprinkle with shredded cheese, and roll as for jellyroll. Fasten each with a toothpick and fry in a small amount of shortening until all sides are brown and crisp; drain. Allow two tacos per per-son; serve on hot plate, cover with sauce, and sprinkle with shredded cheese. Yield: 6 servings.

Tamale Pie

Mush Topping

- 1 cup white cornmeal
- 1 cup cold water
- 2 cups boiling water
- 1 teaspoon salt
- 2 tablespoons butter or margarine

Mix cornmeal and cold water; pour into boiling salted water, stirring constantly. Cook until thickened, stirring frequently to prevent lumping. Cover; continue cooking over low heat for about 5 minutes. Stir in butter or margarine, and let cool while preparing the Filling.

Filling

- 1 onion, chopped
- 1 green pepper, chopped
- 3 tablespoons shortening
- 2 cups canned tomatoes or canned tomato soup
- 2 cups chopped cooked chicken or other meat
- ½ teaspoon salt
- 1 teaspoon chili powder or dash cayenne pepper

Brown chopped onion and pepper in melted shortening. Add tomatoes, chopped meat, and ½ teaspoon salt. Season with chili powder or cayenne pepper. Place a thin layer of mush in greased 2-quart baking dish. Add meat mixture and cover with remainder of mush, or place mush in strips on top of meat. Bake at 375° for 30 minutes. Yield: 6 to 8 servings.

Southwest Stew

    2 cups cubed cooked chicken
    8 cups chicken broth
    1 small onion, chopped
    2 cups whole-kernel corn
    1 cup cooked tomatoes
    2 teaspoons salt
    ⅛ teaspoon pepper
    1 teaspoon Worcestershire sauce
    6 ounces elbow spaghetti
    1 cup cooked okra

Put broth in saucepan; add onion, corn, tomatoes, salt, pepper, and Worcestershire sauce. Cook for about 15 minutes, stirring occasionally. Add spaghetti and cook 10 minutes longer. Add chicken and okra and cook just long enough to heat thoroughly. Yield: 6 servings.

Baked Beans with Tamales

    2 cups finely chopped onions
    1 cup chopped celery
    4 tablespoons butter or margarine
 2½ cups chili, without beans
    6 cups cooked beans
    1 tablespoon sorghum or molasses
    1 teaspoon oregano
    1 teaspoon salt
    2 cups cooked tomatoes
    1 can tamales
       Pimientos

Lightly sauté onions and celery in butter or margarine. Combine all ingredients except tamales. Put mixture into two 13- x 9- x 2-inch pans and bake at 300° for 1½ to 2 hours. Add 1 cup tomatoes or tomato juice if more liquid is needed. Slice tamales and arrange on top about 15 minutes before cooking

time is over. Be sure that tamales are heated through. To serve, make a design of pimientos in shape of poinsettia, if desired. Serve while hot and bubbly. Yield: 8 to 10 servings.

Barbecued Goat Meat

Carefully wipe 1 hind quarter of a fat young goat with a clean, damp cloth; put it into a shallow pan; place in a 250° oven to heat. While meat is heating, mix your favorite barbecue sauce and keep it warm. When meat is thoroughly heated, begin basting with sauce at 30 minute intervals and continue basting until meat is a rich brown color. Turn meat over and baste and brown other side.

Tamales

    2 cups ground chicken or beef
    2 tablespoons chili powder
    2 tablespoons minced onion
    1 clove garlic, minced
    ½ teaspoon cumin seed
    ½ teaspoon red pepper
    1 teaspoon salt
    4 tablespoons beef or chicken broth
       Masa

Mix all ingredients except masa thoroughly. You may buy the masa, but to make your own, add 1 teaspoon salt and 2 tablespoons shortening to 2 cups cornmeal and scald with hot water or hot broth, using enough liquid to make a soft dough. Let set for 10 minutes and work again, adding more water if necessary.

Prepare shucks from long ears of corn by clipping off ends. Put into a large vessel and cover with boiling water. Bring to a boil; cover, and set aside until ready to use. Remove and dry a few shucks at a time. Place shuck on flat surface, and with a spoon spread masa on shuck over area about 3½ inches long by 2½ inches wide. In the center of this, place a rounded tablespoonful of the meat mixture and spread. Roll up the shuck and clip to within 1½ inches of the masa on both ends. Turn ends down. Pack in a container so tamales will be on a rack above water or broth; steam for 45 minutes to 1 hour, or until shuck and dough separate easily when one is unwrapped. Yield: 2 dozen tamales.

Frijoles

1 pound pinto beans
2 medium onions
2 or 3 cloves garlic
  About ¼ pound diced salt pork
1 to 3 teaspoons chili powder (optional)
  Salt to taste

Check pinto beans, removing all stones and faulty beans. Wash through several changes of water. Put into a large kettle, cover with water, and soak overnight. The next day, add more water if needed to cover beans. Add whole onions, garlic, and diced salt pork.

Bring beans quickly to a boil; reduce heat and simmer for 3 to 4 hours, adding more boiling water if necessary. Do not add cold water as this will toughen beans. Add chili powder after beans are soft; then add salt to taste. A few of the beans may be mashed to thicken beans; some Mexican restaurants mash all beans after they have been cooked to the soft stage. Yield: 6 to 8 servings.

Frijoles Refritos

Cook pinto beans until almost dry. Put 2 tablespoons shortening in heavy skillet, add 2 cups mashed beans, and cook at low heat, stirring constantly, until beans become brown and crusty. Serve hot.

Texas Barbecued Chicken

2 broilers or small fryers
1 clove garlic
½ teaspoon salt
¼ cup salad oil
½ cup freshly squeezed lemon juice
2 tablespoons grated onion
½ teaspoon black pepper
1 teaspoon Worcestershire sauce

Wipe broilers with a clean damp cloth and cut in half. Mash garlic with salt in bowl, and stir in remaining ingredients. (This is better if it can be chilled overnight.) Mop chicken with sauce and place on grill. Watch carefully to keep chicken from burning. Turn occasionally, and mop on more sauce. Yield: 4 servings.

Cabrito Guisado
(Goat in Sauce)

Wash well all tripe, tongue, heart, kidney, liver, and head of cabrito. Place in kettle, cover with water, add three or four pieces of celery, and salt to taste. Cook until tender, then remove everything except head; let it cook until meat falls off bone. Let cool and cut into small pieces, saving the liquid. Grind spices in a "molcajete" (a stone mortar and pestle). The following spices are also ground:

6 or 8 peppercorns
1 large clove garlic
½ teaspoon cumin seed

Add tomato, onions, and green pepper so the spices will not become embedded in the rough stone. The flavors also become blended much better.

Sauté all the meat in 3 tablespoons bacon drippings, adding the spices from the molcajete, chopped onions, green pepper, 1 cup of tomatoes, 1 bouillon cube, ½ teaspoon chili powder (for color). Add just enough liquid to moisten well but not make soupy. Simmer slowly for about 20 minutes. Serve over Mexican rice, with guacamole salad, and tortillas.

Chili Con Queso

1 tablespoon shortening
1 small onion, chopped
1 teaspoon chili powder
1 cup canned tomatoes
2 cups shredded cheese
  Dash of cayenne pepper
  Toast

Melt shortening in a heavy pan. Add the onion, and cook slowly for a few minutes. Add chili powder and tomatoes. Cover closely and allow sauce to simmer until it is thick and smooth. Turn heat low and add cheese and cayenne pepper. Serve hot on thin strips of toast. Yield: 6 servings.

Calabaza

1½ pounds zucchini squash
1 medium onion, chopped
2 tablespoons shortening
2 cloves garlic, minced
1½ cups canned tomatoes, drained
  Salt to taste
1 to 2 teaspoons cumin seed
2 or 3 hot green peppers (optional)

Wash squash; cut into 1-inch cubes. Sauté onion in shortening until clear; add squash and remaining ingredients. Bring to boil, reduce heat to simmer, and cook until done, about 15 to 20 minutes. Yield: 4 to 6 servings.

Colache

1 pound shredded string beans
2 tablespoons chopped onion
2 tablespoons salad oil
1 cup tomato pulp or sauce
1 cup water
1 teaspoon salt
¼ teaspoon black pepper

Cook beans and onion in oil for 5 minutes. Add tomato pulp or sauce and water and cook until tender. Add salt and pepper. Yield: 6 servings.

Variation

Add 1 cup chopped green corn or summer squash.

Southwest Succotash

- 1 pound fresh, or 2 cups canned tomatoes
- 1 pint okra, sliced
- 2 teaspoons salt
- 1 teaspoon black pepper
- ¼ cup chopped celery
- 1 cup shelled lima beans
- 1 cup fresh, canned, or frozen corn
- 4 tablespoons butter or margarine

If fresh tomatoes are used, peel and chop. Combine okra, salt, pepper, and celery, and cook for about 10 minutes. Add the lima beans and cook for about 25 minutes. Add corn, and simmer for 8 to 12 minutes. Add butter or margarine the last few minutes of cooking time. The amount of boiling water needed will vary with the maturity of the vegetables, the rate of cooking, and the utensil used. If more water is added after the cooking starts, be sure it is boiling; cold water tends to toughen the vegetable. Yield: 6 servings.

Spanish Corn and Beans

- 1 cup canned whole-kernel corn
- 2 cups cooked green beans
- 2 small green peppers
- 1 small onion
- 1 small red pepper
- ½ teaspoon cayenne pepper
- ½ teaspoon chili pepper
- ½ teaspoon salt
- ½ cup tomato sauce
- 2 tablespoons butter or margarine

Cook corn until tender and drain. Chop beans, peppers, onion, and red pepper. Add to corn and mix. Add seasonings, adding tomato sauce last. Put into skillet in which butter or margarine has been melted, and fry for 10 minutes. Yield: 8 servings.

Dulce de Calabaza (Pumpkin Candy)

Select a round pumpkin that can be cut into uniform slices. Peel pumpkin, remove center, and cut into pieces. Soak overnight in lime water to cover, using 1 tablespoon quicklime for each quart cold water; stir well before pouring over pumpkin. The following morning remove pumpkin from lime water; wash three or more times in clear water. Cover pumpkin with warm water; slowly bring to boiling point; boil for 5 minutes, no longer. Wash twice in clear, cold water; allow to drain for about 1 hour. Pierce each piece in several places with fork (so syrup can penetrate). Weigh the pumpkin; take equal weight of sugar. Place pumpkin in baking dish or pan that has never had fat in it; cover with sugar; moisten with water; cook over very low heat until pumpkin is crystallized (several hours). Carefully move pieces around so all cook evenly. When pieces are tender and crystallized, drain from syrup; dry on waxed paper.

Mexican Rice (Sopa de Arroz)

2 *tablespoons shortening*
1 *medium onion, sliced*
1 *cup regular rice, uncooked*
2 *teaspoons chili powder*
2 *cups cooked tomatoes*

Melt shortening and brown sliced onion in it. Add rice and stir until slightly brown. Add chili powder and tomatoes which have been heated. Cover and cook slowly for about 1 hour or until the rice is very tender. Add hot water when needed. Yield: 6 servings.

Hot Mexican Tomato Sauce

1 *(17-ounce) can solid pack tomatoes, finely chopped*
1 *onion, finely chopped*
10 *green chile peppers, chopped*
1 *teaspoon oregano*
2 *tablespoons wine vinegar*
1 *tablespoon oil*
½ *teaspoon chili powder*
  Few cumin seeds (optional)
  Salt and pepper to taste

Combine ingredients, stir well and heat to boiling. Serve with enchiladas, tacos, or tostados. Yield: 1½ to 2 cups.

Nachos

1 *(11-ounce) can tortillas*
  Hot shortening
1 *(10-ounce) can jalapeño peppers*
½ *pound sliced Cheddar cheese*
  Salt

Cut tortillas in quarters. Fry in deep hot shortening until crisp. Drain. Drain jalapeño peppers and remove all seed. Cut in halves and place on fried tortillas. Cut cheese into strips and place a strip on top of each pepper. Place on ungreased baking sheet and bake at 350° until cheese melts. Sprinkle with salt and serve hot. Yield: 12 to 16 servings.

Mesquite Bean Jelly

½ *bushel mesquite beans*
2 *cups tart plum juice or 1 cup freshly squeezed lemon juice*
3 *to 4 quarts water*
1 *(1¾-ounce) package powdered pectin*
7½ *cups sugar*

Select mature beans that have a red tinge on the pods. (Beans that have fallen on the ground are usually too old and woody.) Wash beans and snap into small pieces into a large saucepan. Add plum or lemon juice. Add 3 to 4 quarts water, and cook for 1 hour. Drain the juice. Measure 5 cups of the juice into a large saucepan; bring to a full rolling boil and add the powdered pectin while stirring vigorously. Bring the mixture to a boil that cannot be stirred down. Add sugar and cook for 5 more minutes. Pour jelly into hot, sterilized glasses or jars and seal.

Crowd Cooking

Southerners gather to eat at the least excuse, from a church supper to a day-long political rally. Entire families have gathered for reunions for generations.

If you have to prepare a meal for a large group, think before you panic. If your usual proportions of ingredients feed four, you've probably often substituted a similar recipe for eight without giving it a second thought. There is no reason, then, why you can't serve from 20 to 100 with an adequately proportioned recipe.

One ingenious mother of five decided that if she fed seven every night there should be little problem in serving her special spaghetti to 70 at a church supper. She not only found a pot large enough to hold it, and adjusted her recipe to serve that many, she also solved the serving problem by buying a rake to dish it out. The only real trouble she has now is finding a place in the kitchen to store the rake between the annual suppers.

Preparing one dish that will serve a multitude of people is infinitely more convenient than the customary covered-dish supper which can result in 20 pots of baked beans surrounding one small bowl of slaw.

Because recipes for crowd cooking aren't suitable for kitchen-testing, we've included in this chapter only recipes from commercial concerns that have been prepared especially for quantity cooking. Also, additional beverage recipes to serve a crowd can be found in the "Beverages" chapter.

Texas Goulash

    10 pounds boneless stew meat
    ½   cup all-purpose flour
    4   tablespoons salt
    1½ tablespoons chili powder
    5   tablespoons bacon drippings
    4   cups chopped onions
    9   cloves garlic, chopped
    1½ cups water
    1½ cups sliced carrots
    3½ cups sliced celery
    1½ cups cooked lima beans
    4   potatoes, cut into eighths
    1½ cups commercial sour cream

Cut stew meat into 2-inch cubes; combine flour, salt, and chili powder. Roll meat in seasoned flour and brown in bacon drippings. Add onions, garlic, and water. Cover and simmer on top of range in heavy, deep pot for about 2 hours, or until meat is tender. Add more water as needed. Put in the carrots, celery, and lima beans during the last half-hour of cooking. Place cut potatoes on top. Cover again and cook until potatoes are tender. Blend in sour cream. Bring just to the boiling point and remove from heat. Serve hot. Yield: 25 servings.

Ham Loaf

    3   quarts ground cured ham
    3   quarts ground pork
    3   quarts dry breadcrumbs
    2   teaspoons pepper
    3   cups eggs (12 to 15 eggs)
    2   quarts milk
    1   cup firmly packed brown sugar
    ¼   cup dry mustard
    ¾   cup vinegar

Combine ham, pork, dry breadcrumbs, and pepper. Beat eggs and combine with milk. Combine both mixtures and mix thoroughly. Equally divide mixture, and form into four loaves. Place loaves in greased 9- x 5- x 4-inch loaf pans. Combine brown sugar, mustard, and vinegar, and pour this mixture over ham loaves. Bake at 375° for 1 hour. Yield: 48 servings.

Chicken à la King

    3   cups chicken fat
    4   cups all-purpose flour
    4   teaspoons salt
    2   cups nonfat dry milk solids
    2   quarts chicken broth
    2   quarts water or vegetable liquid
    4½ quarts diced cooked chicken
    6   (18-ounce) cans green peas
    1   cup chopped pimiento
    4   pounds noodles

Melt chicken fat in large pan. Stir in flour, salt, and dry milk solids. Add chicken broth and water or vegetable liquid, and cook until thickened, stirring constantly. Add chicken, peas, and pimiento, mixing well. Heat thoroughly. Serve on cooked noodles. Yield: 48 servings.

Pancakes

    12 cups all-purpose flour
    ½   cup baking powder
    3   tablespoons salt
    ½   cup sugar
    5   eggs
        About 3½ quarts milk
    1¼ cups melted shortening

Combine dry ingredients. Beat eggs; add milk and melted shortening; mix. Add liquid to flour mixture, mixing only until flour is well moistened. Do not beat. Bake on lightly greased hot griddle, allowing 2 tablespoons batter per pancake. Yield: 50 servings.

Porcupine Balls

    8 pounds ground cooked ham
    4 pounds ground pork shoulder
    ⅓ cup salt
    2 teaspoons pepper
    1 quart chopped onion
    2 quarts uncooked regular rice
    1 cup salad oil
    2 (1-gallon) cans tomato juice

Mix ground meat, seasonings, onion, and rice. Shape into small balls, enough for two per serving. Brown slowly in salad oil for about 15 to 20 minutes, turning several times. Add tomato juice, cover tightly, and bake at 350° for 45 minutes. Yield: 50 servings.

Chili Con Carne

    3   pounds ground beef
    3¾ cups chopped onions
    2   cloves garlic (optional)
    ½   cup shortening
    7½ cups cooked red or pinto beans
    4   cups tomato soup
    ⅓ to ¼ cup chili powder
    3   tablespoons all-purpose flour
    ½   cup water
    3   tablespoons salt
    1   teaspoon cumin seed
    2   teaspoons oregano

Brown beef, onions, and garlic in shortening in heavy frying pan. Put beans and tomato soup into a large kettle. Add beef and cook for 10 minutes. Make a paste of the chili powder, flour, and water. Blend paste into meat mixture and season with salt, cumin seed, and oregano. Cook over low heat for 45 minutes, stirring frequently to avoid scorching. Add more seasoning as needed. Yield: 25 servings.

Brunswick Stew for a Crowd

     3 large hens
     2 pounds calf liver
    12 large onions
     5 pounds potatoes
     2 gallons canned tomatoes
     2 gallons canned corn
     1 gallon chicken stock
     2 quarts milk
     2 pounds butter
     2 (8-ounce) bottles chili sauce
        Worcestershire sauce
        Tabasco sauce
        Salt and pepper

Boil hens for several hours; save stock. Remove meat from bones and cut into small pieces as for hash. Boil and grind liver. Cut onions fairly fine and dice potatoes; mix all together in a large pot (preferably iron). Add tomatoes, corn, chicken stock, milk, and butter. Cook slowly, and after stew begins to simmer, stir constantly for several hours (6 hours is the minimum) or until it thickens well. Add chili sauce. Season liberally with Worcestershire and Tabasco sauces. Salt and pepper to taste. Yield: 40 servings.

Brunswick Stew

     12 *pounds beef*
     10 *pounds of hog head*
      2 *pounds pig liver*
      4 *pounds chicken*
      6 *pounds tomatoes, chopped*
      3 *pounds onions, chopped*
     10 *pounds broth*
      2 *pounds potatoes, cooked and mashed*
      3 *pounds corn*
    3½ *bottles catsup*
      1 *tablespoon black pepper*
    1½ *tablespoons red pepper*
      6 *tablespoons salt*

Boil the beef and hog's head until the meat is ready to fall from the bones; cook the liver until tender, and discard the broth. Strain broth from beef and hog's head and set aside. Remove bones from beef and hog's head and chop or grind the meat. Cook finely chopped tomatoes and onions in broth for 1 hour. Add the mashed potatoes, corn, catsup, seasoning, and meats. Cook slowly for 1 hour, stirring constantly. Yield: 80 servings.

Hamburger Fiesta

     12 *pounds ground beef*
      3 *cups chopped onions*
     ¼ *cup salt*
      1 *tablespoon pepper*
         Shortening
      2 *pounds thinly sliced onions*
      2 *quarts catsup*
      2 *cups vinegar*
     ½ *cup sugar*
      4 *teaspoons dry mustard*

Combine ground beef, chopped onions, salt, and pepper. Shape into 48 patties.

Fry patties in a heavy skillet in a small amount of shortening. When brown on both sides, place in four 13- x 9- x 2-inch baking pans. Cover patties with sliced onions. Combine catsup, vinegar, sugar, and dry mustard to make a sauce, and pour over patties. Bake at 350° for 1½ hours. Spoon sauce over the patties twice while cooking. Yield: 48 servings.

Spaghetti for Twenty

    1½ *to 2 pounds ground beef*
      6 *medium onions, chopped*
     ¼ *pound butter or margarine*
      1 *bunch carrots, finely grated*
      2 *green peppers, finely grated*
      1 *bunch parsley*
      2 *or 3 cloves garlic, chopped*
      2 *cups canned tomatoes*
      2 *(10½-ounce) cans tomato soup*
      1 *(8-ounce) can sliced mushrooms*
    1¼ *pounds spaghetti*
      1 *pound sharp Cheddar cheese, shredded*

Brown meat and onion in melted butter or margarine. Add carrots, green peppers, parsley, and garlic. Add tomatoes and tomato soup, rinsing containers with a little water. Simmer for 40 minutes. Add mushrooms and simmer for 20 minutes longer.

Cook spaghetti in boiling, salted water for about 20 minutes, or until tender. Rinse in cold water. You will need three large casseroles. Put a layer of spaghetti, a layer of sauce, and a layer of shredded cheese into each; then repeat with a second layer. These casseroles may be arranged in the morning and set aside for baking. Bake at 350° for 30 minutes, or until mixture is thoroughly heated and cheese is brown. Yield: 20 servings.

Macaroni and Cheese

4 pounds macaroni
2 cups butter or margarine
2 cups all-purpose flour
¼ cup salt
2 teaspoons pepper
6 tablespoons dry mustard
1 quart nonfat dry milk solids
4 quarts water
6 pounds American cheese, shredded
3 cups buttered breadcrumbs

Cook macaroni in boiling salted water until tender (about 8 minutes). Drain and rinse. While macaroni is cooking, melt butter or margarine in large saucepan. Combine flour, salt, pepper, mustard, and dry milk solids. Add water and cook until thickened, stirring constantly. Add cheese and stir until well blended. Combine cheese sauce with macaroni and pour into three greased 13- x 9- x 2-inch baking pans. Sprinkle with buttered breadcrumbs and bake at 300° for 30 minutes. Yield: 48 servings.

Cheese-Meat Loaf

3 quarts soft breadcrumbs
6 pounds ground beef
1 cup chopped onions
2 tablespoons salt
1 tablespoon celery salt
1½ teaspoons pepper
1 pound shredded processed cheese
3 cups tomato juice
2½ cups eggs, beaten (10 to 12 eggs)

Combine soft breadcrumbs, beef, onions, salt, celery salt, pepper, and shredded cheese in a large mixing bowl. Add tomato juice and beaten eggs; mix well. Evenly divide mixture and form into four loaves. Bake at 350° for 1 hour. Yield: 48 servings.

Panned Cabbage

10 pounds coarsely shredded cabbage
½ pound margarine
1 tablespoon salt
½ teaspoon pepper
½ cup vinegar
6 hard-cooked eggs, sliced

Parboil cabbage in boiling water for 3 minutes. Drain. Melt margarine. Add cabbage and fry until lightly browned, stirring constantly. Add salt and pepper. When tender, sprinkle cabbage with vinegar, and garnish with sliced hard-cooked eggs. Yield: 48 servings.

Corn Pudding

2 quarts fresh or canned corn
10 eggs, beaten
4 teaspoons salt
2 tablespoons sugar
1 teaspoon onion juice
2¼ cups evaporated milk
2¼ cups boiling water
¼ cup melted butter or margarine

Combine ingredients. Pour into greased baking pans, set in pans half-filled with hot water, and bake at 350° for about 30 minutes, or until firm. Chopped green peppers or shredded Cheddar cheese may be added for variation. Yield: 25 servings.

Italian Spaghetti

- 1 quart chopped onions
- 6 cloves garlic, minced
- 1 pint salad oil
- 1 quart chopped green peppers
- 1½ cups canned sliced mushrooms
- 1 quart chopped parsley
- 1 gallon tomato paste
- 1 gallon water
- ¼ cup salt
- 2 teaspoons pepper
- 4 teaspoons celery seed
- 4 teaspoons ground nutmeg
- 4 teaspoons ground oregano
- 4 teaspoons basil
- 4 teaspoons thyme
- 6 bay leaves
- 6 pounds spaghetti
- ¼ cup salt
- 4 gallons water
  Shredded Parmesan cheese

Sauté the onions and garlic in the oil until golden brown. Add the remaining sauce ingredients and simmer for about 1 hour, or until desired thickness. Remove bay leaves and keep mixture hot.

Add the spaghetti to the boiling salted water. Cook until tender; drain and keep hot.

For each serving, place spaghetti on a plate, cover with sauce, and serve with shredded Parmesan cheese. Yield: 50 servings.

Baked Beans

- 4 cups beans, uncooked
- 1 pound salt pork
- 2 large onions, sliced
- ½ cup molasses
- 2 teaspoons salt
- ½ teaspoon pepper
- ½ teaspoon dry mustard

Soak beans overnight in cold water. In the morning drain, cover with fresh water, and simmer gently until beans are ready to burst their skins. Drain and reserve liquid. Place in baking dishes. Bury pork in beans, leaving the rind exposed. Add onions. Mix molasses, salt, pepper, and dry mustard together in a cup and fill with boiling water. Pour this over the beans. Heat reserved liquid to boiling and pour enough over beans to cover them. Bake at 300° for 8 hours. Keep pans covered until last hour of baking. Yield: 25 servings.

Harvard Beets

- 1 cup vinegar
- 12 cups cubed, cooked beets
- ½ cup melted butter or margarine
- ¾ cup all-purpose flour
- 1⅓ tablespoons salt
- ½ teaspoon pepper
- 5 cups hot water

Pour hot vinegar over beets; let stand for 10 minutes. Melt butter or margarine; blend in flour and seasonings. Remove from heat; slowly add hot water, and cook until thick and smooth, stirring constantly. Drain vinegar from beets and add to the sauce. Pour sauce over beets, reheat, and serve. Yield: 25 servings.

Scalloped Potatoes

6 pounds uncooked potatoes
3 cups sliced onions (optional)
1½ tablespoons salt
¾ to 1 cup melted shortening
1 cup all-purpose flour
1 tablespoon salt
1 teaspoon white pepper
2 quarts scalded milk
1½ cups buttered cracker or breadcrumbs

Peel and thinly slice the potatoes. Cover with sliced onions. Place potatoes in baking pan and sprinkle with salt. Melt shortening, add flour, and stir until smooth. Add salt and pepper. Add scalded milk gradually, stirring constantly, and cook over low heat until smooth and thick. Pour hot white sauce over potatoes. Bake at 350° for 1 hour, then cover with the buttered crumbs and continue baking for another hour. Yield: 25 servings.

Candied Sweet Potatoes

16 pounds cooked sweet potatoes
½ cup butter or margarine
2½ pounds brown sugar
1 tablespoon salt
½ cup pineapple or orange juice

Slice peeled, cooked sweet potatoes lengthwise into ¾-inch slices. Arrange in single layers in baking pans. Melt butter or margarine in large saucepan. Stir in brown sugar, salt, and fruit juice. Cook over low heat until sugar dissolves and syrup is formed, stirring constantly. Pour over potatoes. Bake at 350° for 45 minutes, basting occasionally. Serve hot. Yield: 50 servings.

Fruited Yams

15 pounds uncooked yams
3 lemons, thinly sliced
3 oranges, thinly sliced
3 cups crushed pineapple
2 cups flaked or shredded coconut
½ pound butter or margarine
1 pound brown sugar
1 quart dark corn syrup
2 cups pineapple juice
½ teaspoon salt

Cook yams until barely tender, peel, and cut into large pieces. Arrange half the yams in three 13- x 9- x 2-inch baking pans. Arrange lemon and orange slices and crushed pineapple over yams. Cover with remaining yams, and sprinkle coconut over the top. Mix butter or margarine, brown sugar, syrup, pineapple juice, and salt. Bring just to a boil and pour over yams. Bake at 350° for about 30 minutes, or until brown. Yield: 50 servings.

Chicken Salad

2 quarts cooked, chopped chicken
6 hard-cooked eggs
6 cups diced celery
1½ tablespoons salt
½ teaspoon pepper
1¼ cups salad dressing or mayonnaise
6 tablespoons chopped pickles

Cook chicken; remove from stock, and cool. Remove skin and bones; cut chicken meat into bite-size pieces. Combine all ingredients and toss together lightly. Keep refrigerated until ready to serve. Yield: 25 servings.

Tamale Pie

 10 pounds ground beef
  5 cups chopped onions
  5 cups chopped celery
2½ cups chopped green peppers
  6 quarts tomatoes
  4 tablespoons salt
  1 clove garlic, or 2 teaspoons garlic salt
2½ teaspoons chili powder
  3 tablespoons Worcestershire sauce

Brown the beef and onions in small amount of shortening. Add the celery, green peppers, tomatoes, and seasonings, and simmer for 15 minutes. Place the meat mixture in three or four greased 13- x 9- x 2-inch baking pans; cover with Cornbread Topping, spreading evenly. Bake at 375° for 30 minutes, or until cornbread is brown.

Cornbread Topping

  6 cups regular cornmeal
⅓ cup all-purpose flour
⅓ cup sugar
  1 tablespoon salt
  3 tablespoons baking powder
  6 eggs, beaten
  3 cups milk
½ cups melted shortening

Combine the dry ingredients. Add the beaten eggs and milk, stirring lightly until combined. Fold in the melted shortening. Yield: 48 to 50 servings.

Cheese Sandwich Spread

6¼ pounds American cheese, diced
  3 (14-ounce) cans evaporated milk
  1 tablespoon salt
  4 tablespoons dry mustard

Cook and stir all ingredients over boiling water, until cheese is melted and mixture is smooth. Remove from heat. Cover and cool until thick enough to spread. Yield: 100 servings.

Note: Grated onion and chopped pimiento may be added if desired.

Cole Slaw

 12 pounds cabbage
  3 cups vinegar
  3 cups sugar
  3 tablespoons salt
1½ teaspoons pepper
1½ teaspoons paprika
 12 green peppers, chopped
  3 cups salad dressing

Chop or shred the cabbage very fine. About ½ hour before serving, mix vinegar, sugar, salt, pepper, and paprika. Combine with cabbage and let set for 15 minutes, then drain. Cut green peppers into fine strips, or chop fine, and mix with cabbage. Add salad dressing just before serving, tossing lightly to mix with salad. Yield: 50 servings.

Peppery Cole Slaw

  2 cups mild vinegar
2⅔ tablespoons salt
  2 teaspoons pepper
1⅓ tablespoons dry mustard
½ cup sugar
½ cup butter or margarine
  8 eggs, beaten
  1 cup cream
 24 cups shredded cabbage

Heat vinegar, seasonings, and butter or margarine to boiling point. Slowly stir hot vinegar mixture into beaten eggs in top of double boiler. Cook over hot water until mixture thickens. Remove from heat. Beat in cream. While hot, pour over shredded cabbage. Serve cold. Yield: 50 servings.

Mixed Green Salad

- 2 quarts coarsely shredded cabbage
- 7 quarts coarsely shredded lettuce
- ½ cup diced green pepper
- 2 cups sliced celery
- 12 hard-cooked eggs, chopped
- 6 tomatoes, cut in small wedges
- 2½ cups French dressing

Combine cabbage, lettuce, green pepper, and celery. Mix thoroughly. Just before serving add eggs, tomato wedges, and French dressing. Toss. Yield: 30 servings.

Perfection Salad

- 10 envelopes unflavored gelatin
- 2½ cups cold water
- 2½ cups mild vinegar
- 10 tablespoons freshly squeezed lemon juice
- 10 cups boiling water
- 2½ cups sugar
- 1⅔ tablespoons salt
- 5 cups shredded cabbage
- 5 cups diced celery
- 10 pimientos, chopped fine
- 30 small sweet pickles, chopped

Soften gelatin in cold water. Add vinegar, lemon juice, boiling water, sugar, and salt. Stir until dissolved. Set in cool place. When the mixture begins to thicken, add the remaining ingredients.

Pour into three 13- x 9- x 2-inch pans which have been lightly greased. Chill until firm. Yield: 50 servings.

Potato Salad

- 15 pounds raw potatoes
- 2 cups French dressing
- 2 cups chopped celery
- 3 cups salad dressing
- ½ cup chopped parsley
- 1 cup chopped onions (or less)
- 12 hard-cooked eggs, diced
  Salt and pepper to taste

Wash the potatoes and cook in the jackets until tender. Peel. Dice in ½-inch cubes. Pour French dressing over warm potatoes and let stand for several hours. Combine chopped celery, salad dressing, parsley, onions, and diced hard-cooked eggs. Add salt and pepper to taste. Combine with potatoes and mix lightly. Chill before serving. Yield: 50 servings.

Waldorf Salad

- 20 cups diced apples
- 10 cups diced celery
  Freshly squeezed lemon juice
- 5 cups broken walnut meats
- 2 cups salad dressing or mayonnaise
- ½ cup whipping cream
  Lettuce

Combine apples and celery; sprinkle with lemon juice to keep them from darkening. Just before serving, add nuts and mix with salad dressing or mayonnaise, thinned with the whipped cream. Serve on crisp lettuce. Yield: 50 servings.

Tuna Fish or Salmon Salad

8 tablespoons unflavored gelatin
2 cups cold water
6 cups salad dressing or mayonnaise
8 cups tuna or salmon
4 cups chopped celery
4 green peppers, chopped
½ cup chopped olives
4 teaspoons salt
2 teaspoons paprika
½ cup mild vinegar

Soften gelatin in cold water; then dissolve over boiling water. Add remaining ingredients and mix well. Put salad in loafpan which has been rinsed in cold water. Chill well before serving. Yield: 50 servings.

Chicken Salad Sandwich Filling

14 pounds ground, cooked chicken
2 cups sweet pickle relish, well drained
2 tablespoons salt
2 teaspoons pepper
4 (14-ounce) cans evaporated milk

Mix all ingredients. Keep thoroughly chilled and in the refrigerator until ready to serve. Spread on buttered slices of bread. Yield: 100 servings.

Egg Salad Sandwich Filling

1 quart salad dressing or mayonnaise
2 cups evaporated milk
2½ tablespoons salt
¼ cup dry mustard
8 dozen hard-cooked eggs, chopped
1½ pounds chopped, stuffed olives or sweet pickles

Mix salad dressing or mayonnaise, milk, salt, and mustard. Add chopped eggs and olives. Mix thoroughly. Keep refrigerated until ready to make sandwiches. Yield: 100 servings.

James K. Polk Christmas Fruitcake

½ pound blanched, chopped almonds
   Juice of 3 large oranges
1 pound butter
2 cups sugar
12 eggs
1 pound (4 cups) all-purpose flour
1 teaspoon ground cloves
1 tablespoon ground cinnamon
1 teaspoon ground allspice
1 teaspoon ground mace
1 teaspoon ground nutmeg
3 pounds seeded raisins
1 pound citron
1 pound currants
1 pound candied pineapple
2 pounds dates
½ pound pecans
2 cups fruit juice

Put blanched, chopped almonds into orange juice. Cream the butter and sugar, then add eggs and beat well. Brown flour slightly; combine with other dry ingredients and add to creamed mixture. Mix the batter thoroughly with hands, adding the fruit, dredged with flour, a little of each kind at a time. When very stiff, add orange juice and almonds. Later on, gradually add the fruit juice.

Cut brown wrapping paper (double) to fit bottom of tubepans, then cut two strips the width of sides to fit around inside of pan. Grease the pan and paper well and spoon in batter. The batter should be 2 inches from rim to allow for rising. Set a small pan of water in oven to one side to retain moisture. Bake at 150° for 6 hours. Test with straws and when straw comes out clean, take from oven immediately. Leave cake in pan to cool. Yield: 100 servings.

Fruit Cobbler

4½ quarts fruit (cherries, peaches, etc.)
6 cups sugar
1 cup cornstarch
3 tablespoons freshly squeezed lemon juice
4 quarts all-purpose flour
6 tablespoons baking powder
2 tablespoons salt
2½ cups shortening
6 to 7 cups milk

Drain the fruit and heat the juice to boiling. Mix the sugar and cornstarch and sift into the boiling juice. Cook until thickened. Add fruit and lemon juice.

Make biscuit dough. Sift flour, baking powder, and salt together. Cut in shortening, add enough liquid to make a soft, not sticky dough. Knead on a lightly floured board. Roll dough to ⅓-inch thickness, to make a crust.

Fill baking pans half full of fruit mixture. Cover with crust, and perforate to allow the steam to escape. Brush the crust with milk. Bake at 400° until crust is brown (about 20 minutes). Cut into squares and serve with whipped cream. Yield: 50 servings.

Gingerbread

4 cups shortening
1 cup sugar
8 eggs, well beaten
8 cups dark molasses
18 cups all-purpose flour
2⅔ tablespoons soda
1⅓ tablespoons salt
2⅔ tablespoons ground ginger
2⅔ tablespoons ground cinnamon
8 cups boiling water

Cream shortening and sugar thoroughly. Add well beaten eggs and molasses. Sift dry ingredients together and add alternately with boiling water; mix well. Pour into four 13- x 9- x 2-inch baking pans. Bake at 325° degrees for 45 minutes. Yield: 50 servings.

Hot Fudge Pudding

6 cups all-purpose flour
4½ cups sugar
¼ cup baking powder
1½ teaspoons salt
¾ cup cocoa
3 cups milk
¾ cup melted shortening
6 cups chopped walnuts
6 cups firmly packed brown sugar
1½ cups cocoa
10½ cups hot water

Sift dry ingredients into bowl. Stir in milk and melted shortening and mix until smooth. Stir in walnuts. Spread batter in two well greased 13- x 9- x 2-inch pans. Mix brown sugar and 1½ cups cocoa and sprinkle over batter in pans. Pour hot water over all. Bake at 350° for 45 minutes. Yield: 50 servings.

Golden Fruit Punch

4¼ cups sugar
1 quart water
3 cups freshly squeezed lemon juice
3 cups orange juice
2½ cups pineapple juice
2 cups water
1 quart ginger ale

Boil the sugar and quart of water together to dissolve sugar. Chill. Add cold fruit juices and remaining water. Chill. Just before serving, stir in ginger ale and add ice. Yield: 25 servings.

Hot Chocolate

3 cups cocoa
6 cups boiling water
2 gallons milk
1½ cups sugar
1 teaspoon salt

Cook cocoa and water in the top of double boiler over direct heat until smooth. Place over boiling water, add milk, sugar, and salt. Cook until smooth. Beat with rotary beater just before serving. Yield: 50 servings.

Fruit Punch

8 cups sugar
1 quart water
½ cup mint leaves (optional)
1 quart crushed pineapple
1 quart freshly squeezed lemon juice
1 quart orange juice
1 quart grape juice
2 quarts strong tea
2 quarts water

Make a syrup of the sugar and a quart of water. While syrup is cooling, add mint leaves. Let set until cooled; strain out mint leaves. Combine syrup and fruit juices, tea, and remaining water. Serve ice cold. Yield: 50 servings.

Lemonade

6 cups freshly squeezed lemon juice (about 36 lemons)
6½ cups sugar
2¾ gallons water
Chopped ice or ice cubes

Mix lemon juice and sugar. Add water, and stir until sugar is dissolved. Add ice. Yield: 50 servings.

Raspberry Shrub

3 quarts raspberries
3 cups sugar
4 cups water
2 cups freshly squeezed lemon juice
1 gallon water

Cook first three ingredients for about 10 minutes, or until juice is extracted. Strain through a sieve. Cool. Add lemon juice, remaining water, and chipped ice. Yield: 50 servings.

Food Preservation

Women were preserving food long before cooking became an art. The Bible advises: ". . . Eat ye of the old fruit until the ninth year; until her fruits come in ye shall eat of the old store."

Jellies, jams, preserves, and marmalades offer varied ways of retaining both the color and texture of favorite fruits. Visualize a shelf lined with jars of delicate homemade jellies; thick, spreadable jams; textured preserves and conserves and marmalades, holding in gentle suspension small pieces of the fruits which give them flavor.

Jars of pickles and relishes inevitably will be found among the fruits of a Southern summer. Methods of pickle and relish preservation have changed. Old instructions called for the spreading of grape or cherry leaves over pickles before sealing to ensure green coloring, as well as the addition of a few nasturtium leaves to prevent scum formation.

Today's homemaker likely has poignant memories of her mother's jellies enjoyed with the breakfasts of childhood as she attempts to duplicate the taste for her own family. However, in one area of food preservation, freezing, she has a decided advantage. In today's hurried pace, this is an especially appealing way to preserve fruits and vegetables quickly with maximum color, flavor, and nutritive value.

Every fruit and vegetable suitable for home preservation — from oranges to muscadines to okra for pickling — is easily obtainable in the South. Commercially manufactured pectin can simplify the process. And at least one unbreakable rule remains: put up an ample supply because hungry families won't be satisfied with just admiring the jars on the shelf.

Kentucky Apple Butter

      7 pounds tart apples
      4 quarts cider
 2½ cups sugar
      1 teaspoon ground allspice
 1½ tablespoons ground cinnamon
      1 teaspoon ground cloves

Wash and slice 20 to 21 medium apples.
Add cider and cook until the apples are
very tender. Press fruit through a sieve
to remove skins and seed. Add sugar and
spices to the pulp and cook the mixture
until thick and clear, stirring frequently
to prevent burning. When cold, it
should be as thick as good apple sauce.
Determine the thickness at frequent
intervals. Pour into hot, sterilized jars
and seal.

Guava Butter

Wash ripe guavas. Remove blossom and
stem ends with paring knife. If skin is
rough and blemished, peel. If not, slice
unpeeled into sieve to remove seed.
Pulp left from jelly-making may
be used.

Measure pulp. Measure sugar, allowing
½ to ¾ cup sugar to each cup of pulp,
according to sweetness desired, and set
aside. Place pulp in a heavy pan and
cook quickly; stir until it begins to
thicken. Add sugar and continue cooking until very thick. After sugar is added,
stir constantly to prevent scorching.

Butter made from pulp left from jelly
drip gives a darker colored product
than that made from fresh fruit.

Grape Butter

      5 pounds grape pulp and ground hulls
 2½ pounds sugar
 2½ teaspoons ground cinnamon
      2 teaspoons ground mace
      2 drops clove oil

Wash and crush grapes. Separate hulls
and pulp. Heat pulp with juice and put
through a colander to remove seeds;
grind hulls in a food chopper using fine
blade. Combine deseeded pulp, juice,
and hulls. Cook until hulls are tender.
Add sugar and spices. Cook very slowly,
stirring repeatedly, until the mixture is
very thick and has a jellylike consistency. Pack in hot, sterilized jars and seal.

Peach Chutney

      4 pieces ginger root
      1 tablespoon pickling spice
 1½ cups cider vinegar
      2 cups sugar
      1 (20-ounce) can peaches, drained and
          cut into pieces
      1 cup seedless raisins
      1 hard pear, peeled, sliced, and chopped
   12 pitted dates
      1 hot red pepper, broken
      1 teaspoon turmeric
      1 clove garlic, minced
   ¼ teaspoon salt
   ½ pound small onions, chopped

Pound the ginger root, combine it with
the pickling spice, and tie loosely in a
cheesecloth bag. Put it into a large kettle with the vinegar and sugar and bring
to a boil. Drain the peaches. Boil the
peach liquid until there is only ½ cup
remaining. Add the fruits, red pepper,

turmeric, garlic, and salt to the vinegar mixture. Simmer, without a cover, for about 1½ hours, stirring occasionally. Add the onions after the first hour of cooking. When it is thick, remove the spice bag. Pour into hot, sterilized jars and seal.

Carrot Chutney

    4 medium carrots
    8 apples
    1 lemon
    1 onion
    2 cups sugar or honey
    2 teaspoons ground cloves
    1 teaspoon ground ginger
    2 cups vinegar
    ½ cup water

Put the carrots, apples, lemon, and onion through the food chopper. Add other ingredients and cook over low heat until thick, for about 1 hour and 30 minutes. Seal in hot, sterilized jars.

Orange Chutney

    6 thin-skinned oranges
    6 cups water
    3 cups sugar
    2 cups water
    ¾ cup vinegar
    1 (1-pound) can whole cranberry sauce
    2 tablespoons molasses
    ½ cup raisins
    1 tablespoon salt
 1½ teaspoons Tabasco sauce
    1 tablespoon curry powder
    ½ teaspoon whole cloves
    3 (3-inch) sticks cinnamon
    3 pieces whole ginger

Put whole oranges in large saucepan; add 1½ quarts water. Bring to a boil; boil 20 minutes. Drain and cut oranges into eighths. Combine sugar, 2 cups water, and vinegar. Place over low heat and stir until sugar is dissolved. Stir in remaining ingredients. Bring to a boil. Add orange wedges and simmer about 20 minutes. Ladle into hot, sterilized jars and seal.

Pineapple Chutney

    4 cups crushed pineapple
    1 cup cider vinegar
    1 cup firmly packed brown sugar
    2 cups seedless raisins
    1 tablespoon salt
    4 tablespoons chopped candied ginger
    4 cloves garlic, finely chopped
    ¼ teaspoon cayenne pepper
    ¼ teaspoon ground cloves
    ¼ teaspoon ground cinnamon
    ⅓ cup chopped almonds

Cook the pineapple and pineapple syrup, vinegar, sugar, raisins, salt, ginger, the finely chopped garlic, cayenne pepper, cloves, and cinnamon over low heat for about 50 minutes or until thick. Stir frequently and add the almonds just before pouring into hot, sterilized jars.

Assorted Conserves

Use cherry, strawberry, cranberry, Damson plum, grape, peach, apricot, orange, lemon, or lime marmalade. Add ½ cup chopped pecans to 2 cups marmalade and mix well. Serve with any hot, buttered bread.

Pear Conserve

1 orange
2 lemons
5 cups peeled, chopped pears
2 cups raisins
5 cups sugar

Run the orange and lemons through the food grinder, using the coarse knife. Combine ground fruit with chopped pears, raisins, and sugar. Cook slowly until thick. Pour into hot, sterilized jars and seal.

Cranberry Conserve

2 cups cranberry pulp
2 cups chopped tart apples
2 cups quince pulp
2 oranges, grated rind and juice
4 cups sugar
¾ cup nuts

Combine cranberries, chopped apples, quince pulp, oranges, and sugar. Cook rapidly until mixture is thick. Add nuts, and while hot pour into hot, sterilized jars and seal.

Note: Raisins may be used instead of quince pulp.

1-2-3-Conserve

1 pound ripe tomatoes
2 pounds peeled, sliced peaches
3 pounds sugar

Peel the tomatoes and cut fine, removing the hard core at the stem end. Put into a colander; allow to drain, but do not squeeze out any juice. Peel and slice the peaches into narrow strips. Add the sugar. Add the drained tomato pulp to the peaches and sugar. Stir well for 2 to

3 minutes before cooking. Boil the conserve slowly but steadily for 30 minutes. Cool for 3 minutes before putting into hot, sterilized jars.

Note: For a wonderful flavor, add a half cup of chopped crystallized ginger just before sealing.

Plum Conserve

3 pounds Damson plums (after cutting)
1 orange
1 lemon
3 cups sugar
1 pound seedless raisins
1 cup chopped pecans

Slice plums, orange, and lemon; add sugar and raisins, and cook until thick and transparent. Put nuts into mixture 5 minutes before removing from the heat. Pack hot into sterilized jars and seal immediately. Process pint jars for 30 minutes in a hot water bath.

Pear Honey

1 quart ground pears
1 (20-ounce) can crushed pineapple
6 cups sugar

Peel and grind pears. Cook until tender. Add other ingredients and cook until mixture is thick. Pour into hot, sterilized jars and seal.

Ginger Pear Honey

10 pounds pears, peeled and quartered
7½ pounds sugar
4 ounces ginger root or 2 tablespoons ground ginger
3 lemons, grated rind and juice

Wash and prepare pears. Grind through the meat chopper. Place ingredients in kettle and cook until amber-yellow and as thick as desired. Pack into hot, sterilized jars and seal.

Peach Honey

4 *cups sliced, ripe peaches*
4 *cups sugar*
   Juice of 1 lemon

Peel and slice ripe peaches, removing bad spots. Put into large, heavy pan with sugar and cook over medium heat until mixture reaches a good boil, stirring constantly. Add the lemon juice. Continue cooking until thick; stirring constantly. Pour into hot, sterilized jars and seal.

Paradise Pear Jam

4½ *cups prepared fruit (1 orange, 1 lemon, about 2 pounds ripe pears, ¼ cup chopped maraschino cherries, ½ cup finely chopped citron, and one 8½-ounce can crushed pineapple)*
  5 *cups sugar*
  1 *(2½-ounce) package powdered pectin*

First, prepare the fruit. Remove rinds from orange and lemon in quarters; discard about half the white part of rinds. Slice rinds, chop orange and lemon, and discard seeds. Peel, core, and grind about 2 pounds fully ripe pears. Combine all the fruits, including cherries, citron, and pineapple. Measure 4½ cups fruit into a large saucepan.

Then make the jam. Measure sugar; set aside. Stir pectin into fruit. Place over high heat; stir until mixture comes to a hard boil. Stir in sugar at once. Bring to a full rolling boil and boil hard for 1 minute, stirring constantly. Remove from heat and skim. Stir and skim alternately for 5 minutes to cool slightly and prevent floating fruit. Ladle quickly into glasses; cover at once with ⅛ inch of hot paraffin.

Blackberry Jam

  6 *cups crushed blackberries*
  1 *(2½-ounce) package powdered pectin*
8½ *cups sugar*

Sort and wash berries. Crush, and if very seedy, put through a sieve or food mill. Measure crushed berries into a large kettle. Add pectin and stir well. Place on high heat and bring quickly to a boil, stirring constantly. Add the sugar, continue stirring, and heat to a full bubbling boil. Boil hard for 1 minute, stirring constantly.

Remove from heat; skim and stir alternately for 5 minutes. Ladle the jam into hot, sterilized containers and seal immediately.

Mayhaw Jam

Wash and stem mayhaws. Add just enough water to prevent sticking. Cook until soft. Press through sieve. Measure pulp. Then add ¾ to 1 cup sugar for each cup fruit. Boil to the jellying point. Pour into hot, sterilized jars and seal at once.

Strawberry Jam

4½ *cups prepared strawberries*
 1 *(2½-ounce) package powdered pectin*
 7 *cups sugar*

To prepare the fruit, crush completely, one layer at a time, about 2 quarts fully ripe strawberries. Then measure 4½ cups into a very large saucepan.

To make the jam, first measure sugar and set aside. Add pectin to prepared strawberries, and mix well. Place over high heat, and stir until mixture comes to a hard boil. Stir in the sugar at once. Bring to a full rolling boil and boil hard for 1 minute, stirring constantly. Remove from heat, and skim foam off with a metal spoon. Then stir and skim alternately for 5 minutes to cool slightly, and to prevent floating fruit. Ladle quickly into hot, sterilized glasses or jars. Seal at once. Store in a cool place.

Ripe Huckleberry Jam

4½ *cups prepared huckleberries*
    Grated rind of ½ lemon
    Juice of 1 lemon
 7 *cups sugar*
 1 *(6-ounce) bottle pectin*

To prepare fruit, crush about 1½ quarts fully ripe berries. Add grated lemon rind and juice. Then measure sugar and prepared fruit into a large kettle and mix well. Bring to a full, rolling boil over a very high heat. Stir constantly before and while boiling hard for 1 minute. Remove from heat and stir in pectin. Stir and skim alternately for exactly 5

minutes to cool slightly. This prevents floating fruit. Pour quickly into hot, sterilized jars and seal at once.

Peach Jam

 1 *inch fresh ginger root*
 ½ *teaspoon ground allspice*
 2 *teaspoons stick cinnamon, broken into small pieces*
 1 *teaspoon whole cloves*
 1 *cracked peach seed*
 2 *pounds peaches*
 ½ *cup peach juice*
 2 *cups sugar*

Tie spices and peach seed in cheesecloth bag; cook all materials together until a temperature of 222° is reached on jelly thermometer. Remove spice bag. Pack jam into hot, sterilized jars and seal.

Scuppernong or Muscadine Jam

Wash scuppernongs or muscadines, stem, and press the pulp from skins. Chop skins, and boil for 20 minutes in just enough water to prevent sticking. Cook pulp until soft, then press through a colander to remove seed. Add skins to pulp. Measure. Add ¾ cup sugar for each cup scuppernongs. Boil to the jelling point. Pour into hot, sterilized containers and seal at once.

Jellymaking Hints

When making jelly, it is better to prepare small amounts at one cooking. Do not double recipe.

The biggest problem when making jelly without added pectin is to know when the jelly is done.

A jelly thermometer is the most accurate way of testing jelly. To do this, test your thermometer in boiling water to see what temperature is recorded. Jelly should be cooked to 8° above the boiling point of water (220°). For an accurate thermometer reading, have the thermometer in a vertical position and read it at eye level. Bulb of the thermometer should be completely covered with the jelly mixture after it comes to a full rolling boil.

The spoon or sheet test may also be used, although it is not as accurate as the thermometer test. Dip a cold metal spoon in the boiling jelly mixture. Then raise it at least a foot above the kettle, out of the steam, and turn the spoon so the syrup runs off the side. If the syrup forms two drops that flow together and fall off the spoon as one sheet, the jelly should be done.

Fresh Strawberry Jelly

2½ quarts fresh strawberries
  1 (2½-ounce) package powdered pectin
¼ teaspoon salt
  5 cups sugar

Crush strawberries; put through a jelly bag and squeeze out juice. There should be 3½ cups of juice. If there is a shortage of juice, add a little water to the pulp, and squeeze out again. Mix pectin with the juice and bring to a rapid boil. Add salt and sugar and boil hard for 1 minute, stirring constantly. Remove from heat. Skim off foam. Pour at once into hot, sterilized jars, leaving ½ inch space at top of each. Seal immediately.

Quince Jelly

3¾ cups quince juice (takes about 1½ pounds quinces and 7 cups water)
¼ cup freshly squeezed lemon juice
  3 cups sugar

Select about one-fourth underripe and three-fourths fully ripe quinces. Sort, wash, and remove stems and blossom ends; do not pare or core. Slice quinces very thin or cut into small pieces. Add water, cover, and bring to a boil over high heat. Reduce heat and simmer for 25 minutes. Extract juice.

Measure juice into large kettle. Add lemon juice and sugar, and stir well. Boil over high heat until jelly mixture sheets from a spoon. Remove from heat; skim off foam quickly. Pour jelly immediately into hot, sterilized containers and seal.

Berry Jelly

4 cups berry juice
3 cups sugar

Carefully wash and drain berries. Select half of the berries that are just red and the other half fully ripe. Place in large kettle and crush. Bring to a boil and boil slowly for 5 to 15 minutes, stirring occasionally. Let stand for 10 minutes. Drain. Measure juice into a large kettle and place on heat. Bring juice to a boil and add sugar. Stir only until sugar is dissolved. Cook very rapidly until jelly stage is reached. Strain through a layer of damp cheesecloth and pour immediately into hot, sterilized jelly glasses or jars to 1/4 inch of the top. Seal jars immediately. Cover jelly glasses with a thin cloth and allow to remain covered overnight. Then remove cloth and cover jelly with melted paraffin; seal; and store in a cool, dry place.

Ripe Plum Jelly

4 cups plum juice
7 1/2 cups sugar
1/2 (6-ounce) bottle liquid pectin

Crush thoroughly 4 pounds fully ripe plums. Do not peel or pit. Add 1 cup water. Bring to a boil, cover, and simmer for 10 minutes. Place in bag; squeeze out juice. (Sour, clingstone plums make best jelly. If sweet plums are used, substitute 1/2 cup strained lemon juice for 1/2 cup plum juice specified.)

Measure sugar and juice into large saucepan and mix. Bring to a rapid boil and add pectin, stirring constantly.

Bring to a full rolling boil and boil hard for 1/2 minute. Remove from heat, skim, pour quickly into hot, sterilized jars and seal.

Grape Jelly

4 cups grape juice
3 cups sugar

Push pulp from grape skins and drop both into a large preserving kettle. Add enough water to come up to the fruit. Simmer until all juice flows freely. Strain through a colander, then strain through a jelly bag. Place the juice in jars and let stand in refrigerator from 24 to 48 hours. Strain again to remove crystals which may be seen clinging to sides of jar. Measure.

Pour 4 cups juice into large kettle. Boil rapidly for 5 minutes. Add sugar, and boil until it reaches the jelly stage. Pour into hot, sterilized jars and seal.

Fresh Mint Jelly

1 cup mint leaves and stems, packed
1/2 cup apple vinegar
1 cup water
3 1/2 cups sugar
Green coloring
1/2 (6-ounce) bottle liquid pectin

Wash mint. Do not remove leaves from stems. Measure into 3-quart saucepan and press with wooden potato masher or a glass. Add vinegar, water, and sugar. Bring to a boil, and add coloring to give desired shade. Add pectin, stirring constantly. Then bring to a rolling boil, and boil hard for ½ minute. Remove from heat and skim. To remove all traces of mint leaves, pour jelly through a fine sieve into hot, sterilized containers and seal.

Tangerine Marmalade

3 pounds tangerines
  Sugar
3 large lemons

Quarter tangerines, but do not remove peel. Slice very thin, removing all seeds. Add finely shredded or sliced lemons. Grind fruit if you prefer. Measure fruit and add five times as much water. Boil until quantity is reduced nearly one-half, from 1 to 1¼ hours. For light amber marmalade, cook 2 or 3 cups at a time. Add ¾ cup sugar to each cup of boiling fruit and continue boiling until it gives the jelly test. It will take 10 to 20 minutes. Alternately skim and stir. Pour into hot, sterilized jars and seal.

Orange Marmalade

5 medium oranges
  Water
1 lemon
  Sugar

Wash and slice oranges and lemon and cut into shreds. To every pound of fruit add 3 pints cold water. Let stand for 24 hours. Boil until peel is tender, about 45 minutes to 1 hour, stirring frequently. Let stand for another 24 hours.

Weigh, and for every pound of cooked fruit allow 1 pound sugar and the juice of 1 lemon. Place fruit on heat, and as soon as it comes to a boil, add sugar. Cook to 220° or to the jelly stage. Remove from heat and allow to cool to 180°, stirring occasionally so shreds of peel do not settle to bottom. Pour into hot, sterilized jars and seal.

Citrus Marmalade

  Peel of ½ grapefruit
  Peel of 1 orange
  Peel of 1 lemon
4 cups cold water
2 cups boiling water
3 cups sugar
1 cup grapefruit juice
1¾ cups orange juice
⅓ cup freshly squeezed lemon juice

Wash the fruit and extract juice. Remove membrane from inside the peel. Cut peel into very thin strips. Add cold water to the peel and simmer slowly in a covered pan until tender, for about 30 minutes. Drain off and discard the liquid; add boiling water to the peel. Add the sugar and boil rapidly to 220°, about 20 minutes. Add the fruit juices and cook again to the same temperature, about 25 minutes, stirring frequently.

Remove from heat; skim and stir alternately for 5 minutes. Ladle marmalade into hot, sterilized jars and seal at once.

Peach Marmalade

    3 pounds peaches
    2 oranges
    4 tablespoons freshly squeezed
       lemon juice
3 ½ cups sugar

Peel, stone, and cut peaches into ¼-inch slices. Grate rind from the oranges, discard all white membrane, and slice the fruit thin. Combine peaches, orange rind and pulp, lemon juice, and sugar. Bring to a boil, and cook rapidly for about 30 minutes, or until the syrup is thick and the fruit is transparent, stirring frequently. Pour into hot, sterilized jars and seal at once.

Grandmother's Mincemeat

    4 pounds lean boiled beef
1 ½ pounds suet
    9 pounds diced tart apples
    3 pounds raisins
    2 pounds currants
  ½ pound chopped or ground citron
  10 cups sugar
    3 teaspoons ground cloves
  10 teaspoons ground cinnamon
    5 teaspoons ground mace
    1 teaspoon black pepper
    6 tablespoons salt
    4 cups cider and vinegar mixed
    2 cups molasses
       Grated rind and juice of 2 lemons

Chop boiled beef and suet or run through food chopper. Combine all ingredients and cook slowly for 2 hours, stirring frequently. Seal in hot, sterilized jars.

Pear Mincemeat

    4 quarts ground pears
    2 (1-pound) boxes seedless raisins
    4 pounds sugar
    2 lemons
1 ½ teaspoons salt
    3 teaspoons ground cinnamon
    1 teaspoon ground allspice
    1 teaspoon ground cloves

Mix all ingredients. Cook in large kettle until tender. Pour into hot, sterilized jars and seal.

Berry Preserves

    2 pounds berries
    5 cups sugar
    4 tablespoons freshly squeezed lemon juice

Combine berries and sugar and let set for about 4 hours. Bring to a simmering point, and add lemon juice. Boil rapidly for about 12 minutes, or until berries are clear and syrup is thick. Cover, and let stand until cold. Put into jars, seal, and process in boiling water bath for 15 minutes. Pour into hot, sterilized jars and seal.

Mississippi Fig Preserves

    6 pounds peeled figs
       Lime water
  12 cups sugar
    8 cups water
    3 lemons, sliced

Select firm, ripe figs. Peel. Drop into lime water (2 tablespoons lime from hardware store to 1 gallon of water) and let stand for 5 to 10 minutes. This will toughen the figs so they will not cook to pieces. Wash figs thoroughly in three changes of water after taking out of lime water.

Make a syrup of 12 cups sugar and 8 cups water, and when it is boiling hard, drop figs into syrup. Cook with top on container until the figs are clear. Set aside for figs to plump. When cold, pack into hot, sterilized jars and seal.

Old-Fashioned Peach Preserves

Wash, scald, pit, peel, and cut firm, ripe peaches. Weigh. Mix equal amounts of sugar with prepared fruit; let stand overnight in a cool place and then cook (without adding water) until the fruit is tender and syrup is thick. Pour into hot, sterilized jars and seal.

Variations

Add 2 cracked peach seed, or 2 drops almond extract, or ¼ teaspoon vanilla extract for variety.

Pear Preserves

   1 *pound prepared pears*
 ¾ *pound sugar*
 ½ *lemon, thinly sliced*

Select pears that are of good flavor and hold shape. Wash, pare, and cut fruit into uniform pieces, either quarters or eighths; then core. Combine the sliced pears and sugar in alternate layers in a glass or enamel container and let stand

for 8 to 10 hours, or overnight, before cooking. Boil the lemon for 5 minutes in only enough water to cover. Add lemon, with remaining water, to the pear and sugar mixture. Boil rapidly and stir constantly until the fruit is clear and of rich amber color. Pour into hot, sterilized jars and seal.

Damson Plum Preserves

   6 *cups prepared Damson plums, or about*
      3 pounds ripe plums
 5½ *cups sugar*
   1 *cup water*

Sort and wash plums; remove pits. Dissolve sugar in the water and bring to boiling point. Add plums and boil, stirring gently, to 220° or until the fruit is transparent and syrup is thick. Remove preserves from heat and spoon at once into hot, sterilized jars, filling to the top. Seal at once.

Apple and Quince Preserves

 6 *tart apples*
 6 *quinces*
    Sugar

Pare and core fruits, and chop into small pieces before pouring into preserving kettle. Add just enough water to keep fruit from burning. Cover fruit, bring to a boil, and then simmer until fruit is nearly tender. Remove lid, add equal weight of sugar, stir mixture well, and simmer until fruit is thick. Pour into hot, sterilized jars and seal.

Muscadine Grape Preserves

1 *pound seeded muscadine grapes*
1 *pound sugar*

Cook deseeded grapes slowly until hulls are tender, about 15 minutes, adding water if necessary. Add sugar to simmering pulp and hulls. Cook until the jelly stage is reached. It may be necessary to add pectin if grapes are all very ripe. Follow directions on package if pectin is used. Pack into hot, sterilized jars and seal.

Quince Preserves

Allow the fruit to ripen until it is yellow, but still firm. Wash, peel, and quarter; then core. For each pound of fruit, use 1 quart water and 1¾ cups sugar. Dissolve half the sugar in water and bring to a boil. Add fruit, and boil slowly for 1 hour. Let stand overnight; then add remaining sugar and cook slowly until fruit is a clear, reddish color and the syrup passes the jelly test. Pour into hot, sterilized jars and seal.

Cherry-Flecked Peach Preserves

5 *pounds peaches*
3 *pounds sugar*
   Juice of 2 lemons
½ *teaspoon salt*
1 *(6-ounce) bottle maraschino cherries*

Cut peaches into small pieces. If peaches are soft, cut pieces a little larger, as you will want small chunks of peaches in the preserves when done. Cook peaches with sugar, lemon juice, and salt until clear and fruit has cooked down thick.

Drain and squeeze juice from center of each cherry. Cut in half and then cut again into small wedges like tiny slices of watermelon. Drain on paper towels.

Add the prepared cherries to the preserves and cook about 5 minutes longer to allow them to cook into the preserves. Pour into hot, sterilized jars and seal.

Favorite Strawberry Preserves

6 *cups strawberries*
4 *cups sugar*

Wash and sort berries into two sizes, large and medium. Remove overripe berries to use for jam. Place layers of berries and sugar alternately in a heavy kettle and heat slowly, stirring gently until sugar dissolves. Cook rapidly for 15 to 20 mintues or until the syrup sheets from a spoon. Remove and skim. Cool; when cool and before the jelly stage is reached, pack the fruit into hot, sterilized jars. Clean rims of jars, and seal.

Pumpkin Preserves

5 *pounds pumpkin*
8 *cups sugar*
3 *lemons, sliced thin*
1 *orange, sliced thin*
   Salt

Remove peel and cut raw pumpkin into slices ¼ inch thick and about 1 inch long. Place in large crock or enamel kettle. Add sugar and let stand overnight. Drain pumpkin from liquid and boil liquid to the spin-a-thread stage. Add sliced pumpkin, lemons, and orange, and a few grains of salt. Cook until thick and clear. Pour into hot, sterilized jars and seal.

Green Tomato Preserves

Slice small green tomatoes and sprinkle with salt. Put into a stone or glass container. Let stand overnight. The next day, drain off salty water and wash the tomatoes in clear water. To every pound of fruit, add ¾ pound of sugar. Cook until syrup is thick. Pour into hot, sterilized jars and seal at once.

Yellow Tomato Preserves

8 cups small yellow tomatoes

3 cups sugar

1 lemon

1 teaspoon salt

4 tablespoons ginger root or thinly sliced candied ginger

Wash and dry tomatoes. Cut a thin slice from blossom end and press out seed. Combine tomatoes with sugar and salt and simmer until sugar is dissolved. Then boil for about 40 minutes. Add thinly sliced lemon and minced ginger. Boil for about 10 minutes. Pour into hot, sterilized jars and seal at once.

Tomato Preserves

8 cups tomatoes

4 cups sugar

1½ cups water

1 (2-inch) stick cinnamon

1 lemon, sliced thin

2 pieces ginger root

Wash the tomatoes and scald in hot water for 1 minute. Dip into cold water and remove skins. Make a syrup of the sugar and water. Add the cinnamon, lemon, and ginger, and simmer for 20 minutes. Add tomatoes, a few at a time, and boil slowly until the syrup is thick and tomatoes bright and clear. Cover, and let stand overnight. Pack cold tomatoes into hot, sterilized jars. Boil syrup until the consistency of honey and pour over the tomatoes. Seal and process in simmering water bath for 15 minutes.

Watermelon Rind Preserves

1   pound watermelon cubes
8   cups water
2   tablespoons household lime
2   cups sugar
4   cups water
½   lemon, sliced

Select melons that have thick rind. Trim off the outer green skin and the pink flesh, and use only the greenish-white parts of the rind. Cut the rind into ½- or 1-inch cubes, and weigh. Then soak the cubes for 3½ hours in lime water (2 quarts water and 2 tablespoons lime from hardware store). Next, drain and place the cubes in clear water for 1 hour. Again, drain off the water and boil for 1½ hours after fresh water has been added, then drain again. Make a syrup of 2 cups sugar and 1 quart water. Add rind and boil for 1 hour. As the syrup thickens, add ½ lemon, thinly sliced, for each pound of fruit. When the syrup begins to thicken and when the melon is clear, the preserves are ready for the jars. Pack the preserves into hot, sterilized jars, add enough syrup to cover, and seal.

Gingered Watermelon Rind

1   pound melon rind
1½ pounds sugar
1   teaspoon ground ginger
½   lemon

Follow the same method as for melon rind preserves until after the rind has been freshened in cold water. Then drain well and boil rapidly for 15 minutes in strong ginger tea (1 ounce ginger to 1 quart water). Finish cooking in a syrup made by using 4 cups of the strained ginger tea with 4 cups of water and 1½ pounds sugar. Cook rapidly until tender and transparent, about 1 hour. After rind has boiled for 30 minutes, add ½ lemon, cut into thin slices. Cook until rind is tender and transparent. Cool, pack, and process like preserves.

Louisiana Bread and Butter Pickles

6   to 8 medium cucumbers
2   large white onions
½   large green pepper
1¼ cups cider vinegar
1¼ cups sugar
½   tablespoon mustard seed
1   teaspoon turmeric
2   tablespoons salt
⅛   teaspoon cloves

Wash cucumbers and slice as thin as possible. Chop onions and pepper. Combine vinegar, sugar, and spices in large preserving kettle and bring to a boil. Add drained cucumbers. Heat thoroughly, but do not boil. Pack while hot in sterilized jars; seal; and process for 10 minutes in water bath.

Pickled Black-Eyed Peas

4   cups cooked dried black-eyed peas
1   cup salad oil
¼   cup wine vinegar
1   clove garlic
¼   cup thinly sliced onion
½   teaspoon salt
    Freshly ground black pepper

Drain liquid from peas. Pour peas into bowl; add remaining ingredients, and mix thoroughly. Store in a jar in refrigerator, and remove the garlic after 1 day. Store for at least 2 days longer before eating.

Cantaloupe Pickles

2   pounds prepared cantaloupe
2   cups vinegar
2   cups corn syrup
4   teaspoons whole cloves
2   cups sugar
8   (2-inch) sticks cinnamon
1   tablespoon mustard seed

Cut melon into oblong strips. Trim all the seed and rind off. Soak melon in salt water overnight (4 tablespoons salt to a quart of water). Drain, and cook in clear water until tender. Put spices into a bag. Bring syrup and spices to boil; add cantaloupe, and cook slowly until cantaloupe is clear. Pack into hot, sterilized jars and seal.

Sweet Pickled Figs

5   quarts ripe, firm figs
4   cups water
2   cups sugar
4   cups sugar
2   cups vinegar
1   tablespoon whole cloves
1   tablespoon ground mace
1   teaspoon whole allspice
1   (2-inch) stick cinnamon

Scald figs in soda bath, allowing 1 cup soda to 6 quarts boiling water. Drain and rinse. Cook figs until tender in a syrup made of 4 cups water and 2 cups sugar. When figs are tender, add 4 cups sugar, 2 cups vinegar, whole spices (tied in a bag), and the mace; cook until figs are transparent. If syrup is not thick enough, remove figs and boil syrup until it is the consistency of honey. Allow figs to stand in syrup overnight. Next morning, pack into jars, cover with syrup, seal, and process for 15 minutes.

Cold Pack Pickles

     Cucumbers
⅔   gallon vinegar
 2   cups sugar
¾   cup salt
¾   cup dry mustard

Fill clean jars with raw cucumbers, cut lengthwise. Cover with mixture of vinegar, sugar, salt, and mustard. Seal. These stay crisp throughout the winter.

Peach Pickles

4   quarts peaches
6   cups sugar
3   cups cider vinegar
6   (2-inch) pieces cinnamon
4   teaspoons whole cloves

Select medium clingstone peaches. Put peaches into large strainer and dip into kettle of boiling water for about ½ minute; rinse with cold water, and remove peel. Boil the sugar, vinegar, and cinnamon together for 20 minutes. Place about 5 peaches at a time in the syrup, and cook for 5 minutes, or until tender. Pack into hot, sterilized jars, placing a teaspoon of cloves in each jar. Fill jars to top with hot syrup, and seal.

Dilled Carrots

1 (1-pound) package frozen whole baby carrots
2 tablespoons chopped fresh dill or ¼ cup dill sprigs
1 clove garlic, cut into quarters
⅓ cup olive oil
⅓ cup frozen lemon juice
1 teaspoon sugar
1 teaspoon salt
¼ teaspoon freshly ground black pepper

Cook carrots in boiling salted water according to package directions. Drain and place in an earthenware or glass bowl. Add dill and garlic. Combine remaining ingredients; mix well and pour over carrots. Toss lightly to coat evenly. Let stand at room temperature for at least 30 minutes, stirring occasionally. Remove garlic. Serve immediately or refrigerate until ready to serve.

Mixed Pickles No. 1

8 cups fresh green beans
8 cups fresh shelled lima beans
1 bunch carrots, peeled and sliced
1 large head cauliflower
4 ears corn (about 3 cups cut)
2 pounds green tomatoes
5 green peppers
2 pounds small white onions
3 cups sugar
¼ cup salt
3 tablespoons celery seed
3 tablespoons mustard seed
2 tablespoons dry mustard
1 tablespoon turmeric
3 quarts vinegar
2 tablespoons Tabasco sauce

Put whole green beans, limas, and carrot slices into a large kettle. Break up cauliflower, and cut corn from cob. Add to the other vegetables. Add water to cover. Bring to a boil; reduce heat, and cook slowly for 25 minutes. While vegetables are cooking, coarsely chop green tomatoes and green peppers. Peel onions and reserve. Mix together sugar, salt, celery and mustard seed, dry mustard, and turmeric in a deep kettle. Add vinegar. Cook over low heat, stirring constantly until sugar is dissolved. Stir in Tabasco. Add drained, cooked vegetables and other vegetables. Cook for 25 minutes. Spoon into hot, sterilized jars and seal.

Mixed Pickles No. 2

1 gallon cucumbers, diced
2 large heads cabbage
15 large onions
3 dozen peppers
3 pods hot pepper
3 or 4 cloves garlic
¾ cup salt
1 ounce white mustard seed
1 ounce ground white pepper
½ ounce stick cinnamon
1 ounce turmeric
¼ ounce dry mustard
2 cups grated horseradish
2 ounces celery seed
4 to 5 pounds sugar

Brine cucumbers. Grind cabbage, onions, peppers, and garlic. Add ¾ cup salt and let drain in sack overnight. Add seasonings, and cover with cider vinegar. Let boil for about 25 minutes. Add to brined cucumbers.

Sweet Dilled Pickled Okra

3 pounds young, fresh okra
6 cloves garlic
6 teaspoons celery seed
6 pods hot pepper, optional
6 teaspoons dill seed
½ cup salt (not iodized)
1 cup sugar
1 quart water
1 quart white vinegar

Pack washed okra into pint jars. Divide garlic, celery seed, hot pepper, and dill seed among the 6 jars. Combine salt, sugar, water and vinegar in large saucepan; bring to boiling, then pour into jars to within ½ inch of top. Seal jars and place in hot water bath (water to cover jars), and cook for 7 minutes. Remove to wire racks to cool. Yield: 6 pints.

Pear Pickles

2 dozen small pears
4 cups sugar
2 cups water
4 cups vinegar
2 pieces ginger root
2 (2-inch) sticks cinnamon
2 tablespoons whole allspice
1 tablespoon whole cloves

Select firm pears. Pare and leave small ones whole; halve or quarter and core large ones. Boil for 20 minutes in clear water. Boil sugar, water, vinegar, and spices (tied in a bag) for 10 minutes. Add pears. Let stand overnight. Cook until tender. Pack pears into hot, sterilized jars. Cook syrup until thick; pour over pears. Seal and process jars for 5 minutes in hot water bath.

Dill Green Tomato Pickles

1 (6-quart) basket small green tomatoes
4 quarts water
1 cup salt
1 cup cider vinegar
  Fresh dill
  Garlic
  Celery
  Green peppers

Wash tomatoes. Mix water, salt, and vinegar, and set aside. Place a spray of fresh dill and a clove of garlic, 1 stalk celery, and one green pepper, quartered, in the bottom of each sterilized jar. Pack tomatoes into jars. Place dill and garlic on top of tomatoes, if desired. Fill jars with prepared brine and seal jars. Store in a cool dark place for at least 3 months before using.

Crabapple Pickles

2 dozen crabapples
3 cups sugar
3 cups water
4 cups vinegar
2 (2-inch) sticks cinnamon
1 tablespoon ground ginger
1 tablespoon whole allspice
½ tablespoon whole cloves

Wash crabapples, then run a needle through each one. Heat sugar, water, vinegar, and spices (tied in a bag) until sugar dissolves. Cool. Add crabapples, and simmer until tender. Let stand for several hours or overnight. Pack cold apples into hot, sterilized jars. Boil the syrup to the desired thickness and pour over crabapples. Process for 10 minutes in hot water bath.

Hot Pickled Peppers

18 *large green peppers*
 9 *ornamental hot red peppers or Mexican hot peppers*
 9 *cloves garlic*
 9 *teaspoons dill seed*
¾ *cup salt*
 3 *cups vinegar*
 6 *cups water*

Cut green peppers lengthwise into thin strips and pack into sterilized pint jars. In each pint add 1 whole ornamental red pepper, 1 clove garlic, and 1 teaspoon dill seed. Combine salt, vinegar, and water and bring to a boil. Pour over peppers in jars, filling to within ½ inch of the top. Seal immediately. Let stand for a few weeks before serving.

Dill Pickles

1 *quart vinegar*
3 *quarts water*
1 *cup salt*
   Cucumbers
   Fresh dill
   Garlic

Combine vinegar, water, and salt and bring to a boil. Pour over washed cold cucumbers in jars. Add dill and a clove of garlic to each jar. Seal and store.

Pickled String Beans

½ *gallon string beans*
 4 *cups vinegar*
½ *cup sugar*
 2 *tablespoons mixed pickling spices*
 1 *clove garlic*

Wash beans well before removing strings. Do not break. Soak in ice water for 30 minutes. Make a brine to cover, using 1 tablespoon salt to each quart water. Bring to a boiling point, and boil for 20 minutes, or until beans are tender. Drain well. Place beans back in cooking vessel and add the vinegar, sugar, spices (tied in bag), and garlic. Simmer for 10 minutes. Pack beans into hot, sterilized jars and cover with the hot vinegar solution. Seal.

Pickled Okra

   Garlic (1 clove for each jar)
   Hot peppers (1 for each jar)
   Okra
   Dill seed (1 teaspoon for each jar)
1 *quart white vinegar*
1 *cup water*
½ *cup salt*

Place the garlic and hot pepper in the bottom of hot, sterilized pint jars. Pack firmly with clean, young okra pods from which only part of the stem has been removed. Stem end must be open. Add dill seed.

After packing jars, bring vinegar, water, and salt to a boil. Simmer for about 5 minutes and pour, while boiling hot, over the okra. Seal the jars immediately. This amount of pickling solution will fill from 5 to 7 pint jars.

Artichoke Pickles

4 cups chopped artichokes
2 cups chopped onions
4 tablespoons salt
2 cups sugar
3 cups vinegar
2 tablespoons celery salt
2 tablespoons white mustard seed
1 tablespoon turmeric
1 (3-ounce) can pimientos

Chop the artichokes and onions; add salt, and let stand overnight. The next morning, bring sugar and vinegar to a boil. Add artichokes and onions and boil for 10 minutes. Add remaining ingredients, and cook for 15 minutes longer. Pour into hot, sterilized jars and seal.

Pumpkin Pickle

1 (6-pound) pumpkin (weighed before preparing)
5 pounds sugar
3 cups white vinegar
2 tablespoons whole cloves
6 (2-inch) sticks cinnamon

Peel pumpkin and scrape away all seeds and stringy matter from the center. Cut into thin slices. Cover with sugar and let stand overnight.

Next morning, add vinegar, cloves, and cinnamon to sugared pumpkin, and cook together over medium heat until pumpkin is transparent and syrup is thick, about 1 to 1½ hours. Pour into hot, sterilized pint jars, pouring any remaining syrup over them, and seal.

Sam Houston Relish

1 medium cabbage
10 carrots
4 large onions
3 green peppers
1 teaspoon salt
2 teaspoons celery seed
2 teaspoons mustard seed
1 cup sugar
  Red and black pepper
1 cup water
  Vinegar

Grind together the cabbage, carrots, onions, and green peppers. Add salt, celery seed, mustard seed, sugar, red and black pepper to taste, the water, and enough vinegar to cover. Boil well and pour into hot, sterilized jars and seal.

Artichoke Relish

2 quarts artichokes
1½ pounds cabbage
1 quart white onions
4 peppers (2 red and 2 green)
1 cup salt
3 quarts boiling water
1 tablespoon turmeric
4 cups vinegar
½ cup all-purpose flour
3 cups sugar
½ cup dry mustard
2 tablespoons celery seed

Chop vegetables and sprinkle with salt. Add 3 quarts boiling water and let stand overnight. Squeeze dry. Mix other ingredients and let come to a boil. Put in vegetables and cook for 15 minutes, stirring constantly. Pack in hot, sterilized jars and process for 15 minutes in water bath.

Dixie Relish

> 2 cups chopped sweet red peppers
> 2 cups chopped sweet green peppers
> 2 tablespoons mustard seed
> 2 tablespoons celery seed
> ¾ cup sugar
> 3 tablespoons salt
> 4 cups cider vinegar
> 4 cups chopped cabbage
> 2 cups chopped white onions

Quarter peppers and remove seeds and coarse white sections and soak overnight in a brine made of 1 cup salt to 1 gallon water. Freshen in clear, cold water for 1 or 2 hours. Chop separately and measure the chopped cabbage, pepper and onions before mixing. Add spices, sugar, and vinegar. Let stand overnight covered in a crock or enameled vessel. Pack into hot, sterilized jars and process 15 minutes in water bath 180° or simmering temperature, and seal.

Red and Green Pepper Relish

> 2 cups prepared sweet peppers
> 1½ cups apple vinegar
> 7 cups sugar
> 1 (6-ounce) bottle pectin

Cut open about 1 dozen medium peppers and discard seed. (For best color, use half green and half sweet red peppers.) Put through food chopper twice, using finest blade. Drain. Measure 2 cups chopped peppers into very large saucepan.

Add vinegar and sugar to peppers in a saucepan and mix well. Place over high heat, bring to a full rolling boil, and boil hard for 1 minute, stirring constantly.

Remove from heat, and at once stir in pectin. Skim off foam with metal spoon. Then stir and skim by turns for 5 minutes to cool slightly and to prevent floating peppers. If desired, add about 10 drops green food coloring. Ladle quickly into hot, sterilized glasses or jars and seal at once.

Relish for Turnip Greens

> 3 tomatoes, diced
> 1 cup chopped celery
> 1 medium cucumber, peeled, sliced, and finely chopped
> 3 tablespoons finely chopped onion
> 1 medium green pepper, chopped
>   Salt and black pepper to taste
> 2 tablespoons French dressing
> 2 tablespoons vinegar

Mix and chill. Yield: 6 servings.

Chow-Chow

> 1 dozen medium onions
> 1 dozen sweet green peppers
> 1 dozen sweet red peppers
> 4 quarts chopped cabbage
> 2 quarts chopped green tomatoes
> ½ cup salt
> 5 cups sugar
> 4 tablespoons ground mustard
> 4 tablespoons mustard seed
> 1 tablespoon turmeric
> 1 tablespoon ground ginger
> 3 tablespoons celery seed
> 2 tablespoons whole mixed pickling spices (tied in bag)
> 2½ quarts vinegar

Chop onions and peppers fine. Combine all vegetables and mix with salt. Let stand overnight. The next morning, drain well. Combine sugar, spices, and vinegar. Bring to boiling point and simmer for about 20 minutes. Add drained vegetables, and simmer to consistency desired. Remove spice bag. Pack chow-chow into hot, sterilized jars and seal.

Grape Relish

2 quarts grape pulp
4 quarts sugar
1 quart vinegar
½ teaspoon black pepper
1 teaspoon ground cloves

Combine ingredients and boil for 30 minutes, stirring constantly. Pour into hot, sterilized jars and seal.

Texas Tomato Catsup

1 gallon ripe tomatoes, peeled and chopped
2 medium onions, chopped
1 cup sweet red pepper, chopped
2 cups vinegar
¾ cup sugar
1 teaspoon salt
1 teaspoon celery seed
3 (2-inch) sticks cinnamon
1 clove garlic, chopped

Combine chopped vegetables, then simmer for 30 to 40 minutes. Press vegetables through a sieve. Tie spices in a cloth, add to the vinegar and simmer for 30 minutes. Boil sieved tomatoes rapidly until they have cooked to half the original amount. Add spiced vinegar, sugar, and salt to the mixture. While stirring constantly, boil the mixture for about 10 minutes, or until slightly thickened. Pour into hot, sterilized jars or bottles, seal or cap, and store.

Oldtime Grape Catsup

4 pounds grapes
2 pounds sugar
2 cups vinegar
2 teaspoons ground cloves
2 teaspoons ground allspice
2 tablespoons ground cinnamon

Wash the grapes and remove stems. Place them in a pan and steam without water until soft. Put fruit through a sieve or food mill, add the other ingredients, and simmer the mixture for 20 minutes. Pour into hot, sterilized jars and seal.

Chili Sauce

2 quarts (12 to 14 medium) peeled and chopped ripe tomatoes
1 cup chopped sweet red peppers
1 chopped onion
1 small hot pepper, chopped
1 tablespoon celery seed
½ tablespoon mustard seed
1 bay leaf
½ teaspoon whole cloves
½ teaspoon ground ginger
½ teaspoon ground nutmeg
1 (2-inch) stick cinnamon
½ cup firmly packed brown sugar
¾ cup vinegar
1 tablespoon salt

Combine tomatoes, sweet peppers, onion, and hot pepper. Put spices in a thin white cloth and tie. Add spices to tomato mixture, and boil until quantity has been reduced one-half, stirring frequently. Add sugar, vinegar, and salt. Boil rapidly for 5 minutes, stirring constantly. Remove spices. Pack into hot, sterilized jars and seal.

Your Frozen Assets

Marvelous new commercially frozen foods continually appear in our food centers. Ten minutes after you put a "boil in the bag" specialty into a pot of boiling water, you can serve a delectable dish. Foil-wrapped, frozen whole meals — soup, meat, vegetables, and dessert — come in tempting varieties and are ready to serve after 30 to 40 minutes cooking in a preheated oven. And in a matter of minutes between freezer and serving dish, you can offer snacks and tidbits.

By the same token, you can prepare many of your family favorites, freeze them, and be ready for impromptu or long-planned occasions.

Foods That Freeze Well

Quick Breads

Storage life of unbaked breads is shorter than that of baked breads. Frozen unbaked breads do not rise as well and are less tender when baked. Your quick breads will have a better quality if you bake them before freezing.

Use a double acting type baking powder for quick breads that are leavened with baking powder.

Store unbaked breads no longer than 1 month. Frozen baked breads will hold for 2 to 3 months.

To serve frozen baked breads, thaw, then unwrap and heat at 375° for 5 to 10 minutes.

Yeast Breads

Refrigerator type yeast doughs (those with eggs and extra sugar) can be frozen for short periods. Store dough, no longer than 1 month. Plain yeast doughs are usually unsatisfactory for freezing unbaked. Unbaked bread should be thawed at room temperature, kneaded, shaped, and allowed to rise before baking.

Baked rolls and baked yeast breads do freeze very successfully. Cool bread quickly after baking, wrap and freeze. Partially bake brown-and-serve rolls at 275° for 20 minutes. For best freezer management, the recommended storage time for baked bread is 3 to 4 months.

To serve baked bread, thaw, then reheat if desired. To serve brown-and-serve rolls, thaw at room temperature, unwrap and place on baking sheet. Grease the surface of rolls, if dry. Bake at 450° for about 15 minutes.

Cakes

Cakes are of a better quality if baked

before freezing. And cakes that are baked before freezing should be used as soon as possible after taken from the freezer. Frozen cakes have a tendency to dry out more quickly than fresh cakes.

Use your regular cake recipe. Bake, cool quickly, and wrap for freezing. With the exception of cakes iced with a butter frosting, it is more satisfactory to freeze the cakes uniced. They may be iced when taken from the freezer.

To bake and freeze cakes: 1) Line the bottom of the cakepan with greased waxed or brown paper. The cake will rise higher if you do not grease sides of pan. 2) Remove baked cake onto a rack to prevent moisture from forming on the crust. 3) Wrap in moisture-vaporproof wrapping. Place cake on stiff cardboard, cover with cellophane and seal, then cover with heavier freezer wrapping. A box will help protect the frozen cake during storage.

Cakes may be frozen for as long as 1 year if properly packaged, but, for good freezer management, time should not exceed 3 months.

Cookies

You'll save freezer space if you freeze the cookie dough. Rolls of refrigerator cookie dough do not have to be thawed before shaping or cutting and baking, so it is more satisfactory to freeze rolls of cookie dough. Rolled and cut-out cookies are better baked before freezing. Storage time for frozen cookies is 6 months.

Pies

Fruit pies, chiffon, mince, and vegetable pies such as pumpkin, squash, and sweet potato, freeze satisfactorily. Cream pies usually do not freeze well because the cream fillings may separate or spoil. There is a difference of opinion on whether pies should be baked before freezing or frozen unbaked. If a pie is to be served hot, it should be frozen unbaked. Pastry is usually of better quality if frozen unbaked.

You'll need to take special care to prevent soggy under-crust. Roll dough very thin and brush with melted butter or margarine or beaten egg white before adding the filling.

Do not cut steam-release vents in an unbaked double-crust pie until after it is taken from the freezer to be baked.

Fruit and berry pies may need extra thickening before freezing. Treat raw peaches and apples with ascorbic acid to prevent darkening.

Storage time for unbaked pies is 2 months; for baked pies, 4 months.

To prepare for serving, unwrap and place pies in a preheated oven. Do not thaw before heating.

Butter

Freeze only fresh, high-quality butter, preferably butter made from sweet cream. Butter made from sour cream may become strong and rancid within a few weeks.

Storage time for salted butter should be 6 months; for unsalted, 6 to 12 months.

Casseroles

Casserole dishes usually contain many ingredients and they may require a long cooking time. Use your own favorite recipe. You may omit crumb or cheese toppings when preparing casseroles for freezing and add them at the time of reheating.

Storage time for casseroles should be no longer than 3 months. To serve, reheat in oven, on top of range, or in a double boiler. Reheating over direct heat requires careful attention because food must be stirred often to prevent scorching or burning.

Salads

Salads that are usually frozen for brief periods in the ice trays of the refrigerator are best suited for freezing. Salads with a base of cream cheese, cottage cheese, or whipped cream freeze well. Mayonnaise and salad dressings tend to separate during freezing.

When preparing a gelatin salad for freezing, decrease the usual amount of liquid by one-fourth. Gelatin salads tend to get watery after freezing and thawing unless liquid is decreased.

Raw grapes and raw apples do not hold their shape in freezing. Nuts sometimes become bitter. Few vegetable salads are suitable for freezing. Storage time for salads is no longer than 1 month. Salads are generally better served before they are completely thawed.

Sandwiches

Sandwiches with fillings of meat, fish, cooked egg yolk, or peanut butter freeze successfully. Omit cooked egg whites. Omit mayonnaise or salad dressing in large amounts; they often separate during freezing. Instead of using a dressing, spread bread with softened butter or margarine to prevent sogginess. Cream cheese or cottage cheese is often used instead of mayonnaise. Day-old bread is best for making sandwiches. Storage time should be no longer than 3 months.

Foods That Do Not Freeze Well

Some foods do not freeze well, or do not have the quality of the fresh product. The following list gives some of the foods that do not stand up satisfactorily in freezer storage. Check this list against the recipe. In many recipes, a food or seasoning that does not freeze well can be omitted at the time of preparation and added after the package is taken from the freezer.

1. Most fried meats lose crispness and have a warmed-over taste after reheating.
2. Sauces and gravies often separate in the freezing process.
3. Chili powder and salt lose strength. Add the usual amount in preparing the dish for freezing and add more when reheating.

4. Cloves, green peppers, pimientos, celery, garlic, and black pepper become stronger and sometimes bitter when frozen.
5. Onions lose flavor, and curry becomes off-flavored.
6. In making sandwiches, avoid the use of jelly, mayonnaise, or salad dressings. They will soak into the bread and make the sandwiches soggy.
7. Lettuce, salad greens, and raw tomatoes do not freeze well.
8. Macaroni, spaghetti, and some rice will have a warmed-over flavor and often are mushy. Cooking time is so short that these foods can be cooked fresh while food that was frozen is being reheated.
9. Meringues on pies will toughen in freezing.
10. Synthetic vanilla will have an off-flavor.
11. Seven-minute and similar cake frostings do not hold up well in freezing. A butter frosting is best for freezing.
12. Custards and custard-type fillings should be avoided for freezing.
13. Potatoes often become soft and mushy in combination dishes. The secret is to be sure that they are undercooked before freezing. The reheating will cook them to the right stage.
14. Nuts in salads often become bitter and discolored in the freezing process.
15. Poultry should never be stuffed before freezing in the home. In home freezing it takes a long time for the interior of the dressing to become cold, even in the freezer, and spoil-age may result. The dressing may be frozen in small packages separately, or made up just before the poultry is to be baked, but never frozen in the fowl. Commercial stuffed turkeys are flash-frozen and are therefore safe for eating.
16. Cooked egg whites become tough in freezing.

Freezing Fresh Fruits and Vegetables

Fruits

Fruits may be frozen in dry sugar, syrup, or in raw state. It is not necessary to blanch fruit.

Select firm, fresh fruit with no dark or soft spots. Prepare as for serving, since frozen fruits are best served while lightly frozen.

Some light-colored fruits, such as peaches or apples, may need to have ascorbic acid or an ascorbic-citric mixture (available at grocery stores) added before freezing to help retain color. These mixtures can be added to sugar or syrup before fruit is added.

Put fruit into moisture- vaporproof containers. Seal, label with contents and date, and freeze at once.

Vegetables

To get a good product from the freezer, the homemaker must be sure that good fresh produce has been used to put into the freezer.

Fruits do not need blanching, but this is

an essential step in freezing vegetables. Use a large kettle for blanching vegetables, allowing 1 gallon water for each pound of prepared vegetables.

Put prepared vegetables into boiling water as soon as it reaches a full rolling boil. Start counting time as soon as vegetables are put into water. Cool promptly (preferably in ice water), drain, and put into moisture-vaporproof containers. Seal. Label with contents and date, and freeze at once.

Use the following chart for blanching time:

Timetable For Preheating Vegetables For Freezing

Vegetable	Heated in Boiling Water (Minutes)	Vegetable	Heated in Boiling Water (Minutes)
Asparagus,		Corn,	
Small stalks	2	Medium ears (1¼ to 1½	
Medium stalks	3	inches in diameter)	9
Large stalks	4	Large ears (over 1½ inches	
Beans, Lima or butterbeans		in diameter)	11
Small beans or pods	2	Whole kernel and	
Medium beans or pods	3	cream style	heat ears 4
Large beans or pods	4		minutes
Beans, snap, green, or wax	3	Greens,	
Beets,		Beet greens, kale, chard,	
Small	25 to 30	mustard greens, spinach,	
Medium	45 to 50	turnip greens	2
Broccoli, flowerets (1½		Collards	3
inches in diameter)	3	Okra,	
	5 (in steam)	Small pods	3
Brussels sprouts,		Large pods	4
Small heads	3	Peas, black-eyed	2
Medium heads	4	Green	1½
Large heads	5	Peppers,	
Cabbage, medium to coarse		Halves	3
shreds or thin wedges	1½	Slices	2
Carrots,		Pimientos (roast at 400°)	3 to 4
Whole carrots, small	5	Pumpkin	until soft
Diced or sliced	2	Rutabagas, ½-inch cubes	2
Lengthwise strips	2	Squash, summer, ½-inch	3
Cauliflower, pieces (1 inch in		slices, Winter	until soft
diameter)	3	Sweet potatoes	until almost
Celery, 1-inch lengths	3		tender
Corn, sweet, on the cob		Tomato juice (simmer	
Small ears (1¼ inches or		tomatoes)	5 to 10
less in diameter)	7	Turnips, ½-inch cubes	2

Hints & Measures

Time was when mother or grandmother prepared a whole meal without using measuring spoons and cups, relying instead on her own judgment. And the results were delicious time after time.

That kind of judgment comes only from years of experience and probably more than one dish which had a little too much salt or not enough sugar.

Electrical appliances, year-round availability of most foods, and other modern conveniences notwithstanding, probably the most valuable asset a modern woman has in cooking is standardized measuring devices.

Following the exact directions given in a kitchen-tested recipe is as foolproof as cake mix and considerably more timesaving than developing a practiced eye. Level off an exact cup of flour and you've taken a shortcut worth years to grandmother.

Substitutions are often a necessity rather than a shortcut. They should be made with care and as infrequently as possible.

Equivalent Measurements

Use standard measuring cups (both dry and liquid measure) and measuring spoons when measuring ingredients. All measurements given below are level.

3 teaspoons	1 tablespoon
4 tablespoons	¼ cup
8 tablespoons	½ cup
16 tablespoons	1 cup
1 cup	8 fluid ounces
2 cups	1 pint (16 fluid ounces)
⅛ cup	2 tablespoons
⅓ cup	5 tablespoons plus 1 teaspoon
⅔ cup	10 tablespoons plus 2 teaspoons
¾ cup	12 tablespoons
Few grains (or dash)	less than ⅛ teaspoon
Pinch	as much as can be taken between tip of finger and thumb

Handy Substitutions

It is always best to use the ingredient called for in the recipe, but occasionally it is necessary to make a substitution. For best results, use this table only when you do not have the ingredient called for in the recipe.

If Recipe Calls For	You May Use
1 square unsweetened chocolate	3 tablespoons cocoa plus 1 tablespoon butter or margarine
2 large eggs	3 small eggs
1 egg	2 egg yolks (for custards)
1 egg	2 egg yolks plus 1 tablespoon water (for cookies)
1 cup sifted all-purpose flour	1 cup sifted cake flour plus 2 tablespoons
1 cup sifted cake flour	1 cup sifted all-purpose flour minus 2 tablespoons
1 cup honey	¾ cup sugar plus ¼ cup liquid
1 cup fresh milk	½ cup evaporated milk plus ½ cup water
1 cup fresh milk	3 to 5 tablespoons nonfat dry milk solids in 1 cup water
1 cup fresh milk	1 cup sour milk plus ½ teaspoon soda (decrease baking powder 2 teaspoons)
1 cup sour milk or buttermilk	1 or 2 tablespoons lemon juice or vinegar with sweet milk to fill cup (let stand for five minutes)
1 cup brown sugar (firmly packed)	1 cup granulated sugar
Thickening	1 tablespoon quick-cooking tapioca, or 1 tablespoon cornstarch, or 2 tablespoons all-purpose flour

Equivalent Weights and Measures

Food	Weight	Measure
Apples	1 pound (3 medium)	3 cups, sliced
Bananas	1 pound (3 medium)	2½ cups, sliced
		about 2 cups, mashed
Bread	1 pound	12 to 16 slices
Butter or margarine	1 pound	2 cups
Butter or margarine	¼-pound stick	½ cup
Butter or margarine	size of an egg	about ¼ cup
Candied fruit or peels	½ pound	1¼ cups, cut
Cheese, American	1 pound	4 to 5 cups, shredded
cottage	1 pound	2 cups
cream	3-ounce package	6 tablespoons
Cocoa	1 pound	4 cups
Coconut, flaked or shredded	1 pound	5 cups
Coffee	1 pound	80 tablespoons
Cornmeal	1 pound	3 cups
Cream, heavy	½ pint	2 cups, whipped
Dates, pitted	1 pound	2 to 3 cups, chopped
Dates, pitted	7¼-ounce package	1¼ cups, chopped
Flour		
all-purpose	1 pound	4 cups, sifted
cake	1 pound	4¾ to 5 cups, sifted
whole wheat	1 pound	3½ cups, unsifted
Lemon juice	1 medium	2 to 3 tablespoons
Lemon rind	1 medium	2 teaspoons, grated
Milk		
evaporated	6-ounce can	¾ cup
evaporated	14½-ounce can	1⅔ cups
sweetened condensed	14-ounce can	1¼ cups
sweetened condensed	15-ounce can	1⅓ cups
Nuts, in shell		
almonds	1 pound	1 to 1¾ cups
		nutmeats
peanuts	1 pound	2 cups nutmeats
pecans	1 pound	2¼ cups nutmeats
walnuts	1 pound	1⅔ cups nutmeats
Nuts, shelled		
almonds	1 pound, 2 ounces	4 cups
peanuts	1 pound	4 cups
pecans	1 pound	4 cups
walnuts	1 pound	3 cups
Orange, juice	1 medium	⅓ cup
Orange, rind	1 medium	2 tablespoons, grated
Raisins, seedless	1 pound	3 cups
Sugar		
brown	1 pound	2¼ cups firmly packed
powdered	1 pound	3½ cups unsifted
granulated	1 pound	2 cups

Canned Food Guide

Can Size	Number of Cups	Number of Servings	Foods
8-ounce	1 cup	2 servings	fruits, vegetables
10½- to 12-ounce (picnic)	1¼ cups	3 servings	condensed soups, fruits and vegetables, meats and fish, specialties
12-ounce (vacuum)	1½ cups	3 to 4 servings	vacuum-packed corn
14- to 16-ounce (No. 300)	1¾ cups	3 to 4 servings	pork and beans, meat products, cranberry sauce
16- to 17-ounce (No. 303)	2 cups	4 servings	principal size for fruits and vegetables, some meat products, juices, pineapple, apple slices
1 pound, 4 ounce (No. 2)	2½ cups	5 servings	
27- to 29-ounce (No. 2½)	3½ cups	7 servings	fruits, some vegetables (pumpkin, sauerkraut, greens, tomatoes)
46-ounce (No. 3 cyl.)	5¾ cups	10 to 12 servings	fruit and vegetable juices
6½-pound (No. 10)	12 to 13 cups	25 servings	institutional size for fruits and vegetables

How To

Make White Sauce or Gravy

1. Melt shortening or butter in skillet or saucepan.
2. Remove from heat and blend in all-purpose flour, a small amount at a time.
3. Add cold liquid gradually, stirring constantly.
4. Return to heat, and stir constantly until mixture thickens and bubbles.
5. Add seasonings and cook for at least 5 minutes, stirring occasionally.
6. To make dark gravy after frying meat, remove pan from heat, pour off excess fat or shortening, blend in flour, return to heat and stir until brown before adding liquid.

Add Egg Yolks to Hot Sauce

1. Beat egg yolks in a small bowl.
2. Warm egg yolks by stirring in a small amount of the hot sauce.
3. Add yolks to sauce (usually in a double boiler).

4. Cook and stir for a few minutes until mixture thickens and egg yolks are cooked. Do not boil.
5. Sour cream may be added to sauce by this method, also.

Scald Milk

1. Pour milk into a saucepan and place over medium heat.
2. Stir constantly as it heats so that film will not form.
3. Remove from heat as soon as steam begins to rise from the milk.

Measure Dry Ingredients

1. Use a dry measuring cup (without lip), rather than a liquid measuring cup.
2. Sift dry ingredients onto waxed paper or into a bowl. Sift shortly before measuring, as flour tends to pack. Some flour does not require sifting. Read instructions on flour container.
3. Pile sifted ingredients lightly into cup with a spoon (never dip measuring cup into sifted flour or sugar).
4. Level with a knife or spatula.
5. If several dry ingredients are to be mixed, sift them together after measurements have been made.
6. Brown sugar does not need to be sifted, but must be packed into measuring cup or spoon.

Melt Chocolate

1. Place chocolate on waxed paper in a bowl or small pan.
2. Place bowl or pan over boiling water and heat until chocolate is melted.
3. Remove melted chocolate with a rubber scraper.

Fry Eggs (Low Fat)

1. Melt 1 or 2 tablespoons shortening or butter in skillet.
2. Break eggs into cup, and then pour into skillet.
3. Cook over low heat until white is set.
4. Add ¼ to ½ cup hot water.
5. Cover skillet with tight-fitting lid and cook for 2 to 4 minutes.

Hard Cook an Egg

1. Eggs should be at room temperature.
2. Place eggs in saucepan and cover with cold water. Heat until water boils.
3. Remove from heat. Cover pan, and let stand for 20 to 25 minutes.
4. Cool eggs under cold water.

Soft Cook an Egg

1. Eggs should be at room temperature.
2. Place eggs in saucepan and cover with cold water. Heat until water boils.
3. Remove from heat. Cover pan, and let stand for 2 to 4 minutes.
4. Drain off hot water and run cold water over the eggs until cooled.

Beat Eggs

1. Eggs should be at room temperature. Do not beat until just before ready for use.
2. To beat eggs slightly: beat with a fork until texture is broken up.
3. To beat until thick and lemon colored: beat whole eggs or egg yolks thoroughly until they thicken and the color changes to a light yellow.
4. To beat egg whites stiff: be sure there is not a speck of yolk in the whites. Beat with a rotary beater or electric mixer until stiff. The peaks will hold their shape as the mixture is lifted.

Cook Bacon

1. Place overlapping pieces of bacon in a large, cold skillet or on a griddle.
2. Turn heat to low. Separate slices as bacon cooks. Increase heat to medium.
3. Turn as bacon cooks, and spoon off fat as it accumulates. Allow 5 to 8 minutes cooking time.
4. Remove each slice as it browns and place on paper towels or brown paper to drain.

Blanch Nuts

1. Drop shelled nuts into boiling water. Remove from heat and let stand for 2 to 5 minutes, or until skins are loosened.
2. Pour off hot water and add cold water.
3. Pinch each nut between thumb and finger to push off skin.
4. Place nuts on plate or paper towels to dry.

Caramelize Sugar

1. Place white sugar in heavy pan over low heat and stir constantly.
2. Heat until sugar turns to a golden brown syrup.
3. Stir in the hot water (amount given in recipe) and continue stirring until well blended.

Cut Sticky Foods

1. When cutting sticky foods, dip knife or shears into water occasionally.

Section Grapefruit

1. Peel fruit, using sharp knife and a slightly sawing motion. Trim away any white inner peel that remains.
2. Holding fruit in one hand, cut down the membrane side of a segment.
3. Give knife a short twist so that it will slip up the opposite side of the segment.
4. Remove seeds and bits of membrane from each segment before using.

Glossary

À la Mode..............In the fashion of; common usage of pie served with ice cream.

Aspic....................Combinations of meats, fruits, or vegetables molded in unflavored gelatin.

Au Gratin.............With a crust of cheese or breadcrumbs and cheese combined, and browned.

Bake....................To cook food in an oven by dry heat.

Barbecue..............To roast meat slowly over coals on a spit or framework, or in an oven, basting intermittently with a special sauce.

Baste...................To brush or ladle melted fat or other pan drippings over food while it is cooking, to prevent surface from drying.

Beat....................To mix vigorously with a brisk motion with spoon, fork, egg beater, or electric mixer.

Bisque.................A thick soup made of seafood, or a rich ice cream containing powdered nuts or macaroons.

Bland..................Having a mild, pleasant flavor.

Blanch.................Put into boiling water. Let stand for a few minutes to loosen skins of certain nuts and fruits.

Blend..................To mix thoroughly two or more ingredients (usually with a spoon).

Boil....................To cook food in boiling water or liquid that is mostly water (at 212°) in which bubbles constantly rise to the surface and burst.

Bouillabaisse.........A highly seasoned fish soup or chowder containing two or more kinds of fish.

Bouillon..............A clear meat broth, delicately seasoned.

Braise.................To cook slowly with liquid or steam in a covered utensil. Less-tender cuts of meat may be browned slowly on all sides in a small amount of shortening, seasoned, and water added.

Bread..................To coat with breadcrumbs. Food may be dipped in breadcrumbs alone; or dipped in crumbs, then in beaten egg and milk, and then coated with breadcrumbs.

Brine..................A solution of salt and water, used for preserving meats, vegetables, etc. Other preservatives may be added.

Broil..................To cook by direct heat, either under the heat of a broiler, over hot coals, or between two hot surfaces.

The Browning——Used for making gravy in the Carolina Low Country. Put 1 cup white sugar into a hot skillet. Stir constantly over heat until the sugar has caramelized to a dark brown. Add slowly 1 cup boiling water and stir until caramel is dissolved. When cold, pour liquid into bottle. The "browning" adds to flavor and attractiveness of gravies.

Broth——A thin soup, or a liquid in which meat, fish, or vegetables have been boiled.

Caramelize——To cook white sugar in a skillet over medium heat, stirring constantly, until sugar forms a golden-brown syrup.

Casserole——Either a dish used for baking, or a combination of foods, usually with cream sauce, baked in such a dish.

Charlotte——A kind of pudding of custard, fruit, gelatin, etc., enclosed in a mold of cake, cookies, or ladyfingers.

Chill——To cool in refrigerator or other cool place until cold.

Chop——To cut into pieces, usually with a sharp knife or with kitchen shears.

Cobbler——A deep-dish fruit pie without a bottom crust but having a top crust, roof, or covering.

Cocktail——An appetizer. Either a beverage or a light, highly seasoned food, served before a meal.

Compote——Fruit cooked or served in a sugar syrup.

Confectionary——Ordinarily candy; sometimes other sweet foods.

Conserve——A fruit preserve made of a combination of fruits, often with nuts added.

Consommé——A clear broth made from meat.

Cool——To let stand at room temperature until food is no longer warm to the touch.

Court-Bouillon——A highly seasoned broth made from fish; also broth in which fish is to be cooked.

Cracklings——The crisp residue of fat, especially hogs' fat after the lard or fat has been cooked out.

Cream——To work one or more foods until soft and creamy and thoroughly mixed. Usually applies to shortening and sugar; work until no sugar grains are visible.

Creole——A well seasoned tomato sauce containing green peppers and onions.

Crepe——A very thin, crisp pancake.

Croquette——A ball made of diced meat, fowl, fish, etc., coated with eggs and breadcrumbs and fried in deep fat.

Croutons.................Cubes of bread, toasted or fried, served with soups, salads, or other foods.

Cruller.................A doughnut of twisted shape, very light in texture.

Crumpet.................A flat, soft leavened cake made of batter cooked on a griddle or skillet. Similar to an English muffin.

Cube.................To cut into small squares (about ½-inch). Usually applied to meats.

Curry.................A highly spiced dish introduced from India, characterized by the pungent flavor of curry powder.

Cut In.................To use two knives or pastry blender to cut shortening into flour or cornmeal until meal or flour-coated particles are divided.

Daube.................A spicy stew; a larded piece of meat, or one cooked covered with slices of bacon or salt pork.

Demitasse.................A small, after-dinner cup of black coffee.

Devil.................To season a food to make it hot, such foods as deviled eggs, ham, crab, etc.

Dice.................To cut into small (about ¼-inch) dice-shaped pieces. Usually applied to vegetables or fruits.

Dissolve.................To mix a dry substance with liquid until the dry substance becomes a part of solution.

Dot.................To place small bits of butter or margarine on a food.

Dredge.................To sprinkle or coat with flour or other fine-textured ingredient.

Emulsion.................An oily mass in suspension in a watery liquid.

Entrée.................A dish served between the chief courses; also the main dish at a luncheon.

Escallop.................To bake food, usually a mixture, with white sauce and topping of crumbs, or crumbs and cheese in a baking dish or casserole.

Flour.................To coat with flour.

Fold In.................To combine two or more ingredients by passing a wire whip, spatula, or spoon down through mixture, across bottom, and turning mixture over slowly as spoon is brought to top of bowl.

Fondue.................A fluffy preparation made of eggs and milk, usually containing breadcrumbs and cheese.

Frappé.................A liquid mixture frozen to a mush.

French Fry.................To fry in deep fat.

Fromage.................Cheese.

Fry.................To cook in hot shortening.

Glacé.................To cook with a thin sugar syrup cooked to the cracked stage. When used for breads, the mixture may be uncooked or may be cooked a shorter length of time.

Goulash	A highly seasoned stew, usually containing meat and vegetables.
Grate	To obtain small particles of food by rubbing on a grater or shredder.
Gumbo	A soup thickened with okra.
Herb	Aromatic plant used for seasoning and garnishing foods.
Irradiate	To enrich with added Vitamin D.
Jambalaya	Rice and meat or fish cooked together with a creole sauce.
Kedgeree	A combination of rice and smoked fish.
Knead	To work a food (usually dough) with the hands, using a folding-back and pressing-forward motion.
Lard	To place strips of fat through or lay strips of fat on top of lean meat or fish for flavor and to prevent drying.
Macédoine	A mixture of fruits and vegetables served as a salad, cocktail, or dessert.
Marinade	A mixture, usually vinegar or lemon juice and water or oil, in which certain foods are seasoned.
Melt	To liquefy by heat.
Mince	To chop into very fine pieces (about $\frac{1}{8}$-inch).
Mocha	A combination of coffee and chocolate.
Mousse	A type of whipped and frozen dessert that has been stirred during freezing, consisting chiefly of sweetened and flavored whipped cream.
Pan Broil	To cook in a hot skillet with very little shortening. The fat is poured off as it accumulates.
Pan Fry	To cook in skillet in a small amount of shortening.
Parboil	To cook in water until food is partially cooked, usually drained and followed by another method of cooking.
Parch	To brown by means of dry heat.
Pare	To remove outer coverings (as apples) with a knife.
Peel	To pull off outer coverings (as oranges or bananas).
Peppercorn	The whole pepper berry, before grinding.
Pilau or Pilaff	A dish consisting of rice boiled with meat, fowl, or fish and seasoned with spices.
Pit	To remove seeds.
Poach	To cook in water or in a poaching utensil just below the boiling point.
Pot Liquor	The liquid in which vegetables have been boiled.
Pot Roast	To cook larger cuts of meat with liquid added.
Preheat	To turn on oven so that desired temperature will be reached before food is inserted for baking.

Roast................To cook in oven by dry heat (usually applied to meats).

Roux................A blended mixture of flour and melted shortening, browned and used as a thickening.

Salmagundi................A mixture of chopped fish, meat, onions, etc., seasoned.

Sauté................To pan fry quickly in a small amount of shortening.

Scald................1) to heat milk just below the boiling point. 2) To dip certain foods into boiling water before freezing them (also called blanching).

Scallop................To bake food (usually cut into pieces and arranged in layers) which has been covered with a sauce, and often topped with breadcrumbs.

Score................To cut narrow slits or gashes along the edges of meat cuts and into the fat covering on hams to prevent curling of meat in the cooking process.

Sear................To cook at a high temperature for a very short time to brown the surface of meat.

Shredded................Broken into thread-like or stringy pieces, usually by rubbing over the surface of a vegetable shredder.

Simmer................To cook just below the boiling point, at about 185°.

Skewer................To fasten with wooden or metal pins or skewers.

Sliver................To cut long, thin pieces.

Sorbet................A sherbet made of several kinds of fruit.

Soufflé................A spongy hot dish, made from a sweet or savory mixture (often milk or cheese), lightened by stiffly beaten egg whites.

Spatula................A sort of flexible knife with rounded end and without sharp edges.

Steam................To cook with live steam in a covered container.

Steep................To let stand in hot liquid below the boiling point. Container is usually covered.

Stew................To cook slowly in liquid kept below the boiling point.

Stir................To blend food ingredients with a circular motion.

Suet................The firm, white fat of the loin and kidney sections of beef.

Tartar................A mayonnaise base with various additions such as pickles, relish, onions, etc.

Toast................To brown by means of dry heat.

Toss................To lightly blend food ingredients.

Whip................To beat rapidly to increase air and increase volume.

Index